TEXAS
LITERARY
OUTLAWS

TEXAS LITERARY OUTLAWS: SIX WRITERS IN THE SIXTIES AND BEYOND

STEVEN L. DAVIS

TCU Press
Fort Worth, Texas

Library of Congress Cataloging-in-Publication Data

Davis, Steven L.
  Texas literary outlaws : six writers in the sixties and beyond/
Steven L. Davis.
      p. cm.
Includes bibliographical references and index.
  ISBN 0-87565-285-9 (alk. paper)
  1. American literature--Texas--History and criticism. 2. Authors,
American--Homes and haunts--Texas. 3. Texas--Intellectual life--20th
century. 4. Texas--In literature. 5. Cartwright, Gary, 1934-- 6.
Brammer, Billy Lee. 7. King, Larry L. 8. Shrake, Edwin. 9. Jenkins,
Dan. 10. Gent, Peter. I. Title.
PS266.T4 D38 2004
810.9'9764'09046--dc22
                                            2003018984

design and illustration by
Barbara M. Whitehead

Printed in Canada

For those who came before,
Earle and Kathrine,
and those who will come after,
Natalie and Lucia

CONTENTS

PREFACE

This book owes its existence to the Southwestern Writers Collection, founded by Bill and Sally Wittliff at Texas State University—San Marcos in 1986. The collection has come to serve as the leading repository for the personal papers of Texas writers, and among its major holdings are the archives of Billy Lee Brammer, Gary Cartwright, Larry L. King, and Bud Shrake. These materials have been donated by the writers, their families, and their friends, often through the efforts of Bill Wittliff. The collection is a testament to the generosity and vision of many donors. This book is the first major study to emerge from the Southwestern Writers Collection, and it is my hope that it provides some sense of the extraordinary richness of the literary archives housed at Texas State.

Finding a term to define this group of writers is not easy. Others have called them "Mad Dogs," "Mesquite Beats," and "Texas' Merry Pranksters." In New York they were referred to as "The Texas Mafia." After much musing, I finally decided to use a new term, "Texas Literary Outlaws." I don't mean outlaws in the literal sense, of course, although many of the writers did experience a brush or several with the law. Instead, outlaws refers in part to their joyful rebellion in the face of Texas' conservative culture and political establishment. It also emanates from their closeness to the "Outlaw Country" musicians, particularly Willie Nelson and Jerry Jeff Walker. Both groups, the writers and the musicians, often resisted corporate controls as they struggled to create Texas-based artistic visions.

Not everyone appreciates the "outlaw" designation. Dan Jenkins wrote to tell me that he never lived the "outlaw" lifestyle and was not flattered to be included as one here. Billy Lee Brammer's daughter, Sidney, argued against her father's inclusion. She points out that Brammer's own literary scene "was earlier, more establishment, and had to do with politics and postwar existential angst, rather than sixties rebellion and seventies excess." Her father's subsequent involvement with the outlaws, Sidney maintains, "had more to do with easy access to drugs among tolerant pals, rather than a sense of being part of an outlaw literary scene with serious intellectual objectives."[1] Obviously, compelling arguments exist for why individual writers can be classified apart from the "Literary Outlaws." Yet it's also true that the six writers discussed in this book became close friends, they shared a common history and influences, they often supported each other's literary ambitions, and they have long been viewed as a distinct group. To my mind, these arguments for inclusion outweigh those for exclusion. As far as the discomfort triggered by the term "outlaw," I offer my apologies along with the caveat that it could have been worse. I could have stuck with simply calling them "Mad Dogs."

Notes on usage: The Sixties: Like many scholars, I view the sixties as a distinct era, rather than a decade defined by the calendar, and the period lasted until at least 1973. In this way, Bud Shrake's *Strange Peaches*, published in 1972, is considered a sixties novel. Billy Lee Brammer: I have chosen the Billy Lee spelling despite the fact that Mr. Brammer was born Billie Lee. He was known as Bill or Billy Lee for most of his life, although he embraced an ironic return to Billie Lee in his later years. On endnotes: In the interest of readability, I have combined all citations that occur within a given paragraph into a single citation, which appears at the end of the paragraph. The citations that appear in the endnotes follow the chronology of each paragraph.

As with any book, publication would have been impossible without the support and assistance of many friends and colleagues. In this case, I had the exceptionally good fortune to receive constant encouragement and advice from Connie Todd, curator of the Southwestern Writers Collection. I also benefited from the strong support of my academic mentor, Dr. Mark Busby, director of the Southwest Regional Humanities Center at Texas State. Many current and former colleagues have also been instrumental in aiding this project, including Gwynedd Cannan, Dick Holland, Mandy York, Michele Miller, Carla Ellard, Tina Ybarra, Jill Hoffman, Joan Heath, and Carl Van Wyatt. Thanks, too, to Jeff Davis and Lita Fraley for valuable research assistance. Thanks also to Mary Comparetto, Kate Johnson, Ofelia Vasquez-Philo, and A. H. and Cecelia Delgado for moral and practical support.

I remain deeply grateful to Larry L. King, Bud Shrake, and Gary Cartwright for consenting to be interviewed, for allowing me to pester them with numerous follow-up questions, and for allowing me to use quotations from previously unpublished material in their archives. The permissions are especially appreciated considering that the authors did not always agree with my conclusions, and they were also undoubtedly embarrassed at times by csrtain passages that came to light. Yet each remained supportive, and, more importantly, each encouraged my independence and objectivity. Their class is commendable.

The first draft of this book received welcome corrections and criticisms from King, Shrake, and Cartwright, along with Bill Wittliff, Sidney Brammer, Dan Jenkins, Bill Broyles, Jan Reid, Jody Gent, Joe Davis, Jeff Davis, and Marc Wilkinson. Judy Alter and James Ward Lee at TCU Press made many further improvements with their astute editorial suggestions. I'm especially grateful to Judy for her calm, confident leadership in guiding this book toward publication. Special thanks go to my own literary compadre, Donald Lucio Hurd, whose steady editorial hand helped turn a promising idea into a relatively polished manuscript. Finally, I give thanks to my loving, supportive, and guiding wife, Georgia Ruiz Davis, who helped throughout and believed in me every step of the way. Thanks, Sweetie.

TEXAS

LITERARY

OUTLAWS

On the morning of November 22, 1963, Jack Ruby visited the offices of *The Dallas Morning News*. He was not there to register a complaint about the newspaper's coverage of President Kennedy, though certainly Ruby was offended by its full-page advertisement depicting Kennedy as a Communist sympathizer. Instead, Ruby came in to apologize. He had exchanged terse words the evening before with a young *Morning News* writer—a man who happened to be dating the star stripper at Ruby's nightclub. Her boyfriend, the young *Morning News* writer, would find himself in a unique position as events unfolded in Dallas during 1963. Not only was he intimate with Jack Ruby and the city's underworld, he also moved easily through parties hosted by Dallas' right-wing elite, many of whom fervently believed that John F. Kennedy's death was the best thing that could happen to their country. As the writer's later novel would show, Kennedy's murder marked the culmination of a long period of madness and hysteria in Texas' second-largest city.

Across town on November 22, another young writer was preparing to join the presidential motorcade. Once a part of Lyndon B. Johnson's staff, he had already published a novel that became hailed as the definitive portrait of LBJ's personality. Before the day was out, the subject of his book would become president of the United States.

Other young Texas writers also orbited closely around the JFK assassination. One had helped plan Kennedy's trip from Washington, D.C., and in the wake of his beloved president's death, he threw away a successful career in politics to begin life anew as a freelance writer. Another writer, living in Dallas, immediately realized that having a president assassinated "in what was essentially our neighborhood" imbued him with a special responsibility. In the years ahead, he would return often to the subject of the Kennedy assassination, concluding, "My chain of fate is Dallas, 1963."[1]

It seems remarkable enough that so many emerging Texas writers happened to be close to the epicenter of the Kennedy assassination. Yet even more striking is that these four men banded together with two others to form a distinct group—a Texas literary cluster. The events in Dallas 1963 were but one instance in which these chroniclers were at the very center of the action. As Texas moved into the modern era, these six writers closely observed many of the state's defining elements: the transformation from a rural to an urban environment; Lyndon Johnson's rise to national prominence; the civil rights movement; Tom Landry and the Dallas Cowboys; Willie Nelson, Jerry Jeff Walker, and the Outlaw music scene; the birth of a Texas film industry; *Texas Monthly* magazine; the flowering of "Texas Chic"; and Ann Richards' election as governor.

Coming of age in the sixties, in a state largely bereft of a literary tradition, these literary outlaws created their own rules. Several other notable writers with Texas roots also emerged in those years, among them Larry McMurtry, Shelby Hearon, John Rechy, John Graves, James Crumley, William Humphrey, and William Owens. The outlaws became distinctive, however, by forming a single group whose members found their voices in opposition to Texas' inherent conservatism. They led lives of notorious excess, becoming as well known for their raconteuring as for their literary production. They found affirmation in their work but also endured poverty, alcoholism, divorces, censorship, rejections, arrests, and denunciations. In contrast to the backstabbing often found among literary groups, these writers supported each other, inspired each other, and wrote for each other. They are peers, rivals, and have been sometimes friends of Larry McMurtry, but their relationships with Texas' most famous writer have always been ambivalent, and McMurtry has been critical of their approach to life and art.

Not all of the writers survived the turmoil of the times. The group's initial spark, a self-educated intellectual named Billy Lee Brammer, died in 1978 of a methamphetamine overdose. His 1961 novel, *The Gay Place,* inspired in part by Lyndon Johnson, is considered Texas' first modern urban novel. Often viewed as the writer in the group with the most "pure, sparkling, literary talent," Brammer worked as an aide to LBJ for several years in the 1950s, hung out with Ken Kesey and the Merry Pranksters in the sixties, and helped found *Texas Monthly* in the 1970s. In the throes of drug addiction, his writing dissipated, yet he remained an important influence. As Brammer told his friend Larry L. King, "Writing is just so murderously hard for me in recent years . . . though my skull feels livelier than ever."[2]

Though not everyone remembers it, Larry L. King was once better known than Larry King, the talk show host on TV. At a time when literate magazine journalism mattered, King was a star at *Harper's,* America's most relevant magazine during the peak of the sixties. A college dropout from Texas Tech, King became the only writer in America ever nominated for a National Book Award, a Broadway Tony, and a television Emmy. Yet for much of his career, his commercial prospects remained meager until, as a lark, he agreed to help write a stage play. That became the smash Broadway hit, *The Best Little Whorehouse in Texas.* Though *Whorehouse* has come to overshadow his other work, many of King's subsequent plays—*The Kingfish* and *The Dead Presidents' Club,* for example—are superior, and he remains a singular presence in American letters. A brawler from the West Texas oil patch with "a deep and abiding commitment to America and to authentic American values," King possesses rare humor and insight.[3] He is also among the most fearlessly honest writers this country has produced. His 1972 book, *Confessions of a White Racist,* lays bare the depth of white attitudes towards African Americans in twentieth-century America.

Peter Gent is the only writer of the group not born in Texas. A native of Michigan, Gent played five seasons for the Dallas Cowboys during the 1960s, becoming a close friend of teammate Don Meredith. Gent began hanging out with the writers and, influenced by them, later tried his hand at fiction. The result was *North Dallas Forty*, an unflinching look at the dehumanizing corporate culture of professional football. Gent's novel changed forever how many people view the game. He became a literary star, but "didn't always handle fame and fortune as well as friends wished." Soon, Gent was carrying "several loaded guns and believed that the CIA and the Mafia were neck and neck in the race to bring about his end."[4] The stresses on the ex-football player's psyche would eventually fracture his relationships with the other Texas writers.

Dan Jenkins, author of *Semi-Tough*, is the most commercially successful writer in the group. He often distanced himself from the others during the long days and nights of "Mad Dog" excesses, yet he shares a deep connection, primarily because of his common history and long friendships. Born in Fort Worth, Jenkins worked alongside Bud Shrake and Gary Cartwright under legendary sportswriter Blackie Sherrod. Eventually graduating to *Sports Illustrated*, Jenkins became the most influential sportswriter of his generation, admired for his brilliant leads, deadpan one-liners, and sardonic commentary. He turned to fiction at the age of forty-three, and there the Jenkins formula produced a streak of best-sellers that showcase his outrageous humor while largely defying literary conventions. Jenkins, more than any of the other writers, has drifted rightward in his politics over the years, and this personal transformation has coincided with changes in his fiction.

Gary Cartwright is Texas' own "Gonzo" journalist. A longtime writer for *Texas Monthly*, Cartwright began in the 1950s and 1960s as a police reporter and sportswriter in Dallas-Fort Worth. A renowned prankster, Cartwright lived by the ethos, "Writers figure things out, not by logic but by living. Imagination can take a writer great places, but only if he's already been there."[5] From 1967 to 1982, he endured a poverty-stricken freelance career, writing alternately brilliant and horrible stories and suffering crushing rejections. Eventually, his writing voice came to match his extraordinary personal history, giving him a singular advantage over every other journalist in the state.

Edwin "Bud" Shrake is viewed by his peers and a small circle of critics as one of the most accomplished novelists Texas has produced. Yet his fiction has not sold well, and he's largely made his living over the years as a sportswriter, screenwriter, and biographer. He joined his pal Dan Jenkins at *Sports Illustrated* in the 1960s and 1970s; he turned to Hollywood in the 1980s; and he collaborated with Willie Nelson on the singer's autobiography. In the 1990s, he cowrote *Harvey Penick's Little Red Book,* which became the best-selling sports book ever. Though nearly unknown as a novelist, Shrake has produced two books that rank among America's finest since World War II. His 1968 historical novel, *Blessed McGill,* a deeply humorous and spiritually resonant work, is the first "absurdist western" and one of the most original and powerful novels to emerge from the American Southwest. In 1972 Shrake published *Strange Peaches*—a searing portrait of Dallas in the days leading up to the Kennedy assassination. The sixties gave rise to excellent music, journalism, and film, but relatively few great novels were written of the era. Bud Shrake's *Strange Peaches,* though largely overlooked, is among them.

***

For much of the twentieth century, Texas was a mostly inhospitable place for literary artists. There were few presses, no major publishers, and only scattered readers. Young writers felt trapped by the state's confines and found it necessary to leave in order to make their way in the larger world. From the 1920s through the 1950s, Texas letters were dominated by a single voice—J. Frank Dobie, who often seemed more at home around the campfire than in front of a typewriter. Along with his compadres, historian Walter Prescott Webb and naturalist Roy Bedichek, Dobie formed the state's first literary cluster, the Texas Triumvirate. The group's tales of Texas Rangers, buried treasure, bear hunters, coyotes, and Longhorns kept alive a sense of

Texas' rural, mythic past. But their work was far removed from the currents of modern American literature.

Shrake, King, Brammer, Cartwright, and Jenkins grew up aware of Dobie and Webb, but the old-timers' emphasis on the past did not resemble the Texas they knew, a land of fast-growing cities and hard-edged political issues. Their own literary influences became Mark Twain, Ernest Hemingway, F. Scott Fitzgerald, and the Beat Generation. For these emerging hipsters, the choices were clear during years of political and social upheaval. Generations of Jim Crow laws were coming under attack; a conservative state government was challenged by liberal activists; an undeclared war in Vietnam seemed to defy America's basic principles; discredited "objective" reporting was replaced by a New Journalism; and notions of "normalcy" were upended by drugs that provided new ways of perceiving the world.

The literary outlaws chronicled, with daring, wit, and sophistication, the state's culture during a time of rapid social change. In long-lasting, versatile careers, they have produced journalism, fiction, drama, biographies, and screenplays. They helped Texans attain a new awareness of their state. Taken as a whole, their work establishes an authentic Texas vision, one far removed from the fanciful notions promulgated by outsiders and the state's dewy-eyed sentimentalists. Yet much of their work also represents, as one critic observed, "a last ditch stand for what has come to be called male chauvinism."[6]

As full-time writers unconnected to any university, this group showed, for the first time, that professional writers could survive in Texas—though the living was not always easy. They helped develop Austin as the state's artistic hub, and they beat a path to Hollywood for other writers to follow. They changed the state's language and its literary climate. They've recovered from years of drug and alcohol abuse, and their attitudes toward women have largely evolved. Now, as active and engaged writers in their seventies, they continue to provide inspiration. What follows is one version of their story.

PART ONE:

COMING OF

AGE

IN

TEXAS

1.

A Rebel

in West

Texas

L arry L. King was on the verge of getting fired from his third straight newspaper job when he left West Texas in 1954 as the chief assistant to a freshly elected congressman. King has lived on the East Coast ever since, but it is his experience growing up in West Texas that has nourished a lifetime of writing.

King was born in Putnam on January 1, 1929, or, as he terms it, "the first day of the first year of the Great Depression." His family struggled mightily to survive in those years, scratching a living from the land and occasionally joining migrant labor streams. As a child, King demonstrated an unusual facility in language. His mother saw in him the potential for a great preacher, and she taught him to read using the family Bible and a mail-order encyclopedia. By the time he entered the first grade, King was already a voracious reader and writer, composing his own stories on Big Chief tablets. He also knew that his life's ambition was to escape the unrewarding toil of farm labor. In the third grade the local newspaper published his poem, "The Indian Squaw," and the resulting attention made him aware of the possibility of fame as a writer. But the poem also caused conflicts with his peers, and King engaged in the first of several fistfights to prove that, though he was a writer, he was no sissy.[1]

King wrote continuously through his childhood, composing poems for special occasions and distributing his own one-sheet newspaper among schoolmates. He also sent off articles to *Farm and Ranch*, *Progressive Farmer*, and *Livestock Weekly*, none of which ever saw fit to publish his work. King became a voluminous correspondent, mailing unsolicited letters to football coaches, country singers, and even Winston Churchill and Franklin Roosevelt. Though he never received any responses, the very act of writing was liberating, bringing King closer to the big world that he knew lay out there beyond his rural West Texas home.[2]

Growing up as a child of the Depression made King aware of the importance of politics at an early age. He overheard his father and other farmers discussing Franklin Roosevelt's federal programs. To his mind, the president "was keeping people like us alive." The family earned much-needed income through the Civilian Conservation Corps and Works Progress Administration. Conversely, King also absorbed his father's "harsh sermons against the Goddamn Republicans" and how they "didn't give a shit for the little man."[3]

Inspired by the notion that Democratic politics was saving lives, encouraged by his mother's dream that he become a great orator, and driven by his own natural ambition to draw attention to himself, King began to campaign for local candidates by the time he was eight years old. In 1941, when a young New Deal congressman named Lyndon B. Johnson ran for the U.S. Senate, the candidate's grassroots organization included a twelve-year-old volunteer from Putnam. King passed out handbills and made speeches on LBJ's behalf to farmers in the fields. That campaign marked the single high point of what would later become a fractious relationship between Lyndon Johnson and Larry King.

***

In 1944, the family moved to Midland, where King's father took a job for a dollar an hour as a night watchman for Superior Oil. Midland, about halfway between El Paso and Fort Worth, was once a ranching center for those attempting to wrest a living from what was charitably referred to as "semi-desert." With the discovery of abundant oil fields in the Permian Basin, Midland became a white-collar boomtown, transforming itself into a trade and finance center for the oil industry.[4]

The Kings built their own frame house a few blocks north of downtown. The adolescent King had developed into a talented football player, and he was a welcome addition to the Midland High Bulldogs. He also joined the debate team, school newspaper, and drama club. The fact that he was the only football player participating in drama did not escape notice from his teammates. Life became even more difficult when he signed up for a typing class. At first, the other players teased him, jibing, "Take a letter, Miss King." But their glee was short-lived. King decided early on that confrontation would be the best policy. "I'd just pick up something and hit some sumbitch right on the jaw with it. That discouraged smart remarks everafter. The savage poet, I guess."[5]

Though King was popular among his classmates, there was no avoiding the acute sense of "the gap between the nightwatchman's son and the children of Midland's economic royalists." In the summer of 1945 King found work delivering mail for the Midland post office. Walking the treeless streets under the desert sun, he saw his friends from high school whizzing by in their "convertibles or Cadillacs en route to the country club pool or to patio Coke parties."[6]

By his senior year, King's prowess on the football field made him a target for "laying over." A common practice at the time—though now illegal—the scheme called for schoolboy football stars to fall deliberately short of graduating so that they could return for another senior season. King agreed to the plan but then came to regret it after his first senior year ended. Over the summer, he labored in the oil fields but soon tired of "working around hard-drinking, hard-swearing older men . . . despite adventures at poker tables, in beer joints, or in tin-topped hotels where girls were frequently rented."

Realizing that he was almost eighteen and had seen only a small corner of the world, King was anxious to move on. So, two weeks

Twenty-one-year-old Larry L. King in 1950, working as a sportswriter in Midland. *Larry L. King Archives, Southwestern Writers Collection, Texas State University-San Marcos.*

before the opening kickoff of the all-important high school football season, King shocked everyone by dropping out of school and enlisting in the United States Army.[7]

Private King was sent seventeen hundred miles northeast to the Signal Corps Photo Center in Astoria, Long Island. He had been in the army only a few months when he learned that his company had been selected for a unique experiment. President Truman was laying the groundwork to desegregate the armed forces, and the army would begin by integrating a few test units—King's among them. "I could not have been more astonished had [I been told] I would soon be bunking with Martians," King recalled.[8]

The experiment proved to be successful, as most soldiers adhered to army discipline and learned to work together. King was promoted to corporal and worked closely with the unit's top sergeant, Percy D.

Ricks, a black man from Georgia. As Ricks and King attained something of a friendship, King understood that "this was where I first knew black people and where they came to know me. We never had the chance before." He also realized that the common assumptions his friends and family had back home about African Americans were wrong in nearly every respect.[9]

King's awareness was expanding in other ways, too. The army base was just a five-cent subway ride from Manhattan, and King drank deeply of the city's culture, attending museums and Broadway plays. Soon he began dating an aspiring actress who "shortly introduced me to Greenwich Village, where I knew my first show folk, struggling authors, lesbians, marijuana experiments, and revolutionary dialogue; if such a varied show was meant to dazzle a country boy it surely succeeded," King recalled. He was "trying to make some sense of what was being said, trying to key those strange new sermons of life to the contrary preachments of my Texas youth. People casually quoted lengthy passages of what I half-suspected was Shakespeare, or snatches of what I feared might be Marx. . . . Many conversations were so wholly outside my frames of reference or experience that I simply had no mental yardstick by which to measure the moment's philosophy."[10]

King sought to use his proximity to New York to showcase his literary talent for the publishing world. He obtained his high school equivalency diploma and volunteered to write a weekly column for the post newspaper. He continued writing short stories, filling his pages with exotic characters and locales, because he understood that the only way to appeal to sophisticated readers was to appear sophisticated himself. He fired off submissions to New York-based literary magazines, but none of his stories was accepted or even acknowledged.

When his discharge came in July 1949, twenty-year-old Larry L. King left New York, dreaming of returning one day to conquer the literary world. As he hitchhiked through West Texas, he caught a ride that took him to Hobbs, New Mexico, a booming oil town just across the state line. There, he noticed that the *Hobbs Daily Flare*, the smaller of the town's two newspapers, needed a reporter. Inventing just enough of a background in journalism, he "conned 'em out of a job." Over the next few months, King wrote routine news stories and gradually grew more comfortable in his occupation. Then he stepped into the middle of a local political battle. After a federal judge handed down a ruling against the town's mayor, King issued a blistering front-page editorial that came "dangerously close" to libeling the judge. As King later recalled, "It was obviously just a terrible goddamn attack by an ignorant kid who knew nothing about the goddamn law or anything else much." The judge made his displeasure known to the *Daily Flare*'s publisher, who immediately fired King.[11]

He hitchhiked back to Midland to live with his family while looking for another newspaper job. Midland's phenomenal economic boom had continued, and the city would grow to over sixty thousand people by the end of the 1950s. The promise of great wealth in the remote dusty outpost even lured scions of the East Coast aristocrats, among them George Herbert Walker Bush. Oil-rich West Texas was one of the most politically conservative areas of the state, but under the influence of easterners, Midland also began to acquire cultural amenities such as a community theater and a symphony orchestra.

King labored at a variety of grim jobs while sending out fresh inquiry letters to newspapers. He trained as a telephone company lineman, worked the counter at his brother's drive-in restaurant, and even, briefly, shoveled goat droppings for a living. He kept an application on file at the *Midland Reporter-Telegram*, but, with no openings available, he enrolled as a journalism major at Texas Technological College (now Texas Tech University) in Lubbock. It didn't take long for him to realize that he had made a mistake. He found the campus reactionary and intellectually vapid. He could recall "absolutely no conversations touching on politics, social reform, history, literature, or sociology." It was a long way from Greenwich Village. He began skipping classes, staying in his dorm room and writing "some of the world's most hapless short stories." He also sent off inquiry letters to New York-area newspapers, never receiving a response. He soon "lowered [his] sights to include the *Fort Worth Star-Telegram, Dallas Morning News*" and others. The only reply he received was from the *Star-Telegram*, suggesting that he apply to their competition, *The Fort Worth Press*. King recalled that "this so depleted my confidence that I sent no more applications." A few weeks into his second semester, without bothering to withdraw formally, King quit school and returned to his parents' home in Midland.[12]

***

In September 1950 the sportswriter at the *Midland Reporter-Telegram* was called up to fight in Korea, and suddenly, Larry L. King was back in journalism. He also married Wilma Jeanne Casey of Okmulgee, Oklahoma. He earned $55 a week, and she brought in another $18 as a telephone operator. Their first child arrived the next year.[13]

After writing virtually his entire life and receiving only glancing notice, King was thrilled to have a byline in his hometown paper. He was, finally, a *writer*. But the *Reporter-Telegram* was hardly shaking up the journalism profession. It was much like nearly every other Texas newspaper of the era: dominated by Chamber of Commerce boosterism rather than journalistic principles, timid in all respects except for a fierce devotion to promoting its city as an economic mecca. Its view of the business community was that it should be left untaxed, unregulated, and unquestioned. The news desk concentrated on saccharine society tidbits mixed with sensational accounts of car wrecks and violent deaths. Few stories ever appeared about Midland's minority residents unless they were charged with crimes.

Because sportswriters generally had more freedom than other reporters to express opinions, King could experiment with his writing style. He also sought to compensate for his lack of formal education by reading widely, taking full advantage of the Midland County Library. It was there in 1950 that he learned that George Washington and Thomas Jefferson had been slave owners. Shocked, he understood for the first time the extent of the miseducation he had received in school. King thought to himself, "Hell if they lied to me about that, they've lied to me about everything."[14]

At the *Midland Reporter-Telegram*, King decided it was time to change things. He ordered photographs of the black high school's basketball team, "only to be instructed that our paper's policy precluded publication of 'nigger art.'" Later, he wrote a story about Midland High School's first Mexican American varsity football player. His task, as it was explained to him, was to reassure white readers that the young man had "excellent manners, scholastic worth, humility, and all-around ability." But King also pointed out that while the student worked at a local restaurant, he couldn't be served there unless he ate in the kitchen. "That little gem," King remembered later, "was promptly blue-penciled by an agitated editor." King was learning that even sports coverage is political.[15]

Frustrated by the limitations of his newspaper work, King's ambitions remained grand. He continued his creative writing on the side and also found an artistic outlet at Midland Community Theatre. He began showing up at rehearsals, eventually acting in some productions. He also began to work on his own stage play. King frequently joined the cast and crew after hours to talk about the theater, writing, politics, and other subjects.

One person who did not join King during these occasions was his wife. The couple was already experiencing differences over King's literary ambitions. Jeanne resented the time he spent reading, writing, and carousing with like-minded types. In their first year of marriage she threw out some of his books and magazines. King shook a finger in her face and said, "Goddammit, you are NOT going to take reading and writing away from me and if this ever happens again I'm gone!"[16]

King's interest in politics remained acute, and in 1952 he worked on behalf of two losing campaigns: Adlai Stevenson's presidential bid and Texas liberal leader Ralph Yarborough's first run against Allan Shivers for governor. King's superiors at the *Reporter-Telegram* took notice, and the editor demanded that he stop his activity. King responded, "As far as I understand it, the Constitution guarantees freedom of speech even to sportswriters."[17]

His heretical politics were troubling enough, but increasingly King's sports columns, once enjoyed for their often humorous takes on the game, came to be seen as too critical of Midland's minor league baseball team. Despite repeated warnings, he continued to poke fun. As he said later, "If you've got a goddamn baseball team that's 2 and 24 or something like that in a Class D league, how are you going to write about them if you don't write about them critically and funny?"[18]

When King began to complain about the paper's policy of requiring mandatory overtime with no compensation, the *Reporter-Telegram* had seen enough. The managing editor approached King's desk one morning and informed him that he was fired, effective immediately. King, somewhat shocked, began circulating around the newsroom, telling others what had just happened. Then the editor noticed that King still had not left. He came over and ordered King to leave the premises. King snapped. He punched the man in the mouth, knocking him down. The editor in chief came running out of his office, only to be shoved by King back into the oil editor, sending both men to the floor. In a rage, King jumped up onto the counter that separated the advertising and editorial departments, yelling obscenities at people around the room. He concluded his tirade by pointing at the editors, telling them, "You sorry old fuckers, you got no fucking soul."[19]

***

After leaving the *Reporter-Telegram* building, Larry L. King walked five blocks up the street to KCRS radio, where he was a friend of the station manager. Broadcasting at 5000 watts, KCRS was Midland's dominant station and was said to have the strongest signal between Fort Worth and El Paso. The station manager had a well-known hatred of the *Reporter-Telegram*, and, after hearing King's story, decided to hire him to set up and run Midland's first local news program. At KCRS King became far better known in West Texas than he ever had been as a print journalist. He delivered live sports reports in the mornings; he wrote and broadcast a thirty-minute news program at lunchtime; and his taped news summary could be heard every evening. King also broadcast live from a variety of special events—everything from parades to the dedication of the new Greyhound bus station. He also used his position to goad the *Reporter-Telegram* from time to time. Once King solemnly reported that a well-financed out-of-state newspaper chain had sent representatives to Midland to investigate the possibility of establishing a competing newspaper. After a couple of follow-up reports, King eased up, enjoying how the talk on the street was causing some nervous jitters in the offices of the *Reporter-Telegram.*[20]

After seven months at KCRS, the *Odessa American* offered Larry King a job as a reporter at $100 per week, which would make the twenty-three-year-old one of the highest-paid newsmen in West Texas. Odessa, about twenty miles southwest of Midland, was another booming Permian Basin city. The blue-collar counterpart to Midland, Odessa supplied equipment and labor for the oil fields. If Midland was referred to as "the brains" of the oil industry, Odessa proudly considered itself "the muscle." A fierce rivalry developed between the two cities, often expressed through the football games played between their high school teams. Like Midland, Odessa's growth was phenomenal. With just 750 residents before the oil boom, Odessa swelled to over 80,000 by the 1960s.[21]

The *Odessa American* had been acquired five years earlier by R. C. Hoiles, a California millionaire widely considered one of the most reactionary men in journalism. Hoiles was so extreme that he didn't believe in public schools, public parks, public libraries, or public roads. He used his newspapers to promulgate his views and the *American* obligingly ran Hoiles' rabid editorial columns along with a canned twenty-one-part series on "The Income Tax, Root of All Evil." Occasional complaints were voiced in Odessa by those who conceded that they hated Godless Socialism just as much as everyone else, but why were *public roads* and *post offices* such a bad thing? The *American* had a ready response for these complaints: "Next time our friends think we have 'gone too far' we ask them to remember that so long as we can't be in perfect agreement with them all the time, it's better for us to be to the Right of their beliefs than to the Left."[22]

While Hoiles' views dominated the editorial pages, the absentee owner was largely removed from the day-to-day operations, which were guided more by conservative publisher V. L. DeBolt and the pragmatic editors Jim Scott and Brad Carlisle. King, as the local news reporter, covered everything from city hall meetings to car wrecks and honky-tonk stabbings. Riding along with Odessa's cops, he saw first-hand how the white establishment used the police department to sub-jugate the minority population. Though King could never write about it at the time, he saw how officers continually harassed the town's blacks, stopping them on the street and forcing them to stand respect-fully at attention. The police were a constant, threatening presence in black clubs. But in Odessa's white bars, the brawling oilfield workers and ranch hands were subject to police intervention only when the club owners called for assistance. The separate and unequal treat-ment extended to the various forms of gambling. As King later wrote, "Everyone in town knew about the posh gambling house near the Country Club where our high-rollers knew not to expect the sheriff unless he happened by for their votes." At the same time, the police constantly raided small gatherings of the town's black men who played small-stakes card games among themselves.[23]

Taking note of all this, King suggested that the *American* "run a series on double standards in our courts, police operations, hospitals, and other public institutions." King's editor, after several weeks of delays, grudgingly agreed to see a sample story. This was followed by a long silence. Then one evening, as the two men "shared more drinks than was good for secrets," King asked about the series again. "Look," the editor said, "stop spinning your wheels. The publisher hit the ceil-ing when I mentioned your goddamned nigger series. If I turned in that story you wrote he'd probably fire us both."[24]

King understood that police coverage, just like sports at the *Reporter-Telegram,* was shackled by the newspaper's political ideology. While he rarely had a chance to report the news as he saw it, he was gaining valuable experience. As he wrote later, "I believe I was fortu-nate to work for small dailies where young reporters had the opportu-nity to cover everything: city hall, murder trials, sports, labor disputes, oilwell fires, state and regional politics, the police beat." King also learned, as David Halberstam later pointed out, "that the same lies told in city hall or the police station by 'official spokesmen' would later be repeated on a larger scale from the White House and the Pentagon."[25]

Though he felt destined for greatness, King still wasn't sure how to fulfill his ambition. He kept writing fiction in his spare time and maintained his involvement in local theater. In 1953 he finished his first stage play, which told the story of a small-town newspaper taken over by a big chain. The play addressed the "angers and betrayals of people who had been faithful to their jobs and to their newspaper and then got booted in the ass by Corporate America." As King later recalled, "that alleged play must have had a cast of thirty or more and lasted well over three hours in the one staged reading I got in Odessa by several actors from the Permian Playhouse and friends I had roped in. Even I recognized how bad it was fifteen minutes in and wanted to sneak off and hide but, unfortunately, had cast myself in a prominent role and couldn't leave."[26]

***

King's ambitions eventually melded with politics in 1954, bringing to a head his long struggle against the conservatism of his native region. It was a remarkable year, as Joseph McCarthy's Communist witch hunt reached its peak and the Supreme Court issued its landmark *Brown v. Board of Education* ruling. In West Texas, the year's top story concerned Corporal Claude Batchelor, a native son who became notorious as a "turncoat" during the Korean War. Batchelor was captured by the North Koreans and "reeducated" in a prisoner-of-war camp. At the cessation of hostilities, Batchelor became one of twenty-one American servicemen who refused to return to the United States. He explained that his captors "pointed out how this rich country has neglected its poor people . . . and especially its Negro people. . . . I thought about what I had seen back here, and decided it was true."[27]

Batchelor's defection came as a shock to West Texans, who prided themselves on their patriotic zeal. Larry L. King covered the local angle for the *Odessa American* and interviewed Batchelor's parents. "I got to know them a bit and felt more sorry for Batchelor than anything," King said later. Like King, Batchelor had grown up poor and dropped out of high school to join the service. King also understood that, however misguided Batchelor's decision, his criticisms of America had merit.[28]

In January 1954 the news came that Batchelor had changed his mind and had decided to come home after all. King wrote a deeply sympathetic account of the family's reaction to the "joyous bombshell." Noticeably absent in the story was any condemnation of Claude Batchelor himself, who would ultimately be court-martialed and sentenced to twenty years in federal prison. It was this oversight that outraged readers. As King wrote later, "our ultra-conservative newspaper became the target of nuts and kooks who saw a Communist plot in our reporting such 'Red' news." The *American* quickly yanked King off the story, and all further updates on the Batchelor case came through wire-service stories.[29]

In May 1954, just a few weeks after the Supreme Court's *Brown v. Board of Education* decision, King learned of a young black man who planned to enroll in the local junior college. James Robbins, a Korean War veteran, told King that he had always wanted to go to college, "but there wasn't much I could do about it. I didn't have the money to go off someplace to school. . . . Then the Supreme Court came up with the ruling and I decided to take advantage of it." Robbins' application was accepted, and, after some discussion, the *American* decided to carry news of the event on its front page. King followed up two days later with a front-page profile of Robbins, pointing out that the student was occupied with such "normal thoughts" as class schedules and a part-time job. "But Robbins had one more thought to harbor," King told readers, "one that normally doesn't enter into the mind of a student just starting to college. He was getting ready to break the 'color line' of an all-white school."[30]

The next day, King was approached by a deputy sheriff. "Boy, I seen where you give that damn nigger plenty of ink in yesterday's paper." From there, the campaign of police harassment against the would-be student began. Three Odessa policemen claimed that a drunken Robbins had cursed them and attempted to attack them. Two days later, rape charges were brought against Robbins. The young man was notified that all charges against him would be dropped if he withdrew his college application and left town. He did so shortly after. King, who was prevented from publishing any further stories on the matter, went to the local FBI office and asked for a formal investigation. His request was denied, though word of his complaint was quickly passed on to the Odessa Police Department. Suddenly, King found himself viewed with suspicion by the men he covered on a day-to-day basis. Many years later King would discover just how much anxiety he had caused during this period. He had not been the only one to contact the FBI at the time. The bureau had also received complaints about *King,* demanding that *he* be investigated—as a possible Communist.[31]

***

King was still angry about the James Robbins episode as election season descended on Texas. As a one-party state, races were essentially decided in July during the Democratic primary. The year 1954 brought a contentious rematch between conservative governor Allan Shivers and populist liberal Ralph Yarborough. Locally, conservative U.S. Congressman Ken Regan was challenged by moderate State Senator J. T. Rutherford. King was a friend of Rutherford's and had, in fact, helped convince him to make the race. Rutherford appeared to have little chance at the outset against the independently wealthy Regan, who was backed by area oil companies. Rutherford's campaign was so destitute that he had no real campaign manager. But he did have an enthusiastic volunteer—Larry L. King.

Working nights and weekends, King wrote Rutherford's press releases, and together the two men finessed the stories into print and got them aired on the radio. King also suggested to his superiors at the *Odessa American* that the paper could benefit by having a "political writer" during the upcoming campaign season. At the very least, they could show up the Midland paper, which had none. King even volunteered to take on the additional duties himself. The *American* was pleased at the prospect of getting something for nothing, so it accepted King's offer, and he set out to cover the campaigns.[32]

The *Odessa American,* of course, opposed both Ralph Yarborough and J. T. Rutherford and editorialized against both candidates. King, then, felt justified in using his news stories to make up the difference. This would not be easy to get away with. He would have to slant his stories enough to make a difference, but not so much that he would get caught. King proved equal to the challenge. Typically, he would cover candidate forums and focus attention on Rutherford's criticism that the incumbent was an "absentee congressman" who "prefers the cool breezes of vacation resorts to West Texas." This charge, coming as it did during a drought-plagued Texas summer, found a receptive audience. Congressman Regan's responses were generally muted, or, more often, King noted that Regan was not present at the forum to defend himself. This fact, of course, only reinforced Rutherford's basic campaign message.

King also made use of subtle rhetorical strategies. In one story, he noted that El Paso's two newspapers were split over the candidates. He wrote, "The *El Paso Herald-Post* thinks that Rutherford can do no wrong and Regan can do no right." After planting the image that "Regan can do no right" in readers' minds, King simply added, "The *El Paso Times* looks at it the other way." Regan's backers, including the publisher of the *American,* were supremely confident of victory and took little notice at the time of the subtleties in King's reporting.[33]

As Election Day drew near it became clear that the race might indeed be close. Congressman Regan's backers took out full-page ads in the *Odessa American,* but it was too late. J. T. Rutherford won the election by one hundred forty-nine votes out of the fifty-four thousand cast, and the difference came in Odessa, which Rutherford carried by nearly three thousand votes. *Odessa American* publisher V. L. DeBolt was livid. He began thumbing through back issues of his newspaper to find out where he had gone wrong. When he realized what had happened, he demanded that King be fired—immediately. But just as the order was being carried out, DeBolt learned that King had just been hired as the new congressman's chief aide and would in fact be resigning. Larry L. King, now twenty-five-years-old, was at long last headed back to the East Coast, center of the publishing world.[34]

2.

A

TEXAS

OASIS

ustin, whether referred to as "the city with a violet crown" or "The Live Music Capital of the World," has long been considered a cultural and geographical oasis in Texas. The city's setting at the base of the Balcones Escarpment rises to pleasant tree-covered hills cut by clear-running streams. Barton Springs, a natural spring-fed swimming hole, is a particularly beautiful spot that has become a treasured civic symbol. Austin's sense of separateness from the rest of Texas has also been shaped by two important civic affiliations: It is the state capital and home to the University of Texas. Generations of young Texans have succumbed to Austin's charms while attending college, and the university's cultural influence ripened as students over the years have found ways to settle in Austin after graduation. Even today almost twenty-five percent of Austin's residents have college degrees, far above the national average for a city of its size. Austin residents also buy more books per capita than residents in any other city in the country. This concentration of college-educated residents has given Austin a reputation for progressive politics, and the city has certainly been far ahead of the rest of Texas in its environmental activism. Yet in its history of ethnic relations and its sanctioning of official segregation, Austin has been no better than any other southern city.

In addition to the cultural amenities provided by the university and the city's unique setting as the state capital, Austin's pleasant landscape and relatively mild winters have long made it a haven for writers and artists. In the 1880s European-born sculptor Elisabet Ney opened a studio in town, establishing Austin as an arts outpost for the first time. Also in the 1880s William Sydney Porter, later known for his short stories under the pseudonym O. Henry, arrived in Austin. Porter founded his weekly newspaper, *Rolling Stone,* on a printing press he had purchased from William Cowper Brann, who later became notorious as editor of Waco, Texas' *The Iconoclast.* Brann, who "took obvious relish in directing his stinging attacks," has endured as a legend to many independent-minded Texas journalists. Particularly memorable are the circumstances of Brann's death. After being shot in the back by a critic as he walked down a street in Waco in 1898, Brann turned and, before he died, pulled out his own gun and shot his assailant to death.[1]

During the first half of the twentieth century, Austin became the home base of Texas' literary triumvirate, J. Frank Dobie, Walter Prescott Webb, and Roy Bedichek. Dobie and Bedichek, in particular, could often be found hanging out at Barton Springs. In 1995 a large statue of the three men was installed outside the entrance to the city pool—the only public statue in the state commemorating Texas writers. Dobie and Webb both taught at the University of Texas, and Bedichek was employed at the UT extension office. Though all three men have been vilified as racists in the years since their deaths, in their times they held relatively progressive political views. Dobie in particular was an outspoken advocate of liberalism. As the driving force in the Texas Folklore Society, he integrated the organization single-handedly. In 1930 a student he mentored, Jovita González, became president of the organization, a remarkable accomplishment at the time for a woman and Hispanic in Texas. Dobie also supported the work of African American folklorist J. Mason Brewer. As early as the 1940s, Dobie was publicly calling for the complete integration of the University of Texas.

Dobie, Webb, and Bedichek were hardly the only liberals working at UT-Austin, a fact that did not escape the notice of the state's politicians. Though ostensibly aligned with the national Democratic Party, the state's political establishment became increasingly conservative as the country emerged from the Great Depression. Immense wealth was waiting to be extracted from Texas' rich oil and gas fields, and businessmen wanted no government intervention. Texas liberals were initially enthusiastic about the oil discoveries, believing that oil revenues could pave the way for Texas to develop a first-class educational system and stellar social programs. Yet the state's business interests had a different agenda. The very idea of taxing mineral wealth was derided as "illegal confiscation," and soon an "oil depletion allowance" became the law of the land. This extravagant loophole, unmatched in any other industry, allowed oil companies to take a twenty-seven-and-a-half percent deduction on their earnings before being subject to any taxation. The oil depletion allowance became an anathema to liberals and remained the target of failed attempts at tax reform for decades to come.

As Texas' political climate became more conservative in the 1940s, renewed attention was focused on the University of Texas' "liberalism." UT had often seen its appropriations threatened and its teachings scrutinized by legislators seeking to pander to anti-intellectual forces in their home districts. As historian Joe B. Frantz has written, "The University of Texas has the worst reputation of any academic institution in the United States for being ridden, even overwhelmed, by politics—and it is deserved." During the 1940s, regents appointed by governors W. Lee "Pappy" O'Daniel and Coke Stevenson began harassing UT President Homer Rainey. One regent objected to having the university teach social work because it would "create socialists." Another proposed patriotism tests for faculty; still another sought to fire Roy Bedichek because he had presided over rules changes that affected the regent's sons' eligibility for high school athletics. After President Rainey refused to intervene, the regent responded that he would "fight you like hell."[2]

In 1944 the regents sought to remove John Dos Passos' novel *U.S.A.* from literature classes, finding the book "subversive and perverted." Rainey refused. For the regents, this was the final outrage. Rainey was fired. In response huge protests broke out across Austin.

Students boycotted classes and thousands marched from the campus to the State Capitol. The university was excoriated in the nation's press, placed on probation by its accrediting agency, and formally censured by the American Association of University Professors. Among the deposed president's staunchest supporters was J. Frank Dobie. Mindful of the United States's ongoing war against Nazi Germany, Dobie called the regents "native fascists."[3]

Though the Homer Rainey affair had caused national embarrassment, UT's regents seemed to feel little remorse. In 1947 they denied J. Frank Dobie's application for a temporary leave of absence, a request that had routinely been granted to him in the past. Another standoff ensued, and Dobie refused to capitulate. The result was that J. Frank Dobie, the state's most popular writer, found himself effectively terminated from the university he had worked for since 1914.

As conservatives increasingly dominated the state's politics, it was easy to overlook the fact that Texas has always been home to a vibrant, though small, group of Anglo progressives. Though the liberals quarreled and often became factionalized, they were also bound together by their small numbers, their mutual condescension toward the anti-intellectual conservatives, and their implicit understanding of the futility of their enterprise. As the state's capital, Austin was the place where these politically minded provocateurs tended to congregate, if for no other reason than to keep a watchful eye on the conservatives.

These Texans had long worked to make their voices heard, if not by others, at least by one another. A long line of progressive newspapers dated back to the dawn of the twentieth century, and in 1946 the most ambitious forum yet was established. The Austin-based *Texas Spectator* crusaded for civil rights, labor, and education. It covered university politics and featured columns by prominent liberal Texas writers like J. Frank Dobie and Hart Stilwell. The *Spectator* also pinpointed the ways oil and gas interests dominated Texas' public policy. As one progressive wrote, "the men who now control the destinies [of Texas have] a tradition not of moral leadership . . . but of ruthless buccaneering."[4]

By 1948, however, the *Spectator* ran out of money and suspended publication. It was supplanted in the early 1950s by *The State Observer*, which called itself the "Independent Newsweekly of Texas." *The State Observer* was less engaging than the *Spectator* and circulation declined steadily. By early 1954 it was on the verge of collapse.[5]

The 1954 governor's race between Allan Shivers and Ralph Yarborough demonstrated to the state's liberals just how poorly their candidates were treated by the Texas press. Texas was enthralled by Wisconsin Senator Joseph McCarthy's anticommunist crusade, and McCarthy received massive financial support from oil millionaires. Newspapers editorialized in his favor, and McCarthy was often referred to as "Texas' Third Senator."

In the contest for governor, Allan Shivers made red-baiting the centerpiece of his campaign. Shivers, who advocated the death penalty for membership in the Communist Party, linked liberal Ralph Yarborough to a "Communist" strike in Port Arthur. Of the one hundred daily newspapers in Texas, ninety-five endorsed Allan Shivers, and the tone of their news coverage clearly favored the conservative incumbent. The state's media gleefully reported Shivers' smears against Yarborough, while at the same time overlooking ample, concrete evidence of widespread corruption within the Shivers governorship. A major scandal involving the Veterans' Land Board was uncovered not by any of the major Texas dailies but by the feisty *Cuero Record*, which won a Pulitzer Prize for its reporting. Despite Shivers' overwhelming support among the state's business establishment and newspapers, Yarborough nearly pulled off an upset win.[6]

Angered at the state's press, a group of Texas liberals led by Minnie Fisher Cunningham and Lillian Collier decided to fight back. They formed a group of sympathetic investors who agreed to fund a new newspaper to help spread liberal views to Texas voters. They purchased *The State Observer* and merged it with the *East Texas Democrat*, which had been established the previous year. The first task was to find a suitable editor for the new weekly. After some discussion, the board offered the job to Ronnie Dugger, a twenty-four-year-old graduate student studying economics and philosophy at the

University of Texas. Dugger first came to the attention of state liberals in 1950 as the editor of the UT's campus newspaper, *The Daily Texan*. There, Dugger constantly editorialized in favor of integrating the campus at a time when even the state's liberal leaders, including Ralph Yarborough, maintained that they favored segregation. When he was approached about the job, Dugger initially refused, because he did not want to be part of a "hack political organ." But once he received assurances of editorial autonomy, he agreed to take on the job.[7]

The *Texas Observer* published its first issue December 13, 1954, and it made an immediate impact on the political culture of the state. Unlike previous liberal newspaper efforts, Dugger's *Observer* wasn't content just to comment sardonically on the issues. Instead, it investigated them—fiercely. Dugger wrote stories that challenged the state's politicians—and the state's press—in ways they had never been confronted before. Following up on the *Cuero Record*, the *Observer* brought to light major corruption scandals involving state officials. It also ran exposés on racism, segregation, capital punishment, slums, mental hospitals, book censorship, and academic freedom. Dugger also detailed the relationship between lobbyists and legislators, attacking what he saw as the lynchpin of the conservative establishment's dominance of Texas.

Dugger's vision for the *Observer* also included an eclectic approach to covering the state's culture and arts, a concept he had picked up from reading the *Texas Spectator* as an undergraduate back in the late 1940s. Dugger brought in well-known personalities from outside the political spectrum. He gave them the opportunity to write "stories other papers won't touch, and to do them unwaveringly and in whatever depth they believe is demanded."[8] This was a rare opportunity for Texans. Contributors to the *Observer* in those early days included J. Frank Dobie, Roy Bedichek, John Silber, George I. Sanchez, Willie Morris, and Sarah T. Hughes.

Soon the *Observer* became required reading among the political cognoscenti, if for no other reason than to keep abreast of who was being investigated. Though the total circulation remained small, and far below what its backers had hoped, the *Observer* exercised an influence far beyond its modest numbers.

About three months into the *Observer*'s existence a young reporter from the *Austin American-Statesman* began to drift over to Dugger's office in the evenings. At first he merely read through the stacks of Texas newspapers and clipped articles for Dugger's attention. Before long he was writing his own articles, signing them BB or WLB "to conceal his leftist treachery from his bosses downtown."[9] Soon, the reporter, Bill Brammer, resigned from his job at the *Statesman* and became the *Texas Observer*'s first associate editor. Though his tenure at the *Observer* lasted only a few months, Brammer's experiences formed the setting for what would become widely considered Texas' first successful urban novel: *The Gay Place*.

***

Billie Lee Brammer, born prematurely in April 1929, remained small his entire life, topping out at just under five feet seven inches. Brammer was raised in Oak Cliff, a white, middle-class suburb of Dallas. Early on he displayed a strong stubborn streak, evidenced when he refused to spell his name "Billie" as his parents had christened him. Fearful that the spelling was feminine, he began signing his name "Billy" by the time he entered grade school.

Oak Cliff, separated from Dallas by the Trinity River, seemed far removed from the energy of the big city, and Brammer considered his home life boring. Reading books allowed him an outlet, and he quickly developed a voracious interest in reading. When he was twelve years old, he decided to teach himself how to type by rewriting books on his mother's typewriter. His sources ranged from Hemingway novels and Tarzan stories to books by J. Frank Dobie and F. Scott Fitzgerald. It was Fitzgerald who "awakened" Brammer's interest in writing and became his literary hero.[10] Through his love of books and his interest in writing, Brammer became exposed to ideas and works largely absent from his formal education. Though he did not yet know it, he was on his way to becoming a self-educated Texas intellectual.

In 1947 Brammer entered the University of Texas at Austin, but his grades were poor, and he transferred to North Texas State College (now the University of North Texas) in Denton, thirty-five miles north of Dallas. Brammer majored in journalism and wrote a column for the school paper, discussing politics, books, and jazz while poking fun at the school fraternities. His inquisitive intelligence and low-key anarchism gave him the aura of a hipster intellectual, and he was as adept at discussing literary trends as he was dancing in jazz clubs. Soon he met Nadine Cannon, a sultry and beautiful art major from the lower Rio Grande Valley. Nadine was already far more worldly and sophisticated than Brammer. She had a tinge of exoticism, favoring Moroccan sandals and gull-wing sunglasses. Nadine also introduced Brammer to Benzedrine, a stimulant disguised as a "diet pill" that was commonly available along the Texas-Mexico border. Nadine later remembered that Brammer "loved it right away. He said it helped him get into his writing."[11]

After a few months of dating, Bill and Nadine eloped to nearby Lewisville. Brammer got a part-time job on the *Denton Record-Chronicle* and later secured a six-month internship with the *Corpus Christi Caller-Times*. There he worked as a sportswriter under future *Sports Illustrated* staffer Roy Terrell. In Corpus Christi, he and Nadine plotted their move to Europe, where they planned to become expatriates and sit in sidewalk cafés. In the meantime, Brammer found a permanent job. The *Austin Statesman* hired him as a sportswriter at $56 a week.

Money was tight, and when Nadine became pregnant she went to live with her parents in South Texas. Brammer hoped to find a newspaper job near her but was unsuccessful. After giving birth, Nadine returned to Austin with their daughter. At the *Austin Statesman*, Bill Brammer quickly worked his way out of sportswriting and into general reporting. His lighthearted, wryly bemused writing style was popular with readers, and editors often assigned him feature stories. In 1952 the twenty-two-year-old won the *Statesman*'s in-house writing award. Another story earned him first place in the 1953 Texas Associated Press Managing Editors Contest. The *Statesman,* in its report on

Brammer's award, commented that the story was told in his "usual unusual style."[12] Though the young writer had not published any fiction, he was interested in the idea of a novel. He began fashioning a manuscript about his life and the people he knew in Austin.

Bill and Nadine Brammer were among the hippest, most attractive young couples in Austin, part of an intellectually charged social set. Much of the activity centered around the Scholz Garten, a venerable political watering hole that had been operating since 1866. The Scholz Garten was the hangout for conservative politicians and disaffected liberals alike, and the beer, conversation, and gossip flowed freely on the outdoor patio shaded by live oak trees. "There was a real magic in Austin then," recalled Nadine Brammer. "There was lots of excitement and energy, a lot of young people who wanted to try new things—new music, new politics, new ideas — new everything! Those were very exciting, very romantic times."[13]

Even among the group, Bill and Nadine stood out. One of their friends was Robert Benton, a UT student and artist who went on to become an Academy Award-winning director/writer known for his films *Kramer vs. Kramer* and *Places in the Heart.* Benton remembered that Bill and Nadine Brammer were "like creatures from another planet . . . they were far more sophisticated, far more curious, and they were plugged into a whole world that nobody knew in the middle '50s."[14]

Other friends included labor lawyer David Richards and his wife, Ann, who would become governor of Texas thirty-five years later. Another friend was UT student Willie Morris, the latest in a long line of crusading editors at the *Daily Texan.* Morris, who later became an acclaimed writer and editor of *Harper's* magazine, was attracting national attention for his challenges to UT's censorship. Morris recalled that Bill and Nadine Brammer "were like an older brother and sister to me; their honesty and flamboyance were enormously exciting."[15]

The *Texas Observer* was a central part of their crowd, so it was inevitable that the paper, with its editorial freedom and creative energy, would attract Bill Brammer. His friend Bob Sherrill was writing a regular column in the *Observer*. Willie Morris also appeared in its pages, and Robert Benton contributed an editorial cartoon. When Brammer first showed up at the office, Ronnie Dugger recalled, it was mainly to "overhear and to laugh. He was a born spy."[16]

As Brammer began writing for the *Observer*, it became clear that he had little interest in policy issues. He enjoyed personalities and features, just as he had as a reporter at the *American-Statesman*. Brammer was a gifted stylist, and he used delicate humor and keen insight as he wrote profiles of right-wing extremists, political hucksters, prominent journalists, and the state's colorful politicians.

In his first story after formally joining the *Observer*'s staff, twenty-five-year-old Brammer profiled a San Antonio policeman who had been suspended for engaging in white supremacist activities. The cop explained to Brammer, "Any minister who preaches social equality is nothing but a Communist. Anyone who believes it is a Communist. The Jew-Communists are behind the NAACP—that's a Communist-inspired organization—and I know because that's what the Communists want, integration and mongrelization of the races." Brammer's great gift, and what set him apart from the grim tone of much of the rest of the *Observer*, was his whimsical sense of the absurd. As the cop ranted, Brammer described how the policeman's son came charging through the room "with a water pistol, yelling 'Communist, Communist, Communist.'"[17] Brammer, securely in command of his material, enjoyed the mocking parallels between the deadly serious cop and his son's childlike naïveté.

Following this story, Brammer began a four-part series on "The Political Hucksters," bringing to light the men who had directed Allan Shivers' smear campaign against Ralph Yarborough in 1954. Brammer's reporting on Texas' political netherworld included an account of liberal state representative Harold "Barefoot" Sanders, called a Communist by an opponent during a political rally. Brammer reported that "Sanders challenged the fellow—not to a debate but a good old fashioned fist fight."[18] That scene would remain etched in Brammer's mind as he continued work on his novel about Austin.

Brammer's work for the *Observer* gave him an opportunity to explore his interest in fiction. He reviewed Edna Ferber's *Giant*, con-

cluding that it was "a richly conceived and rottenly written book."[19]
In May 1955 the *Observer* published his short story, "The Green
Board," which reads like an excerpt from an early draft of *The Gay
Place*. Addressing the insidious influence of lobbyists, the tale weaves
together a portrait of a boozy legislator who struggles to reconcile his
social conscience with his thirst for alcohol.

Though Dugger and Brammer were friends and colleagues,
Brammer could never become as politically committed as Dugger
wished. Dugger had a strong moral view of government that he
expressed through his work. As such, he became greatly agitated
when he suspected that the *Observer*'s telephones were wiretapped.
But Brammer, for his part, just couldn't believe it. He wrote later,
"Perhaps they were tapped—I've always hoped they were. There's
been precious little intrigue in my life, and at this point I'm inclined
to welcome a really first-rate gang of spies and trenchcoat-flapping
saboteurs." Brammer's sense of whimsy extended to his farcical critique of the *Observer*'s guiding philosophy. In his editorial, "A Fragile
Subject," Brammer conceded that the *Observer*'s "missing ingredient,
obviously, is sex. Whether from sheer ennui or just plain boyish mod-
esty, we have completely forsaken this realm of journalism. Well, let's
live a little." Brammer humorously suggested more "cheesecake"
descriptions in the *Observer*'s pages. He also appealed to readers for
monetary donations, with the promise that "We'll spend it like
crazy."[20]

While Dugger concentrated on ferreting out political scandals,
Brammer continued to aim toward features. When filming for the
movie *Giant* began out in Marfa, in far West Texas, Brammer arranged
to cover the spectacle for the *Observer*. Brammer's dispatches from
Marfa are some of his best work in the *Observer*—indeed, the most
sophisticated writing of any Texas journalist at the time. Brammer
reveled in the contrasts between the full-scale Hollywood production
and the remote Texas village. Describing the Californians' attempts to
dress like the natives, Brammer concluded, "It's something like seeing
a mob of zoot-suited drugstore cowboys." Of the movie set constructed
outside of town, he wrote, "It's as if a vast, traveling circus has broken
down in the midst of this desolation and set up shop." He delighted

in exposing the artifice of moviemaking, pointing out that the Texas tumbleweeds were imported from California. The prefabricated "mansion" constructed for the film, Brammer informed readers, would be used as a hay barn after the filming. There it would host "cattle so sumptuously housed" that they "will probably be gawked at by passersby on the highway for years to come. Coming hard upon it, after mile on mile of endless desert land, you feel it's something of a mirage."[21]

After their return to Austin, Bill and Nadine Brammer continued weekend socializing with friends, though differences between them were beginning to emerge. Nadine's good looks and spirited personality made her enormously popular during the gatherings. Yet Bill Brammer "wanted a conservative personal life but did not find it among his . . . Austin friends," according to Ronnie Dugger. Complicating matters was the family's financial troubles. With two small children and his modest salary as the *Observer*'s associate editor, Bill Brammer was under constant financial duress. His inability to cope with the reality of the situation only made things worse. "When frustrated he'd go on a shopping spree, running up bills he couldn't pay," Nadine recalled. "We had nine cars in six years. . . . I always knew when we were broke—he'd go out and buy a new car. Or he'd buy me a lot of really good-looking clothes, and then we had to go out and pay for them."[22]

At the Scholz Garten rumors were circulating that U.S. Senator Lyndon B. Johnson wanted to add a young liberal to his staff. Most liberals distrusted LBJ and resented him as a "turncoat." Johnson had initially won election to Congress by swearing fealty to Roosevelt's New Deal, yet he had increasingly tacked to the right, aligning himself with conservative businessmen. Though virtually his entire adult life had been spent in public service, Johnson had amassed a huge personal fortune. Obviously a man with national ambitions, Johnson had become the Senate Democratic leader just four years after taking office. He was a master at shepherding legislation through the chamber, and he remains credited as the most effective Senate leader in history. He wanted desperately to become president, yet no southerner had been elected since the Civil War.

Johnson worked closely—too closely, many Democrats thought—with Republican President Dwight D. Eisenhower. Still, he was capable of flashes of liberal conscience. He arranged for the burial of U.S. serviceman Felix Longoria in Arlington National Cemetery, with full military honors, after the segregated funeral home in Longoria's hometown of Three Rivers, Texas, refused to handle the body. Johnson was also the only southern senator who refused to sign the notorious "Southern Manifesto," which called upon southern states to disregard the Supreme Court's *Brown v. Board of Education* ruling. Johnson's complex political maneuverings were then, as now, a source of endless fascination. As Ronnie Dugger later wrote, "No one could say whether his love of the poor or awe of the successful rich is the stronger."[23]

Brammer had been intrigued by Johnson since he first saw him during the U.S. Senate race in 1948, when he covered LBJ's appearance in Denton for the college newspaper. Johnson campaigned that year by helicopter, the first politician in the state to do so. The "machine came churning in just above the rally, noisy and fascinating, circling many more times than was necessary, Johnson leaning from the window and whooping, gesticulating, waving a big white Stetson, which he sailed out into the crowd as the helicopter abruptly sank to a jarring landing."[24] The pure spectacle of Johnson's appearance thrilled Brammer, and he kept an interested eye on the senator over the years.

In August 1955, Brammer learned that Johnson was returning to Texas to recuperate after a heart attack. He went to the Johnson ranch to cover the homecoming for the *Observer*. Though Johnson was often vilified in the pages of the liberal newsweekly, Brammer's report was friendly and earnest. He described Johnson as "kind and obliging" to the reporters, credited LBJ for handling the media well, and he remarked on the "genuine achievements of the Democratic Congress." In truth, Brammer was already politically poised to be sympathetic to LBJ. As much as he appreciated the creative freedom he found in the pages of the *Texas Observer*, he could never march in lockstep to its editorial philosophy. As Nadine Brammer confided to her parents, the Brammers considered themselves more liberal than Lyndon Johnson, but not as liberal as the *Observer* crowd.[25]

Two months later, Brammer returned to the LBJ Ranch, this time to cover the arrival of Adlai Stevenson, who had been the Democratic presidential candidate in 1952 and would represent the party again in 1956. Brammer's portrayal of Johnson was glowing. He described Stevenson as "falling in behind the fast-striding Johnson" and noted that LBJ "looked fit, very much better than upon his return from Washington."[26] The friendly stories on LBJ surely set Ronnie Dugger on edge.

Brammer's next piece in the *Observer* appeared the following week, and it demonstrated his increasing distance from Dugger's publication. Titled "That Old Depleted Feeling," Brammer's column was ostensibly a satire about the oil depletion allowance. But the essay was also self-revealing, as Brammer wrote: "We here at the *Observer*, for instance, are terribly depleted at the moment. We have lost a good deal of our initial momentum. Our enthusiasm at the onset of this experiment has been dulled by too many speeches, too many scandals, and, perhaps, too many crusades against the oil depletion allowance."[27]

That became Brammer's last work as the *Observer*'s associate editor. After two weeks of silence, the last page of the November 2, 1955, issue carried a small final item. The headline read: "Brammer Resigns: Joins Johnson's Staff." The liberal crowd felt betrayed to have one of their own go over to the "enemy," but for Bill and Nadine Brammer, moving to Washington, D.C., as part of a powerful senator's staff was a thrilling opportunity. At the very least, it promised them a sounder financial picture.

3.

THE

GAY

PLACE

Bill and Nadine Brammer and their two young daughters moved to Washington, D.C., in January 1956 for the beginning of the new congressional session. Lyndon Johnson, as was his custom, had also hired Nadine to work for him. Johnson knew from experience that if a wife worked long hours and weekends along with her husband, it curtailed her complaints about his time away from home. The arrangement also contributed to a sense of family among the staff—with LBJ installed as the clear patriarch.

Bill Brammer, as a junior press aide, never became a part of the upper echelon of LBJ's staff. He helped draft speeches, wrote position papers, press releases, and "soothing letters to distraught liberals." Johnson enjoyed great familiarity with his staff, and soon he and Brammer became close. "Lyndon perceived Bill's intelligence," Nadine recalled later. "We were a couple of snobby, prissy intellectuals, and he recognized us right away for what we were. He used to argue with Billy about what a waste of time it was. After a while, you know, he got to liking Billy. I mean he really liked him. He wanted us over at his house all the time in Washington. When we were in Austin we'd go out to the ranch on weekends. Our little girls would play with the Johnson girls, we'd drive around looking at cows, and Bill and Lyndon would talk for hours."[1]

In Washington, Bill and Nadine Brammer became friends with other political staffers, including one congressional aide who came over to admire LBJ's "robotyper." This machine was capable of mass-producing "personalized" messages from Senator Johnson. In this way LBJ could send out "individual" letters of congratulation to every high school graduate in Texas. After Brammer's visitor enjoyed a hearty laugh at LBJ's "unflagging venality," he introduced himself as Larry L. King and "suggested we go drank ourselves a bunch of dranks." Brammer and King hit it off well, especially after they discovered that each was an aspiring writer. They became close friends and their families often joined together for social occasions. Brammer and King also began to exchange manuscripts and give each other critiques.[2]

Though Brammer was making some progress on his Austin novel, there was little time for writing. The staff was consumed with work as LBJ focused on the Democratic nomination for president in 1956. In that year's contentious state convention, he took firm control of the Texas Democratic Party, outmaneuvering both conservative Governor Allan Shivers and liberal activists. Johnson's high-handed parliamentary tactics outraged Texas liberals, further driving a wedge between him and a constituency that he often took for granted because he believed it had nowhere else to go.

Brammer, for his part, was becoming increasingly enamored of Johnson's operating style. He looked up to Johnson—literally. LBJ made unabashed use of body language, and he towered over Brammer, using his imposing physicality to reinforce his points. Brammer came to view Johnson's Machiavellian operating style with admiration, because he saw the senator as a man who was liberal in his heart but had to appear conservative to survive in Texas. Though LBJ was often criticized by Texas liberals for supporting "half-loaf" legislation, Brammer saw that Johnson was at least accomplishing something. The liberals, meanwhile, favored kamikaze missions that were doomed to failure. After the 1956 state convention, Brammer wrote a fawning memo to the senator contending that most liberals supported Johnson, except for incorrigible holdouts.[3]

Brammer's Austin friends became increasingly dismayed by his view of LBJ. Ronnie Dugger received a letter from Brammer telling him, "I'm continually amazed by Johnson." When Willie Morris stopped by to see Brammer on his way to Oxford as a Rhodes Scholar, he reported back to Dugger that Brammer was "enthralled" by LBJ. Brammer, who had initially been hired to help LBJ's image with liberals, seemed now to have abandoned liberals altogether. Liberals saw a Brammer who "waited on [Johnson], rhapsodized over him, toted and fretted and apologized for him. Billy exhibited all the symptoms of teenage dementia, worse even than usual because it was so obviously heartfelt and he was so smart."[4]

After LBJ's 1956 presidential bid collapsed, the climate in his office worsened. Johnson vented his rage and frustration on his staff, often verbally abusing them in drunken tirades. Nadine Brammer wrote Ronnie Dugger that they were no longer close to LBJ, nor was "anyone with any independence. . . . The only good thing is that Bill has time to read, think, write a little." Nadine soon had enough of Washington, D.C., and Lyndon Johnson both. She returned to Austin with their two children while Bill Brammer remained behind in Washington with LBJ.[5]

In 1957 Ralph Yarborough, after years of disappointment, won a watershed election, becoming the junior U.S. senator from Texas. Yarborough offered Brammer a top press relations post. LBJ quickly got word of the contact and wasted no time preventing a defection from his camp. He took his young press aide to his ranch. He "put Brammer and a bottle of Scotch into the ranch jeep. . . . When they returned, Brammer was a reconditioned man." Flush with a $700 raise and promises of an enhanced status within the Johnson office, Brammer solidified his ties to LBJ.[6]

Brammer's loyalty to Johnson also colored his view of Ralph Yarborough. To Brammer, the new senator was a bumbling fool who knew little about the legislative process. In letters to Nadine, Brammer gushed about LBJ's political savvy while expressing contempt for Yarborough's ineffectiveness. Brammer's attitude toward Yarborough intensified the coming political split with his old friends. Brammer declined an opportunity to review a book for the *Observer*, and he wrote to Nadine, "after the lengths to which Ronnie's gone in condemning LBJ, don't think I could write anything for the *Observer* for a long while. . . . Sounds shitty, but I like Johnson, and I can't very well lend my name to paper that calls Johnson a racist and a labor baiter. As much as I respect Ronnie, it's just not true."[7]

Separated from his family in D.C., Brammer found more time to work on his Austin novel, and he slowly amassed material in the hopes of presenting it to a publisher. His demanding work schedule, however, meant that the only free time available was at night.[8]

Called "The Heavy Honeyed Air," Brammer's manuscript featured characters based on his Austin friends. As Al Reinert later wrote, Brammer's creations were "glib talkers sauntering from episode to episode, headed nowhere skeptically, existential as all get-out. It was skillfully written but it had no focus on any level . . . just another clever writer who wished to be an author but had nothing particular to say." Brammer also had stylistic problems. He fretted about his lack of a classical education and believed that those bereft of such training couldn't help but mimic whatever contemporary literature they had recently read. In a letter to Ronnie Dugger, Brammer conceded that he had read so much F. Scott Fitzgerald "that my prose took a turn toward a seedy parody of his style." Brammer also mentioned that he had read Saul Bellow but "the Jewish influence makes my southwest characters talk like Yiddish immigrants."[9]

Brammer missed Nadine and his children tremendously, but the couple's emotional distance only deepened. Back in Austin, Nadine socialized freely in the absence of her husband. "Late in the day the phone would start ringing: Where was the party tonight? Scholz [Garten] was still a magnet for the in crowd's politicos, professors, artists, and writers." Nadine's apparent flippancy regarding monogamy caused Brammer great distress. In his letters home, he often alluded to Nadine's motherly obligations as he complained of her frequent absences. He even appealed to his mother-in-law, writing to her of Nadine's behavior.[10]

The couple's difficulties were compounded by continued financial troubles. Maintaining two residences crippled an already unsteady bank account. The Brammers corresponded regularly in an attempt to keep the bank balances straight, and Brammer often counseled his

Snapshot of Billy Lee Brammer in Larry L. King's D.C.-area apartment in 1961, reading from his just-published book *The Gay Place*. *Larry L. King Archives, Southwestern Writers Collection, Texas State University-San Marcos.*

wife about how to spend money. But, as Nadine maintained, it was Bill who created the household's financial woes with his tendency to make impulsive buys on credit.

Brammer could envision few ways to escape their bleak financial picture aside from publishing his novel. Once he was satisfied with his manuscript, he contracted with a literary agent who began showing "The Heavy Honeyed Air" to publishers. Random House responded with a curt rejection, complaining that the novel had too many characters. Holt also turned it down but was more encouraging. A Holt editor wrote, "Brammer has more wit and facility and sophistication, and larger concerns, than any young writer I've seen in some time; I'd like to work with him; but I cannot pretend that 'The Heavy Honeyed Air' is not a rough, spotty, half-formulated novel that needs a lot of work.'" Brammer returned to the manuscript and tried to create more passion and conflict in an attempt to appeal to commercial interests, but he found that his characters were "all too sophisticated to be moved by tacky melodramas."[11]

Finally, however, Brammer experienced the artistic breakthrough he had been waiting for. It came in his day job. One of his regular duties was to write routine correspondence on behalf of Senator Johnson. His talent for it had been quickly recognized, and Brammer was soon writing "personal" notes to Johnson's friends. He even drafted "fatherly letters to Johnson's daughters." Brammer became so convincing at expressing Johnson's voice that he was eventually asked to write LBJ's mother regularly and sign the letters "Lyndon." For a time, Brammer handled much of Johnson's personal correspondence, even "dashing off spontaneous greetings when whimsy overtook him."[12]

Though Brammer rarely worked closely with LBJ, he did share an office with Johnson's brother, Sam Houston Johnson, who regaled Brammer with tales of his older brother. As Brammer continued to write letters in Johnson's name, while detached from the senator himself, LBJ came to exist more as a fictional character in his imagination. In early 1958 he hit upon the idea of incorporating Lyndon Johnson into his novel, in the form of Texas governor Arthur "Goddam" Fenstemaker. This was the transformative event in his writing, and it lifted his promising manuscript into the realm of literary art.

Brammer began writing furiously as a vision came to him of "Country Pleasures," a novella inspired by his visit to Marfa to cover the filming of *Giant*. He brought Governor Fenstemaker onto the movie set, underscoring the similar illusions practiced by Hollywood and politicians. Rarely socializing now, he stayed awake all night on Dexedrine writing. By Memorial Day he completed the novella in a thirty-six-hour sitting. Several publishers turned down "Country Pleasures," though interest was much more promising than it had been for any of his previous work. Then in the fall of 1958, Houghton Mifflin optioned the novella with the idea that it would form part of a trilogy. Governor Arthur Fenstemaker would straddle all three sections. Brammer made rapid progress on the trilogy by returning to his initial effort, "The Heavy Honeyed Air," recruiting those characters, and recasting them in two new novellas, "Room Enough to Caper" and "The Flea Circus." His writing continued at a feverish pace, and when he completed his manuscript by September 1959 he called Nadine to tell her, "Well, I've finally finished my book. And I owe it all to speed."[13]

The Gay Place comes from a poem by Brammer's literary hero, F. Scott Fitzgerald. Brammer was aware of the coming change in the usage of the word "gay," and he enjoyed poking fun at the title prior to the book's publication. He wrote Nadine that the title was selected, despite his worry that it would conjure up images of a gay community outside of New York City. To Ronnie Dugger, he feigned horror that the title "suggests a queer parlor."[14]

Though his novel was complete, his relationship with Johnson was bottoming out. LBJ was gearing up for another presidential run in 1960, and Brammer was tired of the grind—and the contempt Johnson had for his staff. Though Brammer told others that Johnson remained pleasant to him, it was also true that the senator liked to strike matches off Brammer's suit and call him "Boy." Late in 1959, with his contract from Houghton Mifflin in hand, Brammer left Johnson's staff to take a public relations job in New York with economist Eliot Janeway. The wealthy Janeway was married to a successful novelist, Elizabeth Janeway, and Brammer became a friend of the family. He even lived with the Janeways for a time, attending Manhattan literary parties and riding in the family limousine to his office in the Empire State Building.[15]

In New York, Brammer renewed his friendship with Robert Benton, who was now art director at *Esquire,* an upscale men's magazine in the process of remaking itself into one of the best general-interest magazines in the country. Under editor Clay Felker, *Esquire* was publishing writers such as Norman Mailer, Tom Wolfe, James Baldwin, and Gay Talese. Benton continually tried to aid Brammer, putting *Esquire* editors in touch with him for possible writing assignments.

While Brammer's literary stock rose, his friend Larry L. King struggled. King had originally planned to stay in Washington just long enough to make sufficient contacts and land a job on a major news-paper or magazine. It had now been six years, and he still had no prospects. King had continued to write, staying up late and making the most of whatever weekends he had off. King and Brammer had exchanged several manuscripts over the years, and King had read *The Gay Place* a chapter at a time while Brammer worked on it. Seeing his friend's growing manuscript was a constant source of encouragement. "If Billy Lee can do it," King thought to himself, "by God I can do it." He eventually fashioned part of a novel, "The Secret Music," based on the Korean War prisoners who refused repatriation to the United States.[16]

Once King learned that Brammer was going to be published, he pressed his own manuscript on his friend, pleading and demanding that Brammer help him find a publisher. Brammer agreed, yet King continued to receive curt rejection notices. In one such letter, King found a note from Brammer still stapled to the manuscript. Brammer's note apologized to the editor "for sending along such a confused work," but he explained that he had no choice because of King's "aggressive persistence." For King, learning that even a close friend didn't like his fiction cratered his confidence. It also caused a "temporary rupture" in his friendship with Brammer. King resolved to quit writing forever, and for the next several months held true to his word.[17]

Brammer's work with Eliot Janeway proved unsatisfactory to both men, and after a few months Brammer agreed to be released so he could assist LBJ's efforts to win the presidential nomination at the 1960 Democratic convention. Just before the convention, Brammer received word that his novel had won Houghton Mifflin's in-house award, beating out the work of another promising young writer, David Halberstam. The award was held in high esteem by the publisher and boded well for the book's future. The previous year Phillip Roth had won for *Goodbye, Columbus.* That book went on to win the National Book Award. A few years earlier Robert Penn Warren had received the Houghton Mifflin award for *All the King's Men,* which won the Pulitzer Prize.

Houghton Mifflin had high expectations for *The Gay Place*, and their enthusiasm fed Brammer's own hopes. His editor, Dorothy de Santillana, told him, "This isn't just another 'gifted' first novel to be reviewed and quietly forgotten. It's going to be a big book—our biggest fiction book scheduled so far—and we're excited about the possibilities." Brammer began hearing interest from Hollywood, and there was talk that he could receive up to $75,000 for the film rights.[18] Brammer found it easy to envision his future. He told his agent that his dream was to make enough money to return to Texas and become a full-time writer. The promise of critical and commercial success was tantalizing.

His publisher carefully calibrated the novel's marketing, even going so far as to rework Brammer's name. His editor wrote him in June 1960 to tell him that "No one, I repeat no one, up here thinks 'Billy Lee' is possible. With all respect to your parents who gave it to you with such evident love (and it is a very loving name) it has not the strength and authority for a novel which commands respect at the top of its voice." Ironically, for a writer who had long railed against inauthenticity, Brammer found his own identity swallowed up by the book's promotional campaign. When the publisher decided to describe Brammer as a young writer only thirty years old, Brammer raised no objection though he was on the verge of turning thirty-two.[19]

Flush with confidence, Brammer began working furiously on his follow-up work, "Fustian Days," which began with the funeral of Governor Fenstemaker and would be a sequel to *The Gay Place*. He was one hundred pages into his new novel when *The Gay Place* was released in March 1961.

Reviews were glowing. *The New York Times Book Review* wrote that, "Brammer has an authentic, even lyrical, writing talent. He has as intimate a knowledge of operational politics as any serious American novelist." *The New York Herald Tribune* added that Brammer "shows himself to be one of the ablest novelists now writing in America." David Halberstam ranked *The Gay Place* alongside *All the King's Men* as a classic American political novel and predicted, "It will be read a hundred years from now."[20]

Much of the praise focused on Brammer's brilliant creation of Arthur "Goddam" Fenstemaker, which "caught the voice, the idiom, the excesses, but most of all the Protean vigor of [Lyndon Johnson.]" The governor wears down a recalcitrant legislator with "Bible-belt hectoring," telling him, "World's cavin' in all around us; rocket ships blastin' off to the moon; poisonous gas in our environment; sinful god-dam nation laden with iniquity, offspring, of evildoers. My princes are rebels and companions of thieves."[21]

Johnson's smooth manipulation of the legislative process is cap-tured in Fenstemaker. When an important bill is introduced, Fenstemaker convinces the Speaker of the House to move the bill up on the legislative calendar. "He's a reasonable and honorable man," explained the governor. "All I had to do was threaten to ruin him." Fenstemaker's bill worries the conservatives, who are "all stirred up and worried about taxes and socialism and creepin' statesmanship." He heads them off by persuading a liberal newspaper editor to "Oppose the goddam bill. . . . But just a little bit, understand. . . . You raise hell and your bunch won't go along. They'll introduce their own bill askin' for the goddam aurora borealis. I need their votes, too. Just oppose it a little bit."[22] The governor, of course, gets his bill in the end, and Brammer's depiction of Johnson as Fenstemaker is so acute that he is still credited by many for fashioning the best portrait ever of Johnson's personality.

Sales of *The Gay Place*, however, were a different story. The old-est president in America's history, Dwight Eisenhower, had just been replaced by the youngest. John Kennedy's youthful glamour and sophistication captured the country's imagination. After years of seeming stagnation, people were eager to move forward. Brammer's book was a look back at a southern cornpone politician in a state described as "boondock country." LBJ himself seemed to be disap-pearing into the background of the new administration, and there was little interest in him. Despite the novel's praise from critics, sales never took off. By the summer of 1961, *The Gay Place* was remain-dered in its second printing.

Brammer saw little money from the novel. Even the $1,250 he was expecting for the paperback edition failed to materialize when

Houghton Mifflin discovered that, after accounting for returns of unsold copies of the hardback, the author had a debit balance of $93.33 with the publisher. Brammer wrote to his editor of his financial distress and included a photo of his children. She responded to Brammer's agent, making it clear that he could expect no relief from the publisher. "These terms are incorporated into every contract and ubiquitously applied. He sent me a delightful picture of himself with his handsome children. . . . Will you write him my personal regret that the facts are less than fancy could hope?"[23] Though movie prospects remained tantalizing—at one point Paul Newman planned to play the lead—no film has ever been made of *The Gay Place*.

Brammer had written the novel, as his daughter Sidney later maintained, "as much out of a need to pay the bills and get his estranged wife and family back, as from an overweening ambition to be a Great American Novelist."[24] After it became clear that the novel would not resuscitate his finances or win Nadine back, the Brammers' marriage crumbled for good. They were divorced in June 1961.

***

Despite its commercial failings, Brammer's novel has achieved exalted status in Texas. In the forty years since its initial publication, *The Gay Place* has been reprinted five times, and it remains in print today. In retrospect, it's clear that *The Gay Place* represented a coming of age for Texas letters—it was essentially our first urban novel, populated by sensitive, ironic characters whose sophisticated wit belied the usual stereotypes of Texans. Brammer's work also inspired other young Texans who were interested in making their way as writers—particularly Bud Shrake, Larry L. King, and Gary Cartwright. Brammer "made us understand Texas, and be proud of it," Gary Cartwright has written. "(He) led us out of the dark ages and said, 'See? The place is alive with promise.'"[25]

Brammer's novel has fascinated the Texas literati because it is an unabashed roman à clef, and nearly every character and situation was inspired by real life. As Nadine later said, "Every time I read *The Gay*

Place, I can't believe how much he got in there. He used everything." Willie Morris recalled that after observing the similarities between the novel and real life, he told Brammer, "Billy Lee, at least Thomas Wolfe changed the names and addresses." As the real identities of specific characters have faded, the novel's chief attraction, aside from its still-vibrant portrait of LBJ, is its social history of the Texas intelligentsia during the 1950s. In this way, Brammer provides a prescient view of the cultural transformation that became the sixties. As Don Graham notes in his introduction to the book's most recent edition, "Brammer captures hints of cultural change ahead. Hipsters and politicians talk of Zen and Buddhism and existentialism and jazz. There is a sense of imminent cultural revolution waiting just 'round the corner."[26]

The Gay Place is often read as a bohemian sort of novel, as it bops with beat-inspired dialogue and is infused with diatribes against the artificiality of modern life. The protagonists endure a wry sense of existential ennui. But, underneath the sheen, Brammer's fondness for material comfort is abundant. Strikingly, nearly every character in Brammer's novel is comfortably wealthy. Though Brammer himself had struggled financially for years, the character in the novel most closely based on him, Senator Neil Christensen, has easy access to unlimited wealth. This remains the pattern throughout the novel, as Brammer continually inflates socioeconomic levels far beyond the reality he knew. One of the book's gaudiest scenes is the "Egghead Mixed Doubles Invitational Tennis Tournament and Civil Rights Conference," held at an opulent country estate complete with servants. As in so much of Brammer's book, there was a real-life inspiration for the event—the "First Invitational Egghead Tennis Tournament," organized by *Texas Observer* editor Ronnie Dugger. In reality, Dugger's tournament was not held in palatial surroundings. Instead, it took place at public tennis courts in a middle-class neighborhood in Austin.[27]

While Brammer's novel revels in its images of wealth, relatively little attention is paid to hot-button liberal issues such as the remarkable income disparities in Texas. Indeed, Brammer's gaze often looks past the poor. The novel begins with protagonist Roy Sherwood view-

ing a truck packed full of Hispanic migrant workers, including children, yet there's little indication of their material condition. Instead,
the scene follows Sherwood's trip inside a supermarket, where he
studies the vast inventory "with as much wonder and concentration
as might have been demonstrated in viewing Indian cave mosaics or
a thousand years old cathedral."[28]

Brammer's lack of interest in allowing social criticism to spoil *The
Gay Place*'s patina of wealth is clearly seen in the third novella,
"Country Pleasures," which takes place on the movie set in West
Texas. At one point, a group of revelers, including a movie star and
Governor Fenstemaker, drive into the desert to visit a small village
inhabited by Mexican Americans. Though the narrator has described
the film set in vivid detail, readers are never shown the village itself,
nor is the gap between rich and poor gauged, as Lyndon Johnson himself often liked to do. The meeting between Fenstemaker and the
Mexicanos is played for comic effect, as the drunken governor signs a
proclamation returning the territory to Mexico.

Brammer's lush fondness for material comfort has been mostly
overlooked by reviewers and critics over the years—after all, this
understanding detracts from views of *The Gay Place* as a hipster
novel. But there was one review, published, appropriately enough, in
the *Texas Observer* in 1961, that makes the point. Roger Shattuck
wrote:

> Mr. Brammer lets himself fall into a facility and a flipness
> that begins to sound like a guidebook on how to live in an
> economy of abundance. Cars, telephones, and phonographs
> are as much obstacles to life as its vehicles. Nothing lies fur-
> ther from literature than brand names. True, we fill vast por-
> tions of our lives with cigarettes and liquor and the eternally
> playing TV or jukebox. Yet in a work of fiction, smoking or
> taking another drink (particularly when accompanied by
> elaborate instructions on how to mix it) or tuning the radio
> quickly reveal themselves as narrative fill masquerading as
> vivid detail. This kind of writing should go.[29]

Brammer's frayed relationship with Nadine is also deeply expressed throughout his book. Though the stories are ostensibly about Governor Fenstemaker and Texas politics, just below the surface the novel surrenders to another theme that has also received relatively little attention: infidelity. Specifically, how unfaithful women have hurt the kind, sensitive male protagonists. In each of the three novellas, the major female character is notable, even exceptional, for the easy manner in which she shares herself sexually. While the men generally practice Zen detachment, the one thing that seems to really bother them is the females' behavior. Brammer settled some scores in his fiction—the protagonist of the first novella, Roy Sherwood, was based on a politician with whom Nadine was having an affair. She later commented, "I felt like he ripped me off. He was using all my stuff."[30]

Brammer's feelings about Nadine are most strongly enunciated in the third section of the novel, "Country Pleasures." Jay McGown is an assistant to Governor Fenstemaker, and he accompanies the governor to the movie set. McGown's estranged wife, Vicki, just happens to be a famous movie star who is playing the lead role in the film. Vicki is notoriously promiscuous, and her activity deeply wounds Jay's self-esteem. As he considers her sexual adventures, "Jay had hoped he could pass it off philosophically, but it did not get any better for him—and soon the sensation was very like discovering Vicki in bed with another man, other men, ten or twenty of them, hundreds and thousands [and it] pursued him like some king-sized cuckold in stereophonic sound."[31]

The wronged men in *The Gay Place* have only one recourse it seems—sleeping around themselves. Each of the male protagonists chooses that course of action, each seemingly without much desire. Again, the third novella is the most explicit: Jay McGown "had seen [his wife] leaving with Ben Krueger, and out of self-defense, or possibly a last thundering avowal of his manhood, he had begun to flirt with Evelyn Krueger." After he and Mrs. Krueger end up in bed, they realize that "there was nothing to be done, nothing to savor, no moral bludgeon, even, with which to flail their lovers."[32]

Politically, *The Gay Place* was a stinging rebuke to Texas liberals, who "are scathingly portrayed as a cynical, ingrown coterie that spends most of its time boozing and rutting."[33] As the gulf widened between Brammer and the *Observer* crowd, it wasn't surprising that his novel was critical, yet what must have been unanticipated was its severity. Brammer barely bothers with the right wing—too easy a target, one suspects. He portrays the liberals as far more interested in scoring points among themselves than working for any real change for the state. Their leader, a man with gubernatorial aspirations, turns out to be a corrupt bribe taker and would-be blackmailer. The exposé of corruption is reminiscent of Dugger's investigative reporting in the *Texas Observer*, except that, in his fiction, Brammer indicts the liberals, rather than the conservatives.

Brammer's cynicism about politics, however, recedes before his view of LBJ as Governor Fenstemaker. As Ronnie Dugger has written, Brammer "had, really, only three categories for politicians: fools, whores, and Johnson."[34] In *The Gay Place*, Governor Fenstemaker is the state's dominant politician, condemned by liberals for being too conservative and attacked by conservatives for being too liberal. Yet in his heart Fenstemaker clearly wants social justice. In response to a reporter's question, Fenstemaker concedes that his legislation is only a half loaf, or even a slice of bread. In contrast to the liberals, Fenstemaker is at least taking small, yet concrete, steps toward progress.

In this view, Brammer was right about LBJ's politics in a prescient way that Texas liberals never were. He understood that LBJ's basic liberalism had remained intact, though greatly muted during his reign as U.S. senator. Once he became president, Johnson returned to his New Deal roots and initiated a number of social programs including the Civil Rights Act. With a legacy forever clouded by the war in Vietnam, Johnson remains a complicated and complex figure. Yet as Brammer shows us in *The Gay Place*, LBJ's use of Machiavellian tactics could serve a higher purpose.

Brammer's portrait of Johnson as Fenstemaker is brilliant in many ways, but he clearly neglected many aspects of Johnson's "dark side."

While Brammer condemned the liberals for their corruption, he made no connection between Johnson's long years of public service and his ability to amass a huge personal fortune. Brammer's portrait also misses critical aspects of LBJ's temperament. As Ronnie Dugger later pointed out, Brammer's creation "has almost none of Johnson's demand to be loved, self-serving cynicism, and arrogance of power."[35]

The Gay Place stung liberals deeply, including Ronnie Dugger. Though he and Brammer remained friends, the novel's publication made it clear to Dugger that artists such as Brammer were not reliable allies in the fight against conservatism. Dugger's *Observer* continued to run features on Texas arts and culture, and Brammer occasionally contributed articles. But Dugger never forgot how he had been burned. Later, as Brammer's friends published their own novels, their politically progressive views weren't enough to win respect at the *Observer*. Instead, activism was considered superior to art. Bud Shrake, Larry L. King, and others often found their work pilloried in the pages of the *Observer*. Though relations remained polite on the surface, a subtle new faction emerged among the Texas left—a split between Dugger's *Observer* and the state's liberal writers, who would come of age in the 1960s.

Brammer himself became unmoored after the collapse of his hopes for a best-seller. His publisher's initial enthusiasm for a sequel waned, and his work on "Fustian Days" began to flounder. Brammer became a correspondent for *Time* magazine in 1961, and he went to Atlanta to cover the civil rights movement. He also covered politics in Washington, D.C. When his reporting brought him back into contact with Lyndon Johnson, the vice president took the opportunity to dispense his special form of humiliation. "I tried reading your novel, Billy," LBJ told him in front of a crowd of reporters, "but I couldn't get past the first ten pages because of all the dirty words."[36]

4.

FORT

WORTH'S

NEW

JOURNALISM

A t first glance, the sports pages of the *Fort Worth Press* seems an unlikely place to have spawned three of Texas' best-known writers: Edwin "Bud" Shrake, Dan Jenkins, and Gary Cartwright. The *Press* was, after all, the second paper in a marginal market, housed in a dilapidated old building "within earshot of the railyards and just downwind from the farmers' market."[1]

The *Press* had been publishing since 1921 but evidenced little in the way of financial stability or editorial prestige. A rival reporter described it as having "the social standing of a man living in a trailer house behind a filling station." Gary Cartwright later wrote, "The *Press* was a sanctuary for freaks, for idealists, for demonologists, for outcasts, for drunks, for honest young writers and reporters and curiosity seekers." The newspaper was located "behind the New Gem Hotel, a flophouse used by black prostitutes. Often the hookers propositioned *Press* reporters in the adjacent parking lot. In the dank newsroom, black soot poured down from the floor above through an opening workers called 'the coal chute.'"[2]

Circulation never reached much beyond sixty thousand, placing it far behind the *Fort Worth Star-Telegram*, published by Amon Carter and considered one of the major papers in the Southwest. Carter, who orchestrated Fort Worth's civic affairs for decades, was not above calling major advertisers personally to order them not to place ads in the *Press*. In the early 1950s the struggling paper was reformatted into a sensationalist tabloid, running banner headlines about murders, disasters, and assorted oddities—even though the events themselves often took place thousands of miles from Fort Worth. As one observer commented, "The *Press* considered itself the voice of the people, but, denied access to corporate boardrooms and society ballrooms, it was left to serve those for whom wrecks, rapes, and robberies were life's only grand adventures. The *Press* worshipped the scoop and the ominous headline and the quirky angle missed or ignored by the *Star-Telegram*, and it chased fire engines and murders with fervent urgency."[3]

The *Press* was part of the Scripps-Howard chain, but the corporation invested little in the enterprise. Accounts were frugally managed, often to the point of absurdity. Even pencils were carefully rationed, and when a staffer wore one out, he or she had to return the nub back to the cashier to receive a replacement. Typing paper was also hard to come by. Reporters were issued scrap paper or asked to use the back sides of press releases. Bud Shrake recalled, "Sometimes you would go to the back for more copy paper to write stories on, and find stacks of it cut in the shape of pennants, reject stuff. But if you rolled the paper into the typewriter with the pointy side up, it taught you to write a quick, crisp Scripps-Howard style first paragraph."[4]

As things turned out, it was the *Press'* very marginality, its lack of journalistic ambition, that created the conditions ripe for a flowering of literary creativity. Gary Cartwright noted years later, "We survived on the assumption that no one read our paper anyhow. It is the same feeling you get on a college newspaper or on mind-expanding drugs. There are no shackles on the imagination; there is no retreat, only attack."[5]

Under the tutorship of sports editor Blackie Sherrod, the young staff at the *Fort Worth Press* mounted an inspired challenge to the straight reporting that had come to dominate sports coverage. As Michael MacCambridge writes in his history of *Sports Illustrated*, the

Press' staffers "exhibited a relentlessly impertinent style, a mixture of sensationalism, analysis, irreverence, and showmanship that embraced broad elements of what would later be called New Journalism. At a time when virtually every sports department in the country was sticking to the basics, trying to find out Who, What, Where and When, Sherrod's charges asked Why, and did so with an attitude."[6]

That attitude had a lot to do with being in Fort Worth, a city that had always celebrated a wide-open and rowdy approach to life. Established as a frontier outpost to protect white settlers from Native Americans, Fort Worth became a major supply station for cowboys driving cattle north in the late 1800s. Many hired hands drew their pay and headed straight for Hell's Half Acre, a place where prostitution, liquor, and gambling gave way to fights, dismemberments, and murders. Even after the district was shut down, Fort Worth remained a major center of licentiousness. The 1917 telephone directory listed 178 saloons—and just sixteen churches.[7]

All the while, the growing city looked upon its neighbor thirty miles to the east, Dallas, with a mixture of disdain and jealousy. While Fort Worth reveled in its frontier spirit, Dallas was seen as pretentious, a "department-store culture." Though the two cities projected vastly different images, in reality they often competed furiously for the same resources. After Dallas won the right to host the 1936 state centennial celebration, Fort Worth, led by Amon Carter, responded with Billy Rose's ribald Frontier Centennial, which featured such attractions as Sally Rand's Nude Ranch. The battle cry became, "Go to Dallas for Education, Come to Fort Worth for Entertainment."[8]

During the Prohibition era Fort Worth's Jacksboro Highway became a rekindled version of Hell's Half Acre, home to dozens of illegal drinking and gambling establishments. Amon Carter was among those who flaunted the laws of the time, carrying a whiskey-filled cane that he tippled from regularly. He loved gambling and often hosted high-dollar poker games attended by Fort Worth's elite. Few arrests were ever made for illegal gambling or drinking in the city—unless outside agencies like the Texas Rangers were called.

Gambling became so well entrenched in Fort Worth society during these years that there were even reports of children receiving slot machines as birthday gifts.[9]

In Fort Worth, freedom was prized and held in higher regard than conformity, which ruled much of the rest of Texas. Experimentation was tolerated, even applauded if you could dance to it. It was in Fort Worth that Bob Wills met Milton Brown in 1930, and there they created western swing. The appealing and daring musical hybrid combined Anglo and African-American sounds in a starkly segregated age, blending rural southern fiddle music with sophisticated urban ragtime and jazz. Though dancing was condemned in many parts of Texas, it flourished in Fort Worth's numerous honky-tonks.

Fort Worth had little in the way of high culture or sophistication, but it possessed plenty of free-wheeling energy. This was the environment in which Dan Jenkins and Bud Shrake were raised, and, not surprisingly, it shaped their development as writers in important ways.

***

Jenkins, born in 1929, was the son of a high-profile couple. His mother was described as "a globe-hopping, antique-dealing, chain-smoking daughter of a Fort Worth socialite."[10] His father was a salesman whose inveterate nightclub carousing led to several marriages and divorces. He was also an avid golfer and a founding member of the Colonial Country Club. Jenkins' parents split up before his first birthday, and his paternal grandparents raised him. He grew up in a pleasant neighborhood in South Fort Worth, surrounded by extended family that doted on him. A major preoccupation of the Jenkins clan was sports. By the time he was eight he had played his first round of golf, and he also observed how gambling seemed integral to the game. Golf was becoming increasingly popular among the upper middle class, particularly in Fort Worth, where local talents Ben Hogan and Byron Nelson were on their way to legendary professional careers. Football was also an important part of Jenkins' life. In 1935, he was taken to see the now-legendary game between hometown Texas

Dan Jenkins, left, and Bud Shrake at the *Fort Worth Press*, 1953. *Bud Shrake Archives, Southwestern Writers Collection, Texas State University-San Marcos.*

Christian University and its rival from Dallas, Southern Methodist University. Both teams sported perfect 10-0 records and the national championship was at stake. Though SMU won the contest, the game made an indelible impression on the youngster. In 1938, TCU won college football's national championship. By this time, it seemed to Jenkins that his hometown was the center of the sports universe.

He began keeping scrapbooks filled with stories of local sports figures. He was still in elementary school when his grandmother retrieved an old typewriter from the attic for him. He began by retyping sports stories from the newspaper. Before long, he was rewriting them and then composing his own accounts. Seeing the movies *The Front Page* and *His Girl Friday*, with their romanticized notions of newspaper journalism, also stirred in him a passion to become a reporter.[11]

Other than the irregular dramas of sports, Jenkins' home life was relatively carefree, and he later told an interviewer, "I never had any angst." His family remained comfortable throughout the Depression, and he spent a good deal of time on the golf course, becoming an accomplished player. When he entered Paschal High School in 1944 his family's social status served him well. His grandfather was a U.S. marshal, and as such, was exempt from the gas rationing during World War II. Jenkins was the first in his class to have a car, and he had unlimited access to gasoline. He was already tall, had a deep voice, a pocketful of money, and a brimming sense of self-confidence that girls found appealing. A star athlete at Paschal, Jenkins played for its heralded basketball team and also captained the golf team. He enjoyed high school so much that he took advantage of the same offer that Larry L. King had ultimately rejected in Midland. Jenkins deliberately fell short of graduating so that he could enjoy a second senior year at Paschal High.[12]

During these years, Jenkins' free time, like that of many other Fort Worth youngsters, was spent in the honkytonks along the Jacksboro Highway, where underage drinking was welcomed with a wink. And it was there he met a Paschal High underclassman who would become his lifelong friend and writing colleague.

Bud Shrake was also born into a prominent Fort Worth family. His father was a successful cattle trader and a charter member of both the Colonial and Glen Garden country clubs. The family resided in a large home with live-in servants. They also owned a 640-acre farm southeast of town where they raised horses, cattle, pigs, and chickens. Shrake's mother was the granddaughter of a Cherokee Indian, but she was not proud of the relation, and the family seldom talked of it. Native American heritage was considered a source of embarrassment at the time, as the Indian Wars had been fought within living memory of many. Shrake remembers seeing his great-grandmother only once, when the family drove out to her home at the edge of the Palo Duro Canyon in West Texas. She lived in a hut with a sod roof and sat wordlessly on the porch, looking out over the canyon. "She was ancient, had a headband, and had this great, strong, Cherokee profile," Shrake recalled. "I was fascinated by her and sat at her feet for hours."[13]

Shrake's father became immersed in Fort Worth's gambling scene and drank heavily as his losses mounted. The family fortunes went into decline, and eventually his father's business collapsed. The Shrakes became destitute, and his parents were emotionally shattered. By the time he was eleven, Shrake was working at a grocery store after school to help put food on the table.[14]

From the time he was very young, Shrake had a feeling that he wanted to be a painter or a writer. "But I couldn't envision ever making a living that way," he recalled. "It was not the kind of thing you could come out and talk about." Nevertheless, he began writing down conversations between imaginary playmates soon after he learned to read and write. In the fifth grade, with the outbreak of World War II, he imagined himself becoming a fighter pilot, and he wrote his first short story—an adventure tale of a battle between Japanese Zeroes and U.S. fighter planes.[15]

In 1946, he entered Paschal High School, where Dan Jenkins, two years older, was already a junior. When the two met, they immediately recognized each other as kindred spirits despite the age difference. Both sported senses of humor ranging from the dry to the sardonic. Frequently they were the only ones who laughed at—or even understood—each other's jokes. They soon became inseparable. Both wrote columns for the high school paper, *The Paschal Pantherette*. Each was active in sports, and together they starred in several school plays. Unlike Larry L. King's high school experience in West Texas, in Fort Worth showing off on-stage was no crime. Both Jenkins and Shrake expected to go to New York one day; the only question was how to get there. For a brief time they flirted with the idea of making it as a song-and-dance team, but their talent, while exuberant, was not expansive.[16]

After school, when Shrake was not working, he hung out with Jenkins at places like The Pig Stand and Massey's Café, where they smoked constantly, drank beer whenever they could get away with it, and talked of their grand ambitions. They cultivated a detached cynicism, based as much on role models seen in movies as from their actual circumstances growing up in Fort Worth.

In the spring of 1948, Dan Jenkins wrote a column in the *Pantherette* parodying a sportswriter at the *Fort Worth Star-Telegram*. A stringer for the *Fort Worth Press* noticed the article and brought it to the attention of sportswriter Blackie Sherrod, who was impressed enough to hire Jenkins after graduation at a salary of $25 weekly.

Jenkins was thrilled to work for a real newspaper, though his beginnings at the *Press* were ignominious. He showed up for his first day of work as he imagined a reporter should dress—in a gray herringbone suit from Brooks Brothers. When he walked in, Jenkins was quickly introduced to the *Press'* corporate structure. Puss Ervin, the retired postman who typed a bowling column between sips of bourbon, was sitting at his desk in his undershirt. Ervin glared at debonair Jenkins from across the room and barked, "Who's the damned tap dancer?" Jenkins' editor, Blackie Sherrod, was a World War II veteran who exuded mental and physical toughness. "Blackie was a great disciplinarian," Jenkins recalled later. "I always thought he'd make a good football coach. He commanded respect. I was scared to death of him at first. My first story, I spent all night writing it at home on the kitchen table—cutting, polishing, making it bright. Blackie read the first paragraph and said 'Don't ever write a morning lead for an afternoon paper, dumb ass.'"[17]

Jenkins quickly understood the essence of his first real journalism lecture. Because the *Star-Telegram*, published in the mornings, had already reported the game scores, Sherrod needed to give the *Press'* afternoon readers a different angle—more style and analysis. Or, as he termed it, "punch and juice."[18]

It was still a daring concept in 1948, at least in Texas, but one that Sherrod was well-prepared to carry out. Sherrod was a longtime fan of satirists such as Damon Runyon, Dorothy Parker, and James Thurber.[19] He was also a decorated navy plane gunner who had killed for his country, and he had little patience for those who considered sports contests "life-or-death" affairs. As such, Sherrod's sarcastic, above-the-fray perspective was an inspiring revelation to nineteen-year-old Dan Jenkins, who was just beginning to find his voice as a writer.

Jenkins enrolled at TCU in the fall of 1948 and quickly established himself as a popular figure on campus. He wrote for the student
newspaper and joined the TCU golf team. He also married twice—
both times to the same woman. He and Pattie O'Dell eloped when
they thought she was pregnant. When they learned she wasn't, they
had the marriage annulled. Later they decided to go ahead and get
married after all.[20]

Jenkins' high school buddy, Bud Shrake, graduated from Paschal
in 1949. Shrake had scored 178 on an I.Q. test at the school and
received an offer to go to Yale. But money was a concern, and Shrake
decided he was not ready to leave Texas yet. He chose instead to
enroll at TCU while continuing to work part time. After completing
his freshman year, Shrake collected the money he had saved and
moved to Austin to attend the University of Texas. There, he planned
to "live the life of a student." He majored in government with an eye
toward pre-law, and he gave little thought to his old dream of becoming a writer.[21]

After a year in Austin, Shrake returned to Fort Worth in the summer of 1951, broke and looking for work. His old friend Dan Jenkins
convinced him to visit the *Press* and talk to Blackie Sherrod about a
job. When Shrake walked into the *Press* it was love at first sight: "I
looked around at all the people, and the state editor was over there
eating a can of sardines at his desk at six o'clock in the morning, and
the bowling writer was back there drunk and had set fire to the wastebasket, and the one-legged city editor was threatening people with his
crutch. . . . All of the sudden I walked into a world I knew I belonged
to."[22]

Sherrod agreed to hire him part time, and Shrake, for the first
time, was surrounded by people who were making a living, albeit marginally, as writers. For someone who had long dreamed of writing yet
had received scant encouragement, simply being in the presence of
working writers was an inspiration. As the fall semester approached,
Sherrod offered to put him on staff full time at $30 weekly. With that,
Shrake withdrew from UT and transferred back to TCU. He changed
his major to philosophy and English and began to imagine himself

becoming a writer. Boldly, he predicted to his colleagues that he would publish his first novel by age twenty-five, just like F. Scott Fitzgerald. Failing that, he would at least make it by twenty-eight, like Hemingway. His ultimate goal was to write novels while serving as a foreign correspondent for the *New York Herald Tribune*, then considered a standard-bearer of serious journalism.[23]

Under the tutelage of Blackie Sherrod, Dan Jenkins and Bud Shrake received an education in literature and journalism that transcended their studies at TCU. Sherrod had a formidable knowledge of sportswriting history, and he understood that the field was evolving from a "low art" into a kind of literature. Sportswriting in America had begun a dynamic transformation in the 1920s with the rise of radio. Because broadcasters could announce sports scores immediately, newspapers no longer held a monopoly on results. To remain competitive, papers had to offer more feature and analysis to readers. Suddenly, sportswriters were given free rein to express opinions and develop unique writing styles. At the same time, radio helped ra se the public's awareness of sporting events, increasing the games' pcf-ularity. Sports coverage began to fill more space in newspapers nan ever before.

The rise of sports journalism attracted better writers to the field and popular columnists became syndicated nationwide. Two basic styles emerged in the 1920s: the "Gee whiz" school, led by Grantland Rice, sought to glamorize the games and the athletes that played them. The other group, the "Aw nuts" reporters, adopted irreverent and cynical postures, and their style became the dominant trend by the 1930s. Sports journalism received an additional boost as "serious" writers like Damon Runyon and Ring Lardner reported on games. Both writers made excellent use of the slang vernacular they picked up while covering sports, incorporating the vibrant dialogue and outrageous metaphors into their fiction.[24]

The Great Depression and the outbreak of World War II scaled back many of the advances in sportswriting. Diminished advertising revenues and mandatory rationing reduced available space in newspapers, and the grim times eventually had an impact on the tone of the coverage. By the mid 1940s most stories consisted of conservative play-by-play accounts with little of the breeziness and poetry that marked prewar sportswriting.[25]

Yet with the end of the war, prosperity and increased leisure time fueled a new boom. In 1946, *Sport* magazine was established, joining *The Sporting News* as a nationally distributed weekly. *Sports Illustrated* would follow in the next decade. The flush times also brought new changes to sportswriting that were just beginning to be seen when Dan Jenkins and Bud Shrake joined *The Fort Worth Press*.

By 1951, two of the nation's best-known columnists were Red Smith and Jimmy Cannon. Both were gifted wordsmiths and perceptive observers who chronicled sports events in entirely new ways. Their columns often read more like miniature short stories than traditional sportswriting. By stretching the boundaries of journalism into literary terrain, Smith and Cannon represented early stirrings of what would become a revolutionary movement in American writing in the 1960s—the New Journalism.

New Journalism, in its broadest sense, represents what is now called "literary journalism" or "creative nonfiction." As reporters began recognizing that the time-honored notion of journalistic "objectivity" was a sham, they sought ways to incorporate their own perceptions of events into their stories. As the trend evolved, journalists increasingly used literary techniques such as point of view, dialogue, scene-setting, and narration. The breakthrough came with Truman Capote's true-crime best-seller, *In Cold Blood*, in 1965. Writers such as Tom Wolfe, Joan Didion, and Hunter S. Thompson became stars of the genre, and established novelists such as Norman Mailer also turned to the form. Since the 1960s, most tenets of New Journalism have been absorbed into mainstream reportage. Even as the term itself has faded from use, it remains one of journalism's most significant developments in the twentieth century.

At the *Fort Worth Press* in the 1950s, Blackie Sherrod did not enjoy the stature of Red Smith or Jimmy Cannon. But he had his own unique talent. Sherrod composed brilliant leads, his prose was tough and erudite—he detested pretension—and he was the master of the cutting remark. Though his column wasn't yet syndicated, he was already much admired by his peers. Sportswriters across Texas made a special effort to find copies of the *Fort Worth Press* just so they could steal lines from him. Above everything else, Sherrod's brilliance lay in his attitude. One got the impression from reading him that the games themselves were of little consideration. For Sherrod, sportswriting was merely a vehicle that allowed him to experiment with language and to offer caustic, often funny opinions on a wide variety of topics.

Sherrod was a natural leader and teacher, and he saw great potential in his young staffers. Jenkins and Shrake were both blessed with writing talent, irreverent outlooks, abundant energy, and a willingness to experiment and learn. Sherrod taught his charges what he had learned from great sportswriters of the past—how to hook a newspaper audience by creating great opening lines, how to adopt a strong point of view, and how to find an angle and drive it in. And always, they were expected to jazz up the accounts with clever one-liners. Sherrod himself carried around a little black book so he could scribble down colorful sayings as they occurred to him. The others soon followed this practice.

Under Sherrod, the *Press'* sports department came to function as the equivalent of a college creative writing program—with a dash of boot camp thrown in. The writers were given reading assignments—often books loaned from Sherrod's personal collection. They conducted peer reviews, competed fiercely with one another, and were subjected to withering critiques. The craft of writing was a constant topic of discussion among the staffers. "We read aloud to each other in the newsroom," Sherrod recalled. "S. J. Perelman and H. Allen Smith and Damon Runyon. Mark Twain. Name 'em. And even when we were out drinking, or riding on a Texas League baseball train, we talked about writing headlines or leads or makeup." Jenkins recalled, "We were all ambitious, all writing for each other. So we were writing for the world's toughest audience. We were always eager to stomp on one another."[26]

Through it all, Sherrod was a strict disciplinarian who enforced a strong work ethic. Staffers were expected to report to work by 5:30

A.M. in order to meet the 8:30 deadline. Shrake recalled that "Blackie kept us all scared to death. We liked him, and we hung out with him, but it wasn't even to be considered that you'd be a minute late." If that day's issue had not gone well, Sherrod would grunt his disapproval by refusing to go have breakfast with his writers, telling them, "You guys go ahead and eat. I've got to put out a paper."[27]

Because the *Press* operated on such a limited budget, Sherrod taught his writers that the only way they could beat the *Star-Telegram* was to outwork and outhustle them. "Blackie didn't believe in an idle moment," Jenkins said. "When we weren't working or reading to each other, he'd organize track meets. Chinning contests in the men's room. Fifty-yard dashes on the way to breakfast. Pushups and broad jumping and arm wrestling. I believe we'd have pole-vaulted if Blackie'd had the equipment."[28]

The competitive environment stirred a frenzy of experimental language. Failed efforts were met with derision, mostly in the form of Sherrod's dreaded "bulletin board." If a staffer wrote something that Sherrod disapproved of, he simply posted the piece, without comment, allowing a critical discussion to unfold. Because he knew that Hemingway and Fitzgerald were the biggest influences on the staff, Sherrod kept a sharp eye to train his writers away from mimicry. But he did have one weakness. Writers could break every rule Sherrod set if they could make him laugh.

Even in those early days, it was clear that Dan Jenkins was Sherrod's best pupil. He composed eye-grabbing leads, memorable one-liners, and used cutting humor. Like Sherrod, Jenkins disdained pretension in all forms. And like Sherrod, Jenkins used his columns to ruminate on a wide variety of issues only marginally related to sports. Jenkins also transcended Sherrod's lessons, creating fictional personae to use as sounding boards in his columns. His favorite became Billy Clyde Puckett, a semiliterate ex-athlete who functioned as Jenkins' alter-ego. In his reporting and columns both, Jenkins was making use of a technique that would later become associated with the New Journalism. He transported "himself into the person he's writing about," Sherrod recalled. "He doesn't have to say, 'He thought.' He becomes that person." As Sherrod noted, "Dan Jenkins was doing that when he was nineteen years old, and he didn't know it. It was new and different."[29]

Jenkins had a deep appreciation for colorful slang, echoing the interests of an earlier generation of literary-minded sportswriters— Damon Runyon and Ring Lardner. While at the *Press*, Jenkins "found a sort of eloquence in the ramblings of TCU football coach Abe Martin." The TCU coach "was notoriously suspicious of the new-fangled terminology coming from the pro game. 'They talkin' about pursuit in football,' he told Jenkins once. 'Well, that ain't nothin' but chase 'em and catch 'em.'" Whereas most reporters would clean up Martin's quotes, Jenkins took great pleasure in showcasing the language. In this way the games would be referred to as "a choir practice," "an ear roastin'," or "a story tellin'."[30]

Jenkins pulled all these elements together with effortless self-confidence, though few outside of the *Press*' readership noticed him at the time. Gary Cartwright later described Jenkins as "the coolest guy I ever met . . . polished, and self-confident almost to the point of absurdity. Back when we were working at the *Fort Worth Press*, we assumed that sooner or later New York would call us to the Big Time, and most of us wondered if we could cut it. Not Dan."[31]

For Jenkins and Shrake, being writers represented an attitude as much as a vocation. They hung out in Fort Worth's restaurants, clubs, bars, roadhouses, and honkytonks, practicing their one-liners and honing their barroom philosophies. It was there that Jenkins made his deadpan observation of a gorgeous woman—"Remember—somebody somewhere is tired of her." They also devised the rating system for females that Jenkins later made famous in his novel *Semi-Tough*, ranking women from ten to one just like the college football polls. They often stayed out until three in the morning, even though they were expected to report at the *Press* before dawn and had early classes at TCU. The lifestyle, of course, took its toll on their relationships with women. Jenkins' marriage to Pattie O'Dell ended within a year after she told him, "If you go to Massey's one more time, I'm gonna get a divorce."[32]

At TCU, Dan Jenkins' golf game continued to develop, and he became the captain of the team. He finished second twice in the Fort Worth City Golf Tournament, and Ben Hogan offered to coach Jenkins and help him turn pro. But Jenkins already knew that he was a better writer than golfer, and he was too impatient to spend long hours perfecting the mechanics of the game. He much preferred hanging out at Goat Hills, the ramshackle course adjoining the TCU campus. There, he developed a repertoire of trick shots and picked up extra money hustling bets. His companions, who included Tiny, Easy, Magoo, Matty, Rush, Little Joe, Grease Repellent, John the Bandaid, and Moron Tom, were also there nearly every day, playing in groups of two to twenty-two. They heckled one another along the way, gambling on nearly everything. They practiced drop-kicked tee shots and perfected behind-the-back putting. They played the course backward, entirely out of bounds, or with one club. Matches extended through neighborhoods, city streets, and into the players' apartments, ending with chip shots into an old brown shoe. One time they played through six blocks of downtown Fort Worth, finishing at the Tarrant County courthouse.[33]

Gambling was deeply embedded in the *Press'* culture. Though the young reporters had little money, they bet heavily on football and basketball games. "Our only distinguished visitors," one wrote later, "were Big Circus Face, Puny the Stroller, and Jawbreaker King, who made faithful trips to collect their winnings. The gambling extended to literary matters as well. "When *Life* announced it was going to publish Hemingway's *The Old Man and the Sea,* the *Press* writers started a pool to pick the first word. Shrake won with the dark horse, "He," certain all along that Jenkins choice of "It"—the early line favorite—was going to be the winner.[34]

Jenkins was still at TCU when he married again, this time to Joan Holloway, a graduate student in English. Bud Shrake also met and married a graduate student, Joyce Rogers, a Shakespearean scholar. Though the two friends had both married well-educated and highly intelligent women, neither made much of an attempt to modify their deeply ingrained habit of hanging out with the boys, even as they understood how the behavior crippled their marriages. Joan Holloway Jenkins, for her part, quickly tired of listening to Jenkins and Shrake "talk about their planned conquest of New York City." Finally, she told them, "Listen, you assholes, there's fourteen roads heading out of this town. Why don't y'all just *get on* one of 'em?"[35]

Shrake's marriage was already in trouble by the time he graduated from TCU in 1953. Following Joan's sarcastic advice, he hitchhiked to New York. He took his *Press* clippings with him, hoping to find a job in the city as a writer. First he went to the *New Yorker,* where he was met with laughter. Next he went to the *New York Herald-Tribune.* Much to his delight, the editor closely scrutinized his *Fort Worth Press* clippings and agreed to hire him, telling him that a position would come open within three months. Shrake returned to Fort Worth, immensely pleased with his prospects. Then the Korean War intervened.

While in college, Shrake had enlisted in the army reserves in an attempt to circumvent the draft. He'd managed to avoid service in Korea at the time, but now the army was calling him up for active duty. He gave up his job at the *Press,* put his dreams of New York on hold, and reported to Officer Candidate School at Fort Knox, Kentucky. After months of training, Lieutenant Shrake was just days away from being shipped to the front lines as an infantry platoon leader when news came of the cease-fire. Still, Shrake was obligated to serve out the remainder of his active duty. Eager to see more of the world, he hoped to be sent abroad, preferably to Germany. Instead, the army kept him in Kentucky as a camp instructor, a job he hated. During his active service, Shrake and Joyce divorced, though a year later they married again.[36]

By the time Dan Jenkins was twenty-five he and Joan Holloway split, making it three marriages and divorces for him. He graduated from TCU and grew more confident of his abilities as a writer every day. In August 1954 he saw the inaugural issue of a slick new weekly sports magazine published by the *Time-Life* empire. *Sports Illustrated* was given little chance for success at its debut, and in fact the magazine lost millions of dollars for several years before turning a profit.

But Dan Jenkins immediately understood its potential. Published a week after the games it covered, *Sports Illustrated* was the ultimate extension of the *Press'* role as an afternoon paper. It was all style and analysis. All punch and juice. Dan Jenkins knew that he wanted to work for the magazine, knew that he would work for the magazine. It didn't hurt matters, either, that *Sports Illustrated* was headquartered in New York City.[37]

5.

THE

TEXAS

BEATS

When Bud Shrake was discharged from the army in 1955, there was no longer a job waiting for him at the *New York Herald-Tribune*. Reluctantly, he returned to Fort Worth, only to find no openings at the *Press*, either. He soon found work at a new television station being constructed. The night the station went on the air, Shrake operated the camera. A few months later, a job came open at the *Press*. But it wasn't in the sports department; it was as a police reporter. For a newspaper that thrived on sensationalism, the job promised to be a plum assignment.[1]

His first day of work was unforgettable. He was sent to cover a train derailment that crushed a group of homeless men who had been riding in a boxcar. "When people say someone is as flat as a pancake, you think that's just a figure of speech," Shrake recalled. "But these people literally were that flat. It was the sort of thing I knew I'd never see covering sports."[2]

The *Fort Worth Press'* editorial philosophy remained very simple—create the most sensational headline possible. Even straight news stories appeared in the *Press* under manic headlines. In one case, Shrake reported that a policeman ran over a deer and brought the carcass into the station, where it was handed out as venison. The story appeared in print under the banner "Cops Eat Kid's Pet." Another time, a woman called the *Press* and announced that she was going to kill herself. Instead of calling the police, the *Press* sent Shrake out to get the story. He opened the unlocked door and walked inside. There he found a woman lying on a couch, surrounded by empty gin bottles. "I nudged her and asked if she wanted to kill herself. 'Betcha goddam ass,' she said and went back to sleep." The big headline the next day read, "I Saved Her from Sure Death."[3]

First-person accounts were considered the most eye-grabbing, so police reporters were expected to infiltrate crime or accident scenes whenever possible. They dressed exactly like police detectives and competed furiously with the *Star-Telegram* to be the first on the scene. The goal was to trick victims, witnesses, or survivors into thinking that the reporter was a cop. "I'd just get out my notebook and start asking questions," Shrake recalled. "And they'd tell me everything." Procuring a family photograph of a murder victim from an unsuspecting relative was considered a major coup, and the numerous gangland slayings in Fort Worth during the 1950s provided plenty of opportunities.[4]

Being a police reporter exposed Shrake to a much wider world than he'd ever known as a sportswriter. From crooks and victims to Fort Worth's down-and-out, he came to know people from many walks of life. He became intimate with Fort Worth's underworld, hanging out in the same bars frequented by homicide cops and killers. "In those days it was still a rule of the underworld that you didn't do anything bad to a reporter," Shrake said. "The gamblers, the hoods, the hijackers, and the bank robbers—they all liked good publicity just like everyone else."[5]

One morning in 1956 Shrake was sitting in the police station pressroom when a new *Star-Telegram* reporter walked in, fresh out of the army. The newcomer was intensely competitive, and for weeks he and Shrake jousted for the upper hand. Finally, one afternoon they adjourned to a bar across the street. After a few beers, they concluded that they were making each other work too hard. So they worked out a deal. From that moment on they used a copy boy to alert them if something important was happening. Otherwise, they were content to hang out much of the time, drinking beer and swapping stories. This is how Bud Shrake and Gary Cartwright became friends.[6]

***

Gary Cartwright, born in 1934, was raised in Arlington, halfway between Dallas and Fort Worth. His early life was worlds away from those of Jenkins and Shrake, even though they were just a few miles apart. Arlington was a small country town, "the sort of down-home, chickens-in-the-back-yard place that young people despise and their elders long to recover." Cartwright was blanketed by a solid sense of security with family all around. His cousins were his best friends, doors were left unlocked, and social lives were organized around the church and Boy Scouts. He understood little of the world's complexity, growing up in a place where "experimentation and invention were regarded as offenses against nature."[7] Like Shrake, Cartwright's family had Native American ancestry. He was born with bronze skin, black hair, and dark, almond-shaped eyes—an inheritance from his grandmother, a full-blooded Comanche Indian.

The Cartwrights, however, were staunchly Anglo, and Arlington, like the rest of Texas, was segregated. Cartwright was vaguely aware that African Americans lived in an area north of aptly named Division Street. But it wasn't until he was twelve years old that he ever saw a group of black people. That year he got a paper route—delivering the *Fort Worth Press*—that took him through the area known as "Niggertown" to Arlington's white residents. "It was awful," Cartwright recalled. "A shantytown, unpaved streets full of potholes, houses falling apart. I'd never seen anything like it." He was shocked by the poverty and the sheer numbers of people "who quietly coexisted in the city where he lived."[8]

The protective veil around his life became frustrating to Cartwright during his teenage years. No one he knew drank. Some men, including his father, went off to gamble occasionally, but Cartwright's only knowledge of "fast times and high living came mostly from movies. Movies made me ache to get the hell out of

Arlington." Football was a popular schoolboy preoccupation, but Cartwright soon understood that he was better at writing, and he covered the games for the school paper. In 1951 he graduated and stayed close to home, enrolling in Arlington State Junior College (now the University of Texas at Arlington) as a journalism major. His father bought him a typewriter, and Cartwright became the sports editor of the college paper, the *Shorthorn*.[9]

The next fall he transferred to the University of Texas at Austin. Going to Austin "wasn't just exhilarating, it was revolutionary. I discovered a new world filled with infinite possibilities—music, books, art, politics, travel, cheap thrills." He continued to develop his passion for writing, carrying a notebook in the back of his jeans and "pausing in stairwells to scribble notes or record random passages of poetry, or nursing a beer . . . while composing descriptions of people and things I had encountered." Cartwright joined the staff of *The Daily Texan*, and there he encountered Willie Morris, who was clearly a rising star. "I knew who Willie was," Cartwright said later. "Everybody did, but he didn't really know me at the time."[10]

Cartwright was also introduced to other ethnic groups while in Austin, and that, too, changed his life. It was "the time I became integrated, or as integrated as one got in Texas in those days. Rhythm and blues was big in the early fifties, and so my after-hours hangouts were black hovels on the wrong side of the tracks." Cartwright recalled, "I'd never been a part of anything so exciting. Some of it was the sensual pleasure of sharing an experience with blacks, something I had never done before, a conceit no doubt because we truly weren't sharing anything except the dark corner of a dingy room. These after-hours adventures pierced centuries of bondage, my own if not theirs."[11]

The only thing that Cartwright didn't thrive on at college was the curriculum. "My grades were not that good," he said. "They weren't terrible, but they weren't good. I was drifting, and obviously needed some guidance." After the fall 1953 semester he dropped out and decided to volunteer for the draft. The army quickly obliged, calling him up. "There was a cease-fire by then in Korea. But there was still a high degree of tension, and they were still sending people there. And that's where I wanted to go. I didn't care about the war. I didn't know anything about it. All I knew was that I'd never really been anywhere, and Korea sounded interesting. At least it wasn't Arlington."[12]

Instead, he was assigned to a base in Mineral Wells, Texas—just an hour's drive from his hometown. He worked as the company clerk and wrote a sports column for the base newspaper. After his discharge he enrolled at TCU and sold pots and pans door-to-door. Then a friend told him about an opening as the night police reporter at the *Fort Worth Star-Telegram*. The job paid $55 a week and work hours were abysmal—six o'clock in the evening until two o'clock in the morning. Though he had to get up at seven A.M. for class, Cartwright knew this was an opportunity he could not pass up.[13]

Once Cartwright became a friend of Shrake's, he soon met Dan Jenkins. This new circle of friends marked a profound shift in his thinking. While Cartwright had grown up attending vacation Bible school and earning Boy Scout merit badges, they were gambling, drinking, and dancing in Fort Worth honkytonks. Though Jenkins and Shrake exuded sophistication, it was Bud Shrake's wife, Joyce, who became a major influence on the group's development. "Joyce was our intellectual," Cartwright recalled. "She influenced us as much as we influenced each other. She was teaching English at TCU, and she was always telling us who we needed to read—Henry Miller, John Dos Passos, writers who were breaking new ground. It was Joyce who introduced us to Kerouac and the other Beats. She had an album, *Poetry in the Cellar,* with Kenneth Rexroth and Lawrence Ferlinghetti, the San Francisco Beat poets, reading their poetry to jazz. It just blew us away. That's what we wanted to do."[14]

Though a "Beat Generation" had been percolating in the American underground since the 1940s, it burst into the limelight in 1957 with the widely publicized obscenity trial over Allen Ginsberg's poem "Howl" and the publication of Jack Kerouac's *On the Road*. The Beats rejected the conformity and materialism surrounding them, "trying to look at the world in a new light."[15] They valued personal experiences above "objective" truths, using literature as their form of expression. For the young writers in Texas, imbued with a cultivated cynicism yet devoid of a grander philosophy, this movement was exactly what they'd been waiting for.

Cartwright and Shrake both began thinking seriously about moving to California and taking up with the Beats. Shrake corresponded with Lawrence Ferlinghetti and Kenneth Rexroth, and Cartwright began writing Beat-inspired poetry. "Some of it was pretty good, actually. Even Joyce and some of the English professors were saying so, and they would know. It was more philosophical than political, but it was about as edgy as we could be at that time and place."[16]

Imagining themselves as something of the Beats in Texas, the writers understood that their life experiences could provide the inspiration for their literature. As Cartwright recalled, "the first thing a writer has to do is live like a writer. Writers figure things out, not by logic but by living. Imagination can take a writer great places, but only if he's already been there." The three friends "held the deep conviction that anything worth doing was worth overdoing." When they drank together, they closed "the bars with original songs composed on the spot." Though they'd heard of marijuana and understood that the Beats often smoked it, none of them had any interest in experimenting with it. Shrake had tried it once as a college student in Austin, but it seemed to have no effect on him, though it was difficult to tell for sure because he had also been drunk at the time. As police reporters, Shrake and Cartwright often encountered the drug. A narcotics officer they knew sometimes tossed them bags of confiscated pot as a joke, but they never smoked any of it.[17]

In their work as newspaper reporters, Shrake and Cartwright became increasingly aware of the wide gulf between the world they observed and the stories that appeared in print. "Frequently we saw cops bring suspects in and throw them down the stairs," Cartwright said later. "We saw this all the time, yet we couldn't write about it because our papers didn't want that. Even the *Fort Worth Press*, which was sensational, didn't want stories about police brutality."[18]

Their inability to chronicle life as they saw it was particularly true in the case of Fort Worth's black community. "At no time were we asked to write a story about blacks," Cartwright recalled, "unless a black person had committed some sort of crime against a white person." Shrake added, "We never wrote about blacks unless they were in trouble. Anything that could be construed as positive in any way was off limits—that was called a 'nigger deal.'"[19]

At the *Star-Telegram*, Cartwright learned of "an old black preacher who every day for forty years walked the short distance from his dirt-street hovel to the emergency room at City-County Hospital, there to pray for the sick and afflicted and pass the time with appreciative sisters of his flock." Cartwright believed this "was semiremarkable, since the old man was eighty-two years old and totally blind. Then they built the South Freeway, smack in the middle of his well-trod path. The inevitable happened: He was struck by a car and killed. And there he was when I first saw him, laid out among the weeping and wailing of that same emergency room."[20]

Cartwright wrote up a story "and sent it by copy boy to the night city desk at the *Star-Telegram*, where a frightened and disturbed city editor "read it and called me back. He complimented me on a 'nice little yarn,' then reminded me it was a nigger deal."[21]

In the *Fort Worth Press'* sports department, Blackie Sherrod evidenced little sensitivity toward racial issues. While the *Press* offered Dan Jenkins and other young reporters considerable freedom to experiment with language, harbor points of view, create fictional personae, and express personal opinions, there was a limit. While it was perfectly acceptable to write an entire column complaining about how difficult it could be to open a package of crackers, commentary about racial or political issues was out of the question.

For Bud Shrake, a transformation came when he was sent to cover the violent school desegregation standoff in Mansfield, a small town outside of Fort Worth. In August 1956, one year before the more famous Little Rock incident, Mansfield received a federal court order to integrate its black students, who were previously bussed to Fort Worth and dropped off twenty blocks from a city school. As three young Mansfield blacks prepared to enroll in their local high school, mobs of angry whites surrounded the building, chanting threats and hanging black effigies. Vigilantes roamed through town searching for suspected sympathizers. "Governor Allan Shivers, calling the Mansfield demonstration an orderly protest, defied the federal court order by dispatching Texas Rangers to uphold segregation and authorizing the Mansfield school board to transfer black students to Fort Worth." President Eisenhower, "in the midst of a reelection campaign, did not intervene."[22]

"The Mansfield thing made an impression on me in several ways," Shrake said later. "I wasn't all that hip on civil rights until I saw the racists in action. They woke me up in a hurry, the way they bullied those black kids . . . also it taught me a journalism lesson. At one point a crowd gathered around a Texas Ranger's car, and he told them to get the hell away, and they did. My competition at the *Star-Telegram* reported this as a riot with the Ranger being threatened and driving back the mob with his pistol. My boss at the *Press* was furious at me being scooped. That it never happened was no excuse."[23]

Despite Shrake's failure to sensationalize the Mansfield story adequately, the *Press'* editors were aware that he had a rare talent—he wrote beautifully under deadline pressures. By 1957 Shrake was moved over to the *Press'* rewrite desk. There, Cartwright recalled, Shrake wrote "all the police stories, most of the city and county stories, handled club news, obits, stock markets, call-ins about five-legged dogs and eight-pound turnips. Then in the afternoon [the editor] would let him write features." Shrake estimates that he was writing fifty thousand words a week, the equivalent of a novel. "It was the greatest training I could have had, going to work for a paper that was woefully understaffed and underpaid where I had to do about five different peoples' jobs all at once. Even then I realized that I was learning a lot. I bitched about it, of course, but then newspapermen bitch about everything."[24]

Like his friends, Bud Shrake continued to write fiction whenever possible, mostly in the form of short stories and some failed attempts at novels. The dramatic episodes he witnessed in Mansfield injected a new element into his work. Clearly identifying with blacks as "outsiders"—just as the Beats considered themselves outsiders—Shrake began writing about white-black relationships. An early effort, "Revenge," was based on a real incident he learned of as a reporter but could not publish in the paper. The story tells of a group of whites who kidnap and pistol-whip a black man, whose only "offense" had been to talk to one of the men's wives. The victim's dignity remains intact and at the end, he spits out a bloody tooth and stands up, grinning.

Mansfield also provided enough inspiration for Shrake to complete his first novel. The manuscript was a breakthrough for him because, "I proved to myself that I had the will to write a book all the way to the end, instead of laboring over fragments of a book." Shrake's effort also brought his writing to another level. Though it was never published, the manuscript did get him a literary agent, Carolyn Willyoung Stagg of Lester Lewis and Associates. "Ah, Carolyn," Shrake recalled. "Those were the days—when agents with names like that could impress hicks like me."[25]

***

Gary Cartwright, after two years at the *Fort Worth Star-Telegram*, was ready for a change. He was married and had one child, with another on the way. Domesticity not only interfered with his hopes of joining the Beats, it also seemed to threaten his identity as a writer. My "ambitions were crashing against cold, unyielding reality. Suddenly my future seemed to be an endless procession of $60-a-week paychecks, crying babies, and cars that broke down." In 1957, the twenty-three-year-old Cartwright found a job in Los Angeles with a public relations firm and moved west.[26]

"What I didn't realize until I actually got out there and started working was how much I hated p.r. work. I'd already been corrupted by wanting to be a real writer." Cartwright quit his job and tried to latch on to a newspaper job in L.A. but was stymied. He gave up and returned to Texas, only to find that the *Star-Telegram* refused to take him back. With nothing else available, he began working as a copywriter for Leonard's Department Store.[27]

By 1958, Blackie Sherrod's reputation as a sportswriter was blossoming, and he had outgrown the *Fort Worth Press*. The *Dallas Times Herald* hired him away. Sherrod's departure allowed Dan Jenkins, who had by now spent nine years at the *Press*, to become the new sports editor. In Dallas, the *Times Herald* let Sherrod hire a new staff writer. His first thought was Bud Shrake. Though Shrake had been away from the sports desk for five years, Sherrod knew that he could write.

When Sherrod made his offer, Shrake was ambivalent about returning to the sports beat. He'd always liked the games well enough but had never considered himself a serious fan. He still had his heart set on making it as a New York-based foreign correspondent while writing novels on the side. He asked Jenkins for advice. "Sports pages are where the readers are," Jenkins told him. "If you want to get noticed, writing sports is the way to do it." Though Dallas was only thirty miles away, the *Times Herald* was far closer to the big time than the *Fort Worth Press* would ever be. After some deliberation, Shrake accepted Sherrod's offer.[28]

Back at the *Fort Worth Press*, Jenkins needed to hire a new sportswriter. Gary Cartwright was quickly brought aboard. Cartwright's arrival in the newsroom was immediately noticed by bowling writer Puss Ervin, who saw something sinister in Cartwright's "vaguely Oriental" features. To Ervin, the *Press'* new sportswriter was "that damned Jap kid." From that moment on, Gary Cartwright became known as "Jap" to his friends.[29]

Cartwright adapted quickly to his new beat. "Covering crime had been a good education for journalism, but covering sports was more fun," he wrote later. From "the standpoint of developing a writing style, [it was] more important for what I had in mind. The great thing about writing sports at the *Press* was that nobody expected the story to tell who won and who lost."[30]

Jenkins and Cartwright made a fine team, with Cartwright's imaginative subversion the perfect complement to Jenkins' caustic irreverence. At Jenkins' urging, Cartwright intercepted a National Sportscasters and Sportswriters Survey and responded on behalf of the newspaper. He claimed that twenty-four sportswriters worked for the tabloid, rather than the six who actually did. As a result, the *Press* received twenty-four ballots—far more than any other Texas newspaper—to cast for the first annual "Texas Sportswriter of the Year" award. Cartwright marked each ballot with the name "Crew Slammer." Slammer emerged victorious when the votes were tallied. He was all set to receive the award when it was discovered, just in time, that Crew Slammer, "among his other shortcomings as a writer, didn't exist."[31]

"My specialty at the *Press* was writing cutlines," Cartwright said later. "They had all these old photos and my job would be to invent good captions for them." Cartwright also created fantastical short features, one of which read: "John Doughe made a hole-in-one yesterday at Glen Lakes Country Club when a snake swallowed his tee shot, a dog swallowed the snake, and an eagle carried off the dog, dropping him in the cup after colliding head on with a private plane flown by Doughe's maternal twin." Despite the freewheeling antics, few readers in Fort Worth ever noticed the subterfuge.[32]

Dan Jenkins hoped that his enhanced stature as sports editor would help his chances of signing on with *Sports Illustrated*, but in truth he was growing increasingly worried. Since its founding four years earlier, the magazine had already added two Texans for its staff, overlooking Sherrod's crew each time. The first was Roy Terrell, the sportswriter at the *Corpus Christi Caller-Times* who mentored Billy Lee Brammer. "When Roy Terrell was hired, we were shocked," said Dan Jenkins. "Corpus Christi?! Even people in Texas didn't know him . . . and suddenly, *Sports Illustrated*, the only national weekly sports magazine, hires a fucking guy named Roy Terrell? From Corpus Christi? We thought, 'Well, they must not be as important as they think they are. They're stupid—why didn't they just ask?'" *Sports Illustrated* also hired Tex Maule, a former public relations director for a short-lived professional football team from Dallas. In that capacity, back in 1952, Maule had been victimized by a prank pulled by Jenkins and Shrake. The duo had given away fifty press box passes to patrons of a nearby bar, and Maule was besieged with unwelcome guests, many of whom were obnoxiously drunk. With that in his past, Jenkins could hardly count on Maule to lobby on his behalf.[33]

Still, as sports editor, Jenkins was in a better position to bring himself to *Sports Illustrated*'s attention. He became a stringer for the magazine, sending in items whenever he could. In 1959 he received a huge boost when he received an award from the Golf Writers Association of America for his coverage of the 1958 U.S. Open.

Also that year, a *Sports Illustrated* representative came to Dallas and took Jenkins and Blackie Sherrod to lunch. Sherrod was disdainful, as he didn't care for the condescending attitude he encountered. After that, Sherrod began to refer to it as "Sports Elevated." But Jenkins was impressed—especially by what seemed to be the magazine's unlimited expense account. It was a long way from begging for replacement pencils at a cashier's window. A short time later, *Sports Illustrated* invited Jenkins up for a two-week tour of duty with the magazine. Jenkins was fully aware that he was being auditioned, and he was thrilled. "I thought holy shit, this is big time! Are you kidding me? I'm a fucking stringer, I'm sittin' here lookin' out the window down at Rockefeller Center. I got a guy coming around to shine my shoes. I got a guy bringing me all the newspapers I want. I got people comin' around bringing me donuts and danishes and coffee every thirty minutes, and nobody around here does anything. Except go to lunch."[34]

Once Bud Shrake moved over to Dallas, the writers' long Fort Worth apprenticeship began to draw to a close. Though Dan Jenkins would always look back to Fort Worth in his fiction, Dallas became the new frontier for Bud Shrake and Gary Cartwright. They discovered that, like the Beats, they could incorporate their life experiences into their writing. And Dallas in the early 1960s would offer them much material to work with.

6.

BIG D

MEETS THE

FLYING

PUNZARS

When twenty-six-year-old Bud Shrake joined the *Dallas Times Herald* in 1958, he was immediately thrust into a different world—one that provided him with extraordinarily rich material for his later novels. In the years leading up to the Kennedy assassination, Dallas, Texas, became ground zero for America's far-right movement. Though a clear majority of Dallas residents came to be appalled by the right wing's increasingly ugly tone, the fringe groups—strongly supported by *The Dallas Morning News*—established a climate of hate in the city. In the nation's eyes, as in those of the young writers, Dallas seemed somehow culpable in the president's death. As Bud Shrake said in 2001, "If ever a place was granting a public license to kill Kennedy, Dallas in 1963 surely was that place."[1]

Long a center of banking, insurance, and commerce, Dallas was proud of its close alliance between business interests and civic leaders. The first "Citizens Association" was established in 1907, the same year Neiman Marcus opened its doors for business. Coordinated development efforts often paid off handsomely, and in 1913, Dallas became the Regional Federal Reserve Bank for the Southwest. In the 1930s Dallas won the right to host the Texas Centennial, beating out favorites Houston and San Antonio. The celebration brought national attention to Dallas for the first time, and it was during these years that the city became known as "Big D."[2]

Dallas was perfectly poised to aid the fledging Texas oil industry by making capital available to the men who gambled on oil wells. Those who succeeded did so spectacularly, and Dallas became home to some of the world's richest men, including H. L. Hunt and Clint Murchison. As political debates arose over the proper level of taxation of this newfound wealth, Dallas' ruling interests spoke with a unified voice: none. In fact, many of them favored the abolition of the income tax altogether. Most Texas oilmen considered themselves rugged individualists and despised any governmental intrusions. As such, they strongly supported archconservative politicians.

The far-right movement was a relatively new phenomenon in American politics and represented "the first hate movement chiefly among the middle and upper-middle classes. People of substance and property are confronted with a threatening world." This ultraconservatism blended easily with Christian fundamentalism, and the sense that an epic battle was being waged between good and evil provided a powerful dynamic. Most right-wingers believed that the real threat to America came not from the Soviet Union, but from internal subversion, whether it took the form of fluoridated drinking water or the civil rights movement.[3]

Dallas became so closely identified with right-wing causes that the leader of the American Nazi Party credited Dallas with having "the most patriotic, pro-American people of any city in the country." Political considerations were often uppermost in mind whenever Dallasites had encounters with art, and, as such, museum exhibits were closely monitored. Abstract art was considered subversive, while traditional art was "pro-American." In the mid-1950s, the Dallas Museum of Fine Art, under pressure from local activists, agreed not to display or collect works by "Communist-influenced" artists such as Pablo Picasso and Diego Rivera. The Dallas Public Library also came under attack when a touring exhibit displayed two works by Picasso. The library director quickly removed the offending pieces, and the library board passed a resolution apologizing for its "mistake" in displaying the works.[4]

The city's censorious view of the arts was perfectly aligned with its political posture. Dallas was represented in Congress by that body's most reactionary member, Bruce Alger. First elected in 1954 during the height of the Red Scare, Alger was Texas' first Republican congressman since Reconstruction. He never attempted to pass legislation and instead introduced symbolic bills to withdraw from the United Nations and break off diplomatic relations with the Soviet Union. Alger was the lone "no" vote on dozens of measures, including a plan to provide free milk to needy schoolchildren at lunchtime. After Alger condemned that idea for advancing the cause of socialism, his status as a crackpot in Washington was assured. But in Dallas, the congressman's position made him more popular than ever.

Another notable political figure in the city was former army general Edwin Walker, who was relieved of duty after it was learned that he had been indoctrinating his troops with John Birch Society literature. Walker bought a mansion in a fashionable neighborhood along Turtle Creek Boulevard and established Dallas as his political base. He planned to run for Texas governor and kicked off his campaign by traveling to Mississippi in 1962, where tensions were running high over James Meredith's attempts to integrate the University of Mississippi. The Kennedy administration was insisting that Meredith be allowed to enroll, while the "campus swelled up with angry segregationists, many of them carrying guns, some undergraduates wearing Confederate uniforms." General Walker gave a fiery radio speech comparing President Kennedy to Fidel Castro, helping spark a riot that injured hundreds, killed two, and resulted in an invasion of Mississippi by thirty thousand U.S. troops. Walker was charged by the federal government with insurrection and seditious conspiracy. After his release on bond, he returned to Dallas a hero.[5]

Another prominent figure was H. L. Hunt, America's only billionaire. From his home in Dallas—a replica of Mount Vernon—Hunt bankrolled numerous right-wing initiatives, including a "super-patriotic" radio program called "Freedom Forum." Hunt was also a prolific author, writing tracts with titles such as *Hitler Was a Liberal*. His best-known contribution to literature is his self-published utopian political novel, *Alpaca,* set in a country where voting rights are based on wealth. The more money a citizen has, the more votes he is allowed to cast.

During the closely contested presidential election in 1960, the outcome in Texas was in doubt even though the state's dominant political figure, Lyndon Johnson, was on the ticket. Predictably, much of the opposition to Kennedy-Johnson came from Dallas. Pastor W. A. Criswell, who headed the largest Baptist congregation in the world, warned his parishioners that the election of a Catholic would end religious freedom in America. H. L. Hunt found so much to like about Criswell's sermon that he ordered two hundred thousand copies of it printed up and mailed to Protestant ministers all over the country.[6]

In the last week of frenzied campaigning before the election, Lyndon and Lady Bird Johnson made a stop in Dallas. They were met by nearly three hundred sign-waving protesters, most of them "well-groomed women from the finest homes in the city." Congressman Bruce Alger, who had organized the protest, called the demonstrators "the prettiest bunch of women I ever saw in my life." He stood nearby, holding a sign that read, "LBJ Sold Out to Yankee Socialists."[7]

When the Johnsons stepped out of their car, one woman rushed up to Lady Bird and snatched her white gloves away, throwing them into the gutter. This sparked the crowd, which pressed in on the Johnsons, screaming insults, cursing at them, and waving their placards like weapons. Lady Bird said later that the confrontation was the most frightening she'd ever experienced in politics. Dallas police were on hand and attempted to escort the Johnsons through a side door, but LBJ, taking note of the presence of television cameras, declined. Instead, he "moved with excruciating slowness through the chanting mob and the rain of spit." That evening's national news broadcasts showed riveting images of a frenzied "mink coat mob" hurling abuse upon the Johnsons, while LBJ looked into the cameras "with a martyr's embarrassed smile."[8]

The scene in Dallas changed the dynamic of the presidential campaign. The rest of America suddenly realized that Johnson wasn't quite the racist southern conservative he'd been assumed to be. That

LBJ could inspire such hate in his home state was a revelation. Though Bruce Alger thought the women protesters were pretty, to the rest of the country they seemed shameful. As Lawrence Wright later wrote, "It was the closest election in history, and it was decided that day in the lobby of the Adolphus Hotel. People said afterward that they were not voting for Kennedy as much as they were voting against Dallas."[9]

Alger, despite his popularity among Dallas voters, was beginning to expose a chasm in the long-standing alliance between Dallas' business and political interests. His uncompromising opposition to the federal government jeopardized the city's political clout and economic health. Under his watch, Dallas lost $6.5 million in federal payrolls. Eight federal agencies left town between 1959 and 1963. Likewise, the image of a snarling mob screaming epithets at Lyndon and Lady Bird Johnson threatened Dallas' notions of respectability. City leaders were sympathetic to right-wing causes, but they placed a higher premium on order and steady business growth. Dallas thrived in large part by convincing companies from the Northeast to relocate their corporate headquarters to Dallas. But the campaigns were faltering in the face of its growing reputation as a "City of Hate."[10]

***

One area of expansion that businessmen were interested in was professional football. In 1958, the National Football League was still largely relegated to the Midwest and the East Coast. The league's only "southern" team was the Washington Redskins, whose games were broadcast exclusively on radio stations across Texas and the rest of the South. Texas enjoyed increasing prominence in the nation's economy and politics, and many believed that the state now deserved its own professional sports franchise.

By the end of the 1950s, two sons of prominent Dallas oilmen were attempting to bring professional football to the city. Lamar Hunt, son of H. L. Hunt, petitioned the NFL for permission to launch an expansion team in Dallas. The league, controlled exclusively by a

Gary Cartwright and Bud Shrake at the *Dallas Times Herald*, 1961.
Courtesy of Gary and Phyllis Cartwright.

cliquish group of longtime owners, was uninterested in his offer. The most influential opponent was Washington Redskins owner George Preston Marshall, who saw no reason to give up his exclusive market in the South.

In 1958, Clint Murchison Jr. tried to buy the Redskins franchise, which he planned to move to Dallas. The deal fell through at the last minute when George Preston Marshall insisted on retaining control of the team for ten years after the purchase. Murchison withdrew his offer and instead petitioned the NFL for a new franchise in Dallas. As in the case of Lamar Hunt, the NFL proved to be immune to the lure of the nouveau riche. But the NFL's old guard was also unprepared for the innovative challenges they would face from these two young Texas wheeler-dealers.

In June 1959, frustrated by his failure to gain entry to the NFL, Lamar Hunt announced the formation of an entirely new professional football league that would compete directly with the NFL. The American Football League, as Hunt called it, promised to be more responsive to America's changing demographics and would field teams in cities the NFL had shunned, such as Denver and Houston. Lamar Hunt's own team would be the Dallas Texans. The AFL boasted an exclusive five-year television contract with ABC, and it promised to launch an expensive bidding war to sign the top collegiate talent. Naysayers predicted that Lamar Hunt might lose as much as a million dollars a year on the venture. But the Hunt family seemed unworried. H. L. Hunt was reported to have said of his son, "at that rate he's going to go broke—in 250 years."[11]

Soon after Hunt declared war on the NFL's monopoly, Clint Murchison Jr., received a phone call from the NFL. In the face of new competition in Dallas, the league had decided to reconsider his bid. While the majority of NFL owners understood they had to meet the AFL's challenge, Washington Redskins owner George Preston Marshall remained opposed. And Marshall held veto power over any league expansion. But Clint Murchison had learned a few things since his previous dealings with the Redskins owner. Soon, Senator Estes Kefauver of Tennessee, who chaired the Senate antimonopoly committee, received a very large cash donation from Texas. Shortly afterward, Kefauver's committee ruled that the Washington Redskins' radio network constituted an illegal monopoly. The U.S. government would soon be investigating the Redskins' franchise. Murchison's organization had also, unbeknownst to Marshall, bought the rights to the Redskins' fight song. "Hail to the Redskins" had been played at every team game since 1938, and Marshall cared about it passionately. Clint Murchison Jr. personally informed Marshall that the Washington Redskins would no longer be allowed to use the song—unless the club dropped its opposition to a Dallas franchise. Faced with the threat of government intervention and the prospect of losing his fight song, Marshall gave in.[12]

Dallas, which had been shut out of professional football for so long, suddenly found itself home to two teams, each owned by extremely wealthy men, and each competing fiercely for the fans' attention. Because television was still marginal in terms of its sports programming, good newspaper coverage was crucial in building a fan base. Sportswriters would become the most direct beneficiaries of the new rivalry.

***

With pro football heating up, Blackie Sherrod brought Gary Cartwright over to the *Times Herald* staff in July 1959. Cartwright would cover Lamar Hunt's AFL team—the Dallas Texans. Bud Shrake would cover Clint Murchison's NFL franchise—the Dallas Cowboys. As the lead reporters, Shrake and Cartwright were treated like royalty. "Sportswriters get in free, to sports events or most anything else," Cartwright wrote. "They are fed and liquored and given unusual considerations. There are cocktail parties, and wealthy sportsmen with yachts and planes. . . . The pay is poor, but no one bothers to live on his salary." Lamar Hunt flew several Dallas-area writers in his private plane to Las Vegas. There he put them up in a first-class hotel and gave them money for gambling. Clint Murchison Jr. not to be outdone, flew them out to his private island in the Bahamas for a five-day vacation.[13]

Shrake and Cartwright became increasingly friendly with Hunt and Murchison. Both owners were roughly the same age as the writers, and both proved to be easy to get along with. Lamar Hunt, despite being a billionaire's son, had few pretensions and was an affable fellow. Gary Cartwright, in visits to Hunt's home, was likely to be offered a bologna sandwich and challenged to a game of one-on-one basketball in the driveway.[14]

Clint Murchison Jr. however, was a whole different breed. On the surface, he appeared to be much like any other right-wing Texas millionaire. Senator Joe McCarthy was a family friend, as was FBI Director J. Edgar Hoover. But Murchison also graduated magna cum laude from Duke and held a master's degree from MIT. Possessing a genius I.Q., Murchison was an inveterate prankster and a skilled acrobat. He loved to shock people in first-class restaurants by performing a somersault while walking to his table—without spilling a drop of the drink he was carrying. Murchison enjoyed staging elaborate practical jokes that often reached the realm of bizarre performance art. Once, when his friend and business associate Bob Thompson was out of town, Murchison had a crane place a forty-foot yacht in Thompson's forty-two-foot-long swimming pool. When the Dallas Cowboys traveled to play the Chicago Bears in 1960, Murchison rented a live bear and brought it into the hotel for a photo session. The bear was "shot" by a man dressed as a cowboy. Then Murchison and his gang took the bear up to his penthouse suite, where they got the animal drunk. When the bear became belligerent, they pushed it into the elevator and sent it back down to the lobby, unattended.[15]

Not surprisingly, Redskins owner George Marshall became a continual target of Murchison's pranks, as Murchison never forgave Marshall's opposition to the Cowboy franchise. Murchison's most elaborate scheme came during the December 1961 game between Dallas and Washington. The Redskins owner planned a spectacular halftime show, and the featured event would be a dogsled team pulling Santa Claus around the football field. Murchison purchased dozens of live chickens, which he and his coconspirators hid away in a dugout near the playing field. The plan was to release the chickens at the precise moment the dog team came out onto the field. They were sure that the dogs would abandon Santa to chase the chickens, creating chaos at best and a gory bloodbath at worst. The plan was foiled at the last minute when the chickens were discovered by an alert Redskins official. Marshall was furious and filed a formal complaint to NFL commissioner Pete Rozelle. But Marshall still hadn't heard the last word on the matter. The Redskins owner began receiving strange phone calls at odd hours: Someone would make clucking noises, laugh drunkenly, then hang up. Marshall changed his private unlisted number several times, but Murchison, using his connections with J. Edgar Hoover, always knew the new number before the day was over.[16]

Shrake and Cartwright appreciated Murchison's style, and Shrake wrote several columns about "The Great Chicken Conspiracy," as he called it. Murchison enjoyed partying and carousing just as much as the writers did, and their paths crossed frequently. Murchison often invited them to his house, and he dropped in at their parties. Both sportswriters flew on Murchison's private plane and observed first-hand the culture of business and wealth. "Cartwright and I felt like we were millionaires," Shrake said later. "We ran around with Clint so much that I felt like I was one of them."[17]

The constant drinking and partying kept their domestic situations on edge. Joyce Shrake, not one to look kindly on her husband's long absences, attempted to set him straight. When he came home talking of hanging out with millionaires, she responded, "Why don't you wise up? You're not one of those guys. If you weren't working for the newspaper they wouldn't have shit to do with you."[18]

***

Shrake and Cartwright, who sat at adjoining desks in the *Times Herald* office, were also neighbors away from work. Both families lived in an apartment complex near SMU, where Joyce Shrake taught English literature. Many other couples with SMU affiliations lived there, too. "In this intellectually charged atmosphere, games were played," Cartwright later recalled. "Shrake and I invented a card game we called Naked Bridge, the object being to get everyone naked as quickly as possible. Since our wives refused to participate, we usually played at the apartment of a neighbor." Cartwright reported, "Naked Bridge started with several rounds of drinks and usually ended when either the host or hostess slapped the other and accused him or her of making improper sexual advances to one of the undressed participants. It was good clean fun. But problems started when the neighbors who hadn't been invited began a whisper campaign that Shrake and Cartwright were masterminding orgies."[19]

The Shrakes and Cartwrights remained close to Dan Jenkins and his new wife June. The Jenkins' home on Sunset Terrace in Fort Worth became the scene of several memorable parties. Naked Bridge, naturally, was part of the scene, though the game usually broke up by the time the participants got down to their underwear. In this competitive, riotous atmosphere, Gary Cartwright transcended all expectations. During one such gathering, he shed his clothes entirely, circulating about the party as though nothing was out of the ordinary. Later, he tied a red bow around his penis. In subsequent parties, sightings of a nude Cartwright with a red bow were not that unusual. The behavior almost became routine. During one party, Cartwright approached a table where his wife was chatting with friends. She turned and saw her naked husband standing next to her. She reached out, patted him on the rear, and said absently, "Having a good time, honey?"[20]

By 1958, Shrake and Cartwright became more familiar with marijuana. During one of the parties on Sunset Terrace, a friend from Austin lit up a joint and handed it to them. Soon thereafter, Shrake and Cartwright began to seek out pot at parties. "There might be 150 people at a party, but only maybe three or four smoked dope," Shrake said later. "We had to be very circumspect. It was basically a life sentence to get caught doing that in Texas. In Dallas it was probably the death penalty."[21]

Shrake and Cartwright were also using speed, which Cartwright recalled "was just out in the open in those days. Pro football teams literally had buckets of Dexedrine. You just walked by and grabbed a handful and didn't think anything about it." As sportswriters, Shrake and Cartwright could "hardly avoid offers of free booze. Nearly every luncheon, press conference, or sporting event featured an open bar. Professional teams had hospitality suites. Some p. r guy was always around to pick up the check." The two men tried to be judicious in their use of speed, because the hangovers were always worse afterward. The main reason they used it was "so we could drink more and drink longer hours." In this way, the party could continue on beyond normal boundaries.[22]

As drugs and alcohol became more prevalent, their sense of prankstering, always pronounced, grew more extreme. One evening, at the Riviera Club in downtown Dallas, the two sportswriters joined Lamar Hunt and several members of the Dallas Texans' organization.

Bright red sports coats—the team colors—abounded. Drunk, stoned, and flying on speed, Shrake and Cartwright borrowed a pair of jackets for themselves. Then, affecting Italian accents, they began introducing themselves as "The Flying Punzars," a famous and daring gymnastic troupe touring the United States as a goodwill gesture from the Italian government. One thing led to another, and soon the Punzars were invited onstage to perform the "death-defying triple—without a net!"[23]

Shrake crouched, fingers clasped, and Cartwright "came running at him full speed, leaping at the last second and attempting to engage my right foot in his clasped hands. Instead, my foot landed squarely against his chest, sending Shrake tumbling backward into the drummer. I fell across both of them, knocking over a set of cymbals, which crashed into more cymbals. . . ." The pair "sprang to our feet and began to bow profusely and blow kisses at the audience, which sat stunned in an icy silence."[24] Dallasites, it appeared, were not yet ready for this form of performance art.

7.

A

Gathering

Force

Bud Shrake's sportswriting in *The Dallas Times Herald* brought him far more public attention, just as Dan Jenkins had predicted. Shrake continued to pursue his writing career, finding the first glimmers of success. He sold a script to a TV series called *Medic*. He also published a short story in a ribald magazine called *Climax: Exciting Stories for Men*. His efforts to place a story in the more prestigious *Esquire*, however, failed. As Shrake turned twenty-eight—his initial target date for publishing his first book—he stepped back from the shorter projects and decided to refocus his efforts on a real novel. He had two ideas in mind. One was a western; the other, a "serious" Beat-inspired novel based on the lives of him and his friends. Taking stock of his newspaperman's salary, Shrake decided to focus on the western, *Blood Reckoning*, which would be easier to write and offered more immediate commercial rewards. "I thought that for a writer from Texas to make any money," Shrake recalled, "the novel had to be about John Wayne fighting a whole bunch of Indians."[1]

Shrake's main problem was finding time to write. A full day at the newspaper along with the postwork revelry and family obligations left few free moments. To finish the book he began waking up every morning at three o'clock, writing in the kitchen while his wife and two small boys slept. His agent, Carolyn Willyoung Stagg, who had seen Shrake's serious work and believed in his potential, expressed deep reservations about *Blood Reckoning*. She wrote to him, "I still wish that you had gone along with your original idea of doing that serious novel—it would have brought you so much more in the way of recognition. You are too good a writer to be working in terms of mass appeal."[2]

Once *Blood Reckoning* was finished, hardback publishers proved to be uninterested. His agent eventually turned to the pulp paperback publishers. In 1960, Bantam offered a $3,000 advance to publish the book. Bantam's managing editor, misspelling the author's name as "Schrake," wrote to tell him, "It's a remarkably good first novel . . .we don't intend to do much editing." Shrake's book contract was a cause for celebration among his friends. At last, one of them seemed to be breaking out. Not everyone, however, was impressed. His wife Joyce, who would eventually publish a monograph on Shakespeare, was contemptuous of her husband's adventure tale. Shrake was also beginning to see that, in the new Texas, publishing a paperback western was no longer enough to qualify one as a "real" writer.[3]

At one of the rambunctious parties in Dallas, a bookseller friend introduced Shrake to Larry McMurtry, then teaching freshman English at TCU. McMurtry's own first novel was due to be published in 1961, and word was that McMurtry had created a sensitive and literate work—a "serious" western, as it were. McMurtry had also recently completed a Wallace Stegner Fellowship in Creative Writing at Stanford. There he had met and become friends with Ken Kesey, who would publish his own first novel, *One Flew Over the Cuckoo's Nest,* in 1962.

Soon after, Shrake met another young writer who had recently come to Dallas. Jay Milner, a Lubbock native, had already compiled an impressive record. Milner worked for Hodding Carter's Pulitzer Prize-winning Mississippi newspaper, the *Delta Democrat Times.* From there he'd gone on to the *New York Herald Tribune*—the paper Shrake had long dreamed of joining. Milner's own first novel, *Incident at Ashton,* inspired by the civil rights movement, had just been published.

In March 1961, the most impressive writer of all came to town. Bill Brammer, accompanied by his wife Nadine, visited the *Times Herald* newsroom to talk about his just-published book, *The Gay Place*. "We noticed immediately how cute Nadine was," Shrake said. The Brammers invited Shrake and Cartwright to join them at the press club for drinks, and the group became friends. "Talking to Brammer that day," Shrake said, "I realized that he had been writing stuff that he knew about that happened in Texas. And New York publishers accepted it. I thought to myself, 'Well, it's a whole new world then.'" Inspired by Brammer's example, Shrake returned to his dormant "serious" novel, rewriting it with the lessons in mind that he had learned from Brammer.[4]

* * *

By 1961, Dan Jenkins had been at the *Fort Worth Press* thirteen years. Now in his third year as sports editor, he still seemed no closer to joining *Sports Illustrated*. He had developed some contacts at the magazine and managed to place stories in it from time to time. But nothing further had developed from his two-week tour of duty in New York, and he was growing frustrated. As *SI* continued to keep him at arm's length, Jenkins couldn't help but wonder if it was because he was only at the *Press*, instead of a bigger paper.

Bud Shrake's reputation, in contrast, continued to expand. In 1961, one of his columns was selected for inclusion in the annual *Best Sports Stories*. In October of that year *The Dallas Morning News* hired him away from *The Times Herald*, making Shrake its lead sports columnist. Shrake would now compete directly against Blackie Sherrod. Shrake's arrival at the *Morning News* was announced on the front page of the paper: "One of the Southwest's best-known sportswriters—Bud Shrake—joins the *News* sports crew as he begins his six times a week column. Winner of several sportswriting awards, author of a novel soon to be published and a TV script writer too, Shrake brings more than a decade of sportswriting into this crisp, new column."[5]

Shrake's move created a long-awaited opening for Dan Jenkins at the *Times Herald.* Sherrod quickly hired him to replace Shrake. Sherrod immediately gave Jenkins a more prominent role than either Shrake or Cartwright had enjoyed on his staff. Jenkins not only became the "second" columnist behind Sherrod, his picture also appeared with his column—a designation formerly largely reserved for Sherrod only. While Shrake and Cartwright had covered the pro football beat, Jenkins focused on college football and professional golf. He also wrote feature stories and his trademark humorous commentaries. Dan Jenkins, finally in a bigger league than the *Fort Worth Press,* could begin showcasing his work to a larger audience.

With Jenkins and Cartwright back on the same paper again, the in-print prankstering first begun at the *Press* began to reassert itself. While Sherrod pretended not to notice, suspect box scores crept into the *Times Herald*'s sports pages. During the 1962 high school football season, the fictional East Dozier Bulldozers became the hottest team in Texas history. Led by twin halfbacks, the Bulldozers whipped teams such as "Smallsville" (84-0) and "Pollack" (83-0). They even prevailed over the "Lurid Redskins," which featured its own set of twin halfbacks. The Bulldozers' impressive streak came to an end when they were defeated in a playoff game against the Corbet Comets. The Comets, too, starred a set of twin halfbacks, Dickie Don and Richie Ron Yewbet.[6]

The Corbet Comets eventually became the most famous of the *Times Herald*'s fictional teams, and an entire history was concocted for the town. The Yewbet twins—named after TCU coach Abe Martin's propensity for answering questions "Yew Bet"—were said to date twin cheerleaders at the school. The team's chief booster was a local Ford dealer, E. O. "Shug" Kempleman, who "generously donated the world's largest bass tuba to the Fighting Comet band." After the contest between East Dozier and Corbet, no further fictional game results appeared in the *Times Herald.* As Gary Cartwright later wrote, "Ultimately, our fun and games were frustrated by the fact that nobody ever caught on. What's the fun of being irreverent if the reverent fail to take offense?"[7]

Jenkins and Cartwright did draw attention for their funny one-liners, and it was Cartwright who set a new standard for cutting edge commentary. Area sportswriters had long struggled to find the right adjective to describe Dallas Texans linebacker Sherrill Headrick, who was seen as "earthy" and "brutish." Cartwright, in one of his accounts, simply noted that Headrick had "the face of an Oklahoma chicken thief."[8]

***

For Bud Shrake, the very conservative *Dallas Morning News* was a marked contrast from the playfulness he had known at the *Fort Worth Press* and *Dallas Times Herald*. The *Morning News*—the state's largest and best-known newspaper—was considered a must-read by the establishment. Despite its formidable economic muscle, the *Morning News* was held in little regard within the journalism profession. It had only two correspondents based outside of the state, and it often seemed content to rest on its reputation, rather than devoting real resources to news coverage. At one time, the *Morning News* had been viewed in the best tradition of crusading newspapers. During the 1920s and 1930s, when Dallas boasted the largest Ku Klux Klan membership in the country, *The Dallas Morning News* led the campaign against the Klan—even in the face of boycotts and a precipitous drop in circulation. In the early days of the Roosevelt administration, the *Morning News* was a strong supporter of FDR's New Deal programs. But with the rise of the oil industry and the business community's fierce resistance to governmental regulation, the *Morning News* gradually became more conservative.[9]

By the 1950s the *Morning News*, under publisher Ted Dealey, had developed an ultraconservative editorial philosophy. The newspaper, in fact, was so right wing that it became, like Congressman Bruce Alger, something of an embarrassment to the city's business establishment. The paper's editorial board railed against the civil rights movement, condemning it as a Communist plot. The Supreme Court was derided as "Courtnik," and Washington, D.C., was considered "the Negro capital of the U.S." The few tentative steps toward civil rights

Dallas Times Herald sportswriters Blackie Sherrod (left) and Gary Cartwright, early 1960s. *Courtesy of Gary and Phyllis Cartwright.*

progress in the new Kennedy administration were harshly condemned, and the paper's language toward the president became increasingly rabid. Kennedy was described as "a crook, a Communist sympathizer, a thief, and 'fifty times a fool.'" Publisher Ted Dealey's own columns referred to JFK as a "weak sister" in dealing with Communism. When Kennedy held a press luncheon at the White House, Dealey showed up and lectured the president, "We need a man on horseback to lead this nation, and many people in Texas and the Southwest think you are riding on Caroline's tricycle." One of Dealey's colleagues at the *Times Herald* was so chagrined by the exchange that he sent Kennedy a note assuring him that the *Morning News* publisher didn't speak for all of Dallas. Kennedy, in response, replied, "I'm sure the people of Dallas are glad when the afternoon [publication of the *Times Herald*] comes."[10]

Bud Shrake, tucked away in the sports department, felt largely immune from the political climate at the *Morning News*. He exercised political self-restraint, avoiding commentary about the increasingly dominant issue in sports—the integration of black athletes. Shrake concentrated mostly on football, and he continued to cover the "millionaires' standoff" between the Dallas Cowboys and Dallas Texans. The NFL's entrenched strength was proving to be of great benefit to the Cowboys. Their games were played against well-known teams and star players, and many fans, including Shrake, viewed the Cowboys as a "major league" franchise. The Texans, meanwhile, were considered a minor league team. An element of class consciousness also crept into the rivalry. The city's upper classes began to associate themselves with the Cowboys—whose tickets cost more. The Texans became heroes to the blue-collar crowd. Working against the Cowboys was the fact that the team performed dismally, suffering a succession of humiliating losses. The Dallas Texans, meanwhile, compiled an impressive record and won the league championship in 1962. The rivalry between the AFL and NFL had spawned, just as observers predicted, a bidding war for college players. In 1962 the Cowboys scored a major coup by signing a hometown star, SMU quarterback Don Meredith.

Shrake was enjoying the high point of his newspaper career. His face appeared on the front page of the sports section six times a week, his column was read by hundreds of thousands of people, and he became a Metroplex celebrity. But the work itself was distinctly unrewarding. "Writing those columns was the hardest thing I've ever done," he said later. "Until you do it, you don't realize how hard it is to come up with topics, day after day." Another problem for Shrake was that, unwittingly, he became identified with *The Dallas Morning News'* editorial philosophy. Once, after he made an offhand reference to the *Texas Observer* in a column, a reader wrote in, "Isn't Bud Shrake quoting from the *Texas Observer* sort of like General [Edwin] Walker quoting from the *Communist Worker?*"[11]

In 1962, Shrake's novel *Blood Reckoning* was published by Bantam. On the advice of his agent, he agreed to be credited as "Edwin Shrake" rather than "Bud Shrake." *Blood Reckoning* departs little from the western formula, with flat characters and a plot that relies heavily on coincidence. But Shrake's depictions of the Native Americans are of interest. Parts of the story are told from the perspective of the Comanches, and Shrake excels at capturing nuances of life inside the Indian camps. No apologies are made for the Comanches' brutal murders of whites, and there is deep respect for the way the Indians defended themselves in the face of overwhelming odds. Shrake had come earlier to understand Beats and African Americans as "outsiders." In *Blood Reckoning,* he found a new expression for this alienation from mainstream society—Native Americans.

Marketed in drugstores and truck stops, *Blood Reckoning* did very well as an original paperback, eventually selling over 100,000 copies. Shrake received moderate royalties, and the book remained in print for two years. The novel also became something of a cult phenomenon in Italy. Published as *Vendetta di sangue,* it remained popular for several more years. As late as 1976, Shrake continued to receive annual royalty checks from the Italian edition.[12] Yet having published a paperback western soon became something of an embarrassment to Shrake. As he concentrated on his "serious" novel, he began referring to that work as his first book. References to *Blood Reckoning* were omitted from several of his subsequent novels.

The publication of *Blood Reckoning* coincided with other changes in Shrake's life. His relationship with Joyce finally cratered for good. He had used most of his advance from Bantam to buy a white Cadillac El Dorado, a decision hooted at by his friends and condemned by Joyce, who considered the car vulgar and refused to ride in it. After the divorce, Joyce kept the house and the children. Shrake maintained possession of his prized Cadillac, which he lived in for several weeks, sleeping in *The Dallas Morning News* parking lot, until he could find an apartment.[13]

* * *

In late 1962, the also-divorced Bill Brammer returned for a visit to Dallas, where he quickly renewed his friendship with Shrake, Cartwright, and Jenkins. Like Shrake, Brammer's life had undergone extensive changes. Work on his sequel, *Fustian Days,* had floundered as the financial failure of *The Gay Place* became more apparent. His publisher lost enthusiasm for the book, and Brammer's agent tried to talk him out of it. *Fustian Days* also lacked the vital presence of Governor Fenstemaker, who had been the driving force of much of *The Gay Place.* Brammer wrote to Larry L. King that he had rewritten his opening chapter of the novel nearly two hundred times, and he joked that the book would probably be published only posthumously.[14]

Brammer's job with *Time* magazine had not gone well. While his clever, highly personal style clearly anticipated the emerging New Journalism, it was also the antithesis of *Time*'s conservative approach to newswriting. Brammer resented his treatment at the hand of *Time*'s editors, and he tried to catch on at other, more literary magazines. *Esquire* offered Brammer $750 to write a profile of Arthur Schlesinger Jr. a prominent historian serving in the Kennedy administration. But Brammer's superiors at *Time* nixed the deal, invoking a clause that forbade him from reporting for anyone but them. Brammer did write a short parody of J. D. Salinger's *Franny and Zooey,* recasting it in a Kennedyesque White House and titling it "Glooey." *Esquire* bought the piece and scheduled it for the May 1962 issue. Yet, again, Brammer's luck failed. *Esquire* had already set the story into type and was on the verge of publication when it heard from Salinger's agent, who protested that the author would be seriously offended by the piece. "Glooey" was canceled. Brammer's agent tried to sell it to *Playboy,* which also declined. Eventually, with nowhere else to turn, Brammer published the satire in the *Texas Observer.*[15]

Brammer continually received offers to work for Texas politicians, and in early 1962 he quit *Time* and returned to Austin. There he became a speechwriter for Tom Reavley, who was running for state attorney general. Reavley not only lost the race, he also refused to pay

Brammer. Brammer had also signed up for the campaign of Woodrow Wilson Bean, the El Paso County judge who was a leading candidate to be elected to Congress—until it was revealed that Bean had not paid income taxes in over a decade. Bean, too, lost, and Brammer's much-anticipated paychecks failed to arrive. Meanwhile, his child support obligations lay in arrears and creditors from New York, Atlanta, and Washington, D.C., were pursuing him.[16]

On a visit to New York, Brammer met Gloria Steinem, who was then engaged to Robert Benton. Steinem was just beginning her career as a journalist, contributing short, unsigned pieces to *Esquire*. Steinem was also director of Independent Research Service, a CIA-funded nonprofit foundation that sought to increase American participation in the International Youth Festivals sponsored by the Soviet Union. Because the United States was beset by ugly racial violence in the South, its stature as a world moral leader was threatened. The youth festivals drew delegates from all over the world and provided the Soviets with rich propaganda. The United States sought to counteract the Soviet strategy by sending groups of young Americans, who could demonstrate that the United States, too, was interested in social justice.[17]

Steinem was making arrangements to attend the upcoming festival in Helsinki, where she would publish a newspaper to offset the official organ produced by the Soviet Union. She hired Brammer as a reporter. The two-week job offered impressive wages, and Brammer received a thousand-dollar advance. Thinking that a lengthy journey might allow him an opportunity to make progress on *Fustian Days*, Brammer booked a voyage aboard a freighter. Unfortunately, the ship made several unscheduled stops en route, and by the time he arrived in Helsinki, the festival had ended, everyone had gone home, and he went unpaid. Now out of money, he pleaded with his literary agent for an advance, and he wandered through Northern Europe, cadging money from new acquaintances and digging for change in the sofas of hotel lobbies. He learned that an old girlfriend of his, Diana de Vegh, a New York socialite who had once been linked to John Kennedy, was in Paris. He contacted her, and de Vegh immediately wired him $100 to join her.

In late 1962 Brammer returned to Texas. Though work on his second novel was not going well, his stature as a prominent Texas writer remained secure. In an essay for the *Texas Observer*, Brammer self-consciously chronicled his return to Dallas, poking fun of himself as a "Famous Arthur." Frankly admitting that he was alienated from Dallas, Brammer observed, "I see these savage, self-made enterprisers all over town, building their own post offices, dredging the Trinity River, dropping coins into pay toilets, underwriting the crash-program development of their own nuclear weapons."[18]

***

While Brammer was in Europe, Bud Shrake finished a draft of his "serious" novel, which focused on rebellious young Texans battling the corrosive influence of an older generation. Though Shrake's agent had initially been very encouraging of this work, she became much more critical when she saw the entire manuscript. Perhaps not realizing that the characters were largely drawn from Shrake's own social world, she complained that the book was about "a group of ugly wastrels whose preoccupation is sordid sex and drowning themselves in alcohol." The next day, worrying that perhaps she had been too critical, his agent wrote again, making it clear that she still had "great hopes for the novel," but asserting that it needed substantial revisions. Explicitly mentioning Brammer's *The Gay Place,* she warned him that his work might be too "similar in theme and treatment." She agreed to show the manuscript to publishers with the proviso that he would begin substantial revisions. Later she reported that *Harper's* had turned the book down, worrying that the novel would end up being too much about "adult delinquents." Still, they saw promise in his work, and considered Shrake a writer to cultivate.[19]

Shrake soon had an idea how to expand his novel's scope substantially. While his friends Dan Jenkins and Gary Cartwright would eventually transform their years of sportswriting into sports-based novels, Bud Shrake took a different approach. He made profound use of the social connections sportswriting allowed him access to; particularly, the millionaire class in Dallas. Just as Bill Brammer had used Lyndon Johnson to bring life to his "Austin" novel, Shrake turned to the business elite he had become intimate with in Dallas—men who were represented by, among others, Clint Murchison Jr. In this new fictional landscape, Shrake would blend his youthful Fort Worth acquaintances with the world he had come to know in Dallas.

Soon after beginning his revised novel, Bud Shrake was playing host at one of the rowdy, seemingly omnipresent parties held in his bachelor apartment. "I was lying on the floor wearing a big sombrero. Someone had put a cigarette on the crown of it and it had caught on fire. But I hadn't noticed that yet, because I was in the middle of making a bet that I could piss on the ceiling while lying on the floor." Shrake's friend Bill Gilliland, a bookstore owner, walked in with a stranger. A while later, after he lost the bet, Shrake went into his bedroom, where he found Gilliland and the stranger reading his manuscript. "I was pretty pissed off, until Bill introduced me to the guy." The guest turned out to be Ken McCormick, editor in chief of Doubleday. After McCormick finished reading he told Shrake that he wanted to buy the book.[20]

"He asked how long it would take me to finish it and I told him six months." Soon thereafter, Bud Shrake had a contract for his "serious" novel. McCormick was excited about Shrake's work, and the editor corresponded often, telling Shrake that he had the potential to become "the voice of your generation."[21]

All Shrake needed now was some extended time to finish the book—a nearly impossible task given his demanding schedule at the *Morning News*' sports desk. Sensing that he was on the verge of a breakthrough, he decided to ask for a year's leave of absence. He wanted to travel through Europe while finishing his novel. The *Morning News* turned down his request. Shrake was about to resign when a new idea was suggested. The *Morning News* was interested in prestige—it just didn't want to have to pay for it. Shrake could become the paper's "foreign correspondent" if he agreed to send them stories from Europe occasionally.[22] Though it wasn't exactly the *New York Herald-Tribune*, Bud Shrake had just become a foreign correspondent as well as a novelist. His dreams were coming true.

8.

A LONG

WAY

FROM

BEAUMONT

A s Shrake departed for Europe, Dan and June Jenkins were packing to move to New York City. Earlier in 1962 Jenkins, along with several other stringers, was asked to submit anecdotes for a story on putting. Instead, Jenkins wrote up an entire article, "Lockwrists and Cage Cases," and sent it in. His story began, "The devoted golfer is an anguished soul who has learned a lot about putting, just as an avalanche victim has learned a lot about snow." Jenkins got quotes from many of the game's top golfers about putting, and he added his own humorous insights. Jenkins' piece impressed editor André Laguerre, and *Sports Illustrated* ran the story in full. Readers responded with raves, and soon thereafter, Jenkins got the call to join the magazine.[1]

In January 1963, after a series of going-away parties, Dan and June Jenkins and their three children loaded up the car and drove the nearly sixteen hundred miles to New York. As much as Jenkins had prepared himself for the move, it still came as a shock to encounter bagels, pizzas, and other cultural oddities. It was a big change, Jenkins later recalled, for someone who "used to think Beaumont was an exotic dateline."[2]

Jenkins adjusted very quickly to his new life. His *Sports Illustrated* colleague Roy Terrell said later, "Dan, we used to call him Broadway, because from the minute he landed in New York, he was more of a New Yorker than anyone I ever saw." Jenkins understood that thriving in New York depended on "whipout." Money—taking care of the wait staff, door people, and others who took care of you. Jenkins learned right away that P. J. Clark's was the hottest spot in town. "You had to be somebody to get in that back room. That first week, Dan introduced himself to Jimmy, who guarded the door. . . . As soon as Dan had slipped Jimmy a twenty, Dan became somebody and got a table near Ed Sullivan. After that, it only got better." Soon, there "wasn't a restaurant, there wasn't a bar, there wasn't any place in New York where the owners and the maître d's and waiters didn't throw people out of tables when Dan Jenkins walked into the room."[3]

Jenkins loved the corporate culture at *SI.* Though his salary didn't compare to what writers made at other New York-based magazines, the expense accounts were stupendous. His workload, too, was a welcome change from the years at daily papers in Fort Worth and Dallas. Jenkins sent Shrake a series of letters in Europe, describing how writers took three-hour lunches and dreamed up story ideas that allowed them to spend long periods of time away from the office. This left about eight people, Jenkins joked, to put out the magazine, and they did it in twenty minutes.[4]

But there were drawbacks. For his first story, Jenkins was sent to cover a college football gambling scandal involving the University of Georgia and the University of Alabama. Editors drastically reworked his version of events, and a sober account appeared under his name. Jenkins was not pleased at how "group journalism" often ruled at *Sports Illustrated,* and he was already chafing under the restrictions.[5]

Dan Jenkins did manage to transform the magazine by successfully arguing that it was not covering college football properly. As Michael MacCambridge writes in his history of *Sports Illustrated,* "The magazine had yet to cover the long season as a continually unfolding drama, a multi-act play toward a specific end, replete with significant elements of tragedy that would result in one team being coronated at the end of the season with the mythical national championship."[6] Editor André Laguerre put Jenkins on the beat he coveted—college football, and in SI's preseason issue, Jenkins boldly picked the University of Texas Longhorns to win the national championship. His prediction came true a few months later, and Jenkins' stature at the magazine was assured.

Jenkins proved to be more than an exceptionally knowledgeable sportswriter. He also won accolades for his feature stories. The breakthrough came with his November 11, 1963, story, "The Disciples of Saint Darrell on a Wild Weekend." Writing as a genial, slightly condescending anthropologist would of a primitive culture, Jenkins' affectionate, closely observed portrait of a quartet of Texas football fans was a delight. The abundant humor is evident in the title— which refers to the University of Texas' winning football coach Darrell Royal as a "Saint." Jenkins' Texans seem to live for football, beer, gambling, and country music, while their wives and children were of secondary importance. The men are also "modern Texans," which means that they "might not recognize a cow pony if it were tied on a leash in [the] back yard." Jenkins' assured tone was evident throughout the piece, and he had no reservations about making outrageously bold statements. "Waco, Texas is noted for only two things," Jenkins told SI readers. "One is that it is the home of Baylor University. The other is that Waco, from time to time, has tornadoes."[7]

Jenkins was quickly proving that he could excel at the national level. In New York, he was contacted by Doubleday editor Ken McCormick at the suggestion of Bud Shrake. Jenkins and McCormick discussed the possibility of eventually publishing a collection of Jenkins' best *Sports Illustrated* pieces. Jenkins had no immediate plans to become a novelist, but he liked the idea of doing an anthology. He also had another idea in mind. He began to think about a way to have his best friend Bud Shrake join him on the staff of *Sports Illustrated*.[8]

* * *

Bud Shrake was in Europe when he heard the news that one of his sports columns had been selected for the second consecutive year to appear in *Best Sports Writing*. But sports was far from Shrake's mind at the time. In his journey to Europe, Shrake was following a well-trod path of American writers. Ernest Hemingway's spirit loomed large and Paris' Lost Generation of the 1920s held a timeless appeal for young artists. Writers from Texas' own World War II generation, including John Graves and Terry Southern, had already gone to Europe for lengthy sojourns.

Shrake wrote relatively few stories as a foreign correspondent, but those that he did publish were far more provocative than his sports reporting had ever been. In Spain, Shrake's reporting drew parallels between that country's right-wing government and Dallas' own ultra-conservatism. Shrake wrote, "But beneath the surface glitter of a city like Barcelona is the reality of the Fascist dictatorship of General Franco. . . . There is a fine new Picasso Museum in Barcelona [but] there is no name on the door. For Franco, the fact that Picasso has been a Communist is more important than the fact that Picasso is the greatest living Spanish artist and perhaps the greatest living artist of any nationality."[9] Though Shrake's article never mentioned Dallas, alert readers understood the connection—Picasso's own work had been banned in Dallas for the very same reason it was denigrated in fascist Spain.

Back in Dallas, the *Morning News* hired Gary Cartwright to fill in for Shrake, with the promise that both men would have jobs when Shrake returned. In his newly prominent position, Cartwright's reporting grew bolder by the day. He began using his forum to write about a previously taboo subject—black athletes and the inevitability of integration. Whenever possible, Cartwright wrote straight news stories on attempts to integrate Texas universities. He also used his opinion column to prepare readers for the inevitable changes. "We've all watched too much Amos 'n Andy," he began one column. And that, he concluded, "begats ignorance." Cartwright delighted in writing about local blacks who had been shut out of Texas colleges but went on to star in other parts of the country. These "Texas Negro athletes," Cartwright wrote, "would have been credits to any Southwest Conference school, both as athletes and citizens."[10] Not content merely to discuss issues of race, Cartwright also sneaked in unflattering references in his columns to Dallas congressman Bruce Alger and Texas' Republican senator John Tower.

The *Morning News* was alarmed and disturbed by the turn their new sports columnist was taking. Cartwright wrote Shrake in Europe that one editor complained, "I write too much about niggers." Cartwright also mentioned, "The only letters I get are from the Ku Klux Klan [which is] offering me a million dollars if I can define for them the term integration. I am still thinking up an answer. I'm glad they understand I don't come cheap." Cartwright's editors began keeping a closer eye on his work, deleting controversial references to politicians. They also clamped down on his reporting. In March 1963, a surprise announcement rocked the sports world. Mississippi State University, a bastion of segregation, chose to defy its state's politicians and compete in the NCAA basketball tournament, even though that meant they would play—for the first time ever—against black athletes. Cartwright, calling sources on the phone for quotes, promptly wrote up a story. But the piece was killed, and an editor told him, "If it were a wire-service story, maybe it would be different. But this story . . . this story is written by our own man. Our own man!"[11]

***

From Spain, Bud Shrake traveled through Paris and then on to Frankfurt, Germany, where an old friend from Fort Worth, Dick Growald, was the United Press International bureau chief. There, in Growald's apartment, Shrake finished his novel in a great rush, thanks in part to the speed he was taking. The book was called *But Not for Love*. He wrote to Brammer in Texas, downplaying his accomplishment. "It nearly made me throw up but anyhow Doubleday is going to publish it . . . and we can have a mass throwing up." Shrake also feigned horror that the "one big trouble was, I noticed that there's no Indians in it. That's the thing about heart medicine [speed]: here I was going along furiously and finishing, and then I found out I had left out the Indians. What kind of goddamn book is that, without Indians?"[12]

Despite Shrake's attempts at self-effacement, Doubleday was immensely pleased with the novel and began planning a substantial promotional campaign. But Shrake, despite his hopes for becoming a successful novelist, could not get himself interested in the machinery of publicity. He initially refused to fill out Doubleday's routine public-ity questionnaire, feeling that it was demeaning. Finally, after editor in chief Ken McCormick intervened, Shrake submitted a short biogra-phical statement.[13]

When he returned to Dallas in May 1963, Shrake and the now-divorced Cartwright moved into an apartment together. "We were night people," Cartwright recalled. After the clubs closed, people seemed to find their way over to their apartment, and "on any given night the living room would be full of famous athletes, coaches, bil-lionaires, nightclub acts, artists, hoodlums, drunks, writers." Entertainers from local clubs performed after-hours at the apartment, and touring artists such as the Kingston Trio also showed up. Cowboys quarterback Don Meredith was a frequent guest, as was Cowboys owner Clint Murchison Jr. The lure of celebrity wasn't enough to pla-cate some neighbors, who filed noise complaints. The Dallas police were always very genial in breaking up the parties, though once their suspicions were aroused because of a report that a naked man was seen in the area. That turned out to be Gary Cartwright, who sought refuge in the swimming pool.[14]

After his return, Shrake resumed his duties as the *Morning News'* lead sports columnist, writing six columns a week. He and Gary Cartwright covered pro football, and the big story that year was that Clint Murchison's Dallas Cowboys had prevailed in their battle against Lamar Hunt's Dallas Texans. In early 1963 Kansas City offered Hunt several incentives, including a guarantee of twenty-five thousand season ticket holders. Hunt may have had his heart set on Dallas, but he was a businessman, after all. He agreed to relocate, and his team became the Kansas City Chiefs.

Shrake's return to Dallas was noticed by the city's reclusive elderly billionaire, H. L. Hunt, who issued Shrake an invitation for lunch.

During their meeting, Hunt lectured Shrake on the vices of unhealthy eating, and he talked of the wonders of the aloe vera plant. Hunt rubbed several ounces of aloe vera lotion into his skin as he told Shrake how he had discovered the herb in "Bible Country," as he called the Middle East. Ever since, Hunt had been trying to corner the world market and sell it as a tonic in the United States. In the midst of his monologue, Hunt suddenly dropped to the floor. Shrake rushed to his aid, only to be waved off. Hunt was going to demonstrate his "creeping"—crawling along the floor like a baby. It was this practice, he claimed, along with the aloe vera, that kept him young. The conversation ended abruptly when the butler stepped in to announce that it was time for Hunt's nap. Lunch had never been served. Shrake left the Mount Vernon replica never knowing why he'd been invited, but the scene remained in his mind when he wrote his subsequent novel about Dallas, *Strange Peaches*.[15]

Shrake continued to hang out with Murchison and his band of rowdies. On one occasion they descended on a housewarming party hosted by Dallas millionaire Jim Ling. Shrake had first met the millionaire some years earlier when Ling was a young businessman helping to revive the Dallas Open golf tournament. In the intervening years, Ling became fabulously rich, but in the process had butted heads with Dallas' more established wealthy class. In 1961, Ling had won a fierce fight to take control of Chance Vought aircraft. This battle gave him a "reputation as a ruthless and reckless industrialist." In fact, it was Jim Ling, along with Clint Murchison Jr. who had inspired Shrake's establishment characters in his forthcoming novel, *But Not for Love*.[16]

Ling's new mansion was appropriately gaudy for Dallas sensibilities—the bathrooms boasted solid gold toilet fixtures and the grounds featured a "Versailles-palace arrangement of terraces, statues, and fountains." Accompanying Shrake and Murchison to the party was Eric, Murchison's half-tame turkey, contemptuously named after Dallas Mayor Eric Jonsson. Eric had Dallas Cowboy stickers plastered all over him, and he had also shared a good deal of alcohol with his owner. Eric, who was ill-tempered under the best of circumstances, turned mean when drunk. The barefoot Murchison carried his turkey into Ling's party but soon lost control of the bird. This scene would also make its way into Shrake's "Dallas" novel, *Strange Peaches.* In the book, the turkey has been renamed "Lyndon," and it stumbles drunkenly through the party, "hissing viciously, crapping every few seconds and pecking at bowls of peanuts." Several people join in a chaotic chase and Lyndon knocks over a statue that the party host "was buying on advice from a New York gallery." "My God, he's broke my ort!" the man screams. Soon, Lyndon finds himself facing the barrel end of a shotgun.[17]

Shrake and Cartwright and other friends often made trips to Austin, where they looked up friends including Billy Lee Brammer. Another writer living in Austin at the time was Larry McMurtry, who had become friends with Brammer. McMurtry's own first novel, *Horseman, Pass By,* had upended the Texas literary establishment by winning the Texas Institute of Letters Award for best novel. In 1963 McMurtry's novel was made into a successful film, *Hud,* starring Paul Newman and Patricia Neal.

McMurtry and his wife often hung out at the Scholz Garten with Brammer and others in the circle. When McMurtry's wife abruptly left him to run off with a poet to the West Coast, McMurtry and Brammer decided to share a house together. McMurtry continued to come down to the Scholz Garten, bouncing his baby son James on his lap. McMurtry recalled that Brammer "was at that time the local culture hero" because of his Austin-based novel. "He was thus a natural target for anyone in Austin who was aspiring, frustrated, or bored. The inrush of wives threatened to wrench the hinges off the door, and Mr. Brammer faced it with the courteous and rather melancholy patience with which he would have probably faced a buffalo stampede."[18]

To McMurtry, it seemed "that Billy's enthusiasm had run down. He wasn't getting anything back from his writing. He was working on his sequel then, *Fustian Days,* and I read everything he had. The first hundred pages or so, starting with Fenstemaker's funeral, was just wonderful, actually better than most of *The Gay Place.*" From there,

McMurtry said, Brammer's effort "petered out pretty quickly as far as its narrative interest. There were maybe another hundred pages, but it was pretty bad. I felt that it was running down already. Billy felt it too, which didn't help. It just seemed like he was bored with it."[19]

When McMurtry's friend Ken Kesey came to town to visit, speaking of the mind-expanding possibilities of psychedelic drugs, he found a ready convert in Billy Lee Brammer. When Kesey extended an invitation to join him in California, Brammer accepted, moving to the West Coast in the summer of 1963.

9.

DALLAS,

1963

As fall 1963 approached, Shrake and Cartwright met Dallas club owner Jack Ruby, who came to *The Dallas Morning News* and handed out free passes to his strip joint, the Carousel Club. Ruby loved having newspapermen and cops around, feeling that they brought an aura of respectability to what he considered a "fucking classy joint." A few days later, Shrake and Cartwright showed up. Because they were well-known columnists, Ruby made sure their drinks were free.[1]

Ruby's star stripper was Jada, a striking orange-haired woman whose "act consisted mainly of hunching a tiger-skin rug and making wild orgasmic sounds with her throat. As a grand climax Jada would spread her legs and pop her G-string." After that first night at Ruby's club, Bud Shrake and Jada began dating.[2]

Jada was, as Gary Cartwright later wrote, "the most interesting and exotic woman I ever met. She traveled with an entourage of mysterious people who always seemed to have just returned from Ankara or Beirut." Jada loved playing the part of a star, and one of her "great pleasures was driving around Dallas in her gold Cadillac with the letters JADA embossed on the door, her orange hair piled high on her head, wearing high heels and a mink coat and nothing else." Once Jada drove her car into the U.S. from Mexico "with a hundred two-

pound Girl Scout cookie tins of marijuana in the trunk. Her companion, who knew nothing about the contraband, was a state politician.
The first thing she did at customs was fall out of the Cadillac with her
mink flaring open, revealing to the startled customs officers far more
than any customer at the Carousel ever saw." By the time they met
Jada, Cartwright and Shrake were no longer smoking pot merely on
social occasions. It became an everyday part of their lives, and it contributed to their feeling that they were living life "on the edge."
Spending time in the company of Jada only reinforced the impression.[3]

Shrake and Cartwright soon realized that Jada and Jack Ruby
couldn't stand each other. Though Ruby operated a strip club, he
remained something of a sexual prude. He considered Jada's act "vulgar," and during the climax of her performance he would often turn
off the lights and hustle her offstage. Jada, for her part, treated Ruby
with contempt, calling him "a pansy and worse." She complained
about the dogs Ruby kept in the Carousel's kitchen, and she often
told customers that the hamburgers served by the club "were con-
taminated with dog shit." When Shrake would come to the club to
pick up Jada after her last performance, he'd frequently find her and
Ruby yelling at each other.[4]

***

While Bud Shrake and Gary Cartwright were immersing themselves in Dallas' underground culture, the city's political climate was
becoming increasingly tense. Once it became clear that President
Kennedy's plans for a Peace Corps would become a reality,
Congressman Bruce Alger appeared on TV, denouncing it as "welfare
socialism and godless materialism." *The Dallas Morning News* continued to heap scorn on the president. General Edwin Walker, who had
lost his race for Texas governor in 1962, remained an active political
force. In April 1963 a gunman fired a shot at General Walker inside
his home, narrowly missing. It was later concluded that the would-be
assassin was Lee Harvey Oswald.[5]

The civil rights movement was taking on increasing urgency. In August, Martin Luther King Jr. delivered his "I Have a Dream" speech to some two hundred thousand people in Washington, D.C. The next month, a black church in Birmingham, Alabama, was bombed, killing four young girls. Shrake and Cartwright, after years of being vaguely sympathetic to the cause, became more directly involved after meeting David and Ann Richards, who had moved to Dallas after graduating from UT-Austin. David Richards worked for a law firm that represented organized labor. Ann Richards, while raising their children, was a "a political activist and a famous force of nature among our state's small, gritty band of liberal Democrats." She helped found the Dallas Committee for Peaceful Integration, which soon found itself harassed by local FBI agents. Freedom marches were taking place across the South, and Ann Richards' goal was to have plenty of white people marching alongside the blacks in Dallas. "She made sure that Shrake and I joined the marches," Cartwright said later. Though Dallas newspapers refused to carry any news of the events, management was certainly aware that they were taking place. "I remember one march that carried us right by the front of the *Morning News* building," Cartwright said. "Bud and I did our very best to become as inconspicuous as possible at that moment."[6]

In October, the U.S. ambassador to the United Nations, Adlai Stevenson, announced that he would travel to Dallas and give a speech for UN Day. The United Nations was an object of particular hatred in Texas, as it was considered "an instrument of the worldwide Communist Conspiracy" by right-wingers. "Get the U.S. Out of the U.N." billboards became common throughout the state, and earlier in 1963 the Texas legislature had passed a bill making it a crime to display the United Nations flag in Texas.[7]

U.N. ambassador Stevenson's challenge to Dallas would not go unanswered. Governor John Connally was persuaded to proclaim October 23—the day before Stevenson's visit—U.S. Day. General Walker held a boisterous U.S. Day rally the evening before Stevenson's speech—in the same building where Stevenson would appear. Walker told the twelve hundred in attendance that it was their patriotic duty to disrupt Stevenson's visit, and the crowd roared its assent.

When Stevenson arrived for his speech the next day, "a band of men in black shirts, black pants, and black boots goose-stepped up and down the sidewalk in front of the auditorium, giving the stiff-armed salute." When Stevenson began to speak, the audience erupted with catcalls, and "he was drowned out by an orchestrated pack of women who jangled their charm bracelets so loudly he was forced off the stage." Several in the audience attempted to restore order, but it proved impossible. "One man screamed, again and again, 'Kennedy will get his reward in hell! And Stevenson is going to die! His heart will stop, stop, stop! And he will burn, burn burn!'"[8]

Stevenson left the building to find a group of hecklers waiting for him. The Dallas police formed a protective cordon around Stevenson but lost control as the crowd closed in, spitting and yelling curses. The ambassador, a believer in reasoned discourse, attempted to engage a woman carrying a sign that read, "If You Seek Peace, Ask Jesus." She responded by slamming her placard down on his head. The police pushed Stevenson into a car, and the ambassador "wiped the spit from his face with a handkerchief and asked aloud, 'Are these human beings or animals?' The crowd responded by rocking the car. At that moment it seemed likely that Stevenson would be murdered on the streets of Dallas, but the driver gunned the car and burst through to safety."[9] The entire episode was captured by news cameras and played before a national TV audience.

City leaders were mortified and quickly issued an official apology to Stevenson. But the far-right groups remained defiant. Congressman Bruce Alger called the protesters "proud" and "courageous." General Walker told reporters, "Adlai got what was coming to him." When Walker heard news of the city's formal apology, he responded by flying his American flag upside down, a sign of military distress.[10]

As the political hysteria in Dallas ratcheted up during the fall of 1963, Billy Lee Brammer returned to his hometown under extreme financial duress. He had made very little money during 1963 and had, in fact, done very little work. His child support payments were far behind, and his ex-wife Nadine was threatening to sue over money Brammer had received for a proposed film version of *The Gay Place*. In Dallas, he could count on the love and support of his parents while being close to friends Bud Shrake and Gary Cartwright. Brammer also returned as something of a cultural avatar. As a result of his stay with Kesey, Brammer had become one of the first Texans to experiment with LSD. On his return home, he brought news of an imminent psychedelic revolution.

In November it was announced that President John F. Kennedy would make a trip to Texas—and Dallas was on his itinerary. Kennedy, with an eye on his 1964 reelection campaign, wanted to make peace within Texas' fractured Democratic Party. An open feud had developed between liberal Senator Ralph Yarborough and the party's conservative wing, led by Governor John Connally and tacitly supported by Lyndon Johnson. Several people, including Adlai Stevenson, warned JFK against coming to Dallas, but Kennedy refused their advice. To him, avoiding Dallas would have been seen as an act of cowardice.

Once Kennedy's trip was set, Dallas' business establishment decided it was time to crack down on the political extremists who were giving the city such a bad reputation. A well-coordinated public relations campaign was launched to convince Dallasites that the president of the United States deserved complete respect during his visit, even if people disagreed with his policies. The newspapers were enlisted in the effort, and even *The Dallas Morning News* grudgingly went along with the plan. But not everything went smoothly. The week before the visit, *Times Herald* columnist A.C. Greene speculated about why so many people hated the president. The editorial outraged anti-Kennedy forces, and members of the American Nazi Party staged a demonstration in front of the *Times Herald*, marching around a man in an ape suit. The ape wore a sign that read "A.C. Greene." As Gary Cartwright recalled, the *Times Herald* didn't print a story about the incident, "possibly because it didn't want to offend any Nazi subscribers, and the *News* didn't print the story because it happened in front of the *Herald*."[11]

The weekend before November 22, Gary Cartwright married an airline stewardess whom he had known for three weeks. Not quite sober, he and his bride were driven to Oklahoma by a man named Richard Noble, whom Cartwright also barely knew. Noble supervised everything, paying for the license and blood tests and volunteering a Stanford class ring for the wedding band. When the newlyweds returned to Dallas, Jada gave them a "two-pound cookie tin filled with manicured marijuana" as a wedding present.[12]

Bud Shrake and Jada were continuing their love affair, despite Jack Ruby's increasingly angry protestations. On the evening before Kennedy's visit, Shrake received a phone call at his apartment. On the line was Jack Ruby, asking if Shrake had seen Jada. Shrake said no. Then Ruby told him, "Don't let that woman in your apartment anymore. You better stay away from her if you know what's good for you."

"Are you threatening me?" Shrake asked.

"Oh, no, I didn't mean for you to take it that way," Ruby said. "I'm just telling you for your own good."[13]

* * *

On the morning of Kennedy's visit, *The Dallas Morning News* undid everything for which the business establishment had worked. The newspaper prominently displayed a full-page advertisement, in a bold black border, from a fictitious organization. The advertisement read, "Welcome Mr. Kennedy, To Dallas." From there the ad listed twelve specific grievances, almost all of which accused Kennedy in some form of selling the country out to the Communists. Even more chilling was a privately distributed handbill that appeared on the front doors of homes throughout the city—an effort coordinated by General Walker. The handbills read in large type, "Wanted for Treason." Underneath the headline were two "mug shots" of John Kennedy, along with angry language denouncing Kennedy as a traitor.

Shrake reported to work at the *Morning News,* and shortly after his arrival Jack Ruby approached his desk. "I just want you to know that I'm not angry at you," Ruby told him. "I just want to warn you about Jada. She works for the mob, you know, runs cash for them and runs dope for them. She can get you in really big trouble in no time." Ruby was telling Shrake the truth, and Shrake had, in fact, begun formulating his own suspicions about Jada by that time. He and Ruby chatted for a few minutes more, and then Shrake left to find Gary Cartwright so they could go watch the presidential motorcade.[14]

Despite the last-minute attempts by Dallas' right wing to sour Kennedy's visit, the crowds along the motorcade route were large and exuberant. Shrake and Cartwright got themselves a place in front, and as the president rode by they were so close they could almost reach out and touch him. Cartwright later wrote, "Kennedy looked directly at us, his famous grin flashing like a polished diamond, his hand flickering a sort of salute of recognition, as though to say 'I've heard all about you two Cole Avenue rogues!'"[15]

Bud Shrake, in *Strange Peaches*, describes the scene through the eyes of John Lee Wallace, the narrator. Wallace is filming the motorcade:

> The president's gray eyes looked directly at me leaning out from the curb, took me all in with an instant's deep gaze, and looked squarely into my lens, and his lips moved a bit, the smile broadening, and he raised a finger and pointed at me, and I took my eye away from the viewfinder and looked straight into his eyes, and a communication flashed from him to me that said there you are you freak what a time you must have among these people I like you for it don't give up. At the same second he was sending me that message I was receiving it and thinking as well, with surprise and embarrassment that I would have such a thought, that if I'd wanted to hurt the man, I was so close I could crack his skull with a five-iron or couldn't conceivably miss with a pistol. But I could tell this perverted thought never reached him. He had trained himself to tune out small paranoias. I smiled at him as he looked at

me, and his right eye squinted very slightly as if it occurred to him that he had seen me before but could not recall where. Then his eyes left me and held their place in the crowd. . . . I didn't wait to film Lyndon Johnson or any of the others. To me they were just politicians, not great men, just part of the crowd the same as me, and I still didn't care for all this big-ass politics, but I knew a great man when I saw one.[16]

A few minutes later, their hero was dead. JFK's murder was a life-changing moment for many people, and its impact has also reverberated through Texas letters. Gary Cartwright and Bud Shrake found their lives and work profoundly affected by the assassination. Billy Lee Brammer, after a long downward slide, suddenly found a reversal of fortune. But the tragedy changed more than anyone else the very course of Larry L. King's life.

PART TWO:

TOO MUCH

AIN'T

ENOUGH

10.

A

New

Beginning

arry L. King was scheduled to accompany the Kennedy entourage to Texas in November 1963. As the chief aide to Congressman Jim Wright of Fort Worth, King had, in fact, helped plan the Kennedy trip. But he had come down with strep throat and remained behind. By the twenty-second, he felt well enough to return to the office, and he was having lunch with former Congressman J. T. Rutherford in a small club across from the House Office Building. Sitting nearby was House Majority Leader Carl Albert and other D.C. power brokers.

King had been in Washington for nearly ten years, and he was enjoying a successful career by most standards. His annual salary of $17,000 was good money, and he had managed to ingratiate himself into Washington's political society, which was far smaller and more intimate than it is today. King was originally starstruck when he came to the capital, enthralled at the opportunity to meet luminaries such as former president Harry Truman. But, eventually, being around powerful politicians became routine, and there were few figures that aroused great emotion in him. One of those was John F. Kennedy, whom King had come to know when Kennedy was still a senator. King much admired Kennedy's poise, wit, and intellect. King had joined Kennedy on a campaign trip to Texas in 1960, where he observed firsthand the candidate's coolness under pressure. It was quite a contrast to the unseemly bluster of Texas' own Lyndon Johnson.

King worked eight years for Congressman J. T. Rutherford, who gave him broad latitude in his job. King often conferred with constituents and politicians about substantive matters. He also helped nudge Rutherford in liberal directions, and the congressman, representing a very conservative district, supported public housing, the minimum wage, and national park status for Padre Island. Most notably, Rutherford voted in favor of the 1957 Civil Rights Bill, making him one of the few southern congressmen to do so.[1]

The political life also required a lot of drinking and after-hours socializing with colleagues, which took an inevitable toll. King later wrote of those years, "What we did not notice much was that our homes and families were being taken for granted, were sorely neglected, while we schemed [during these occasions] to improve the general lot of mankind."[2]

Rutherford's tenure came to an abrupt end in 1962 when it was discovered that he had taken a check from Billy Sol Estes, a Lyndon Johnson operative who became the key figure in an emerging bribery scandal. Rutherford was defeated, and King needed a new job. Like Brammer, he was courted by Senator Ralph Yarborough. Instead, he signed on with Jim Wright, an ambitious young congressman who would eventually become Speaker of the House. One of King's first acts after joining Wright's staff was to hire a black man, the first African American to work in any Texas congressional delegation. King was also making concerted attempts to integrate his own life. He consciously sought out blacks for friendships and hosted interracial parties in his white D.C. neighborhood. When neighbors complained, he responded by pointedly inviting even more blacks to his home. When Martin Luther King Jr. delivered his "I Have a Dream" speech, Larry L. King was among those in attendance.[3]

Congressional assistants—including Lyndon Johnson himself—often went on to become congressmen. As such, there was some talk in West Texas that King might make a run at J. T. Rutherford's old seat in 1964. But in reality, King was becoming tired of politics. The reason he had come to Washington in the first place was to launch his writing career. "My original plan was just to stay three years in politics. I thought I'd get up here and get a job on the *Washington Post* or *Washington Star* or some big-ass paper, but I quickly found those folks just weren't interested in me. My only credentials were a couple of small papers from Texas and New Mexico." Undeterred, King expected to accumulate literary contacts that he could call upon as he wrote short stories, magazine articles, and novels in his spare time. But as it turned out, his job "required twelve-hour days Monday through Friday, a half-day or more on Saturday, some Sunday afternoon conferences." King's life was becoming encircled on all sides. He and his wife now had three children, making it even more difficult for him to find time to write. "Though the days dragged by, the years somehow sped," King wrote later. "I had yet to find time to begin the first of what surely would prove to be a string of triumphant novels."[4]

King began retreating to the attic of the family home on nights and weekends, typing furiously while his wife kept the children from disturbing him. Through these efforts he eventually fashioned *The Secret Music*, a novel based on the Korean War prisoners who refused to return to the United States. This was the manuscript that King had asked Billy Lee Brammer to send to publishers on his behalf. Though Brammer disappointed him in that regard, his friend was more helpful in introducing King to other writers. In this way, King gradually began to develop a circle of literary acquaintances. One was David Halberstam, who had finished second to Brammer in the Houghton Mifflin in-house contest for best first novel. Brammer also introduced King to Warren Miller, a novelist, journalist, and screenwriter who was the book page editor of *The Nation*.[5]

After abandoning *The Secret Music* and giving up on writing for several months, King returned with a focus on a new novel, *The Back of a Bear*. Several rejection notices later, he at long last received the phone call for which he'd been waiting. An editor at St. Martin's Press told him that they were interested in publishing it. Shortly afterward, the editor came to town and took King out for drinks, talking up the prospects of the book. When King asked about a contract or an advance, the editor dismissed his concern "with a limp wave. . . . All that remained was for a couple of other in-house editors to gorge themselves on its poetic beauty, and then the formality of a contract." King was thrilled at the prospect of finally becoming a published novelist and, "told all my friends, many bewildered strangers in bars or at bus stops and—you may be sure—a few enemies with special relish." Months passed with the occasional encouraging note from the editor, but still no contract. Finally, ten months after the initial phone call, King received a package in the mail. It was his manuscript, along with a two-sentence rejection notice.[6]

By 1963, King was a frustrated husband, father, and failed novelist who saw his life crumbling away. Writers his own age—and younger—were becoming rich and successful in ways he had once dreamed of. King wrote to his friend Billy Lee Brammer back in Texas in January 1963, employing gallows humor to discuss his writing prospects:

> Is there a market for the Unfinished, Unpublished Works of Larry King? I can include, appropriately indexed with puzzling little footnotes, the following: a rather carelessly-done complete 400 page novel about a lil kid and Texas-type thangs; three different versions of the first quarter of a book about a turncoat; about 30% of a story about a fellow who got caught selling horsemeat for human consumption (the first of a trilogy . . .), nine pages of a budding novel about a political race between an Earl Long and a General Walker complicated by the riotful integration of a State University, thirty-eight short stories ranging from a low of 2% to a high of 7% completed, a dirty poem and eight years of ghosted newsletters sponsored by a former member of Congress from West Texas.[7]

King's literary friends were well aware of his ambition, and they also saw in him great potential. King's friend Warren Miller mentioned to an editor friend of his, Robert Gutwillig at McGraw-Hill, that Larry King was a writer worth checking into. In September 1963,

Gutwillig sent King an inquiry letter, asking if he had anything to show him. King had done precious little subsequent work on his "political" novel featuring characters based on Earl Long and General Edwin Walker, but in response to Gutwillig's inquiry he "spun out a rough plot for a political novel, finding a title—*The One-Eyed Man*— by flipping through *Bartlett's Familiar Quotations*. I claimed to have been slaving on the nonexistent book for about eight months; after ninety days of polishing I would send along representative chapters."[8]

Gutwillig responded immediately, telling King, "If you write a novel like you wrote the letter, both of us may become rich and famous." Gutwillig wanted to see King's manuscript, so King called in sick for a week at Jim Wright's office and put together a thirty-six-page chapter. A few hours after he showed the manuscript to Gutwillig, McGraw-Hill offered King a contract with a $1,500 advance. As King later said, "I would have accepted $1.98."[9]

By November 22, Larry King was becoming increasingly restless at work and home. Though he and Congressman Wright got along well personally, Wright managed his staff much more closely than Rutherford had, leaving little to King's discretion. The tension increased when Wright caught King working on his novel during office hours. At the same time, King's domestic situation was falling apart. He and Jeanne, who had been leading separate lives for so long, were barely speaking. King was spending more and more evenings away from home, often in the company of other women. The situation got so bad that Jeanne began locking him out of the house and forbade the children to open the door for him.[10]

King dreamed of quitting his job to make a living as a full-time writer, but there was little to encourage him. Aside from a contract for an unwritten novel, he was a complete unknown in the literary marketplace. One intriguing connection he did have was with Willie Morris, whom he had met earlier that year. Morris, after a sojourn as a Rhodes Scholar, served as editor of the *Texas Observer* from 1960 to 1962. There, he continued the aggressive muckraking established by Ronnie Dugger. Morris and King had spoken several times on the phone when King passed along tips to the *Observer*. They also had several mutual friends including Billy Lee Brammer. But they had never met in person. In 1963 Willie Morris was hired as an associate editor at *Harper's,* America's oldest magazine. Despite its venerable history, *Harper's* was being left behind as the New Journalism, led by *Esquire,* swept the country. *Harper's,* under editor John Fischer, seemed to be guided by caution, both in its editorial policies and its pay scales. By hiring the twenty-eight-year-old Willie Morris, the magazine hoped to rejuvenate its image.

Soon after beginning at *Harper's* Morris made a trip to Washington and came to Jim Wright's office looking for Larry L. King. King recalled, "I asked Willie out for coffee and headed for the House Office Building cafeteria. On the way he asked, 'Do they sell Bloody Marys there?' So instead we stepped across the street to the Filibuster Room in the Congressional Hotel and commenced sipping at about eleven A.M I think it was two P.M. by the time I got back to Congressman Wright's office, and by then Willie and I were brothers." Morris and King continued to see each other socially whenever possible, and Morris loved the off-the-record stories King told him about D.C. politics. King remembered that Morris kept saying, "You must write that for me!" Both men understood that King couldn't—as long as he remained a congressional aide.[11]

On November 22, while King and J. T. Rutherford were having lunch, the news came on the television that President Kennedy had been shot. King remembered, "Suddenly I found myself at the bar, hitting it so hard my hand later swelled, cursing and—I think—crying and shouting 'They got him! The sons-of-bitches got him!' It was my presumption that some Right Wing nut had shot the President." That evening Kennedy's body arrived back in Washington, and King went to meet Jim Wright. The two men burst into tears upon seeing each other, but they went on to have very different reactions to the tragedy. Wright responded by furiously immersing himself in the duties of the office. King, however, was completely deflated. The following week, he didn't show up for work, nor did he bother to call in. "Jim Wright was furious with me. But I didn't care. My hero was dead, the dream was gone, I knew politics held no more hope for me."[12]

Larry L. King, left, enjoying a moment with U.S. Senator Ralph
Yarborough, 1958. *Larry L. King Archives, Southwestern Writers Collection,
Texas State University-San Marcos.*

King returned to work after several days, but he continued to
meditate on Kennedy's fate. Though the president had died too
young, JFK had at least accomplished a great deal before his death.
King, in contrast, had done very little of what he initially set out to
do. So, in the wake of the Kennedy assassination, King decided to
start a new life for himself. He served Jeanne with divorce papers, and
later he turned in his formal resignation to Jim Wright. At thirty-five
years of age, he was going to start over as a freelance writer.

His career change was crippled immediately. He had moved out
with just a suitcase, planning to return later to collect his things.

When he did, he discovered that Jeanne had burned everything he'd ever treasured: his manuscripts, his outline for *The One-Eyed Man,* his old clippings, his correspondence, photographs, his football letter jackets and other "precious trash." King's departure from Jim Wright's office was also met with bleak portents. When he called his editor, Bob Gutwillig, to inform him of his resignation, Gutwillig was dismayed. "Goddammit, King, are you crazy? . . . Do you know the odds against making a living as an unknown, *unpublished writer?*"[13]

He began to feel better after talking to Willie Morris, who told him, "Larry, I'll buy all the articles from you I can, and not only that, I'll encourage other editors to buy from you." Morris proved to be true to his word, and Larry L. King, who had never before published anything outside of oil-patch newspapers, suddenly found himself assigned to write an article about his years in Congress for *Harper's.* Other friends also came to his aid. Warren Miller sent King books to review for the *Nation.* The reviews paid only $40 each but provided much-needed exposure. Ronnie Dugger, too, commissioned articles from King for the *Texas Observer.* Dugger's pay scale was even less— only $15 per article. At this rate, King knew, it could be a long time before he saw $17,000 in a single year again.[14]

As a gesture of his newfound independence, King grew a beard— a highly provocative act in 1964. King remembered that friends laughed at first, thinking that perhaps he had lost an election bet. The beard also drew its share of hard stares from strangers, particularly in Texas and the South. At one D.C. party where the liquor flowed freely, a Florida congressman's wife began insulting King, telling him that he must be hiding a weak chin. Deciding that his beard must be a fake, she reached out and yanked it hard. King slapped her in response, drawing an angry confrontation with the congressman.[15]

King was dating Rosemarie Coumaris Kline, who worked as a secretary on Capitol Hill and had previously been married to a jazz musician. King and Rosemarie enjoyed many things in common, including a fondness for marijuana. King had a long acquaintance with pot, having first experimented with it as a fifteen-year-old back in 1944. Marijuana was also a part of the Greenwich Village scene he'd explored while in the army. King and Rosemarie hung out with jazz musicians, and marijuana was a regular part of the scene. Rosemarie also introduced King to speed, which he realized could help him remain alert for extended periods of time. That came in handy for a freelance writer. King's immersion in this new world also carried certain risks. At one point he was picked up and quizzed by a narcotics officer, whom King suspected was put on to him by his ex-wife. The officer also "called upon Rosemarie *and* her boss to ask pointed questions about the same thing."[16]

By mid-1964 he was halfway through his *Harper's* article and had published a few articles and reviews. He was also "trying to finish that goddamn novel, of which I am very sick by this time." It was clearly impossible to keep up with his child support obligations, not to mention his car payment and the necessary allowance for beer and cigarettes. With few other options available, King returned to physical labor for the first time in fifteen years, taking whatever day jobs he could find. He unloaded boxes, joined construction crews, worked as a busboy, and delivered produce. The worst job of all was installing seats in a newly constructed football stadium. The backbreaking labor under the August sun seemed even more grueling than roughnecking in the West Texas desert. Adding to his humiliation was the fact that the other workers, "none older than twenty, called me Pops."[17]

In the fall of 1964, King finished his *Harper's* piece and turned it over to Willie Morris. Then he watched in awe as Morris went to work editing it. Morris coolly excised the superfluous language, pedantic statements, repetitions, and whatever other irritations caught his eye. By the time he was finished, King estimated that Morris had improved his writing some forty percent. "That was a real eye-opener," King recalled. "I began studying how he edited and that quickly helped me become a much better writer, because I could train myself to anticipate the criticisms."[18]

Morris also found it necessary to protect King from *Harper's* editor John Fischer. King's story contained a sentence reading, "As one who attended several of Billie Sol Estes's Washington dinner parties, I am sure they had more fun at the Last Supper." Fischer, worried about offending religious readers, deleted the line. Only after Morris intervened did Fischer grudgingly restore the sentence. The editor

Larry L. King in 1964, after he left politics to pursue his writing career. *Photo by Rosemarie Coumaris King. Larry L. King Archives, Southwestern Writers Collection, Texas State University-San Marcos.*

also decided that there was no need to pay King the $500 initially promised for the piece. Instead, he offered $250. Again Willie Morris intervened, and after some negotiation, *Harper's* agreed to pay King $400.[19]

King's article appeared in the January 1965 issue of *Harper's* as "Second Banana Politicians." In this candid and often humorous look at Washington's political society, King offered a self-deprecating take on his life as a congressional underling. "My lot was to be one of the faceless young men, with that 'passion for anonymity' which [Franklin Roosevelt] demanded of his brain trusters," King wrote, "but lower down on the social register." He described how House Speaker Sam Rayburn often called him "Ritchie" by mistake, and how a retired

State Department employee mistook his "receding hairline, horn-rimmed glasses and shapeless form" for discredited Senator Joseph McCarthy.[20]

King's humor was charming, but the article's impact came through his sharp insights into Washington society. He analyzed the scarcity of women in positions of power and why so much adultery is committed in D.C. He also exposed the insidious nature of lobbying, describing how relationships are built up over time. He pointedly identified specific lobbyists, giving *Harper's* reporting a newfound edge. When these lobbyists receive preferential treatment, King wrote, "it is less for tangible gain than out of a vague and mellow social obligation. Here the currents run treacherous and deep, and a Congressman or his [Administrative Assistant] may be in over his head before he knows he has left the shallows."[21]

King's first fan letter came from distinguished Harvard economist John Kenneth Galbraith, who wrote, "Your piece in the current *Harper's* is particularly fine. I haven't enjoyed anything by anybody else so much in years."[22] The high-caliber exposure in *Harper's* also brought King to the attention of other major magazine editors. Though he would make only $2,000 from freelance work in his first year, other offers were coming in. King was beginning to gain the confidence that he could make it as a writer after all.

11.

THE

DOORS OF

PERCEPTION

When Bud Shrake and Gary Cartwright heard the news of the Kennedy assassination, they knew instinctively how to respond. They jumped in a car and, along with their friend, Pete Dominguez, drove out to General Edwin Walker's mansion. Certain that the right-wingers had killed their president, they went looking for a fight. On the way over, the car radio informed them about Lee Harvey Oswald, along with the news that he had once been a Communist defector.[1]

It was almost too much to absorb. As Gary Cartwright later wrote:

> The subtext of everything I've written over the past thirty-something years cannot escape the gravity of the 60s, specifically the unparalleled weirdness a lot of us experienced when John F. Kennedy was assassinated in what was essentially our neighborhood. I think of the event as a great power outage . . . the best of times transformed into the worst of times. Or was it the other way around? All I know is that until the assassination, everything in my world seemed clean, transparent and orderly. Nothing has seemed clean, clear, or orderly since.[2]

In the wake of the presidential assassination, events were canceled all across the country. Though a great tragedy, JFK's death was also the biggest news story local journalists had ever seen. *The Dallas Morning News,* in an unprecedented display of ambition, sent reporters out across the city. But Shrake and Cartwright were kept shackled to the sports pages, especially after NFL commissioner Pete Rozelle made a controversial decision—the league would play its games as scheduled on Sunday, two days after the murder. Bud Shrake was among those critical of Rozelle, writing a *Morning News* column headlined "No Day For Games." The morning after Kennedy's murder, the Dallas Cowboys and their entourage flew from Dallas to Cleveland. "We were the first group to travel outside of Dallas that was publicly identified with the city," Gary Cartwright said later. "It was terrible. People were spitting at us, calling us murderers. We weren't exactly proud to be from Dallas at that moment."[3]

Once the team arrived at the stadium on Sunday morning, Gary Cartwright went with the players to the locker room while Bud Shrake accompanied Clint Murchison Jr. on a visit to Browns' owner Art Modell's executive offices. There they watched live television images of the Dallas city jail, where Lee Harvey Oswald was due to be transferred to another facility. This would be the world's first good look at the murder suspect. Oswald, escorted by a squad of officers, entered the room, looking defiant, when suddenly a man darted from the crowd and shot Oswald. When he realized who the gunman was, Shrake leapt up and ran to tell Gary Cartwright the news. He met him in the parking lot and said, "Someone just shot Oswald and you'll never guess who did it." Cartwright, on gut instinct, answered, "Jack Ruby."[4]

***

By the time of Kennedy's death, *Sports Illustrated* had finally established itself as a major publication. Editor André Laguerre's aim was to make *SI* "the best written and best looking weekly magazine in the world," and, indeed, it was "emerging as an innovative, ground-

breaking magazine." In late 1963, former Texan Roy Terrell was promoted to assistant managing editor and the magazine wanted to hire
another full-time staff writer. Dan Jenkins recalled, "I told [Terrell]
that Bud Shrake was the best sportswriter in the country who wasn't
already working for us. . . . I didn't mention that he'd been my best
friend since Paschal." Terrell was no fool—he knew that Jenkins and
Shrake had worked together and were friends. But Shrake had much
else to recommend him: He was the lead sports columnist in the
largest newspaper in the South, and his work had been included in
Best Sports Stories for the past two years. Shrake was also as keenly
knowledgeable as anyone about the struggle between the AFL and
the NFL. Professional football was becoming increasingly popular, and
SI was looking for another writer to help cover the sport. Shrake's
forthcoming novel from a major publisher was also a plus. Though
Sports Illustrated was a sports magazine, it was also interested in literary prestige.[5]

In January 1964 Terrell called Shrake and expressed interest in
seeing some of his clippings. Soon thereafter, Shrake received word
that editor André Laguerre wanted to meet him. He flew to New York
the following weekend. His interview consisted of "going to the bar
and drinking with André. As far as I could tell, if you could stand
there at the bar and drink with André, and carry on a conversation
for several hours, and he found you amusing, you were in."[6]

Two weeks later, thirty-two-year-old Bud Shrake was packing up
to move to New York. His buddy Dan Jenkins was out of the country,
covering the Olympics in Innsbruck, Austria. Jenkins was thrilled at
the news of Shrake's hire, and he wrote to offer Shrake their home
until he found an apartment. Jenkins also advised Shrake on *SI*'s
office politics. Well aware that his friend would rather be a novelist
than a sports journalist, Jenkins pointed out that *Sports Illustrated*
offered a great base and would allow him to travel all over the world.
All Shrake had to do, Jenkins counseled, was write decently and let
the editors think they're brilliant.[7]

***

Shrake moved to New York just as his novel, *But Not For Love*, was published. The novel was indeed intended to be serious literature, and Shrake's title came from Shakespeare's admonition, "Men have died from time to time, and worms have eaten them, But not for love." An obvious heir to Brammer's *The Gay Place*, Shrake's novel charts a group of hip young Texans who reject the conformity around them. Influenced by the Beats, they explore casual drug use and sexual relations. They also embark on quasi-spiritual odysseys, seeking new understandings about the nature of existence. The old ways are being left behind. As one comments, "Christianity roasted at Hiroshima and Auschwitz."[8]

Anticipating the tumult of the sixties, conflict erupts between the young rebels and the entrenched establishment figures. The novel opens along the Texas coast, where two swashbuckling millionaires take a subservient U.S. senator deep-sea fishing. Out in the Gulf of Mexico, they plot a corporate takeover with antitrust implications. Back in Fort Worth, a boisterous birthday party is thrown for thirty-year-old Ben Carpenter, a young lawyer poised nearly single-handedly to challenge the businessmen's deal. Carpenter's party extends far beyond Fort Worth as the group charters a bus to Nuevo Laredo, Mexico. There his rowdy friends instigate a small riot in Boystown (the red-light district) and eventually meet up with their establishment adversaries in a surreal showdown at the "Plaza del toros"—the bullring.

Doubleday's high expectations for *But Not for Love* were somewhat muted by concern over the novel's language and its frank treatment of sex. While the novel is by no means graphic, it never shies away from describing intimate encounters. Then there was the novel's "obscenity." The first section of the book ends with a character saying the word "motherfucker." The United States was just coming out of a period when books with similar language and content had been banned, and one Doubleday editor warned Shrake to prepare himself for denunciations from reviewers. He, in turn, jokingly suggested that Doubleday should encourage newspapers to damn the book on the editorial page, thus ensuring a healthy notoriety that would spur sales. But any hope that Shrake's novel would achieve notoriety died when two long-banned books debuted in the United States that same year: Henry Miller's *Tropic of Cancer* and Terry Southern's and Mason Hoffenberg's *Candy*.

As it turned out, few reviewers worried about *But Not for Love's* obscenity, and the novel instead received glowing reviews. The *Los Angeles Times* declared it, "Brilliant, sexy, astonishing" and lauded Shrake as "a major novelist." *The Phoenix Gazette* called it, "a major novel. . . . Shrake records the strident sound of the 60s as well as John O'Hara caught his world." But the country's most influential publications— those based in New York—ignored Shrake's novel. Still, *But Not for Love* did modestly well, selling about seven thousand copies in hardback. Avon paid Shrake $13,250—then a handsome sum—for the paperback rights, and the novel went through five printings in paperback, selling over 100,000 copies. The novel turned Shrake into one of Texas' best-known novelists, and he had every reason to feel good about what he had accomplished, especially after he received a complimentary letter from Herb Wind at *The New Yorker*. "[Your book] recalled for me something of the mood and shape of [Hemingway's] *The Sun Also Rises*," Wind wrote, adding, "You have a great deal of talent, Bud, and I have a feeling that as fine as this first book is, you will go on to do some really outstanding things in fiction."[9]

As Wind and other reviewers noted, Shrake's novel is largely successful. Funny, perceptive, and wise, his prose crackles with energy as he portrays an emerging urban Texas, still clinging to its rural roots. Rough-edged businessmen are leaving oil behind to go into electronics; politicians are contemplating liberalizing antiquated liquor laws; and members of the black underclass are taking small, yet deliberate steps to assert their equality. Texas' young whites—experimenting with marijuana, casual sex, and alternative spirituality—represent the first stirrings of sixties culture in the state. The ambitious novel overreaches at times, particularly as the rabble of characters blurs together during the extended party sequences. As in Brammer's novel, Shrake's characters express their angst best when they're partying. Shrake himself conceded later, "for a while the book turned way too Billy Lee-ish, and never entirely found its way back."[10]

Yet *But Not for Love* transcends *The Gay Place* in important ways. It offers a nuanced, richly detailed view of Texas' upper classes, far surpassing Brammer's fanciful notions. Shrake also zeroes in on gender relations, just as Brammer did. Yet Shrake's characterizations are far more candid and searing than Brammer's, which have a whiff of petulance about the women. In *But Not for Love*, Shrake's insight is unflinching as he explores the absurdity in how men relate to women. The men acknowledge that they are "scum," yet they can't seem to help themselves. The women, however, are beginning to battle back.

Much of the male mindset is described through Jason, who guiltily leaves his wife and children at home so that he can spend time at the Oui Oui Club. There he listens to old drunks who complain of sinus infections, bronchitis, pink eye, dandruff, and colon troubles. As Jason contemplates his beer, he thinks to himself, "How many nights had he spent exactly like this? How many of these lonely, wasted nights when he couldn't have explained reasonably why he was here and not at home with [his wife]. Could it be the possibility of adventures that hardly ever happened?" His wife eventually moves out and takes their children. She leaves him a note that ends ominously: "If you try to see me or them again I will shoot you."[11]

Ben Carpenter, the thirty-year-old leading the fight against the corporate raiders, has his own limitations. He confides to a woman he is falling in love with, "I want the same thing every man wants. . . . What I want is a woman who's an extension of myself. Somebody who doesn't give me a hard time and who thinks I'm great. I want a woman that I can feel like it's you and me against the world, baby, and screw all them people out there." She responds, "You don't know how to love. You may have the capacity for it, but you haven't learned how to do it."[12]

The millionaire businessmen have their own difficulties in relating to women, and along the way Shrake draws some nicely understated parallels between the spirit of business conquest and the act of sexual pursuit. The wide gulf that separates reality from desire can be crippling to the psyche, and for these Texans, the dim, unfocused pain is best soothed by continuous drinking.

By the late 1960s, *But Not for Love* was out of print, generally forgotten by the public, and seldom discussed by Texas scholars. Curiously, Shrake's novel continued to be overlooked even as critics decried the lack of "urban" novels dealing with modern Texas. In 1986, James Ward Lee, in his *Classics of Texas Fiction,* resurrected *But Not for Love,* writing, "It was a daring novel that spoke volumes to the young people of Texas who had felt repressed by their elders and by the political climate of the country after World War II."[13]

In 2000 TCU Press published a new edition of the book. *But Not for Love,* read now forty years after it was conceived, retains much of its immediacy and vibrancy. As James Ward Lee writes in an afterword to the new edition, "Like Hemingway and many other writers who trained on newspapers, Shrake took the best features of journalism and incorporated them into his fiction. His work is spare, clear, rapidly paced." It is also apparent, reading the book forty years later, that Shrake captured something of the Zeitgeist, providing a remarkably clear social portrait of early 1960s urban Texas.[14] Though *But Not for Love* falls short of the artistic achievement of two of Shrake's subsequent novels, the book offers an important contribution to Texas letters that is just now beginning to be recognized.

***

When Bud Shrake arrived in New York City in 1964, he was somewhat ambivalent about leaving his close circle of friends in Texas behind. But he quickly established himself at *Sports Illustrated,* where the culture of sportswriters was similar to what he had experienced in Dallas and Fort Worth. "I remember the first thing I saw when I got off the elevator was people in the hall playing hockey," Shrake said. "They had a tennis ball and they were using real hockey sticks." Writer Liz Smith, another Texan living in New York who later became a well-known gossip columnist, also worked for *Sports Illustrated* during the 1960s. In her memoir she describes the climate as "hard-drinking, hard-driving, sports-soaked fanatics, competing for Laguerre's attention and approval. It was a world of testosterone at the top of the Time/Life building. . . . It was the last gasp of male superiority, masculine ego and grown-up adolescence run rampant."[15]

Staff members often accompanied Laguerre for three-hour-long lunches at a nearby bar. Laguerre considered the sessions working lunches, and it is true that story ideas and current events were often discussed. But mostly it "was also a place for the sort of esprit de corps that energized Laguerre." Dan Jenkins recalled, "André drank Scotch and water and he drank a lot of 'em. But he never got drunk. I don't think any of us got drunk—we just got brilliant."[16]

Laguerre was well aware of Shrake's literary ambitions, and he assured his new writer that he would have opportunities to travel widely and do stories only marginally related to sports. Shrake's early work for the magazine reflected these interests. He wrote about a backgammon tournament in the Bahamas and profiled a Native American oil millionaire from Oklahoma. In December 1964, Shrake wrote a long feature on Buffalo Bills star Cookie Gilchrist, a thoughtful and rebellious running back who told Shrake "People think I'm an oddball because I'm a Negro who speaks up."[17] The story, focusing as it did on racism and Gilchrist's criticisms of the football business, was the sort of article that had been impossible for Shrake to write in Dallas.

In addition to the changes in his professional life, Shrake's personal life underwent a transformation when Billy Lee Brammer came to New York, bringing along vials filled with a mysterious blue liquid. At Brammer's urging, Shrake tried one, thus beginning his first LSD trip. A few days later, he and Brammer visited Millbrook, the private estate outside of New York where former Harvard professor Timothy Leary had established an acid colony. There, they saw "Leary in a white robe wandering through piles of totally doped out people on the vast lawn in the middle of the night."[18] Shrake never saw much in the acid "scene" that appealed to him, but he became very interested in the drug itself. Though he hadn't written directly of metaphysical matters, Shrake had long been fascinated by spirituality. Christianity seemed somehow inadequate to him. LSD, dissolving the ego state and opening up "the doors of perception," offered a provocative new way of viewing the world. Ultimately, acid would come to be recognized as a metaphor for spiritual insight instead of the actual journey. But Shrake's expanded awareness opened up new literary terrain that he would make use of for the rest of his life.

***

That it was Billy Lee Brammer who introduced Shrake to LSD was no surprise to anyone who knew Brammer. Not only was Brammer a profound literary influence on Shrake and other young Texas writers, he was a mentor in other ways, too. "We learned a lot of things from him," Shrake said. "He was the one who first told us about Bob Dylan and the Grateful Dead. He was always plugged in; he always knew what was going on. Whenever you saw him at his place, every TV, radio, and everything else was always on."[19]

When Brammer came to visit Shrake in New York in 1964, his own life was going through big changes as the result of the assassination of John F. Kennedy. Prior to Kennedy's visit to Texas, Brammer's literary stock had been dwindling as his second novel floundered and journalism assignments began to dry up. Staying with his parents in Dallas in November 1963, Brammer did find temporary work covering the presidential tour. He was riding in the second press car in the motorcade, not far behind the president. Brammer was at Parkland Hospital when President Kennedy was declared dead, and he was at the Dallas city jail two days later, where he witnessed Jack Ruby shooting Lee Harvey Oswald. In the aftermath of the assassination, Lyndon Johnson—the subject of Brammer's novel—was no longer a minor figure in American politics. Instead, Brammer's highly praised book was about the man who had just become president of the United States. As such, the author was in demand.

Brammer received a contract from Random House to write a biography of LBJ. He also agreed to write a profile of Lady Bird for *Ladies Home Journal.* Brammer enjoyed the newfound financial comfort that came from the generous advances publishers paid him, but he also complained of feeling guilty, knowing that it was Kennedy's death that had caused the sudden reversal in his fortunes.[20]

The month after the Kennedy assassination, Brammer married Dorothy Browne, a University of Texas coed he'd met in Austin earlier that year. In January 1964, Bill and Dorothy Brammer moved to Washington, D.C., so that he could begin work on his book. He planned to call it *The Big Pumpkin*—the nickname LBJ's less reverent staffers used for the Great Man. Media interest in Brammer's work was intense, and expectations were high. Bud Shrake reported to a friend that *Harper's*, for one, was eager to publish an excerpt from it.

Brammer, somewhat naively, expected to make use of the contacts he had developed during his years on LBJ's staff. He planned to interview his old colleagues, Johnson himself, and make full use of internal documents. Instead, Brammer learned from George Reedy, now the new press secretary, that LBJ had forbidden any cooperation with the author. Brammer was even denied press credentials to the Johnson White House—making him the only journalist singled out for exclusion. Dorothy later said, "Billy just couldn't believe it. Hardly anyone would talk to him. People he'd known for years. Everyone said it was . . . because of Lady Bird, but he never really knew. He never got near Johnson." Brammer's profile of Lady Bird fared no better. None of Mrs. Johnson's staff would talk to him. Then he learned that the *Ladies Home Journal* had decided to cancel the assignment.[21]

Finding it impossible to make progress on the book he had envisioned, Brammer returned to Austin after a few months. He ostensibly continued work on the LBJ biography, but in truth he was accomplishing very little writing. He was, however, already becoming legendary among the Austin subculture for his astounding intake of mind-altering substances, whether speed, LSD, or marijuana. Brammer had received large advances for his abandoned biography and magazine article, but he quickly ran through the money as the partying continued day after day, week after week, month after month. In the meantime, he neglected to keep current with his child support payments, nor did he catch up on the back support due. His ex-wife Nadine was not amused, and friends saw that Billy Lee and Dorothy were "obviously in a rut."[22]

Brammer did set aside enough of his advance money so that he and Dorothy could rent a large house in the Mexican resort town of Manzanillo, along the Pacific Coast between Acapulco and Mazatlán. There, Brammer planned to continue to work on his LBJ book. But as he confided in a letter to Shrake, he wasn't particularly hopeful about his prospects for finishing. One positive aspect of Mexico, Brammer wrote, was that he could at least find plenty of drugs there.[23]

***

While Billy Lee Brammer seemed to be fleeing the world of literature, Bud Shrake was becoming immersed in New York's literary scene. He became friends with George Plimpton, cofounder of the *Paris Review* and literary man-about-town. Shrake attended the frequent parties at Plimpton's apartment, and there he began to meet and mingle with other writers. One of the first he met was Norman Mailer. When Mailer learned Shrake was from Texas, he called him a racist and challenged him to a fight. Shrake managed to defuse the situation or at least confuse the somewhat tipsy Mailer, by telling him that he was a Catholic.

Shrake and George Plimpton frequently made the rounds together. One night in mid-1964 Plimpton took Shrake to a small restaurant and bar at Eighty-eighth and Second. "This," he told Shrake, "is where writers are gonna hang out."[24] The restaurant had opened the year before and was run by the matronly Elaine Kaufman. The place was, simply, Elaine's. This was where Bud Shrake and several other Texas writers in New York would spend much of the next twenty years.

Dan Jenkins and Bud Shrake, working together at *Sports Illustrated*, soon developed a regular pattern. Already loosened up by their lunch and afternoon drinking with André Laguerre and their *Sports Illustrated* colleagues, they left the Time-Life building in the afternoons and went to Toots Shor's for a few more drinks. Then they stopped at P. J. Clarke's, a bar that served "great bacon cheeseburgers, which we devoured by the thousands." After that, the duo would head over to Elaine's, "setting consumption records and strewing havoc along the way."[25]

At Elaine's, Shrake became reacquainted with Willie Morris, whom he had first met at the Scholz Garten in Austin. It was Willie Morris who told Shrake about an expatriate Texan living in Washington, D.C., who was writing for *Harper's* and getting ready to publish his first novel. At Morris' urging, the next time Shrake went to D.C. he paid a visit to Larry L. King.

12.

LITERARY

COMANCHES

L arry L. King and Bud Shrake wouldn't come to appreciate fully each other's writing for a few years yet, but they did form an immediate bond. "Meeting Bud was like meeting a brother," King said later. "Just instant kinship." The connection of the two men drew their colleagues into a real literary cluster. Artists born in Texas had succeeded before in the larger world, generally by leaving their Texan identity behind. But this group was different, because, even though they were embarrassed by their home state's backwardness, they also reveled in their unique identity as Texans who knew a thing or two about art. This tension between Texas provincialism and literary ambition would drive much of their lives and careers. As Larry L. King said, "I learned very early on that New Yorkers were suckers for people who said 'aw, shucks' and had Texas accents—but who could also quote a few snatches of Shakespeare. So I melded the literary with John Wayne, and I did it to call attention to myself."[1]

Shrake remembers how people responded to him as a Texan. "They acted like we were some kind of freaks, like we had three legs or something." Willie Morris, in his memoir *New York Days*, said that his Texas friends "were the closest the nation had then to Australians." The "Obscure Famous Arthurs," as they jokingly referred to them-

selves, cultivated the dopey-savvy, hick-intellectual persona first artic-
ulated by Billy Lee Brammer. They prided themselves on their progressive politics, yet they also breezily used epithets like "nigger" and
"meskin," intending to be satirical.[2]

This emerging group of writers from Texas, led by Shrake and
King, consciously chose to support one another whenever possible—
a rare exception in literary cultures notorious for backstabbing and
rivalry. Though the Texans often lived in different cities, they kept in
close contact through phone calls, visits, and frequent letters. As they
struggled for acceptance among the East Coast literati, their close
bonds provided a significant support network. In time, they became
viewed among New Yorkers as the "Texas Mafia." But for the Texans
themselves, "mafia" wasn't the term that came to mind. Instead, they
viewed themselves as outsiders. Jay Milner, the writer who moved to
Dallas in 1961, wrote to Bud Shrake, "I figure we Comanches oughta
stick together and pretty much do."[3]

Just as Dan Jenkins had helped Bud Shrake get hired at *Sports
Illustrated*, Shrake in turn lobbied for his other writer friends. Billy Lee
Brammer landed occasional assignments, and Jay Milner received
$1,200 for an article that *Sports Illustrated* chose not even to publish.
Larry L. King, shortly after meeting Shrake, sent him a story on boxer
Sugar Ray Robinson. King, in his naïveté, had written the piece with-
out any prospects for publication. Once the story got into Shrake's
hands, it wound up on the cover of *SI*, becoming King's first-ever
cover story.

Sports Illustrated paid King $1,000 for the article, twice what he
was making at *Harper's* and his largest payday yet. By 1965, King's
freelance career was heating up. He was publishing regularly in
Harper's, and his work also appeared in *Esquire*, *The Progressive*, and
The Nation. He continued to write regularly for Ronnie Dugger's *Texas
Observer*. The magazine work was keeping him busy, but he was barely
making enough money to survive. He kept up with his child support
payments, but other creditors fell by the wayside. King got an unlisted phone number and began to answer the door warily, only after
ascertaining that it was not a bill collector.[4]

As the magazine offers continued to come in, King realized that it was necessary to have an agent. He signed up with Sterling Lord, a high-profile agent who also represented Jack Kerouac and Ken Kesey. Lord was shocked to learn that his new client had accepted only $1,000 from *Sports Illustrated* for a cover story. He immediately contacted the magazine and renegotiated the fee to $1,750.[5]

Though King continued living in Washington, D.C., he began making frequent trips to New York, often staying at either Bud Shrake's apartment or that of his other new friends, Dan and June Jenkins. King caroused with Shrake, Jenkins, and Willie Morris at a number of nightspots and private parties. But the main hangout was Elaine's.

On the surface, Elaine Kaufman's bar had little to recommend it. Located in a rough neighborhood, it was a dark, seedy-looking place. The food, décor, service, prices, and seating were all unrewarding by sophisticated New York standards. But Elaine had one thing going for her that other bar owners didn't. She actually liked writers. Elaine, who called herself "Big Mama," considered the writers her "boys," and she allowed them to run up large tabs. Elaine created a hospitable, comfortable place where writers could feel at home.[6]

By the mid-1960s, Elaine's virtually became a writers club. In addition to Shrake, Jenkins, and Willie Morris, regulars included Tennessee Williams, Norman Mailer, Kurt Vonnegut, Terry Southern, Gay Talese, David Halberstam, William Styron, and many others. Woody Allen became a regular, too, though he steadfastly refused to interact with others. David Halberstam recalled that though Elaine's was called a literary salon, there wasn't really that much serious literary conversation. Mostly it was shoptalk—money, royalties, agents, sales. Another regular at Elaine's was a hot young editor named Bob Gutwillig, who was said to throw around big advances—as much as $25,000. When Larry King heard about that, he naturally began to wonder about his own standing with the editor who signed him, considering that King's own advance had been only $1,500.[7]

As word began to spread about Elaine's, the club naturally attracted the attention of outsiders looking to rub elbows with famous writers. The first to come were those in the movie business—actors, producers, directors, screenwriters. Elaine became more choosy about whom she allowed in, and she began guarding the entrance personally. Despite her efforts, and a growing reputation for snobbishness, more and more gawkers came to the restaurant in the hope of seeing real live celebrities. Sometimes the gawkers could be found among Elaine's own crowd, particularly among certain relatively unsophisticated writers from Texas. One was Larry L. King, who saw that Lauren Bacall had just been seated by Elaine at a table adjacent to his. Goaded by Shrake, who assured him that Bacall *loved* the attention, King summoned up his courage and approached her table. He started to introduce himself, but Bacall cut him off sharply. "Fuck off, buster," she said.[8]

***

In February 1965, with his divorce from Jeanne final, King and Rosemarie Coumaris Kline married. Just a few months later Rosemarie noticed a small lump in her breast, which turned out to be cancerous. She quickly underwent a masectomy, which the Kings' health insurance plan did not cover, and her long-term prognosis was not good. The best therapy, one physician suggested, was to take her south to the sunshine. King had no way to do so, as it was all he could do to keep up with his basic expenses.

Work on *The One-Eyed Man* was proceeding slowly, partly because King was so busy with his magazine work, taking care of Rosemarie, and his gregarious socializing. Still, he kept cranking out the pages, because the novel offered his best hope for rescuing himself from poverty and establishing himself as a major writer. As he wrote later, "I was all but certain [that the book] would win the highest literary honors, become a runaway best-seller, and cause sleepless nights for Norman Mailer, William Styron, Irwin Shaw, Eudora Welty and John Steinbeck—among other gifted novelists—as they worried about being displaced by the new kid on the block."[9]

The One-Eyed Man was a fictionalized reimagining of an actual historical event—James Meredith's dramatic attempt to integrate the University of Mississippi in 1962. Meredith's action, backed by the

United States government but ferociously opposed by Mississippi's white establishment, created a tense standoff that was front-page news for weeks. Mississippi governor Ross Barnett had personally blocked Meredith's attempts to register, and President Kennedy sent U.S. marshals to escort Meredith to school. The riot precipitated in part by Dallas reactionary General Edwin Walker was quelled only after thirty thousand federal troops invaded Mississippi.

King's novel, capitalizing on the drama, seemed to offer immense commercial possibilities. Unlike his friend Bud Shrake, who seemed to pride himself on his anticommercial sensibilities, King lusted after commercial success. He wrote to his publisher's marketing director, "I am more than willing to go anywhere, do anything, sing any song, that will sell books. I am promotion minded, besides which I dote on public preening, and am of rather strongly held views that books are for selling." King concluded his pitch with these lines: "What you must understand is that I will do damn near anything to be rich. It is my oldest ambition."[10]

King's editor, Bob Gutwillig, left McGraw-Hill for New American Library, and arranged to take King's novel with him. *The One-Eyed Man* was scheduled for publication in the fall of 1965, but when New York newspapers went out on strike NAL decided to postpone it. That turned out to be a blessing, because in November King learned some astonishing news that seemed to confirm his hope that the novel would make him rich. The Literary Guild, the nation's second largest book club, had chosen *The One-Eyed Man* as its alternate selection. King received a $10,000 check in advance of sales.[11]

"We're gonna take the whole damn wad and blow it wintering in Florida," King told Rosemarie, who was back in the hospital. Upon her release, the Kings relocated to Sarasota, where they lived among a writers' colony that included McKinley Kantor, John D. McDonald, and Borden Deal. King, his literary status seemingly assured, quickly ingratiated himself with the group, joining them for poker games, drinking, and socializing. Wintering in South Florida gave him a taste of the good life he would have as a successful writer—if *The One-Eyed Man* followed through on its promise.[12]

13.

THESE

HAPPY

OCCASIONS

As Bud Shrake entered his second year of living in New York he continued to feel uneasy about his occupation as a sportswriter. "In my practical field I have one of the very few top jobs in the country," he wrote to a friend. "But it is not satisfying. Of course I work on novels and that can be, and I hope will be, the ultimate satisfaction. And I hope to wrangle around with a couple of deals and escape New York."[1] Shrake's plan was to win a multi-book contract from his publisher that would allow him to resign from *Sports Illustrated* and become a full-time novelist. Shrake explored the idea of moving either to Santa Fe or Austin, and he told editor André Laguerre that he might quit after the football season.

Dan Jenkins and Laguerre both counseled Shrake against leaving *Sports Illustrated.* Laguerre also suggested that Shrake might not necessarily have to live in New York in order to write for the magazine. "You travel so much anyway there's no real reason for you to be here," he told him. Laguerre promised to see if he could arrange an accommodation. In the meantime, the editor gave Shrake a long leash and continued to allow him to travel widely and write stories that appealed to him. In early 1965 Shrake took an extended vacation through Mexico, staying in Acapulco, Mexico City, Mazatlán, and Durango. He made a special stop in Manzanillo to visit Billy Lee Brammer.[2]

Shrake also went to Texas, where he spent three weeks in Austin researching an article on the Hill Country, then becoming known as "LBJ Country." The story, published in May 1965, was a revelation. In contrast to Shrake's competent, yet often workmanlike sports reporting, "The Once Forbidding Land" was a journalistic tour de force. Shrake's survey began, appropriately enough, in the pickup truck of Hondo Crouch, the man who would later become famous for resurrecting the tiny town of Luckenbach. Shrake also stopped in at Johnson City to talk to residents about their famous native son. Noting that the president had often been photographed astride a horse in recent years, Shrake asked an old-timer if he'd ever seen LBJ on a horse. "Used to see him ridin' a jackass to school," came the reply. Shrake's article incorporated riveting historical data, with tales of Comanche raids, Mormon wanderers, and German farmers who supported the Union during the Civil War. The depth, scope, humor, and vibrancy of the work ranked with the best magazine journalism in America at the time, and Shrake's colleagues were deeply impressed. The upper echelon at Time-Life also took notice and proposed publishing the story as a coffee table book with photographs. Despite the acclaim among industry insiders, Shrake's article made little impression upon *Sports Illustrated*'s readers, who expressed more interest in that week's rugby coverage.[3]

Once he returned to New York in April 1965, Shrake resumed work on a new novel. Titled *These Happy Occasions,* the story was inspired during his visit to Rome in 1963 while working on *But Not for Love.* There, he had read of the canonization of Mother Frances Xavier Cabrini, who in 1946 became the first American saint. Shrake, as a lark, invented his own saint—a figure from the American Southwest named McGill—and he began writing about a group of five Americans who came to Rome for McGill's beatification. "That was the idea, at least," Shrake said later. "But in actuality all they were doing for the first two hundred pages were sitting in bars and talking. I thought it was brilliant at the time."[4]

As Shrake prepared to submit his manuscript to Doubleday, he signed on with the same agent Larry L. King had just chosen—

Bud Shrake in Chihuahua, Mexico, 1966. *Photo by Shel Hershorn. Bud Shrake Archives, Southwestern Writers Collection, Texas State University-San Marcos.*

Sterling Lord. With his new agent's blessing, Shrake submitted a portion of his manuscript to Doubleday's editor, Ken McCormick. Shrake's intention was to win a three-book contract and a large advance. This would allow him to resign from *Sports Illustrated*. The publisher's response was cool. McCormick rejected outright any notion of a multi-book deal, and he told Shrake that the best advance he could offer would be in the $5,000 to $7,000 range. That seemed insulting to Shrake, who had earned some $15,000 from his previous novel for Doubleday. The problem, according to the publisher, was the material Shrake had submitted to them. Shrake wrote to his agent, "About the pages I turned in, [they are] very nervous . . . they think the work so far on this new book is superficial . . . I think it escaped them that much of it is supposed to be funny. . . . I felt strongly inclined yesterday to tell them all to go fuck a rope, but instead I kept my mouth shut."[5]

McCormick suggested that Shrake set aside *These Happy Occasions* for the time being and instead work on a different project that Shrake had once mentioned—a novel called *Dallas* that would lead up to the assassination of John F. Kennedy. Shrake wrote to Brammer back in Texas with the unhappy news: "Doubleday thinks my new book, of which they read 15,000 words, stinks. What they want me to do is write BUT NOT FOR LUST again. I was considerably dejected about it for several hours until I reasoned with [myself] and decided they are stupid. There is no other conclusion I could come to and stay sane. They will publish it if I insist, they say, but they want a novel about Dallas. I think I may go elsewhere."[6]

Soon after, Shrake notified McCormick of his intention to leave Doubleday, telling him, "after re-reading the manuscript, I still think it is good." Shrake meditated deeply on his novel over the next few days and, suddenly, the formerly murky outlines of the saint he created, McGill, began flowing into his head. "It's as if it came from heaven," Shrake said later. McGill's captivating story transcended the bright chatter of the café set, and Shrake realized that he needed to change his plans. Five days after announcing he would leave Doubleday, Shrake wrote to his agent: "Dear Sterling: I know when you read this you are going to think you are dealing with a lunatic, and perhaps you are—especially in view of all the squabbling I raised over that fifteen thousand words of *These Happy Occasions*. But I have thought about it constantly for the last three days, and it has struck me that I am writing the wrong book." Shrake went on to explain that he wanted to write *The Secret Journal of Blessed McGill*. This novel would take the form of a journal left behind by the nineteenth-century adventurer, who "became a saint in spite of himself, and for different reasons than those supposed by the Church."[7] In this novel, Shrake would unify the western and historical elements of his first novel with the literary ambition of his second. He would also inject it with a sense of spiritual relevance, creating one of the most powerful and original novels to emerge from the American Southwest.

Shrake received no advance in the absence of a manuscript. Nevertheless, he resolved to work on the book without a contract while continuing his employment at *Sports Illustrated*. Laguerre was pleased that Shrake would stay on staff, and he made it a point to send him on coveted assignments that suited Shrake's appetite for travel. Thanks to Laguerre, Shrake went to London, Paris, and South America. He was all set to go to the Soviet Union until the Russians canceled his visa at the last moment without explanation. The magazine also gave Shrake wide latitude to work on stories that clearly overlapped with his literary interests. In May 1966 *Sports Illustrated* sent him to Chihuahua, Mexico, to write about the Tarahumara Indians, renowned for their long-distance endurance running. The Tarahumaras would also play a key role in *Blessed McGill,* and Shrake was able to accomplish his field research while living among the Tarahumaras for several weeks.[8]

***

While Bud Shrake worked on his novel, his friend Dan Jenkins had no immediate plans to pursue fiction, for he was enthralled by working for *Sports Illustrated*. Unlike Shrake, who viewed journalism as just a job, Jenkins poured all of his energy into his reporting. As the magazine's chief college football correspondent, Jenkins vastly preferred it to the pro game, observing, "College football has become a geographical, historical and social event, and sometimes all three." Jenkins reveled in reporting on the regional differences between teams, writing, "Sophisticates . . . may not like it, but college football is Michigan playing Minnesota for the Little Brown Jug, a street brawl in downtown Dallas the night before the Texas-Oklahoma game . . . and that annual Wall Street Block Party and Raccoon Coat Parade known as the Yale-Harvard game."[9]

Sports Illustrated was becoming increasingly popular, and Jenkins' arrival was a big event in college towns. His name appeared on hotel marquees and people fell over themselves to do favors for him.

"'When you heard that Dan Jenkins and *Sports Illustrated* were coming into town for a game, everyone got a bit more excited," said a sports information director at Nebraska. Jenkins "would arrive in town a couple days before an event, interview the coaches and a few key players during the day, and hold court at the hotel lounge at nights, picking up every check in sight."[10]

Jenkins took note of the teams' training regimens, and he absorbed bits of background color, which always seemed to inform his reportage. He also kept a keenly analytical eye on the games. But it was his inspired wordplay that drew the raves from readers and created a devoted following for his stories. When number one-ranked USC and number two UCLA clashed in 1967, Jenkins' game story began, "Here is the way it was in that college football game last week for the championship of the earth, Saturn, Pluto and Los Angeles: UCLA's Gary Beban had a rib cage that looked like an abstract painting in purples and pinks, and USC's O.J. Simpson had a foot that looked like it belonged in a museum of natural history."[11]

Jenkins' jaw-dropping lead sentences delightfully usurped readers' expectations, and his humorously keen reportage always came across as the absolutely last word on the subject at hand. As Michael MacCambridge notes in his history of *Sports Illustrated*, "Jenkins's distinctive style would help to shape and inform the prose of those within the magazine as well. [George] Plimpton would call him 'one of the great writers of first lines that there has ever been,' and many of the staffers at the magazine tried to match him, if not directly in style then in tone and attitude." Jenkins' irreverence, always assured, struck a responsive chord in readers. Just a few short years into his tenure at the magazine, he was already emerging as one of its biggest stars.[12]

While Jenkins' football coverage drew more attention, it was his golf writing that probed deeper, largely because of his intimate knowledge of the game and his unrivaled access to the players. Jenkins knew the golf scene as well as many of the professional golfers, having a near professional-quality game himself. Traveling together with the same group of players, seeing them at tournament after tournament, year after year, allowed him to develop deep and fruitful relationships with many of them. One *SI* reporter covering the Masters Tournament recalled how Jenkins seemed to fit right into the pro golf game: "We were all seated on the veranda there, having drinks; Dan was with us. First round was over, and Dan quietly got up and walked off, and I looked over and he was on the putting green with Jack Nicklaus." The reporter remembered "being so impressed that he could approach Nicklaus and that it clearly wasn't an interview. Nicklaus was leaning on his putter, chatting and smiling and waving, gesticulating with his hands. Jenkins was talking to him, and he was clearly getting a just-between-friends kind of view of what was going on. The rest of the reporters would have killed for that kind of access. Dan had it because of who he was and the way he wrote."[13]

One aspect of pro golf always bothered Jenkins—the solemnity with which many of the players competed. He kept an eye out for underdogs and the unusual, and he delighted in reporting on it. When Gay Brewer surprised the field in the 1967 Masters, Jenkins wrote that the winner was "a guy in his mid-30s developing a paunch, a man with a loopy swing who has been strolling along on the PGA for 10 years achieving no more of an identity than, oh, Julius Finsteraaron." When highly quotable and free-spirited El Paso native Lee Trevino emerged from obscurity to win the 1968 U.S. Open, Jenkins was thrilled. Trevino charmed the press galley with remarks like, "I used to be a Mexkin, but I'm makin' money now so I'm gonna be a Spaniard." Jenkins delighted in contrasting Trevino to the "visor-gripping [players], most of whom seem to have graduated from the yep-and-nope school of public relations." For Jenkins, Trevino's real accomplishment was to "shoot more life into the game of golf than it has had since Arnold Palmer . . . came along."[14]

Jenkins writing was too popular to confine him to football and golf, and he found himself doing more and more lighthearted feature stories as the years went by. The magazine's editors saw early on that Jenkins was gifted in a way their other writers weren't. He had a rapport with younger people, and his ear could instinctively recognize which expressions would go on to gain wider currency. Much as Billy

Lee Brammer awed his friends by knowing which albums or books would become important, Jenkins did that with slang. As publisher Garry Valk noted, Jenkins "was the first of our writers to use the term 'teeny bopper' in a story—so far ahead of the common usage of today that nobody had even heard it."[15]

Jenkins, in addition to serving somewhat as an arbiter of the cool to the aging crew at *Sports Illustrated*, was also establishing himself as a very high roller at the magazine. Laguerre had always subtly encouraged his staffers to inflate their expense reports to make up for the mediocre salaries, and Jenkins tested the boundaries as no one had done before. He became a first-class traveler, staying in the best hotels and eating at the finest restaurants. He always picked up the check. His expenses became legendary within the company. One dinner totaled over $2,000. The magazine's accountants were agog when they received the bill.[16]

Though the accountants and some editors complained about Jenkins' lifestyle, his image also made him the natural choice for certain feature assignments. When Laguerre wanted a profile of "Broadway" Joe Namath, a New York football star with a taste for the high life, who better than Dan Jenkins, who hung out at many of the same clubs? Jenkins came through in fine form. His story began, "Stoop-shouldered and sinisterly handsome, he slouches against the wall of the saloon, a filter cigarette in his teeth, collar open, perfectly happy and self-assured, gazing through the uneven darkness to sort out the winners from the losers."[17]

Jenkins' flair for extravagant spending and his wife June's status as an ex-fashion model made him the perfect choice to write a story on Jack Hanson, a former baseball player who had become a woman's clothing designer. Hanson had outfitted Audrey Hepburn, Jacqueline Kennedy, and Marilyn Monroe, and his social set in California included the very rich. Jenkins reported on the opulence, somewhat mesmerized. Hanson's home, he told readers, also included a "formal garden leading lazily to an arbor underneath which sits the dollhouse that F. Scott Fitzgerald wrote about in *The Last Tycoon*."[18]

Increasingly, Jenkins was living the life of a star. He was staying in first-class hotels, and he was intimate with talented and wealthy winners. Sometimes, given all that, it was a bit annoying to remember that one was only a sportswriter, with a commensurate paycheck. Jenkins' thoughts occasionally turned to fiction, but he couldn't yet envision how to create a novel the way his friends Shrake, Brammer, and King had.

14.

THE

ONE-EYED

MAN

I n the spring of 1966 Larry and Rosemarie King returned to
Washington, D.C. Flush with his acceptance at the writer's
colony in Florida, King continued to make contacts with
other writers. His transformation from a one-time congressional aide
to real writer was becoming complete. At a "Southern Dogwood
Party" held at Willie and Celia Morris' house, King met Robert Penn
Warren, a leading southern intellectual and author of *All the King's
Men*—widely regarded as the most important American political
novel of the twentieth century. In the hope of soliciting praise for
King's forthcoming novel, his publisher had earlier sent Warren an
advance copy of *The One-Eyed Man*. Warren's response—"It seems
your author has been writing in my sleep"—would not be quoted on
the dust jacket. Despite the put-down, Warren remained a literary
hero to Larry King.[1]

At the Southern Dogwood Party, Warren did not realize that King
was the author of the novel he had recently dismissed, and King certainly wasn't about to tell him. Instead, he carefully opened up conversation on other fronts. At one point Warren asked King about his
own literary ambitions. King, defensive in the face of the older man's
scholarly and literary accomplishments, blurted out, "I have little formal education and feel so goddamned *ignorant!* There's so much that
I just don't understand."[2]

Warren's answer was not only soothing to King, it became prophetic. He replied, "Well, if you did understand . . . I doubt whether you'd be very successful at the creative process. I've always found that I write to learn as much as I do to tell or instruct. I don't think a writer is really having a creative experience when he merely tells: there should be in his work a great seeking."[3]

In June 1966, Larry L. King's The One-Eyed Man was finally published. The first-time author was thirty-seven years old. The event was celebrated in Washington with a high-profile book release party hosted by congressmen Jim Wright and Morris Udall. The party was proceeding well when a disturbing news bulletin quieted the crowd. James Meredith had been shot by a sniper while leading a civil rights march outside of Memphis. Initial reports indicated that Meredith had died, though later it was learned that he would recover. King's editor, Bob Gutwillig, no less cynical than anyone else in the book business, understood immediately the impact renewed publicity about Meredith would have on his author's novel. He leaned over to King and said, "I knew Ole James would come through." Unfortunately, the public address system was on, broadcasting Gutwillig's comment to the assemblage.[4]

King's novel, in contrast to Bud Shrake's But Not for Love, received prominent reviews in major publications. Unfortunately, the notices were not positive. The first review appeared in Book World, a literary supplement carried by the Washington Post, New York Herald-Tribune, and several other newspapers. Critic R. Z. Sheppard noted the similarities between King and another Texan who had worked in politics and written a novel—Bill Brammer. But while Brammer had written "a first-rate roman a clef," Sheppard saw King's effort as "a static, often pretentious, and derivative assemblage of cliches which at times reads as if Mr. King were parodying Robert Penn Warren and even Brammer himself." Sheppard conceded that the novel had some good moments, but to get to them "the reader must be prepared to wade through far too many swamps of local color, hoked-up dialogue and bargain sentiment."[5]

The excoriating review sent King into despair. "I prowled and cursed for hours, tossing down a fresh beer about every three minutes, alternately smoking dope and nicotine. Periodically I issued long, wailing moans like some poor wretch on the rack being pulled apart a rib and a tendon at a time." As the other reviews came in, King could take comfort in the fact that he also received several good notices. He began keeping score. As he wrote years later, "The novel received eleven truly 'bad' reviews, about ten indifferent ones, thirty-two 'good' ones and five 'raves.' Unfortunately, the better ones appeared in places like Wheeling, West Virginia, and Casper, Wyoming."[6]

One place that King expected to receive a glowing review was in the pages of the *Texas Observer.* After all, he had written a politically liberal novel and had been contributing articles to the *Observer* for two years now, maintaining his loyalty to Ronnie Dugger's enterprise despite the low pay and limited circulation. But the mutual support society found among the emerging Texas writers did not extend to the *Texas Observer.* There, King's book was reviewed by a young man he had never heard of—Dave Hickey, a brilliant and ferocious young critic. Hickey found even less to like about King's novel than R. Z. Sheppard had, and his review appeared just as King was arriving in Texas on his publicity tour. King quickly let Ronnie Dugger know how he felt at being run "plumb through with a dung-smeared spear." Dugger responded by writing his own favorable review of *The One-Eyed Man,* which appeared on the front page of the *Observer*'s next issue.[7]

From a distance, it's easy to see now that reviewers such as Dave Hickey and R. Z. Sheppard, however brutal, were more accurate in their assessment of King's first novel. In *The One-Eyed Man,* Larry L. King had not yet found his writing voice. He was so anxious to show off every funny thing he'd ever heard—every anecdote and joke and colorful phrase and wisecrack—that the narrative quickly buckles under its own weight. This "Redneck Rococo," as Dave Hickey called the effect, "is originally cute and finally deadening." *The New Yorker* offered the same diagnosis: "as frantically entertaining as a resort director on a rainy day."[8]

Comic patter aside, King's novel, like Shrake's *But Not for Love,* owes a great deal stylistically and thematically to Billy Lee Brammer's

The Gay Place. The One-Eyed Man, in fact, can very nearly be read as a sequel to Brammer's novel. *The Gay Place* ends at the precise moment it becomes clear that official segregation is crumbling. King's story picks up at the very next moment in history—the actual attempts to integrate an all-white institution. Though King's novel is largely based on James Meredith's case, it also takes into account his more personal experience—the story of James Robbins, who attempted to integrate Odessa Junior College in 1954. King's novel also makes knowing use of his decade of experience as a political assistant.

The One-Eyed Man is narrated by Jim Clayton, a former journalist who is the chief aide to Governor Cullie Blanton. The governor, though largely modeled on Louisiana's Earl Long, is also reminiscent of an earlier fictional creation: Arthur "Goddam" Fenstemaker in *The Gay Place*. A coarse, shrewd, political operator whose control of his state's political infrastructure is legendary, Cullie Blanton, like Fenstemaker, wears conservative armor to remain in power. Yet he also works in roundabout ways to achieve the liberal goals of social justice. Most similar between Blanton and Fenstemaker is the language, full of Old Testament phrasing and rhythms:

> "Corruption and evil-doin' all around," the Governor boomed. "Half the world in rubble and the other half bound for hell in a paper sack. Heathens in the pulpits and love for sale on sinful streets. Knaves and fools violatin' the sacred temples of public trust. Nation's goin' bankrupt shootin' rocket doodads at the moon. Jaded police officers winkin' at the high crime of litterbuggin' the public's paved primrose path. Shameful, sinful, goddamn thing! How long, America? O, how long?"[9]

King makes his debts to Brammer clear in the novel, dropping in Brammeresque phrases like "cornpone Buddhas" and slyly inserting the title of one of Brammer's novellas, "Room Enough to Caper," on the second page of his book. But what King intended as an homage, others saw as something more sinister. Bud Shrake, in a letter to Jay

Milner back in Dallas, commented on the issue: "Am reading L. King's book which Billy Lee has underlined passages of and claims they were lifted verbatim out of Gayly Places. Myself I have not noticed that close—word for word, I mean, although the characters of the Govs are of course close—but B Lee says you have to have almost committed his book to memory to notice and so I fail there. Billy seems upset about it . . . but I stay out of those things. Especially when I missed it anyhow."[10]

In actuality, Brammer was far too defensive about King's novel. Partly this was because King was a writer clearly on the way up, while Brammer had gone five years without publishing another book. There was natural jealousy and competition. But while there are certain surface similarities between the novels, King's is very different. Drawing heavily from his work experience, King tells numerous political stories, and his narrator revels in political strategies and shenanigans. *The Gay Place*, though it's considered a "political" novel, is in truth a documentation of a social group, not a political one. Politics is merely the backdrop of Brammer's book. In *The One-Eyed Man*, politics is the whole.

Though he was upset by the reviews, Larry L. King "toured the country for a month, touting my crippled book." It didn't take long for him to conclude, "Book Promotion is the nearest thang we got left in this Wunnerful Country Of Ours to debtor's prison." NAL's publicity department fell far short in King's estimation. As he wrote to David Halberstam, "They send me to [John] Birch Country to promote a book that calls for Brotherhood to Man in its special wacky way. We will not sell enough to pay for the gas." When King arrived preening for his autograph party in his old hometown of Odessa, "the first person who showed up . . . was a bank official come to seek satisfaction on an ancient $300 note I had conveniently forgotten."[11]

By August, sales of *The One-Eyed Man* in hardback peaked at around 7,500 copies, and NAL decided to abandon further advertising. King lobbied strenuously against it, and Gutwillig reluctantly agreed to purchase one more ad in an upcoming issue of *Harper's*. But King's "editor and top boss had not concealed their opinions that my book had failed them both commercially and critically." Though *The One-Eyed Man* did reasonably well by first-book standards, King had held extraordinarily high expectations for his novel. When they weren't met, it was easy for him to conclude that, "it was a miserable flop."[12]

15.

COWBOYS

AND

INDIANS

By early 1966, Bud Shrake was thirty-four years old and had completed his second year at *Sports Illustrated*. He felt sure that André Laguerre would follow up on his promise and allow him to move away from New York. But when the magazine's senior football writer, Tex Maule, suffered a heart attack, Shrake glumly noted, "That makes my presence here more necessary, at least for this autumn." While at *Sports Illustrated*, however, Shrake did meet Charlene Sedlmayr, known as "Doatsy" to friends. She worked as a fact checker at the magazine and was from a well-to-do New York family. As he wrote to one friend, "She is beautiful, 23, straw-blond, from Long Island, flies a plane, has just been initiated into the mysteries of our dark circle and took to them like a mountain goat, and is obviously insane." By the end of 1966, the couple married.[1]

Shrake continued to make frequent visits to Dallas, and he maintained his friendship with Gary Cartwright. The pair easily rekindled the prankstering spirit of their earlier days. Texas writers were already gaining a reputation in New York literary circles for their relentless partying and exuberant practical joking. In contrast, conservative, uptight Dallas was easy pickings for Shrake and Cartwright, and their alcohol and drug-fueled escapades began to take on an aura of legend in the city.

For Shrake, who appreciated a good show, Gary Cartwright was the perfect instrument for creating chaos. Peter Gent later recalled that Cartwright "was at the tail end of that Dan Jenkins-Bud Shrake-Blackie Sherrod era, and Shrake particularly played him. Shrake would egg him on into doing awful things, not just in his column, but in his daily life, incredible shit." Cartwright himself admitted, "I would have done almost anything to please them. I did do almost anything." Shrake, in a letter to a friend, noted, "Anywhere Jap goes, there is possibility of disaster. They ought to announce him on a TV chart, like the weather. Board up the windows, folks, Jap is moving into your area. Heh heh. That's one reason we love him."[2]

One of Cartwright's best-known episodes was his prank that took dead aim at Fort Worth's Colonial Country Club's "first [and last] annual poolside luau and fashion show." Shrake had received an invitation, but Cartwright had not, so Cartwright dressed as a waiter to infiltrate the party. The setting was extraordinarily pretentious. Guests dined on freshly roasted pig under Hawaiian torches as "the current Miss Universe conducted a fashion show on the one-meter boards." Floating orchids bobbed in the pool below. Cartwright, dressed in a white waiter's jacket and carrying a wicker basket full of rolls, began to circulate through the crowd. Club Manager Virgil Bourland, taking notice of his only non-black waiter, tried to intercept Cartwright. But it was too late. Cartwright began climbing the ladder to the high diving platform, the handle of the wicker basket firmly clamped between his teeth. Miss Universe and two other models were posing on the low boards. The crowd hushed as Cartwright walked out to the end of the platform and bounced lightly, testing its spring. Then, holding the basket high, he leapt out into the water, spraying dinner rolls among the floating orchids. He climbed out casually and then ran like mad, disappearing over a fence before the club manager or anyone else could stop him. Most onlookers were shocked or appalled. Among the few who laughed was Bud Shrake. It was Shrake, in fact, who had originally suggested that it would be funny as hell if someone pulled a stunt like that. Cartwright later concluded, "I ruined my wristwatch, but got a good newspaper column out of it."[3]

On several occasions Shrake and Cartwright teamed up in their revelry and in the spring of 1966 they went on a performance art rampage through polite Dallas society. Shrake, dressed as an Indian, and Cartwright, outfitted as Robin—Batman's sidekick—"went calling on various rich people." They crashed a debutante party, where they claimed to be folk singers. Once they began making music, however, those present knew otherwise.[4] On their next outing Cartwright, too, appeared as an Indian, and he and Shrake staged a "raiding party" across the city. *Dallas Times Herald* columnist Dick Hitt was among those visited by the pair, and he described the experience for his readers as "one of the more grotesque events this side of Saigon." Though Hitt mentioned no names, it was easy enough to recognize the subjects of his column:

> . . . a shortish character with a faint Oriental cast to his face, which in turn peered from under a floppy Army campaign hat—also with a feather and beadwork band. He wore a waistlength, vestlike garment, which appeared to be a tailored horse blanket, khaki pants and suede chukka boots. He carried a matching canteen. He is widely known in the area as a sportswriter, though not under his new Indian name of Dancing Hawk. Right behind Dancing Hawk came . . . an instant Indian towering about 6-6. He was dressed in one of the blanket things, a stiff straw hat, sunglasses, calf-high Indian moccasins, and a band of Indian bells strapped around his knee. He is likewise known in writing circles, although he now lives in White Man's Big Village on Manhattan. Indian name: Big East Wind.[5]

At Hitt's apartment, Dancing Hawk and Big East Wind explained, "We have just reclaimed the city of Dallas and all environs, including mineral rights, for rightful owners, Indians. Have white leaders turn over keys by two moons, one sun, or Wednesday noon, your time." As they prepared to leave, Big East Wind explained, "We not much for liturgy, so we end with brief rain dance." Then they left, "driving south on Turtle Creek in an Impala convertible." Hitt took pains to mention that, four hours after the ceremony, the rain dance paid off with a rain shower. The storm did nothing to hurt Shrake and Cartwright's growing legend. By the following year *Sports Illustrated* was describing the pair's rain dance as resulting in "one of the worst floods in Dallas history."[6]

For Cartwright, the wild behavior played right into his conception of himself as an outrageous writer, and he reveled in the notoriety of his public image. His activity was also an integral part of life in the sixties. "All these things were happening," Cartwright said. "Civil rights protests, the Kennedy assassination, Vietnam. The old world was turning upside down and you had to make your choice. For me the choice was clear."[7] Cartwright's sensibilities were, more than ever, in direct opposition to those of his employer, and he was growing increasingly frustrated in his newspaper work.

Time after time, Cartwright was on the verge of breaking important news stories, only to find out that the *Morning News* refused to print them. One year, he learned that the Dallas Country Club would cancel its annual tennis tournament rather than open it up to black star Arthur Ashe. Though news of the tournament itself "was displayed by both Dallas newspapers as you would display WORLD WAR THREE," Cartwright's story about its cancellation was deemed unnewsworthy. The paper's competition, *The Dallas Times Herald*, also declined to carry a story about the matter. Eventually news of the controversy appeared in *Sports Illustrated*, which would have embarrassed the two Dallas-area newspapers had they any sense of shame.[8]

Cartwright was at the Dallas Cowboys' California training camp when the Watts riot broke out in nearby Los Angeles. Cartwright immediately left to cover the story firsthand for the *Morning News*. Thirty-four people would die, and the Watts riot was front-page news across the country. But *The Dallas Morning News* didn't *want* a reporter on the scene. Cartwright's phoned-in story was buried deep in the paper's first edition and then was removed from subsequent editions. When Cartwright returned to Dallas and asked what had happened, he heard a familiar refrain: "We want to have coverage of the riot, but we can't have our own man covering it."[9]

As the 1960s progressed Cartwright's sports columns encompassed more and more political commentary. To combat this, the *News* assigned an editor to censor his prose personally. "It was a good challenge in a lot of ways," Cartwright said later, "trying to see what I could slip past them." Though the *Morning News* forbade any political perspectives in its sports reporting, it did welcome critical commentary about athletes themselves, believing that it created reader interest. Cartwright was only too happy to supply the criticism. "We thought that anybody who took sports seriously was an idiot," he said later. "A lot of sportswriters of the time were 'homers,' meaning that they referred to the home team as 'we.' That was embarrassing. I was the antithesis of that. I felt it was my duty to be critical, so I went out of our way to criticize, to be cutting edge."[10]

Increasingly important in Cartwright's coverage were the Dallas Cowboys, who had managed to transform themselves from a lowly expansion team into the NFL elite in just a few short years. Part of the reason for the Cowboys' success was their new approach to the game. The team was the first in the NFL to use computer analysis to rank players. Coach Tom Landry was widely regarded as a brilliant, though sometimes obtuse, strategist. General manager Tex Schramm and head scout Gil Brandt often looked outside of the usual talent pools to find players, and they brought aboard new stars that caught the rest of the league off guard. The Cowboys lured Olympic sprinter Bob Hayes, "the fastest man in the world," to the team. They also signed Cornell Green, a basketball star at Utah State who became an All-Pro football player.

While the team was tightly controlled by Landry and Schramm, the undisputed leader on the field was Don Meredith, a star quarterback who had all the talent in the world, yet possessed a seemingly casual approach to the game. Tom Landry could not bear Meredith's irreverence, whether it involved singing made-up country songs in the huddle or sneaking drags off a cigarette between plays. Meredith became a close friend of Shrake and Cartwright, and he enjoyed partying, even on the nights before games. A teammate recalled how Meredith spent $400 one evening buying drinks for himself and several others. When Meredith was asked why he blew so much money, Meredith responded that he had, in fact, just made $400—because he had "$800 worth of fun."[11]

While Landry was critical of Meredith's attitude, there was no questioning the quarterback's guts. During the 1964 season Meredith played the entire year with torn cartilage in his knee. Even Landry, who rarely complimented players, called it "perhaps the most courageous and gutsy season any professional quarterback ever played." But behind the scenes, few outsiders realized the depth of the struggle for the team's soul between Don Meredith and Tom Landry. It was the classic confrontation between individuality and conformity. "Tom Landry's whole theory . . . was industrial," as Peter Gent later pointed out. "Football was a machine with replaceable parts." Landry's intricate offensive scheme required that players surrender the on-field control that they were accustomed to. Instead, they were directed by a coaching staff that computed averages and based their decisions on quantitative data.[12]

"Dandy Don" Meredith, perhaps more than any other player in the league, was the epitome of an instinctual player; the sort who could read a situation and respond correctly. Tom Landry's task was to strip Meredith of those feelings and create a remote-controlled quarterback. During their struggle, Meredith was supported by most of the players, who respected his courage and talent as much as they were suspicious of Landry's emotional detachment.

When the Dallas Cowboys struggled on the field, it was Don Meredith who got booed by the fans. Meredith even found himself booed when he went out to eat at Dallas restaurants. Meredith's teammates saw, as few others realized at the time, a different side of the story. From their perspective, Coach Landry was disingenuous in allowing reporters to blame his players, even in those cases when the mistakes were clearly the result of coaching errors. Middle linebacker and pro football hall of famer Lee Roy Jordan bluntly noted years later, "Coach Landry never took any blame, and he let the players take all of it, and at that time Don Meredith took the criticism for the entire team not being successful."[13]

In 1964 the Cowboys' scouting system identified Michigan State basketball star Peter Gent as a potential prospect. Basketball in the Big Ten Conference was only slightly less physical than professional football, and Gent was invited to try out for the Cowboys. The National Basketball Association had offered Gent a contract worth $8,500, but the Cowboys promised that if he made the team they would pay him $12,000.

When Peter Gent arrived in the Dallas Cowboys' training camp, Gary Cartwright immediately noticed him. "Gent just got the shit beat out of him, every day," Cartwright said. "You never saw a gutsier guy. He could never get beat up bad enough to miss practice. Multiple injuries and all, he'd still go out and compete." Cartwright wasn't sure if Gent would even make the team, but he took a liking to him and wrote about him several times in his column. Gent was a tough, capable receiver, and the coaches appreciated his competitive attitude. Gent made the team, and soon his injuries began to rival Meredith's. As one teammate later recalled, "We often wondered who was going to get off the plane and get in the ambulance first, Meredith or Gent."[14]

Gent was a fierce competitor, but he never fit into the Cowboy mold. Sarcastic and antiauthoritarian, he often questioned orders and he openly mocked those in charge. Tom Landry, a deeply religious man, ex-military officer, and a political conservative, believed strongly in a firm chain of command. To Landry, Gent represented everything that was wrong with younger players. The two men feuded constantly, foreshadowing the increasing difficulty Landry would have in the years ahead with new generations of players.

Peter Gent became the first Cowboys player to grow long hair, and it was his presence that brought the sixties to the Dallas Cowboys. No longer was the establishment's word automatically accepted. When the Cowboys organization sent a questionnaire to players and promised that the responses would be anonymous, Gent didn't believe it. "The only way I kept up with Landry, I read a lot of psychology—abnormal psych," Gent said. "I had just gotten through reading how you could send out supposedly anonymous questionnaires, but they could find out who was actually answering by coding the return

address in pinholes, and not two weeks later here comes this questionnaire from the Cowboys. I held that son of a bitch up to the light,
and there are the fucking pinholes."[15]

If Don Meredith was irreverent, Peter Gent was insouciant.
During one training camp Gent walked up to a rookie player struggling to make sense of the complicated Cowboy playbook. "Don't
bother reading it, kid," Gent told him. "Everybody gets killed in the
end." Much to management's dismay, Peter Gent and Don Meredith
became best friends. Before long, Gent was also hanging out with
Cartwright and Shrake. For someone who claimed not to drink,
smoke, or do drugs before arriving in Dallas, Gent quickly made up for
lost time. By the 1965 season, he and Don Meredith were smoking
pot together on the team's chartered airplane.[16]

***

Gary Cartwright, while covering the Dallas Cowboys, was also
working on what would become his first novel, *The Hundred Yard War*.
Cartwright's burgeoning work described a team very much like the
Dallas Cowboys. Its protagonist, Rylie Silver, was modeled on Don
Meredith. By mid-1966 Cartwright had completed a hundred pages of
his manuscript, and Bud Shrake helped arrange for Sterling Lord to
become his agent. Larry L. King was eager to lend assistance, as well.
He wrote Cartwright and asked, "Would you like my publisher to look
at that novel you are working on? Say the word." As it turned out,
Shrake's own publisher, Doubleday, offered Cartwright a contract on
the book. Cartwright responded to King, "I start tomorrow on the second part of the novel which, I think, will go damn well. Anybody asks,
tell them you heard the great American novel has been half-writ-
ten."[17]

While the thirty-two-year-old Cartwright worked on his ostensibly "inside" look at professional football, his caustic reportage caused
him to be excluded from the team's inner circle. Covering the
Cowboys as a jaded drama critic might review stage plays, Cartwright
largely missed the story playing out behind the scenes. The Dallas
Cowboys organization in the 1960s represented the Establishment as

clearly as the White House or the Pentagon did. Yet Cartwright and other journalists failed to grasp the connections between politics and pro football at the time. The diagnosis would only become clear several years later when Peter Gent published his novel, *North Dallas Forty.*

Cartwright was on friendly terms with Meredith and Gent, but many of the Cowboys openly disliked him. Running back Pettis Norman said later, "a lot of players felt Gary was someone who would criticize everybody on everything, and who was there just to tear people down." Buddy Dial called him "'Poison Pen' Cartwright" and told an interviewer, "Gary was a wormy little old devil. I mean, he breathed an ill wind. Cartwright killed. He was so negative about everybody."[18]

In his coverage of the Cowboys, Cartwright came to violate Blackie Sherrod's first rule of journalism—stay aloof from the events on the field. "I sensed early on that I spoke for Cowboy fans," Cartwright said later, "that my anguished cries of disappointment and betrayal reflected their own." Though Cartwright and Meredith were friends, the reporter often heaped scorn on Meredith, reinforcing the fans' tendencies to blame Meredith for the team's woes. Meredith rarely communicated his displeasure with Cartwright, but other players took note of it.[19]

In a pivotal playoff game against the Cleveland Browns, the Cowboys got a big break late in the game when the Browns fumbled near their own end zone. The crowd roared its approval as Don Meredith trotted on to the field with the Cowboy offense. On first down from the one-yard line, Meredith dropped back and threw a quick pass—right into the hands of a Cleveland defender. The Cowboys, on the verge of a great victory, had suffered a crushing defeat. In the locker room, sports reporters' questions naturally focused on Meredith's pass. Tom Landry, true to form, told reporters that the play had been "poorly executed." The blame, obviously, lay with Meredith.

Gary Cartwright's lead story in the next day's issue of the *Morning News* echoed a famous lead written decades earlier by legendary sportswriter Grantland Rice. Cartwright's story began, "Outlined against a gray November sky, the Four Horsemen rode again: Pestilence, Death, Famine, and Meredith." The lead was reprinted widely across the country, including the pages of *Sports Illustrated*, and it did more than any other single sentence to bring Gary Cartwright fame as a sportswriter. "People still come up to me at parties and talk about that lead," Cartwright said in 2001.[20] However humorous, Cartwright's judgment was wrong. It was Tom Landry, not Don Meredith, who had ordered the play. Meredith, rather than following his own instincts, had thrown the ball to a specific spot on the field just as he had been ordered to do. It was not Meredith's fault that the Cleveland Browns player had failed to follow Landry's playbook.

The other Cowboys players knew where the real blame lay—as far as they were concerned, Tom Landry had outcoached himself again. While they resented Landry's refusal to accept responsibility, they were livid about Cartwright's story. Pettis Norman recalled that the article "was devastating to Meredith. It angered a lot of players." Lee Roy Jordan said, "After Cartwright wrote that article about the Four Horsemen, some of the players wanted to beat him to a pulp. I was one of them. Gary deserved it several times and never got it the way he should have." Peter Gent said, "I've never known that kind of fury against any reporter . . . he doesn't know how close he came to guys dragging him to the back of the plane and just beating the shit out of him. Guys were still on speed, man. They were half-drunk. They wanted to kill him." But one man intervened on Cartwright's behalf—Don Meredith. He calmly explained to the others that Cartwright was "just doing his job like we're doing ours." Cartwright reported later that Meredith thought the Four Horseman story "was funny." None of the Dallas Cowboys remembered it that way.[21]

Though Cartwright's style was not appreciated by the Cowboys players, his daring prose brought him increasing national attention. In early 1967 he received a phone call from the *Philadelphia Inquirer*. "They offered me a job paying double what I was making in Dallas, and it was more prestigious besides," he said.[22] Philadelphia, halfway between Larry L. King in D.C. and Shrake and Jenkins in New York, seemed like the perfect opportunity for Cartwright. He accepted the offer and by June was on his way to the East Coast.

Political unrest was growing more pronounced every day, and Cartwright was increasingly swept up in the drama of the time. Students were demonstrating, ghettos were erupting in anger and violence, and the fabric of the nation seemed to be tearing apart. Cartwright's apartment in Philadelphia was just a few blocks from a ghetto, and he could see the looting and burning from his windows. Covering ballgames seemed more trivial than ever, and Cartwright was coming to realize something that he'd only had a vague awareness of in Dallas—he was getting tired of sportswriting.

"Philly was a very traditional sports town," Cartwright said. "But I was doing anything I could to get out of writing a sports column. I'd write about the janitor of the building I lived in, and how he wanted to be a bullfighter." On July 4 Cartwright went to Independence Square and interviewed war veterans, asking them about the Vietnam War. His resulting column may have been of interest to some readers, but it was not sports reporting. On his eighty-ninth day of employment at the *Inquirer,* one day before his union benefits kicked in, Gary Cartwright was summoned to the editor's office and fired.[23]

16.

HARPER'S

ON THE

RISE

arry L. King slid into a depression after *The One-Eyed Man*, partly because of "them old post-creative blues" but mostly because the novel had not brought him the wealth and fame he'd hoped for. NAL had already signed him to a second novel for a $22,000 advance, yet King was making little progress. He began a book about a television evangelist called *The God Business*, but it was soon abandoned. Two subsequent novels met similar fates. King wrote later that his disappointment with his first novel "probably had a great deal to do with being unable to write a second."[1]

While his fiction was floundering, King's magazine journalism was taking off. King's articles for *Harper's* were outstanding, brimming with humor and insight. His version of New Journalism openly acknowledged the inherent tension between reporter and subject, and King's directness created controversy. His provocative profile of William F. Buckley, "the aging *enfant terrible* of rightward-listing politics," caused Buckley to comment, "Larry King has serious deficiencies as a gentleman." But the rewards for readers were immense.[2] In Willie Morris' estimation, King was "writing wonderfully uproarious and poignant pieces for *Harper's*, blends of H. L. Mencken and Mark Twain and his fellow Texan, one William Cowper Brann, the Iconoclast." Morris saw that, "even at his most cutting, [King's] writing would be characterized by a commitment to authentic American values—almost to an older and vanished America."[3]

King wrote tenderly and humorously of his hometown, Putnam, in "Requiem for a West Texas Town." The article provided a firsthand look at Texas' ebbing rural tradition while chronicling the small-town residents' absurd struggles to stave off the inevitable. The article drew raves from readers, and Willie Morris told King, "People will be reading that piece fifty years from now."[4]

For his story on Louis Armstrong, King spent a month hanging around Atlantic City with the famed bandleader. Reading the story, it was easy for *Harper's* readers to imagine that they were right there, on the scene, as Armstrong and King walked out onto an ocean pier after a concert:

> Pops lit a cigarette and leaned on a restraining fence to smoke. For long moments he looked up at the full moon, and watched the surf come and go. The glow from his cigarette faintly illuminated the dark old face in repose and I thought of some ancient tribal chieftain musing by his campfire, majestic and mystical. There was only the rush of water, gently roaring and boasting at the shore. "Listen to it, Pops," he said in his low, chesty rumble. "Whole world's turned on. Don't you dig its pretty sounds?"[5]

King's profiles were often praised for capturing the essence of his subjects' humanity. Those who knew Louis Armstrong agreed, and when Armstrong died a few years later, King's article was reprinted in the program issued at the funeral service.[6]

In October 1966 *Harper's* published "My Hero LBJ," a fascinating personal account that traces King's "evolution from a starry-eyed farmboy" who idolized Lyndon Johnson to the congressional assistant who observed firsthand the temper tantrums, the sulking, the massive ego, the "Johnson treatment," the micromanagement, the way he berated his staff, and also, his political genius. Johnson was so consumed by politics at all times that John Kennedy had to interrupt a tirade during the 1960 presidential race to advise his running mate, "Settle down, Lyndon. It's a long time until November."[7]

King astutely analyzed Johnson's political behavior, noting, "If any man had the power and finesse to move Texas toward a more moderate, enlightened political climate it was Lyndon Johnson." Yet LBJ cast his lot with the oil interests and Texans "so conservative they did not fully approve of indoor plumbing." Reviewing Johnson's tenure as Senate majority leader, King granted that LBJ "saved Eisenhower's chestnuts time after time. It seemed apparent, however, that many of Senator Johnson's [legislative] shows suffered from overdirection." King also deconstructed Johnson's failed presidential bid in 1960, concluding that "Johnson's advisors mistakenly assumed that tactics successful in Texas would prove workable nationally."[8]

"My Hero LBJ" was the most provocative of King's articles yet. None of his political friends questioned its accuracy, but every one of them questioned his judgment in being so revealing about the notoriously thin-skinned Johnson. The article appeared at a time when LBJ still enjoyed relatively good press coverage, and it was the first salvo in what eventually became a torrent of negative coverage. The story, King later wrote, inspired in LBJ "a sense of outrage toward me that didn't die until he did." One of Johnson's staffers, Harry McPherson, called King from a pay phone, telling him that Johnson had called the article "a dirty story." Noting that King had once been invited to lunch at the White House, Johnson had railed, "I don't want that lying, bearded son of a bitch down here eating my groceries anymore."[9] King, far less naïve about Johnson's political machinations than his friend Billy Lee Brammer, predicted to friends that the IRS would soon be auditing him. The prophecy turned out to be accurate.

Despite the growing acclaim for King's magazine journalism, he received few financial rewards. In 1966 he made about $15,000—a vast improvement over his first year in the business but still less than what he'd been making as a congressional aide. King wrote for many magazines, but his best work appeared in *Harper's*. That was because of Willie Morris, and "the way he nurtured and edited me. Morris had a way of engaging writers in conversation on diverse subjects; when the writer began to glow and verbally roll, he would simply say, 'Write about that for me.'"[10]

While Morris had made several improvements to *Harper's*, his task remained difficult because the magazine's pay scale was so far behind its competitors. Larry L. King knew about that firsthand. Once, after being summoned to meet editor John Fischer in New York to discuss a potential assignment, King was shocked to find that he was expected to pay half the dinner bill. Another time, King's payment for a completed story arrived, but he was not reimbursed for his travel expenses. When he complained, Fischer told him that the magazine's offer had included the expenses. No other publication worked that way.

Eventually, King wrote Willie Morris "a desperate letter begging for a raise and predicting that in the absence of more money I soon would be required to shave my chin whiskers and seek a job in the straight world."[11] Morris confided that he might be taking over as editor in chief, even though he was still only thirty-one years old. Once that happened, Morris told him, he planned to hire King as a staff writer.

While King enjoyed receiving dozens of offers from magazine editors each month, he began to worry that "such small piecework might be wasting time better spent weaving the fabric of a big new novel. . . . Now and again I paused to ask myself where all the scrambling about to produce magazine pieces was taking me as a writer. I felt the need to have a plan, some grand design or purpose."[12]

King was suffering from an affliction common to magazine journalists. While hundreds of thousands of people might read and appreciate his words, within a few weeks the magazine was in the wastebasket, tossed aside in favor of the newest issue. The problem could be solved by writing books, which took years to craft and might sell only a few thousand copies. How to achieve the permanence of a book while retaining the readership of a national magazine? To King, the answer was simple: publish a collection of his best magazine articles.

His editor at NAL, Bob Gutwillig, was unenthusiastic. "Collections don't sell for shit," he told King. Gutwillig asked King to write a novel about pro football instead. It's "on the verge of exploding as the next big fad," he said. "Take us behind the scenes in a novel full of the violence, the pressures, the gambling, the deals, the sex. There's a damn big book in that." When King declined, Gutwillig grudgingly agreed to publish the nonfiction collection. But he complained, "I once thought you would be a big-money writer. Now here's this!"[13]

While relations with his publisher were fraying, King's journalism career continued to soar. In the summer of 1967 John Fischer retired as the editor of *Harper's* and was replaced by Willie Morris. Morris immediately hired two new contributing editors, David Halberstam and Larry L. King. King, at last, had a salaried position at a prestigious magazine.

Once Morris took over *Harper's,* he had very definite ideas about what he wanted: "a truly *national* magazine . . . willing to fight to the death the pallid formulas and deadening values of the mass media . . . young and courageous enough to carry the language to its limits, to reflect the great tensions and complexities and even the madnesses of the day, to encourage the most daring and imaginative and inventive of our writers, scholars, and journalists—to help give the country some feel of itself and what it is becoming."[14]

Morris also recharged *Harper's* by investing heavily in luring the country's best writers to its pages. A major coup was Norman Mailer, who had earlier rejected Morris' overtures, telling him that *Harper's* "was so arid it would not take anything of his anyway."[15] Soon after Morris became editor, Norman Mailer deliberately got himself arrested at the Pentagon while protesting the Vietnam War. *Harper's* published Mailer's account of the incident in the March 1968 issue. At ninety thousand words, it was the longest magazine story ever printed. Later published in book form as *The Armies of the Night,* it won both a Pulitzer Prize and a National Book Award. Willie Morris' editorship was paying off.

17.

OBSCURE

FAMOUS

ARTHURS

Working for *Harper's* brought Larry L. King to New York frequently, allowing him to cement his friendships with Bud Shrake and Dan Jenkins. Though King and Shrake became close friends, King was barely familiar with Shrake's writing. The two exchanged letters regularly, but they rarely discussed the intimacies of their literary activities. Instead, they planned ways to get together and party, or regaled each other with tales of parties that the other had missed.

One thing King and Shrake shared was a desire to help their friends. Both made repeated attempts to improve the fortunes of Jay Milner, who had not published anything in years and was losing confidence. Shrake tried several times to get Milner writing assignments at *Sports Illustrated*. King, who had obtained a copy of Milner's latest attempt at a novel, prodded several editors to read the manuscript. As the rejection notices piled up, King offered encouragement to his friend, writing to him, "I have said before, and will say again, that if you will relax and write it like you talk it you have got absolutely no trouble in this world."[1]

A much more difficult assignment for Shrake and King was thirty-seven-year-old Billy Lee Brammer, who had once been among the most heralded emerging writers in the country. As Brammer's writing muse dissipated, he became increasingly wily in capitalizing on his one-time literary prestige. By 1966, Brammer completely abandoned his LBJ book. He and Dorothy moved every few months, often migrating among New York, San Francisco, and Austin.

In California, Brammer got a job at the *San Francisco Chronicle,* yet the position was short-lived. He tried to hook up with Kesey and his Merry Pranksters again, but the acid scene no longer had the intimacy that he had known in 1963. Kesey's "Electric Kool-Aid Acid Tests" were drawing thousands of teenagers eager to experience the psychedelic revolution. Brammer was not part of Kesey's inner circle, and he drifted along on the margins. From San Francisco the Brammers moved to Denver, where they managed a rock-and-roll ballroom until it became clear that Brammer's business instincts were inadequate to the task.

Returning to Austin, Brammer rented a dilapidated Victorian mansion, which became "a way station for intellectuals, artists, musicians, writers, and politicians and other power trippers. If anything," Gary Cartwright later asserted, "the conversation at Brammer's was wittier than it was at Gertrude's, while pot, speed, mescaline, acid, and peyote were served rather than eau-de-vie." Brammer became a prominent figure in the city's counterculture. Artist Gilbert Shelton lived behind the mansion in a garage apartment. There, inspired by the LSD Brammer brought back from California, Shelton invented the underground comic sensations "Wonder Warthog" and "the Fabulous Furry Freak Brothers."[2]

Brammer remained a sexual force among Austin women. "He had coeds climbing in and out of his bedroom window all hours of the night. It was incredible. The women just loved him." His wife Dorothy, who would divorce Brammer in 1969, recalled, "He would do this thing about, 'I'm impotent. . . .Well, honey, you can try, but I don't know if it's gonna work.' Lots of young girls fell for that. *Lots* of young girls."[3]

One constant problem, however, was money, and Brammer's writing prospects continued to dwindle. Desperate, he appealed to Bud Shrake for assistance in landing a position with *Sports Illustrated.* In a letter signed "Billy Bob Cunnilinguis age 36-1/2," Brammer wrote that he needed money to pay back child support, private school tuition for his eldest daughter, and Dorothy wanted to leave Austin. He wanted a tryout at *SI* without any guarentees and promised Shake that he would even give up doping for such a chance. He admitted, however, that he would need to finish his two-thousand-capsule supply of speed first.

Shrake wrote back to tell Brammer, "As for jobs, I do not know of any but will ask around. I'll tell Roy [Terrell] of course, but the magazine is dead against hiring any more Texans. However there might be a couple of assignments you could pick up and thus earn goodly money." True to his word, Shrake managed to get Brammer some freelance assignments for *Sports Illustrated.* But the *SI* editors quickly soured on Brammer. His reporting and prose were subpar, and his expense reports were stratospheric, even by *Sports Illustrated*'s usual plush standards. As Shrake wrote to a friend back in Texas, Brammer's expenses have "got the folks here agog." Instead of them owing him $197, it turns out that he owes them $623."[5]

Shut out of *Sports Illustrated*, Brammer decided to go for a larger score. In 1966, he contacted Larry L. King and told him that he was nearly done with *Fustian Days,* his long-awaited follow-up to *The Gay Place.* Brammer claimed that he had so much material that he could conceivably publish two novels from the manuscript. He was interested in changing publishers, and he wondered if King could put him in touch with the powers at NAL. King did so, and NAL was very interested. Brammer flew up to New York with his manuscript. Staying at Bud Shrake's apartment, he arranged "great stacks of paper on the floor in a way that suggested that he had fifty chapters outlined."[6] NAL was impressed and bought the novel.

King wrote to David Halberstam later:

> You say if I see Brammer tell him hello. There are millions wanting to tell him much more than that, only no one can find him. He has disappeared into Texas Limbo again, after

having conned NAL (with my help) into buying him out from Hootin'-Mifflin' and, of course, without writing a single one of the many lines he pledged to write if they would buy him. He has got his parents trained so that they will not admit to knowing his whereabouts, nor even admit blood kin with him. One of these days when the Sheriff is gaining on him fast he'll pop out of the toolie bushes all goggley-eyed and abstracted and wanting to borrow $5 and to be hid-out. And of course I will loan him the $5, even if I have to borrow it, and will hide him out. For I am a Fool.[7]

It was becoming increasingly clear to others that Brammer was in the grip of serious writer's block. His letters to friends became less frequent, and correspondence that did arrive was difficult to follow. Words, sentences, even entire paragraphs were scratched out. Brammer recognized his problem, and he wrote to Larry King in January 1967, obliquely apologizing for the publishing scam he'd run on King in the previous year. Of his writing, Brammer conceded that it was difficult for him to write coherently because thoughts popped in and out of his head so quickly.[8]

By late 1966, Brammer landed a job writing promotional copy for the Hemisfair in San Antonio, though few of his ideas were actually used. He wrote to Bud Shrake, telling him that he had suggested that the fair include a "Pavilion de Dope Fiend" featuring drug users in action, "preferably being executed by young, pre-pubescent noodie females who might also be available for few quick turns of trick (percentages for the house.)" When that suggestion failed, he proposed a "Pavilion a Gone-Gone" "aimed at capturing the spirit and the enormous appeal of apple-cheeked, snug-dugged, tight sphinchtered Teeny-Boppers and Apprentice Hippies."[9]

By early 1968, Brammer was again eyeing possibilities in the New York literary marketplace. He wrote Larry L. King again and explained that he had reformed and would love to get back into regular writing. Brammer didn't have anything to show, of course, but he promised to work hard if someone hired him. King responded warmly and contacted several publications, but he found little interest in Brammer. By this time, few editors even recalled Brammer's novel from the beginning of the decade. Most of those who did know of him had heard stories about Brammer's propensity to swindle editors out of advances. King also attempted to resuscitate Brammer's reputation in his own work. In a 1968 article on "Lyndon Johnson in Literature" for *The New Republic,* King wrote, "The best book about Lyndon B. Johnson is, of all things, *The Gay Place,* a novel published in 1961."[10]

While none of the major magazines would hire Brammer, King did manage to get him an assignment at *Status* magazine, which offered only $500. Brammer eagerly awaited the money, and when it was slow in coming he became worried. Fearful that *Status* had learned of his past, Brammer asked King to intervene for him. He also reassured King that he was serious about resurrecting his writing, and there would be no more of the scams he had pulled before.[11]

In addition to his efforts on Brammer's behalf, King also sent his friend an impassioned letter urging him to write:

> You know and I know and every bone in you knows that you were by talent and design meant to be a writer. . . . I think the [problem] holding you up now is that writing isn't "fun." Well, fuck it being fun—it's more than that, it's important [because] you got more talent than most of us. Than all of us from what folks call "The Texas School." . . . You can write circles around Ronnie Dugger and Willie Morris and William Humphrey and the Bode Boys and Larry L. King and the only Texan I rank in your class is Larry McMurtry. You simply use the language better than the rest of us; you are better at form and technique . . . [But] all that is so much shit unless you work, Billie Lee.[12]

In his letter, King outlined a specific, step-by-step plan for Brammer to recover his writing voice. He suggested that his friend begin by contributing small pieces to the *Texas Observer.* From there,

Larry L. King at the Scholz Garten in Austin, 1968, at the book signing
party for *. . . and other dirty stories*. Behind King, holding a drink, is Billy
Lee Brammer. *Larry L. King Archives, Southwestern Writers Collection, Texas
State University-San Marcos.*

King hoped, Brammer could eventually move on to larger projects as his confidence grew.

King and Shrake talked about Brammer's possible rehabilitation. Both hoped it would happen, though each was a realist. Shrake wrote to King, "Billy has never wrote a magazine story in his life, though God too knows that he has had many opportunities to do so, including here at this very place [*Sports Illustrated*] where I sit."[13]

Brammer still had one other hope to cash in on his former renown as a "famous arthur." He had some friends on the faculty of the University of Texas at Austin. At their urging, he applied for a teaching position for fall 1968. When he was turned down, Brammer was devastated. He wrote to King that the job was important to him not only for financial reason but also for his self-respect.[14]

***

While Brammer's stock continued to decline, acclaim grew for Larry L. King's work. *Harper's* under Willie Morris "was gaining a reputation as a showcase for lively, excellent writing." Responding to the freedoms and challenges posed by the sixties, American journalism was taking off, adding fresh new voices to the national dialogue. King was being seen as "a very top banana figure in the murderously competitive field of magazine journalism." He was besieged with offers from editors; prominent universities solicited his literary papers; and publishing houses approached him with book projects in mind. In 1968, King was inducted into the Texas Institute of Letters. He appreciated the honor, though he noted that he was "dunned . . . $5 for dues. That took a little of the glamour out of it."[15]

Television also expressed an interest in King. In 1968 CBS was preparing to launch a weekly news program called *Sixty Minutes*. Journalist Mike Wallace suggested to producer Don Hewitt that King could provide short, humorous commentaries for the program. Hewitt agreed and King was scheduled for a segment on the show's debut episode. King wrote to a friend, "I may be too high strung or countrified or something to make a TV star but I'd like to take a shot at it."[16]

In his on-air essay, King planned to connect the war in Vietnam to the domestic war on hemp. He would finish by flashing the peace sign at the camera. After some debate, CBS decided not to air King's segment after all.

By 1968, massive demonstrations were erupting over the war in Vietnam, and Larry L. King's role as a very vocal critic of President Johnson became even more prominent. In the April 1968 issue of *Harper's*, King wrote a guest editorial, "Epithet for LBJ," in which he urged the embattled president to resign. *Harper's* was besieged with angry phone calls and letters. Yet a few days after King's column appeared, Lyndon Johnson made a shocking announcement: He would not run for reelection after all. King, suddenly, had a reputation as a political seer, and Willie Morris' *Harper's* again proved itself bold and daring.

LBJ's resignation had an unfortunate impact on King's forthcoming book of magazine articles, which was to be titled *My Hero LBJ and other dirty stories*. King's editor called to tell him, "Now that the old boy's quitting, it might look like we're pissing on the corpse." Because the dust jacket was already in production, the title was truncated to *. . . and other dirty stories*. This tentativeness soured promotion efforts for King's book. Instead of capitalizing on the author's link to LBJ, the re-titled book was instead met with confusion. Some reviewers grumbled "about a nonsensical title, and old ladies who ran bookstores [hid the] book under the counter with their soft porn."[17]

Published just as the full extent of the New Journalism was becoming apparent, King's book is a fine representation of his contributions to the field. Included are his profiles of Lyndon Johnson, Sugar Ray Robinson, William Buckley, Louis Armstrong, and other political and cultural figures. All of the stories are enhanced by fascinating commentary, as King tells the stories behind the stories, illuminating the process of magazine journalism. King's confidences are riveting and direct. He even tells readers of his own editor's reluctance to publish this very book because it "won't sell for sour apples."[18]

One of the book's aims is to show the long distances King has traveled to become a writer. His introductory article, "Confessions of an Obscure Famous Arthur," picks up on the "famous arthur" term first used by Bill Brammer in 1962. King relates his long journey from the West Texas desert to the literary lights of the East Coast. Here are the first glimmerings of King as "a professional Texan," living on the East Coast and appropriating his native state for his literature. King pleads guilty to the crime. "The last thing a Texas boy should do is poke fun at Texas in print," he confesses. "I never would have done it if it hadn't been for the money."[19]

Neither King nor his publisher was prepared for the massive outpouring of critical acclaim that greeted the book. The first inkling came when *The New York Times* carried a rave review. This was shocking, since the *Times* hadn't even acknowledged King's earlier book. Other accolades poured in, and, this time, the country's most influential publications were cheering King's work.

Among those impressed were the other "famous arthurs" from Texas. Billy Lee Brammer sent King praise far beyond what he had ever offered in the past. He told King that . . . *and other dirty stories* ranked among the best works currently in print aside from Tom Wolfe's *Electric Kool-Aid Test* and Norman Mailer's *The Armies of the Night*. Brammer promised to review King's collection for an upcoming issue of the *Texas Observer*. This news prompted King to write to Jay Milner, "If Brammer finishes the article, that alone will make me feel like progress has been made and old wounds healed. From recent exchanges with him, I do think he seriously is on the verge of a comeback."[20] Brammer did in fact review King's book. This became his first published article in several years.

Thanks to the effusive critical reaction, the first printing of . . . *and other dirty stories* sold out immediately. Eventual sales were modest, though respectable, and the book did much better than anyone at NAL had expected. Basking in the glow of the critics' praise, Larry L. King still had not become a best-selling author. Yet he had won a decent consolation prize—he was now a darling of the East Coast intelligentsia.

As *Harper's* new reputation grew, it was thrilling for King to be part of a publication at the center of progressive American journalism. But for King to survive financially, he was also forced to accept dozens of assignments from other magazines to which he felt no emotional connection. By 1968, his life "seemed to have become nothing but deadlines and travel. Some days I felt incapable of producing even one more piece. I felt, too, that almost before the ink was dry my work disappeared into a bottomless maw. Perhaps much of that hurried work fully deserved to be forgotten quickly, but that knowledge was less than comforting to the author of such perishable goods."[21]

King approached his friend and editor Willie Morris, telling him, "I haven't got a thing but fatigue to show for all those magazine pieces."[22] After discussing King's dilemma, Morris came up with a novel idea. Why not send his forty-year-old contributing editor, a dropout from Texas Technological College, to Harvard?

18.

ABSURDISM

IN THE

SOUTHWEST

I n 1967 Bud Shrake completed work on *Blessed McGill,* one of the most striking novels ever to emerge from the American Southwest. Peter Hermano McGill is a nineteenth-century "scalp hunter, buffalo shooter, gold seeker, brawler, gambler, and family man." McGill is raised as a Catholic, but he is more comfortable living alongside Native Americans. In his journal, McGill chronicles his various adventures as he prepares to meet his death at the hands of his boyhood friend, a Comanche Indian named Octavio. The novel is buttressed with an intricately layered philosophical structure, and in the wake of Peter McGill's "martyrdom," he becomes the first American to be declared blessed by the Catholic Church.[1]

McGill's story is related with a tight, humorous edge. Shrake sidesteps the usual pitfall of historical fiction—the tendency to overexplain. Instead, influenced by the Beat writers, Shrake plunges us into the immediacy of each moment. McGill's seemingly offhand comments about the Indians' dress, customs, gender relations, and religious beliefs add up to, as the *New York Review of Books* later termed it, a "sophisticated anthropology."[2] The historical detail in McGill's "journal" comes across as so realistic that many people, including two Catholic priests and Shrake's own editor, believed that McGill was a real person.

Shrake's agent, Sterling Lord, arranged for a rapprochement with Doubleday, which agreed to publish the novel. But it was obvious that Doubleday's enthusiasm for Shrake waned in the face of what it saw as a "western." He was no longer considered the voice of his generation. Shrake only realized the full extent of his publisher's inattention when he saw the proposed dust jacket. He wrote to editor in chief Ken McCormick complaining about the errors, which included the misspelling of a major character's name and misplacing the book in time. Even more worrisome to Shrake was the fact that "the copywriting was utter garbage." He told McCormick, "I don't think I am being too vain when I say this, but this is a very complex novel that does have many levels to it . . . . The copywriting, however, makes it sound like a Max Brand Western. I hope to Christ it is not being presented as such to the booksellers, but I fear that selling it from the jacket copy . . . will sink this book before anybody ever reads a page of it."[3]

Shrake had every reason to worry about Doubleday's marketing campaign, which turned out to be halfhearted and misdirected. Shrake's own public relations gambits paid off better than Doubleday's efforts. He showed the novel's galleys to his editor at *Sports Illustrated*, André Laguerre, who promptly decided to run a chapter-long excerpt, the second piece of fiction ever published in the magazine. Larry L. King was among those who read the excerpt, titled "The Buffalo Hunt," in the December 25, 1967, issue of *Sports Illustrated*. King was familiar with Shrake's *But Not for Love*, but he had never read Shrake's first novel, *Blood Reckoning*. King wrote to Jay Milner in Dallas, telling him, "I liked it, though it is a far different type of book than I expected from Shrake. I do not know where he learned so much about cowboys and injuns."[4]

When *Blessed McGill* was published in January 1968, George Plimpton hosted a book release party in New York. Literary celebrities, journalists, and show business personalities turned out in force. Shrake arrived early with his wife Doatsy, and they saw that Terry Southern was already there. Southern was busy putting up posters for his own new book, *Red Dirt Marijuana and Other Stories*. When Shrake asked what he was doing, Southern explained, "Let this be a lesson to you. You got to fight for your turf up here, and if you're going to invite me to your party then I'm going to put my posters on the wall, not yours."[5]

The year 1968 was not a good time for a sportswriter from Texas to publish a historical novel about a rough-hewn frontiersman. Lyndon Johnson had become an object of widespread loathing, and there was little interest in historical fiction as America descended into chaos after the murders of Martin Luther King and Bobby Kennedy. *Blessed McGill*'s sales were disappointing, confirming Doubleday's expectations and destroying Shrake's hopes of becoming a full-time novelist. In a copy of the novel inscribed to Sam and Virginia Whitten back in Texas, Shrake joked that they were "among the 34 owners of this book." When Larry L. King asked Shrake how things were going with the novel, "he reached in his coat pocket and handed me two reviews . . . . they were both small papers, one in West Virginia, one in Nebraska or wherever. One said it was a fine book and one said it wasn't worth a shit. That was his way of saying, 'I'm not getting much attention.'"[6]

Though sales of *Blessed McGill* were meager and the critical reception was spotty, there were some breakthroughs. One of the country's most influential publications, *The New York Review of Books* carried a review hailing Shrake's "high adventure," and it argued that *Blessed McGill*, "might be put alongside Norman Mailer's *Why Are We in Vietnam?* as a novel about the problems of being a Texan." Shrake said later, "I hoped that piece might change things. But it didn't. It did make me feel better, having at least one classy place take me seriously."[7]

The most effusive praise came, naturally, from Texas. Yet those familiar with Shrake seemed taken aback by the book's metaphysical reaches. No one expected this from the hard-living, hard-partying sportswriter. A. C. Greene, writing in *The Dallas Times Herald*, called McGill "a frontier hippie" and saluted his "integrity and sense of rightness." Yet Greene also wondered if he might be "reading a bit more into the story than the author meant, perhaps." The state's major newspaper critic, the discerning and difficult-to-impress Lon

Tinkle, wrote, "Bud Shrake's third novel is a brilliant performance, one of the most virtuosic novels by a Texan in many a moon, and superior to his earlier vivid novels just because it does have the added dimension of meaningfulness." Larry McMurtry, who was already becoming known as Texas' major novelist, reviewed the book for the *Houston Post*. Unlike the others, McMurtry expressed no interest in the novel's religious elements. Instead, he viewed *Blessed McGill* as "a very readable contribution to a promising genre"—the "Black Humour Western." To McMurtry, McGill's stories were "the usual sort of butcheries—scalpings, brawls, pillage and mutilation common to the Old West." McMurtry judged the book's appeal in terms of "McGill's ability to recount [his story] amusingly. . . . To have a good Black Humour Western you need a frontiersman with wit, and McGill has it."[8]

Yet there was one publication that took a different approach. *The Texas Observer* carried no review of the novel until eleven months after publication. Then, in November 1968, it ran a scathing essay by Gaines Kincaid, an amateur historian working at the Austin Public Library. Kincaid wrote that Shrake "has fed upon secondary sources like a starving vulture in a slaughter pen, picking up anything and everything that happens to be lying around." Accusing Shrake of "abusing history," Kincaid contemptuously ticked off the four historical errors he found in the book. Shrake, for example, had placed McGill passing through the town of Creel, in the Mexican state of Chihuahua, in 1874. Yet as Kincaid points out, Creel wasn't established until 1907. "Can't win that game," Shrake remarked later in response to Kincaid's criticisms. Near the end of his essay, Kincaid did grudgingly admit that Shrake's novel might be acceptable to "casual and occasional readers who do not object to authors who are casual researchers and haphazard dabblers."[9]

The Texas Observer notwithstanding, in the years since its publication *Blessed McGill* has become recognized as a classic of Texas fiction. It circulates in prominent "best of" lists, and it has been reprinted twice—in 1987 by Texas Monthly Press and in 1997 by the University of Texas Press. Though widespread sales have never taken off, its status seems assured in the state. Yet *Blessed McGill*'s lack of commercial success means that it has been overlooked as a truly remarkable American novel. Larry L. King saw that quite clearly. Two and a half years after the novel was published he finally had a chance to read it, and what he found changed his view of Shrake forever. He wrote to his friend:

> Shrake, when I read "Blessed McGill" shortly after publication I was more than mildly impressed. I read it a paragraph here, however, and a page there, and in good weeks a chapter, on account of I had a complicated life in them days and many deadlines. . . . Last week . . . I re-read it, sitting down and blowing right on through, stopping only to let key paragraphs soak in, or to read certain select passages aloud to [Rosemarie], and have concluded it is one of the best goddamn novels ever and was shat on by the most inattention I ever have saw. What you did, you sly thang, and what no critics I read even suspected, was you showed how goddamn silly is the myth of religion, and how absurd it is, and how the Catholics and Baptists are as goddamned ignerent and ritualistic as the savage Redman. . . . And everybody took it for a goddamn adventure story. Well, it was a Big Theme and it was Nobly Done, and I am full of Admiration and say again that of all us Texas Writers you got the most Novelist potential.[10]

While some reviewers had noted *Blessed McGill* takes on "meaningful" themes, none ever elaborated on them. Despite the high regard for Shrake's novel among the Texas literati, no extended critical treatises or even adequate writings have appeared on the work. Of the little writing on *Blessed McGill*, much has been made of the novel's exceptionally vivid historical detail, and for good reason. *Blessed McGill*'s well-told adventures are enough to recommend it, but the novel's transcendence emerges in Shrake's subtle manipulation of the form. In one sense, as Larry McMurtry noted, *Blessed McGill* is a successful black humor western. As such, it is an heir to Thomas Berger's *Little Big Man*, published in 1964. Yet *Blessed McGill* also represents something more spiritually resonant than simple irony. It is, in fact, America's first "absurdist western."

As a philosophical precept, absurdity gained currency among French existentialists following World War II. Scientific understanding had invalidated many religious explanations for natural phenomena, and humanity's self-inflicted horrors—the Holocaust and atomic bomb among them—called into question the very existence of a supreme being. The universe was seen as indifferent and chaotic, mocking humans' longing for unity, order, and absolutes. Absurdity results as humans recognize that there is no meaning to life, yet continue to struggle on in any case. The chief strategy for dealing with the dilemma is to live fully in each moment, just as Zen Buddhism suggests.

Existentialism and absurdity quickly gained favor in the western world, and in the United States, the Beats and other writers integrated relevant portions of the philosophy into their works. An "absurd hero" developed as something of an archetype in American fiction, much commented on by literary critics, and is seen in the works of Saul Bellow, John Updike, and J. D. Salinger, among others. One of the most effective treatments is Bellow's picaresque 1955 novel, *The Adventures of Augie March*, a book that captivated Bud Shrake.[11] *Augie March*, like *Blessed McGill*, is related by a first-person narrator in an easygoing style that conceals its strong sense of purpose.

In the character of Peter Hermano McGill, Bud Shrake brings the absurd hero to the American Southwest for the first time. Much of McGill's journey involves leaving behind the religion in which he was raised, and spiritual struggles occur throughout the narrative. Christianity's relevance is questioned early. As a youngster, McGill witnesses a group of criminals attempting to hang a German farmer in the presence of the farmer's son. The farmer pleads for divine intervention, and the ruffians do in fact have great difficulty carrying out their task. At one point the tree limb supporting the noose breaks off, causing everyone to tumble in a heap. This inspires the farmer's son to speak up: "Thank you, God," he says. But eventually, through a series of blunders, the farmer is killed in a bizarre accident. This leaves his son with only one thing left to say: "That God up there is useless." No one contests the point.[12]

McGill's mother, devoutly Catholic, gradually retreats from the world to live out her life in a small room in a San Antonio mission. When she remarks how much she enjoys being cloistered, because it allows her to defeat the devil, McGill tells us, "Well, I thought, the old lady is cracked."[13]

Though he remains polite to his mother, McGill has little patience for Christians in general. During a buffalo hunt with some Comanche friends, McGill and the Indians are interrupted by a party of white hunters, who shoot at the Indians for sport. Two Comanches are killed and another nearly dies. The Indians, with McGill in tow, stage a retaliatory ambush. The whites are quickly overrun. The lucky ones are killed immediately. The captives will be tortured to death. As it dawns on them what their fate will be, one, a sixteen-year-old boy, stares accusingly at McGill. "You're no Christian," he says. McGill recalls, "He had one of those churchgoing attitudes that confers its own order upon things." To McGill, there is no such order, and "God didn't have anything to do with it." Instead, the whites had created their own fate by foolishly choosing to shoot at the Comanches. McGill's rejection of Christianity has its roots in something his father told him as a child: "Birth is real, death is real, and all between is a game." Existentialism, by whatever name, turns out to be far more practical for frontier life than Christianity could ever hope to be.[14]

McGill's spiritual understanding undergoes a transformation, however, as a result of his participation in the Indians' peyote ceremonies. Peyote, like the LSD Shrake experimented with, creates insights that many users view as mystical or religious. When Peter Hermano McGill takes the drug, he has the same out-of-body sensation he'd felt earlier during a near-death experience, complete with the same "Whoom Whoom" sound. As he looks upon the group he is sitting with, McGill notices a man he had formerly thought of "as a very scurvy-looking individual, with a long scar on his cheek and villainous eyes." But when McGill looks again, the man's face "seemed quite pleasant, radiant even, with the blanket over his head and his eyes looking out softly as the eyes of a Madonna." As he returns to his body, McGill understands that "I knew there was unity if we would seek it . . . I knew that vanity caused all the trouble and made life what it is, and I had lost my vanity and had died but yet was living somehow."[15]

Thanks to the peyote, which McGill continues to use for the rest of his life, he understands that, contrary to being absent of meaning, the world is instead infused with meaning, as "I have seen there is unity in all things."[16] Both views—the meaninglessness of existentialism and the meaningfulness of a "cosmic consciousness"—evoke the same behavioral response. As an existentialist, McGill had refused to impose a false order upon a world that he believed was devoid of a guiding consciousness. Meaninglessness had subverted hierarchy and order. Now that he recognizes the interconnectedness of all life, there is still no reason for him to impose a human-centric hierarchy ruled by a "God." A cosmic consciousness transcends hierarchy and order. In either case, Christianity is irrelevant. McGill reacts to his environment just as he did as an existentialist—by living fully in each moment. But a profound spiritual evolution has taken place, and McGill's expanded awareness brings him a deep serenity absent from mere existentialism.

Near the end of his chronicle, McGill's recognition of the universe's infinite unity helps him understand that "Every accident of my life had worked in combination to bring me here, and there was no way out."[17] In a novel stuffed full with ironic humor and absurdist insights, the final irony comes as McGill's own sense of right and wrong, as it turns out, happens to coincide finally with that of the Catholic Church. That, in the end, is how he becomes beatified as the Blessed McGill.

***

Just as with *But Not for Love,* Bud Shrake made a major move as his novel was published. By the end of 1967, André Laguerre told Shrake that he could leave New York and live anywhere he wanted in the country and continue writing for the magazine. "I really wanted to go to Santa Fe," said Shrake. "But because I'd be traveling so much I needed to be close to a major airport. I also loved Austin and the

Hill Country and I had several good friends here." Shrake had also concluded that the New York literary establishment "contained so many unattractive people. . . . I cannot conceive of ever wanting to be part of it. If I want to be among nasty, inbred boobs I had as soon select the uneducated ones of Texas as the educated ones of New York."[18]

19.

BUSTED

IN THE

OASIS

Soon after Bud and Doatsy Shrake settled into their new residence in Austin, they learned that a good friend would be joining them. Gary Cartwright, after his brief foray in Philadelphia, was moving to town. In 1968 Austin was the cheapest city of its size in the country, and the hipsters who lived there considered it "the best-kept secret in America." The University of Texas remained the dominant cultural institution, and its official enrollment of more than forty thousand students was complemented by scores of graduates, dropouts, and other hangers-on who had remained in town. The large and vibrant youth culture had turned the city into the South's leading hippie enclave by the late 1960s. "When I moved to Austin in 1968," Gary Cartwright wrote later, "the city was already evolving into the pop-culture capital of Texas, and the easiest place to score an unbelievable variety of drugs."[1]

Austin boasted a number of counterculture amenities. It was home to several vocal and well-organized student groups, including an active chapter of the Students for a Democratic Society. *The Rag,* established in 1966, was considered the South's first "underground" newspaper. Love-Ins and music festivals were staged around town. At nearby Lake Travis, a nude swimming area became known as Hippie Hollow. In 1968, a character from one of Gilbert Shelton's acid comics, "Oat Willie," was drafted to run for governor. Oat Willie lost the race but became an enduring inspiration to Austin "freaks." Later a head shop opened under his name with the motto, "Onward Through the Fog."

A burgeoning music scene was also developing. An Austin-based band, the 13th Floor Elevators, invented the psychedelic rock genre, ahead of the Grateful Dead and the Jefferson Airplane. But the commercial payoff in Austin was thin, and groups such as the 13th Floor Elevators and the Sir Douglas Quintet moved on to San Francisco at the first hint of success.

Bud Shrake and Gary Cartwright were joined by other new arrivals, as old Dallas friends David and Ann Richards moved to Austin. David Richards opened a law practice and soon began taking on high-profile cases affecting Austin liberals. Eventually, he would argue before the U.S. Supreme Court after the University of Texas sought to ban sales of *The Rag* on campus. Shrake and Cartwright also became friends with Jerry Jeff Walker, a well-traveled folk troubadour who wrote his best-known song, "Mr. Bojangles," during one of his frequent visits to Austin.

By 1968, Billy Lee Brammer, now thirty-eight years old, had returned to town with his wife Dorothy. With Bud Shrake, Gary Cartwright, and Billy Lee Brammer living in the same city, those familiar with the writers understood what lay ahead. Shrake's friend Darrell Royal, coach of the University of Texas football team, wrote to him, "Edith and I will be looking forward to your housewarming, although I am sure we will not be able to stay for the entire party if it lasts eight years. Maybe you will permit us to come and go."[2]

With Shrake and Cartwright living nearby, Brammer seemed to become more serious about his writing. He told others that he was writing a great deal, and Bud Shrake reported to Larry L. King that Brammer had finally resumed work on *Fustian Days*. Brammer was also working on a rock-and-roll novel titled *Rock of Aegis*. The protagonist was based on Texas musician Doug Sahm (of the Sir Douglas Quintet), whom Brammer had come to know in San Francisco. In November 1968, Brammer's literary resurgence gave rise to a new essay that he published in the *Texas Observer*. Titled "Apocalypse

Now?" Brammer addressed the growing distance between his "middle age" and "Today's New Youth." His cynicism about political activism seemed complete, as he characterized "the golden era of my own Radical Youth . . . as a dull, headachey interlude generally occurring between high school graduation and the onset of stupefying installment debt." Brammer suggested that, despite the current generational divide, "America would forgive its youth, provided young people trim their hair, dress respectably, get some sort of job, and exhibit sufficient zeal for incinerating Vietnamese peasants." As for himself, Brammer concluded, "I am tuned in, turned on, and almost entirely bereft of any emotion save for such as might apply to geriatric disorders."[3]

This *Observer* essay, coming as it did just a few weeks after his review of King's . . . *and other dirty stories*, indicated that Brammer was indeed following the literary path prescribed to him by Larry L. King. Billy Lee Brammer's long-awaited comeback seemed to be taking shape.

***

Gary Cartwright, moving to Austin after being fired by the *Philadelphia Inquirer*, was at least as grateful as Billy Lee Brammer for the city's cheap cost of living. He scratched out a living as a freelance writer, drawing inspiration from the card his wife Mary Jo gave him, which remained on his bulletin board for years to come: "A year ago I couldn't even spell 'author' and now I are one."[4] Thanks to assistance from Shrake and Jenkins, Cartwright received occasional writing assignments from *Sports Illustrated*. There he provided memorable coverage of the first-ever Terlingua World Championship Chili Cookoff in West Texas. More regular work, however, came from *SI*'s main competitor, *Sport* magazine. For Cartwright, sports was his natural segue into the world of magazine journalism, but it hardly satisfied his literary ambitions.

Any doubts about Cartwright's ability to write compelling journalism were erased when he published a remarkable essay in *Harper's*, "Confessions of a Washed-Up Sportswriter." Just as Larry L. King had launched his own freelance career by reviewing his years in Congress, Cartwright signaled his entry into the field by recounting his long years as a sportswriter. In a series of memorable vignettes, he chronicled the numerous pranks, the fights with editors, the pervasive idiocy that infects most sportswriters, and the hazards of the occupation. "Sportswriting should be a young man's profession," he wrote. "No one improves after eight or ten years, but the assignments get juicier and the way out less attractive. After eight or ten years there is nothing else to say. Every word in every style has been set in print, every variation from discovery to death explored. The ritual goes on, and the mind bends under it."[5]

Cartwright's *Harper's* essay brought him to the attention of other editors, who began offering him magazine assignments. Yet despite this early success, it became evident that Cartwright's freelance journalism was of inconsistent quality. Several subsequent stories were rejected, and Cartwright grew increasingly frustrated. As cash became scarce his telephone was disconnected, and his ex-wife tried to have him jailed for back child support.[6]

Just as with Brammer and King earlier, Cartwright saw his soon-to-be published first novel as his potential salvation. *The Hundred Yard War* was scheduled for release in the fall of 1968 to coincide with the start of football season. Ken McCormick, editor in chief at Doubleday, had already told several people that he expected the book to become a best-seller. As Cartwright awaited his book's publication, he found employment in Austin that seemed to suit his political interests. Fagan Dickson, an Austin attorney, had decided to challenge LBJ's handpicked heir, Jake Pickle, for the U.S. Congress. Cartwright joined Dickson's campaign staff and helped formulate their battle cry: "Bring Lyndon Home."[7]

On the evening of March 28, 1968, two "hippies" knocked on the door of the Cartwright's rustic home in the hills west of Austin. The men introduced themselves by explaining that they had mutual friends. Cartwright invited them in and, as was the custom at the time, rolled a joint for his guests. After some polite chatter the men asked Cartwright to sell them some of his stash until their own supply came through. Cartwright explained that he never sold dope, but he would be happy to give them a joint for the road.[8]

The next morning, Cartwright was getting ready for work when a squad of federal narcotics officers and local police descended on his home. Cartwright, his wife, and their two-year-old son were all taken to jail, despite the Cartwrights' pleas to have their child left with a babysitter. The charges against the thirty-three-year-old Cartwright were potentially devastating. At the time in Texas, possession of marijuana was a felony, with penalties ranging from two years to life in prison.

Rumors swirled around Austin in the aftermath of the much-publicized arrest of a "famous arthur" and Fagan Dickson campaign aide. Many people assumed that Cartwright had been set up because he was working for a political opponent of LBJ. "I recognized this as a time-honored method of operation in LBJ cronyland," Cartwright wrote later. News reports of Cartwright's arrest gave the most damning picture possible. A local radio station even reported that Cartwright had been arrested for selling LSD to minors.[9]

Cartwright's attorney, Sam Houston Clinton, got the family released from jail, and a group of friends gathered at Scholz Garten, all pledging their support. The Cartwrights faced several immediate problems. Their landlady had evicted them, and the bank repossessed their Volkswagen van. Fagan Dickson, in the wake of his aide's arrest, withdrew from the race. Cartwright would receive no more paychecks.

Bud Shrake was among those who came to Cartwright's defense. Shrake offered financial support, and he also solicited contributions from others. As he wrote to one friend, "Whatever Gary needs, I will certainly raise, not only because we are friends but also because there is no doubt in my mind that his pro football novel is going to have him rolling in cash before Christmas. One movie producer told me two months ago in Palm Springs that he is eager to buy the book. And all he knows about it is the advance reputation it is already getting in New York."[10]

Cartwright's legal case received an immense boost when Warren Burnett, one of the state's most prominent defense attorneys and a close personal friend of Larry L. King, offered to represent the defendant for free. Also joining the defense team were David Richards and state senator A. R. "Babe" Schwartz. Schwartz requested and received a legislative contingency, which delayed the trial for several months while the defense gathered information. With the financial assistance and the superb legal support behind him, Cartwright began to feel on increasingly solid ground. He even regained possession of his car. Of the case against him, he began to tell people, "All I want them to do is apologize and give me my dope back."[11]

Cartwright's prospects also improved when Doubleday offered him a modest advance for a second novel. With the money, the Cartwrights went to Mexico, spending four months in Zihuatanejo, a village where Timothy Leary had earlier established an LSD colony. Leary's International Psychedelic Research Center was quickly shut down by the Mexican government, but Zihuatanejo had lingered in the minds of many in the counterculture, mostly because the area was known for its abundance of high-potency marijuana.[12]

Bud and Doatsy Shrake and Dan and June Jenkins later joined the Cartwrights in Mexico. The group spent a month in Acapulco, sharing a large Pacific Coast villa once owned by Mexican movie star Dolores del Rio. Bud Shrake and Gary Cartwright made a special trip back to Zihuatanejo to procure what they referred to as "Pure Green Overkill." The summer would prove instructive in how the different writers approached their craft. While Dan Jenkins and Gary Cartwright did a bit of writing, the Mexican idyll largely served as a welcome respite from life in the States. For Bud Shrake, however, his and Cartwright's adventures in Zihuatanejo would inspire part of the narrative of his subsequent novel *Strange Peaches*.[13]

When Gary Cartwright returned to Texas, he learned that his trial had once again been delayed. He was also broke again, but with his novel on the verge of release, he felt upbeat about its prospects. Cartwright had one positive review in the bag already, and it appeared on the front cover of the book. Edwin Shrake of *Sports Illustrated* wrote: "Certainly the best novel ever written about pro football . . . an accurate picture of the sort of men who play the game, who coach it, and who run it, and of what it does to their lives."[14]

The Hundred Yard War is a kaleidoscopic view of the Dallas Troopers, a professional football team much like the Dallas Cowboys. The team is led by its "brilliant, erratic" quarterback Rylie Silver, who enjoys singing country and western songs, late-night carousing, and bedding available women. Silver, of course, is largely modeled on Don Meredith, though he also contains touches of Cartwright and Peter Gent. While Silver is the most interesting character, he only emerges as the novel's protagonist about one hundred pages into the book. Though the dust jacket promises to tell the stories of the "brutal gladiators" and women who swim naked in private swimming pools, the novel opens with a lengthy, excruciatingly dense and technical reconstruction of the convoluted process by which players are chosen in the annual college draft. From there, the novel tracks various players, scouts, coaches, sexy women, the team owner, sportswriters, and other assorted characters as it explores contract negotiations, sexual adventures, practice drills, game strategies, play-by-play recaps, and assorted other digressions—including a long discourse on a vegetable, the pea. Soon it becomes abundantly clear that *The Hundred Yard War* is, as Tom Pilkington wrote in his 1998 book *State of Mind: Texas Literature and Culture*, "a sprawling train wreck of a novel."[15]

Cartwright, like Larry L. King before him, tried to stuff everything he possibly could into his first book. Like King, Cartwright had not found his voice as a novelist, and his overwritten book goes to great lengths to impress readers with every single sentence. Characters don't just talk to one other. Instead, the narrative describes "Words careening down a greased pole, splattering on the valley of his mouth, bending and tilting and gyrating like a hula hoop."[16] Blackie Sherrod and his former crew might have enjoyed the rambunctious wordplay in every paragraph. But in a book-length work, the appeal to readers and critics was limited. Despite Doubleday's initial hopes, *The Hundred Yard War* never became a best-seller.

In the years since its publication, Cartwright's novel has been mostly forgotten, and rightfully so. Cartwright himself later said that he reread the novel about six months after it came out and was embarrassed by it.[17] But the novel does retain some historical value for literary scholars. Cartwright's work offers a distinct preview of the cultural terrain mapped by three later novels. In its pointed political satire and criticisms of Dallas' right-wing environment, *The Hundred Yard War* introduces material found in Bud Shrake's *Strange Peaches* and Peter Gent's *North Dallas Forty.* Dan Jenkins, too, obviously learned a great deal from Gary Cartwright's earnest, ambitious failure. When Jenkins began working on his own pro football novel, he understood what mistakes to avoid. For one thing, Jenkins would steer clear of any long explanations about the game's technical aspects. Dan Jenkins understood, just as Blackie Sherrod had always maintained, that sports readers wanted things kept bright and simple.

20.

HARVARD'S

"WHITE

RACIST"

In 1937, Harvard University launched a new program to improve the standards of journalism. The ambition was, as Larry L. King noted, "then and now, pregnant with potential." The Nieman Fellowship, as the program was called, offered a paid stipend so that selected journalists could engage in classroom studies for a full year. Newspaper reporters were preferred and the unofficial age limit was thirty-nine. King, a magazine journalist, had already turned forty, but Willie Morris encouraged him to apply in any case.[1]

Aware that his chances of being accepted into the Nieman program were small, King took stock of his other options. After the tussle with NAL over . . . *and other dirty stories*, King decided it was time to seek out a more supportive publisher. He became a free agent, and Sterling Lord arranged for a bidding session. When it was over, King agreed to sign with Viking. He received a $30,000 advance to write a new book, which would expand upon the idea he had explored in his "Requiem for a West Texas Town." With his wife, Rosemarie, King planned to spend 1969 traveling around small-town and rural America "to record what was happening to towns being bypassed by the network of new superhighways."[2]

His first stop was North Carolina, where a friend helped him find a job in a tobacco factory. But the "hostile redneck foreman" demanded that King shave his beard, and King himself knew that, "What I really wanted . . . was to be in Manhattan partying at Elaine's with my writer buddies." Soon, he realized that while his book idea "sounded romantic on paper, I found myself unwilling or unable to live through it. What I had forgotten was that the reason I had so enjoyed visiting the old farms and towns of my youth was the fresh opportunity to celebrate having escaped them."[3]

When the Kings returned to their Washington apartment, a surprising piece of news was waiting for them. Harvard University had indeed accepted him for the coming school year. "I whooped and yelled, 'Saved by the school bell!'" Because journalists were not supposed to publish work while enrolled, King and Rosemarie decided to spend the summer at the beach so that he could work up several magazine articles in advance.[4]

The first piece he began evolved out of a conversation he and Willie Morris had several months earlier. In the wake of Martin Luther King Jr.'s assassination, rioting broke out in many American cities, including Washington, D.C. King and Rosemarie had been greatly shaken, watching helplessly as the street violence advanced dangerously close to their apartment home. Martin Luther King's philosophy of nonviolence had already come under fire from a new generation of black leaders, and King's murder seemed a final brutal rebuke of his methods. A new era of black militancy emerged, led by the Black Panthers and others who believed that racial integration in America was an impossible dream. Instead, the best hope for achieving justice was black separatism, and all white people were viewed with suspicion. White sympathizers who had long been a part of the civil rights movement suddenly found themselves rejected.

Larry L. King was dismayed by this turn of events, and he became critical of blacks who no longer bothered to distinguish "good" whites like himself from "overt bigots and flaming white racists." King's article would be called "How I Became Whitey." He planned "to take a wounded tone: 'Here I am, a white liberal who has always done the best he could within the racially split society to learn, to grow, to be an activist, to be of human stuff, to be a worker for true brotherhood. And now, suddenly, I'm being cursed as Whitey, Honky, Beast, White Devil, and so on. And I resent it.' My purpose was to show how this foul thing had come about."[5]

As King began writing, he reviewed the numerous good things he had done on behalf of black people. Yes, he had hired the first black person to work in the Texas congressional delegation. But then he promptly hid the man in the back. Yes, he had contributed to causes and candidates, rebuilt inner-city playgrounds, marched a few times, and argued with overt bigots. But as he added up his accomplishments, it "soon developed that the list was so short as to be embarrassing. . . . This was painful information requiring rethinking."[6] Just as Robert Penn Warren had once advised him, King saw that his writing was not merely an explication—it became an act of discovery. Later, King explained the process to John Carr in *Kite-Flying and Other Irrational Acts: Conversations with Twelve Southern Writers:*

I realized I was writing and thinking pure white man's bullshit. I belatedly realized that I held the same attitudes that far too many white people harbor: "Oh, I have done so much for those poor downtrodden people, and now they throw rocks at me." The more I tried to write about what I had done for black people, the more I realized I had done zilch. The more I got into it, the more it dawned on me that I was guilty of the unthinking practices I had always assigned to other white bigots. So I thought, "How does one with my good intentions find out at this late and crucial time of life that he's not done a damn thing really, in areas where he had considered himself accomplished? What forces in society and what old poisons in my heart shaped me into such a disappointing and self-serving creature?" This sent me on a voyage back to my mind's most private country: When had I first become aware of black people? Who was the first black person I saw? What were my thoughts then? What did my social

or political institutions and my family teach me of black people, by word or deed or example? As a result there evolved an
article, and then a book, with the almost exact opposite viewpoint that I had originally intended to reflect. This was certainly the most basic and important discovery I have made
about myself in forty-one years of living. And it was made at
the typewriter by a man stumbling and feeling his way. I sat
down to write a lie and the truth got in the way.[7]

King, now consumed by this one essay, spent the entire summer
researching, rethinking, and rewriting. By the time he left for Harvard
it was finally complete. It would be published in *Harper's* as
"Confessions of a White Racist."

Larry L. King arrived in Cambridge in August 1969. He and
Harvard University were a mismatch from the beginning. Willie
Morris recalled, "Rumors proliferated among his many friends and
foes that he would major in astrology and Christian Science. . . . I was
with him his first day there when he drove his car into a service station near Harvard Square and asked the attendant, 'Which way is the
schoolhouse?'"[8] King enjoyed rebuking what he saw as Harvard's pre-
tentiousness, and he took distinct pleasure in tormenting university
president Nathan Pusey. As King wrote to a friend, "I have not made
a friend of Harvard's President Pusey, who is picky about the way I
pronounce his name. When I *do* pronounce it correctly, he takes
exception—perhaps because I pronounce it correctly only in using it
in the following sentence: 'You been getting any good Pusey lately?'"
King even printed up and distributed three hundred bumper stickers
with that line, and they quickly became an underground hit in
Cambridge.[9]

King arrived at Harvard with the notion that he might receive
some compensatory education, but, as it turned out, he had little
patience for the classroom environment. He came to realize that his
many years of intensive reading had given him as solid an educational
foundation as he could ever hope for. Despite the welcome hiatus
from the constant pressure of making a living as a writer, King grew

restless. The academic life seemed irrelevant as events in the larger world outside continued to erupt. Richard Nixon, who had campaigned in 1968 on the promise of a "secret plan" to end the war in Vietnam, instead escalated American involvement after taking office. Antiwar protests became a daily occurrence on the Harvard campus, and often found among the marchers was a bearded, forty-year-old famous arthur.

King also bristled at the conservative tone of the Nieman program itself. He openly challenged its director, Dwight Sergeant, whose roster of guest speakers was often "Establishment or Administration pablum."[10] In response, King brought his own "underground" speakers, including Norman Mailer, William Styron, and Congressman Morris Udall.

During the long New England winter King's wife, Rosemarie, became increasingly ill from cancer and chemotherapy treatments. Rosemarie didn't want anyone else to know of her condition, so the Kings often retreated to the privacy of their apartment, abandoning many of the formal Nieman activities. As he cared for his sick wife, King had plenty of time to contemplate the astonishing reaction to his "Confessions of a White Racist" essay. After its appearance, five publishers approached him with offers to expand the article into a full-length book. King eventually settled on Viking, and in early 1970 he began working feverishly on the project despite his pledge to refrain from writing during the Nieman fellowship. In truth, King believed he had gotten everything he could out of the program, and he was eager to return to work. Three weeks before the end of the spring semester, Larry and Rosemarie King were sitting together in the apartment when Rosemarie mentioned that she'd heard "spring is bursting out all over Washington." King "took one look at the still-wintry New England landscape—muddy from slow-melting snows; trees and bushes still bare." The next day the couple slipped away, headed back south.[11]

21.

LAND

OF THE

PERMANENT

WAVE

As the 1968 football season peaked, Bud Shrake made a bold, well-publicized prediction in the pages of *Sports Illustrated*. Though no AFL team had ever won the Super Bowl, Shrake argued that the AFL's New York Jets would become the first team to do so. A few weeks later, the Jets, led by quarterback Joe Namath, pulled off a stunning upset. A few days after the game, Bud Shrake was drinking with André Laguerre at their regular bar. Talk eventually turned to the fast-fading British Empire, which was in full retreat from the Middle and Far East. Laguerre knew that in its long years of colonial rule, Britain had developed an enviable sports infrastructure. He wondered aloud what would happen to the sports facilities once the British pulled out. He also wondered who among his staff might be willing to spend three months touring Asia to write the story. A few days later, Bud Shrake was on his way to Singapore.[1]

Shrake's journey eventually took him to Thailand, Malaysia, Cambodia, and Hong Kong. He also made side trips to Japan, Algeria, and Lebanon. Being away from friends and the constant expectations for partying, Shrake found far more free time than he was accustomed to. He began taking his portable typewriter with him into hotel bars, where he sat typing for hours at a time. When he returned to the United States, he had nearly finished a new novel. This one was a little different from *Blessed McGill*. Titled *Boneyard*, it recasts Petronius' classic Roman satire, *The Satyricon*, in modern Texas. Shrake obviously saw many parallels between the extravagant decadence of imperial Rome and life among Texas' oil millionaires. The original *Satyricon* is related by Encolpius, a cultural advisor to Nero who feuds with a longtime friend over the affections of a servant boy. In Bud Shrake's version, the story is narrated by a bisexual interior designer from Dallas.

"Writing from a bisexual's point of view didn't bother me," Shrake said. "But it sure worried a lot of other people, including my mother." His agent, Sterling Lord, thought the book was tremendous. Lord knew that Herman Gollub, the editor at Harper's Press, was interested in Shrake's work, so he sent the manuscript to him. Gollub reactednegatively, Shrake reported in a letter to Larry King. He "greeted it with remarks such as 'trash . . . a waste of time . . . a conceit.'" The novel "is I guess perplexing," Shrake added. "[Gollub] was I think looking for Western Gothic and got instead a faceful of faggots and it made him jumpy."[2]

Word began to spread in New York literary circles about Shrake's work, and homosexuality was making a lot of people nervous that summer. In June, patrons at a gay bar in Greenwich Village battled back against police harassment, precipitating the Stonewall Riot and launching the modern gay rights movement. Though liberal New Yorkers proclaimed a commitment to civil rights, prejudice against gays remained widespread. Shrake began to realize how difficult it might be to find a publisher when an editor at Random House approached his table at Elaine's one evening. "If you publish this book," he told Shrake, "your career as a writer is ruined."

"Why do you say that?" Shrake asked.

"For one thing, the book is such a piece of shit—it's about the worst thing I've ever read, and besides that everybody's going to think you're a homosexual." Recalling the conversation later, Shrake said, "By the time he finished telling me why I shouldn't publish it, I was determined to do so." But finding someone willing to publish the book was another matter.[3]

* * *

Shrake's article on his trip to Asia appeared in *Sports Illustrated* that summer, but the story told only a fraction of what he had observed and learned in his travels. Though he had more freedom to comment on political matters than at *The Dallas Morning News*, *Sports Illustrated* was still very confining. To compensate, Shrake published a subsequent article in the *Texas Observer* titled "A Story of Thailand." In it, Shrake told of a country caught in the grip of a U.S.-backed military dictatorship. He described the capital, Bangkok, as "a monstrosity which myopic travel writers persist in calling 'The Pearl of the Orient.'"[4]

In the fall of 1969, Shrake asked André Laguerre to let him write a story on the Big Thicket region of East Texas. He wanted to focus on the area's deforestation at the hands of the timber industry, and as such the article would complement the numerous conservation-minded features *Sports Illustrated* had published over the years. Laguerre agreed, and Shrake and Doatsy traveled together throughout East Texas. It quickly became apparent that the long-haired couple was not welcome.

"We were spooked," Shrake said later. "Cops followed us everywhere, motels wouldn't take us, restaurants wouldn't serve us. There was this mumbling everywhere that made me increasingly paranoid." Finally, one morning, Shrake had an inspiration. He opened the trunk of his car "and put on a battered, well-crushed cowboy hat I have owned for years. As I turned back toward the coffee shop, there stood the cop. His mean face slowly resolved into a baffled, respectful expression, like that of a weasel facing a trap." Later, Shrake was congratulated by a friend for "having lived for a week bareheaded in East Texas without getting beaten with a tire iron."[5]

By the time Shrake submitted his story to *Sports Illustrated* in late 1969, the magazine's ownership had changed. A Texas lumber company had become a major shareholder in Time, Inc. Upper management decided that Shrake's story might offend the new owners, and André Laguerre was ordered to kill it. This would be the only article ever written by Shrake that the magazine refused to publish. At

Elaine's, Shrake talked to Willie Morris about the situation. Before long he was rewriting the story for *Harper's*. Morris recalled that Shrake "sat down and changed the main angle of the story from the mercenary destruction of the Big Thicket to his and his young wife Doatsy's travels through Lufkin and on down to the Thicket, about permanent waves and long hair in the Sixties and cowboy hats and rednecks and cops and the fumes from paper mills."[6] The essay, titled "Land of the Permanent Wave," appeared in the February 1970 issue of *Harper's*. Shrake's rare gifts as a narrative journalist are on display throughout the piece, and it anticipates the social milieu covered in his later novel *Strange Peaches*.

Willie Morris was among those who admired Shrake's story. In his memoir *New York Days*, Morris ranked "The Land of the Permanent Wave" as one of "two pieces among the many that gave me special pride." Morris wrote that Shrake's story, "struck a chord in me that I have never quite forgotten, having to do with how clean, funny, and lambent prose caught the mood of the moment in the country and mirrored with great felicity what we were trying to do at *Harper's*. To me few finer magazine essays have ever been written."[7]

***

By 1969, Billy Lee Brammer's comeback was losing momentum. "I was under the impression that he was writing more than he really was," said Gary Cartwright. "A lot of people probably got that impression. He didn't like to talk about writing at all. As it turned out, he *was* writing a lot, but it was just gibberish." His wife Dorothy recalled, "He'd written a whole essay about angst, but it never got anywhere. . . . He had an X on his Selectric typewriter, and I'd wake up, and he'd just be holding it down, X-ing out everything he'd written. . . . He'd write all night and have four sentences of it left by the morning."[8]

Brammer started several projects. He began compiling what he called a "Devil's Dictionary of Drugs." The project lost momentum after he completed the entries for speed and grass. Many of Brammer's writing ideas began as puns and wordplays. Most became incoherent and were abandoned after a few lines. A short story, "Can

There Be Life After Meth?" began with an extended digression and was soon abandoned.[9]

Brammer's friends much admired what they saw as his nonjudgmentalism. But Brammer's emotional detachment, reinforced by heavy drug use, became a deeply rooted ambivalence about everything—so much so that it paralyzed the ego-driven self-assuredness needed to choose words to represent reality. "Billy just accepted everything," Dorothy said. "I think he really rejected wisdom. He saw all sides. He could not come up with a moral philosophy, or a standard—he simply couldn't believe anything." His friend Al Reinert later acutely diagnosed the problem in a *Texas Monthly* article. "He did more speed than a punk-rock band and all he could show for it were reams of stray impressions, run-on sentences, midnight digressions. He couldn't concentrate his attention for more than a page or two. Speed, after all, is only a stimulant. What Billy lacked was inspiration."[10]

Though he'd worked on articles for various magazines, Brammer still had not completed anything outside of his two short pieces for the *Texas Observer* the year before. In the summer of 1969 he got an assignment from *The New York Times Magazine*. Bud Shrake wrote to Larry King on the situation:

> [He] claims he is in truth going to write the story and get $750 and re-establish hisself and publish novels with high frequence. Says *Fustian Days* is back up to 200 pages and his rock novel is about the same. I have no doubt that if he ever were to finish *Fustian Days* it would be a good novel. . . . Billy is amazing. About the time we left [for Mexico] he was in as bad shape as I ever saw him, with eye & marital trouble and overloads of chemicals. Now he is coherent, can see and if he writes this stuff will probably save his marital troubles as well.[11]

But Brammer never finished the article. Soon, he and Dorothy separated for good. Just when it seemed he had hit bottom, a new opportunity came his way. An old friend, Jay Milner, was hired by Southern Methodist University to become the acting head of its small journalism department. Milner, in turn, promptly hired Billy Lee Brammer to teach a class. "Billie seems serious about wanting to do good so he can stay in teaching," Milner wrote to Larry King. "It could be a good deal for both of us. If it got him in shape to finish a novel, it would be worth much."[12] Brammer moved to Dallas to begin a new career as a college professor.

Also living in Dallas at the time was Peter Gent, who had just been forced out of professional football after a five-year career. The Dallas Cowboys' 1968 season had ended in frustration when Tom Landry benched quarterback Don Meredith during a playoff loss. Many of the Cowboys believed that Landry had given up on his quarterback and his team too easily. After the game, Meredith decided not to fly back to Dallas with the Cowboys. Instead, accompanied by Gent, he caught a flight to New York with sportscaster Frank Gifford. According to Gent, Meredith was so devastated by the loss and Landry's treatment of him that he lit up a joint during the flight, not caring whether he was arrested or not. A few weeks later, a startling announcement shook the sports world. Don Meredith, one of professional football's most exciting and talented athletes, announced his early retirement from the game.

Peter Gent planned to continue playing, but the Cowboys organization had other ideas. For much of his career in Dallas, Gent had been insulated because of his friendship with Meredith. But with the team leader gone, Gent was vulnerable. He had heard rumors that a teammate had reported him for using illegal drugs. Gent began to suspect that he was under surveillance by NFL security agents. On one occasion he caught someone who appeared to be looking at his house through binoculars. Another time a car blatantly followed him as he drove across town.[13]

Gent's stock with the Cowboys had also diminished because of the multiple injuries he'd suffered over the years. Initially, general manager Tex Schramm offered to sign him for another season—if Gent would agree to a ten percent salary cut. After Gent refused, Tom

Landry called him into his office. There, Landry informed him that he was cut from the team. According to Gent, Landry seemed to derive great pleasure from delivering the news personally.[14]

Gent co-owned a printing company in Dallas with former Cowboy teammate Bob Hayes. Through Cartwright and Shrake, Gent had already become friends with Jay Milner and Billy Lee Brammer. He didn't necessarily need a job, but he was looking for something different to do, and he did have a degree in advertising from Michigan State University. Milner, seeking to beef up his department, decided to hire Gent to teach an evening advertising class.

At SMU, Milner quickly revived the somnambulant journalism program. He launched a new campus magazine, *The Rap,* and he asked Larry L. King to contribute to it. He also asked King to solicit stories from Norman Mailer and William Styron. King sidestepped Milner's rather extravagant requests but did agree to write a letter of support and serve on an advisory board. King also arranged to bring Milner to Harvard, at Harvard's expense, for a two-week consultation to improve SMU's journalism program. King also made sure to stop by and visit with Milner's journalism students whenever he came to Dallas.

Life as a journalism professor remained a rather abstract notion to Billy Lee Brammer. As Milner reported to King, "Billie keeps asking me, because he is rather forgetful these days, what it is the course is about." At times Milner found it necessary to dispatch "a husky pair of varsity football players who were taking journalism classes to ensure that Mr. Brammer got to class on time." Before too much longer, Brammer "was regularly either missing class altogether or bumbling his way through them."[15]

As the fall 1970 semester approached, Milner believed that his superiors were poised to fire Brammer. So, at Milner's urging, Brammer accepted a long-standing offer to become a writer-in-residence at Bowling Green State University in Ohio. "In his typically passive manner, Billie Lee allowed Pete and Jody [Gent] to put him on a plane . . . although he grumbled all the way to the airport that he'd prefer to stay and teach at SMU." Shortly afterward Milner received a letter from Brammer, who wrote, "This place is pretty, pleasant, seemingly safe from hippie peril and riot squad assault." Brammer was clearly unhappy, referring to himself as a "Rotter in Residence." "My god I'm suffocating in all this interminable wholesomeness. The pitiful kiddies largely drink . . . this place doesn't even stock Zig Zag papers!" Before the semester was over, Brammer abandoned Bowling Green and was back in Dallas. He promised to become a responsible and productive faculty member—if SMU would only give him one more chance.[16]

22.

MAD

DOG,

TEXAS

By 1970 Austin's counterculture was in its ascendancy. Protests, boycotts, and marches were a regular occurrence, and the demonstrators' numbers grew larger every day. In April the United States invaded Cambodia, further widening its war in Southeast Asia. In response, massive new protests broke out on college campuses across the country. At Kent State University, National Guard troops fired on unarmed demonstrators, killing four and wounding several others. Activists in Austin responded by burning Richard Nixon in effigy. By the end of the week, some twenty-five thousand protesters filled Austin's streets, the largest antiwar rallies ever seen in the city.[1]

Texas conservatives exploited the political chaos and launched their fiercest challenge yet to Senator Ralph Yarborough. During his fourteen years in office, Yarborough had been a most curious anomaly—a liberal senator from Texas. In the Democratic primary, well-funded conservative challenger Lloyd Bentsen ran television ads with footage of riot-ravaged cities, linking the violence to Yarborough's support of civil rights legislation. Bentsen won the race, and Larry L. King was among those who sent condolences to Yarborough. "You're still my senator," King wrote. "I never had one from Texas except you . . . my main regret is that such a good man could become a victim of the times."[2]

Though civil rights and the Vietnam War remained a vital part of America's domestic resistance, new issues were also gaining strength, including women's liberation and the ecology movement. But as hippie numbers swelled, the most passionate dissent seemed to come in response to marijuana prohibition. *The Rag* remained Austin's counterculture voice, and each issue carried an array of stories, comics, and advertising designed to capitalize on the hippies' pro-marijuana feelings. *The Rag* promoted such schemes as the "First Annual Marijuana Mail-In and Cross Country Toke-Down." The idea was for every dope smoker to send joints through the mail to nonsmokers, including police chiefs and public officials. As a result, "The USA will come together in psychedelic harmony at last. Amerika will break out in one huge smile and everyone will be stoned, high, fucked up, jacked out of shape, mellow, blasted."[3]

Austin's hippie community was much like that of other major college towns. But there was also something different brewing here, an odd mix of the freak culture and Texas' ingrained ranching heritage. Rednecks across the state were notorious for "hippie-bashing," but in Austin, the two groups were coming to coexist more and more—largely in their mutual appreciation of good music. A beer joint owner named Kenneth Threadgill was viewed by many as the one who "fused relationships between hippies and cedar choppers."[4] In the early 1960s, Threadgill encouraged students from UT to participate in small weekly jam sessions. Janis Joplin was among those who got her start at Threadgill's place before moving on to San Francisco.

By the late 1960s, Austin's leading music venue was the Vulcan Gas Company, which featured local psychedelic favorite Shiva's Headband as well as touring blues legends like Muddy Waters. But increasingly, other groups such as the Hub City Movers came to share the stage. These musicians exuded a hippie ethos, with long hair and beards. But countervailing elements were also present—cowboy hats and western boots. Another local venue, The Cactus Club, was also hip to the emerging trend. Its advertisements in the pages of *The Rag* read, "Where the heads and the [red]necks get together."

Bud Shrake and Gary Cartwright were nearly twice the age of most Austin hippies by 1970. But they had long hair, smoked dope, and they, too, favored cowboy boots. And as Shrake learned during his sojourn to East Texas the preceding year, a cowboy hat was a mighty handy thing to have when faced with suspicious stares. Living in Austin, making friends among those in the counterculture, the two men became caught up in the swirl of energy. In 1969 they envisioned holding an "Intracontinental Smoke-O-Rama Festival," which never progressed beyond the talking stage. But on a plane flight from Los Angeles to Austin, they began discussing the need to do *something* in the face of the American government's war against Vietnamese peasants abroad and peaceful dope smokers at home. "We decided that it was necessary to form a 'peoples' lobby,'" Cartwright said later. "After all, the corporations had lobbies. Why couldn't the people? When we got back to Austin we arranged to speak to a government class at UT. It was total bullshit—we were just winging it. But they got all excited."[5]

Cartwright was already a cause célèbre among Austin hippies because of his bust for pot. In February 1970, nearly two years after his arrest, his long-delayed trial finally opened. On the surface, his prospects looked bleak, as the Travis County district attorney's office had won sixty-six convictions in its previous sixty-seven cases. But the prosecutors had never before faced a defense team led by Warren Burnett and buttressed with Sam Houston Clinton and David Richards. The defense had already punched several holes in the prosecution's case during pretrial motions. On the eve of the trial, the state offered Cartwright a deal: In exchange for a guilty plea he would receive two years' probation. The offer was refused.[6]

Warren Burnett loaned Cartwright some money to buy a suit, and the defendant arrived wearing a dark blazer and a tie. But he refused to cut his hair. The courtroom overflowed with spectators, many of whom were hippies who turned out in a show of support. Several others were law students who came to watch Warren Burnett in person. Still others were professional lawyers themselves, who came for the same reason. Cartwright's case attracted statewide publicity, as he was still well known from his days as a *Morning News* sportswriter.

Once the jury was seated, it didn't take long for the prosecution's case to fall apart. Under Burnett's questioning, the agents admitted that they had insufficient evidence to obtain a search warrant, so they had practiced deceit by disguising themselves and then lying their way inside a private home. One of the agents slipped during cross-examination and said that Cartwright had sold, rather than given them, the marijuana cigarette. This testimony contradicted the arrest warrant. Shortly thereafter, the judge said, "I have not been happy with the way the case was presented. I think a mistrial is in order." A few weeks later, the district attorney quietly dropped all charges against Cartwright. Despite the intensive publicity Cartwright's initial arrest had generated, the media made little mention of his case's ultimate dismissal.[7]

***

On April Fool's Day 1970, just a few days after the conclusion of Cartwright's trial, Bud Shrake received a suspicious telegram at his home in Austin. It purported to be from movie star Cliff Robertson, and it contained an unusual offer: Robertson was looking for someone to rewrite his screenplay about a rodeo star. "It was called *Ride the Wild Lighting* or something silly like that," Shrake recalled. He telephoned Gary Cartwright, who denied being the source of a prank. A few hours later Cartwright called Shrake back. He, too, had just received the same telegram. As it turned out, the telegrams were authentic. Cliff Robertson had just seen Shrake's story, "The Land of the Permanent Wave," in *Harper's*. He'd also read Cartwright's article in *Life* on the filming of *Viva Max*. Somehow he got the notion that either writer could bring some much-needed authenticity to his script. He had no idea that the two men knew each other.[8]

Robertson's message came at an opportune time for Shrake, who was becoming increasingly serious about movies. He had always been interested in screenwriting and had made several tentative forays into the medium over the years. Though none of his projects had developed beyond the planning stages, the success of other Texans was encouraging. Larry McMurtry's first novel had been made into the memorable *Hud*, starring Paul Newman. McMurtry had since been called to rewrite several Hollywood scripts. One of Shrake's acquaintances in New York, Texas expatriate Robert Benton, had left his job at *Esquire* and cowritten the hit film, *Bonnie and Clyde*. Benton received an Academy Award nomination and became much sought after in Hollywood. In 1969, Texas-based journalist Jim Lehrer's farcical Alamo novel, *Viva Max,* was made into a successful film starring Peter Ustinov.

Though Shrake's *Blessed McGill* had not sold well, its critical praise generated some serious film interest. In May 1968 the *Hollywood Reporter* carried a front-page story on United Artists' intention to film *Blessed McGill.* A screenwriter was hired, and the film was projected to have a release date in 1970. Shrake was initially very enthusiastic, writing to a friend that the studio has "a substantial amount of cash invested. They can get it back only by making the movie." But over the next year little progress was reported on the film. Finally, after several months, Shrake received a call from the studio. The producer assured him that that the screenplay was coming along well. But then he told Shrake, "Of course we had to take out all that religious shit." Another long period of silence followed. Eventually the project was abandoned.[9]

In 1969 Shrake went to see a just-released film, *Butch Cassidy and the Sundance Kid.* The movie was a huge hit, and Shrake, for his part, was amazed at how easy the story and dialogue seemed to come off. "Hell," he thought to himself, "I can do that." He went home and immediately began writing a screenplay. He had no idea how a script should be structured, but bookstores were selling paperback copies of William Goldman's script for *Butch Cassidy.* So Shrake bought the book and copied Goldman's form.[10]

A few weeks later, his screenplay was nearly complete. "I was amazed at how easy it was," he said. "Writing a script was a lot more fun and so much easier than writing a novel. Writing a novel's the hardest thing I've ever done in my life." The script, titled *Dime Box,* told the story of a misfit outlaw who attempts to go straight in a slightly addled Texas town at the dawn of the twentieth century. The hero works in a factory that produces sombrero-shaped ashtrays. But trouble is never far away, and he hatches a plan—with help from some dope-smoking Comanche friends—to make one last score.

Shrake was editing and revising his *Dime Box* screenplay when he received Cliff Robertson's telegram. Cartwright and Shrake arranged to work together on Robertson's script. A few weeks later, they met Robertson in Dallas so they could tour the rodeo circuit together. They also made the rounds of several parties with Robertson but soon soured on their new partner. "We took Cliff to a party at Peter Gent's house in Dallas," Shrake said. "But he turned out to be a real prick. He didn't want to be recognized, so we started introducing him as 'Biff' instead of Cliff. But then he got upset when people didn't recognize him."[11]

After Robertson flew back to Hollywood, Shrake and Cartwright began working on the screenplay in earnest. They ended up throwing out most of what Robertson had written and created their own, titling it *J. W. Garrett*. When it was done, Robertson came to Austin to review the script. He accompanied them to several more parties but seemed to grow increasingly ill at ease in their presence. Perhaps it was the disorienting psychedelic light show he was exposed to. Or maybe the phone call Shrake received at 3:00 A.M. warning him that the cops were on their way to raid his house for drugs. In any case, Robertson quickly returned to California, screenplay in hand, pledging to find a studio that would back the project. They didn't hear from the actor for several months, and then one day he called Shrake with some bad news. "He said he was sorry, but that everyone in Hollywood turned down our script. He said that he worked his ass off, and that we were great guys, but it's just not going to work. He said that he hoped we'd stay friends. He also said that he didn't have the money to pay us the rest of what he owed us for the script, but that this is the kind of thing that happens in show business."[12]

"So we said, 'Oh, yeah, Cliff, we're sorry too, and sure, we're buddies.'" A few months later Bud Shrake noticed a small item in a syndicated gossip column: Cliff Robertson was thanking the executives at Columbia Pictures for allowing him to make his movie, *J. W. Coop*, in total secrecy, because there were two other rodeo movies being made at the same time.[13]

"That's when I decided to join the Screenwriters Guild," Shrake said. "I got a copy of the script, and sure enough, it was the same one

Jap and I wrote, only it had Cliff Robertson's name on it."[14] Soon thereafter, Shrake and Cartwright sued the Hollywood star. Austin lawyer David Richards, against his better judgment, agreed to represent the two writers. Richards would only realize two years later, when the case finally came to trial, how difficult it would be to make his clients look sympathetic in a Travis County courtroom.

***

By May 1970, Bud Shrake and Gary Cartwright figured out a way to merge their interests in literature, film, political reform, and drugs. They officially formed a new organization, Mad Dog, Inc. Shrake deposited $500 in a bank account, and attorney David Richards drew up the articles of incorporation. Ostensibly, the company would "make, produce, and distribute motion pictures and other entertainment." In reality, Mad Dog served as a rallying point for the "writers, lawyers, artists, radicals, politicians and other ne'er-do-wells now living in Austin . . . plus their friends in other parts of the country." Several divisions of Mad Dog, Inc., were proposed, including the Institute for Augmented Reality, the All-Night General Store, the Mad Dog Foundation for Depressed Greyhounds, a Freak Nursery, a church, and the Mad Doggeral Vanity Press. The Mad Dogs sought to produce "the world's first literate and nonhysterical underground newspaper" as well as a novel, to be titled *Sweet Pussy*. Another project was to produce thirty-minute porno movies with just enough socially redeeming value—calculated by attorney David Richards—to elude prosecution.[15]

Charter members included David and Ann Richards, Peter and Jody Gent, Billy Lee Brammer, Larry L. King, Dan Jenkins, Willie Morris, George Plimpton, David Halberstam, and several others. Stationery and business cards were printed up with the Mad Dog motto: "Doing Indefinable Services to Mankind." The credo became "Everything that is not a mystery is guesswork." As new members were inducted in the years ahead, an initiation ceremony of sorts developed. It "consisted of passing around a bottle of tequila, after which the new member was given a Mad Dog card, two pesos, and a kiss on the cheek."[16]

Bud Shrake wrote to Larry L. King with news of Mad Dog, and he explained that "our first project, outside of buying a ping pong table for the office" would be staging a Mad Dog Masked Ball at the Vulcan Gas Company. The group also planned to publish a magazine, *Mad Dog Ink,* which would devote its first issue to the Dallas stripper Candy Barr, who had been sent to jail on trumped up marijuana charges. They also planned to publish Candy Barr's prison poetry.[17]

Mad Dog Ink never got off the ground, but on May 23, 1970, the Mad Dog Masked Ball came off as planned, billed as a benefit for the Citizens Lobby. The advertised guest list included Ken Kesey and Don Meredith. The Masked Ball also featured a return of the Flying Punzars, who had not performed in public since Shrake and Cartwright had destroyed a drum set while wearing red Dallas Texan blazers. The Punzars had new costumes—green tunics with a backward, winged "P," and brilliantly colored red-and-yellow caps. Gary Cartwright wrote later that "we spoke broken English and told stories of how we had represented our country at the 1952 Olympics, only to be disqualified when we failed the gender test. Our dream was to do the impossible—the death-defying Triple Somersault, without a net, of course."[18]

The Mad Dogs' most sustained effort involved their attempts to buy their own town, which would have "municipal codes that reflect the most progressive and enlightened sociolegal thinking in the country." Or, as David Richards termed it, "Gary and Bud felt that if we owned a town, and perforce controlled the town's law enforcement, a sanctuary could be set up as a barrier against foolish laws, such as the state's drug laws." It was also suggested that "gambling, saloons, prostitution . . . dueling, spitting in public, lascivious carriage, cohabitation and every other wholesome vice known to man" be made legal. The town, once purchased, would naturally be renamed Mad Dog, Texas.[19]

The first choice was Shafter, an abandoned mining village in the Big Bend region of West Texas. Its location near the Mexican border seemed ideal, and Shrake told *Playboy* magazine that it had potential for "heavy tourist traffic in expatriates, the smuggling of Chinamen and extensive trade in the Far East in jade, fine silks, and frankincense."[20] But Shafter was an eight-hour drive from Austin, and it was uncomfortably close to Presidio, known to weather watchers as the nation's hot spot.

The next target was Sisterdale, a small settlement in the Hill Country. The asking price of $6,000 was within Mad Dog, Inc.'s financial reach. But the sellers turned recalcitrant at the sight of the long-haired potential buyers. Suddenly, the price became $60,000, and the deal was off. A final stab was made at Theon, northeast of Austin. As the group discussed the proposal at a place called The Squirrel Inn, Bud Shrake took what he thought was a pitcher of water out of the refrigerator and poured it into a glass of scotch. Then he swallowed it all in one big gulp. The "ice water," as it turned out, was kerosene. With Shrake ailing, the group rushed back to Austin but was stopped by the highway patrol. Cartwright got into an argument with the cop, and the Mad Dogs ended up spending the night in the Williamson County jail. A doctor friend was called to come check on Shrake. After a cursory exam, he gave Shrake a handful of pills and told him to swallow them all. Those turned out to be speed. "He thought that would make me feel a lot better," Shrake recalled. "And I guess it must have. My heart exploded about twenty-five times and I bounced around the walls of the cell for a while."[21]

After Theon, the Mad Dogs abandoned their attempts to buy a town. But they did get their own office space, which happened to be right in the middle of Austin's newly emerging counterculture headquarters. For several years, Austin artist Jim Franklin had become increasingly obsessed by a modest marsupial, the armadillo. His drawings in *The Rag* focused lovingly on the creature. In *The Rag*'s cover commemorating the lunar landing in 1969, Franklin's drawing shows the space capsule hovering over a curved surface. Just before the margin of the page, the gradually curving surface flares to reveal a small ear, and then, the beginning of an armadillo's snout. Soon, Franklin's armadillo obsession would become shared by many in Austin and in the rest of Texas.

Shrake and Cartwright were friends with Eddie Wilson, an ex-marine turned beer distributor and hippie entrepreneur. Wilson managed Austin's best known acid-rock group, Shiva's Headband, which played regularly at the Vulcan Gas Company. The Vulcan had been forced to close in the summer of 1970 after the landlord raised the rent in response to concerns about the club's hippie clientele. A few evenings later, Wilson gazed upon an old red brick National Guard armory, sitting vacant on the banks of the Colorado River. This, he decided, would be the perfect place for a new club.[22]

By August 1970 Austin had a new live music venue: The Armadillo World Headquarters, a cavernous building decorated throughout with Jim Franklin's armadillo-inspired murals, as well as paintings by other hippie artists. The Armadillo's opening was announced in a two-page spread in *The Rag*, and readers were promised diverse music—"rock, folk, country—any music people want to hear in a relaxed . . . atmosphere." Mad Dog, Inc., was one of the Armadillo's initial investors, and the organization was given office space next to the stage.[23]

True to its promise, the Armadillo featured performers ranging from Earl Scruggs and Ravi Shankar to Lightnin' Hopkins and Jerry Jeff Walker. The Armadillo capitalized on Austin's growing appreciation of eclectic music, but it also became something more than just a concert hall. Envisioned as a community arts laboratory, the Armadillo featured crafts workshops, artists' wares, and its own record label. It also had a bakery, kitchen, and a vine-covered beer garden. Soon, "the Armadillo was widely recognized as Austin's social, musical, and artistic hub."[24]

The Mad Dogs made their presence felt on the scene. As Gary Cartwright recounted later, "On occasion, Bud and I would put on our Punzar capes and Ann [Richards] would dress as Dolly Parton— a gigantic blond wig, tight red dress, rolls of cotton stuffed in her bra—and we'd head out to Armadillo World Headquarters for an evening of Austin culture. The home of David and Ann Richards "became a sort of Mad Dog sanctuary and the scene of some of our city's most memorable parties." It was there that visiting *New York Times* editor Abe Rosenthal was invited to a dinner party one evening. He was greeted at the door by Ann Richards, dressed as a giant Tampax. Inside Rosenthal discovered Bud Shrake, wearing a large afro wig and claiming to be basketball star "Dr. J."[25]

Though the deal to buy the town of Shafter had fallen through, a fictitious writer named M. D. (Mad Dog) Shafter took on a life as the pen name of choice for the Mad Dogs. This was particularly useful for Cartwright after the IRS placed a lien on his earnings for back taxes. He wrote several stories under the name and even published a few.[26]

The Mad Dog mentality could test the limits of friendship. Dan Jenkins, for one, was uncomfortable at having his name publicly associated with Mad Dog. After a *Playboy* article on Mad Dog that contained several quotes from Bud Shrake, Jenkins wrote to Larry King, complaining that the publicity would land them all on government watch lists. He predicted that the CIA would monitor them, and the IRS would begin auditing their tax returns every year.[27]

Larry L. King, in a visit to Austin shortly after Mad Dog's founding, wrote to Billy Lee Brammer that neither Shrake nor Cartwright "made real good sense." King was particularly put off by Cartwright's "scheme where I am supposed to sell his and Shrake's novel drawn from an original screenplay, claiming to my agent and editors I had discovered a live-wire writer named M. D. Shafter who had wrote a great novel."

Cartwright and Shrake planned to have their friend Fletcher Boone pose as the novelist, and then after publication they "would sue [Boone] for stealing their idea, or he would sue them, or maybe they would sue one another jointly; I forget just how it worked. Anyhow, I hoo-hawed and smiled and acted friendly and never gave them the satisfaction of an answer about doing their dirty work for them, and escaped town before they could press me a second time. They are crazy."[28]

23.

KING'S

ROAD

By the time Willie Morris entered his fourth year of editing *Harper's* in 1970, the magazine was viewed by many as America's most vital monthly. A number of the nation's best writers appeared in its pages, including Ralph Ellison, Robert Penn Warren, Joan Didion, Arthur Miller, James Dickey, John Updike, Phillip Roth, and Truman Capote. *Harper's* daring journalism often set the tone for national debate. In May 1970 it published a thirty-thousand-word investigative report by Seymour Hersh on the massacre of Vietnamese civilians by American soldiers in the village of My Lai. The events were so shocking that many people refused to believe it, and "Nixon himself ordered a secret investigation of Hersh in order to discredit him."[1] But Hersh's report was eventually corroborated, vindicating *Harper's* and winning the reporter a Pulitzer Prize.

Harper's circulation had also been on the rise ever since Willie Morris took over. One hundred thousand new subscribers had joined in the previous three years. But the magazine's owner, John Cowles Jr., who had initially supported Morris, began to worry about rising editorial costs. Morris defended his budget by pointing out that *Harper's* writers were still paid less than their colleagues at other publications. Morris even offered to take a pay cut if the magazine's business manager, William Blair, would also agree to do so. The suggestion was rejected, and relations between the magazine's editorial and business sides deteriorated. Soon, Cowles restructured the organization so that the business manager, William Blair, became Willie Morris' direct supervisor.[2]

In truth, Morris' editorship was messy. He often overpromised himself to his staff writers, leading each of them to believe that their own article would be the magazine's cover story for an upcoming issue. His drinking, always pronounced, became even heavier after his wife, Celia, left him in 1968. Increasingly, Morris found solace at Elaine's restaurant, which became like a second home. "Often I would even hide at a corner table and read manuscripts there," he wrote later. He spent so much time at Elaine's that he even began receiving mail at the restaurant and negotiated "various magazine assignments on napkins."[3]

Morris was often so drunk that his friends considered it a miracle if he remembered any part of their conversations the next day. At least once he lost a writer's manuscript during a cab ride home. Still, his writers continued to support him, because Morris had exceptional editorial instincts, and he empowered them as writers. "We knew that we could take, within reason, whatever length we needed to do a story," Larry L. King said later. "You could really plumb the depths of your subject." The result, King believed, was "a national journal free of the sneering provincialisms of New York, one that spoke in several strong voices, one that allowed the writer to extend the language and himself as no other journal has done in our time."[4]

As the tension mounted in *Harper's* offices between the business and editorial sides, Morris believed that much of the friction resulted from his magazine's anti-Vietnam War posture. As such, "this was only representative of the generational and political divisions taking place all over the country in those years." William Blair, for his part, found it difficult to control *Harper's* independent-minded journalists. In a conversation with Larry L. King, Blair referred to himself as "the boss." King responded, "You're not my boss . . . I'm not a goddamn accountant. I'm a writer. Willie Morris is my boss."[5]

In 1970 the economy dipped into a recession, and by the end of the year *Harper's* circulation declined by some twenty-five thousand. Though it was still substantially up from the outset of the Willie Morris era, *Harper's* business hierarchy saw an opportunity to make Morris and his writers understand that *Harper's* was their magazine, not his. Morris was summoned to Minneapolis for a meeting with *Harper's* management. There, his editorship came under a fierce attack. One of the executives commented, "No wonder it's such a failure. Who are you editing this magazine for? A bunch of hippies?" At the close of the meeting, William Blair recommended a number of editorial cutbacks, including laying off all the staff writers—Larry L. King and David Halberstam among them.[6]

Morris decided to call their bluff. Aware that *Harper's* had acquired a sterling reputation under his leadership, he offered his resignation. Much to his surprise it was immediately accepted. When the *Harper's* staff learned what had happened to their editor, they demanded a meeting. But it quickly became apparent that the owner was in no mood to compromise. Cowles explained that he wanted the magazine to go in a new direction, and he suggested that market research and reader polls should determine what articles to publish. At this point Larry L. King interrupted. As Willie Morris later described it, King told the owner, "If you can find one single goddamn self-respecting writer worth the ink of his by-line who'll work on terms like that, John, I'll kiss your ass till your nose bleeds."[7]

Soon it was clear what course of action the writers should take. It was King who stood up first and said, "Then fuck it, there's no reason to stay here. I resign." King left the room, and every other staff writer except for one—Louis Lapham—followed him. As word spread, the mass walkout grew. The magazine's managing editor and executive editor also quit in protest. Other writers who had published in *Harper's*, including Norman Mailer and William Styron, announced that they would no longer appear in its pages.[8]

Ironically, the May 1971 issue of *Harper's* was already at the printer by the time the staff walked out. So one last issue came out under Willie Morris' tenure. And it was in this issue that *Harper's* published "The Old Man." It became Larry L. King's most celebrated piece of magazine journalism ever, a story that, Larry McMurtry later asserted, "puts everything else he has written in the deep shade."[9]

For years King had regaled Willie Morris with stories about his father, and that "peculiar mixture of love and resentment, of pride and shame, of tenderness and gruffness, and the other complex emotions that we—like many fathers and sons—had experienced." Morris had asked King on several occasions to write about his father, but every attempt failed.[10]

In the summer of 1970, King's wife Rosemarie, whose own health was deteriorating as her cancer spread, begged him to take his eighty-two-year-old father on a long-promised trip to see the Alamo and the state capitol in Austin. Though his father had lived in Texas his entire life, he had never visited either place. A few days later, King and his father were driving away from Midland together. King quickly realized how special this trip would be. His father, taciturn in most respects, "began a monologue lasting almost a week . . . he gestured, pointed, laughed, praised the land, took on new strength."[11]

During their journey, King and his father reached a new accommodation with each other, connecting far more intimately than they ever had before. After returning to Washington, King tried once again to write about his father, but the piece would still not come together. A month later, drinking in a bar with Willie Morris, King "morosely confessed failure," telling Morris, "Goddammit, I'm intimidated by it. I guess I just don't understand him well enough." A few days later, Clyde King suddenly died. King flew to Texas for the funeral, "openly and carelessly puffing several sticks of pot between Washington and Dallas, and seeing mystical, tantalizing, undefinable clues to what it was all about in the puffy drifting cumulus formations outside the sealed window." When Willie Morris telephoned his condolences, King blurted out, "Willie, I can write it now."[12]

King structured the essay around the final trip he and his father took together. "The Old Man" describes, in King's honest, searching style, how his "blindly adoring period of childhood" eventually developed into open confrontation, capped by a "savage and ugly" fistfight that produced no winners. Yet little by little, over the ensuing years and decades, a reconciliation and acceptance of sorts occurred, a warming that continued to grow.[13]

In his essay, King recalled how he awoke in his Austin motel room to find his father waiting outside. The Old Man complained, "Folks sure must be sleepyheaded around here. . . .Went over yonder to that governor's mansion and rattled the gate and yelled, but didn't nobody come to let me in." King, "moderately appalled," asked, "Did you *really?*" The Old Man responded, "Thunder, yes, I'm a voter . . . Democrat, at that." King wrote, "Then the sly country grin flashed in a way that keeps me wondering in the night, now, whether he really had."[14]

King's understanding of his deep connection to his father became clear during their visit to San Antonio. King wrote:

> Now it is late afternoon. His sap suddenly ran low; he seemed more fragile, a tired old head with a journey to make; he dangerously stumbled on a curbstone. Crossing a busy inter-section, I took his arm. Though that arm had once pounded anvils into submission, it felt incredibly frail. My children, fueled by youth's inexhaustible gases, skipped and cavorted fully a block ahead. Negotiating the street, The Old Man half laughed and half snorted. "I recollect helpin' you across lots of streets when you was little. Never had no notion that one day you'd be doin' the same for me." Well, I said. Well. Then: "I've helped that boy up there"—motioning toward my distant and mobile son—"across some few streets. Until now it never once occurred that he may someday return the favor." "Well," The Old Man said, "he will if you're lucky."[15]

Gauging the distance between himself and his father, King wrote that The Old Man's "time extended from when 'kissin' wasn't took lightly' to exhibitions of group sex; from five years before men on horseback rushed to homestead the Cherokee strip to a year beyond man's first walk on the moon . . . from the first presidency of Grover Cleveland to the mid-term confusions of Richard Nixon." Though King's father "had plowed oxen in yoke, he never flew in an airplane.

He died owing no man and knowing the satisfaction of having built his own house."[16]

The article, evoking the universal chords of father-son relationships and rural-urban tensions, is the most affectionately loved of all of King's work. It drew "the most and the best mail I have received in my writing life," King said later. "The Old Man" was eventually translated into several languages, including Russian, and it became his most widely anthologized story ever. But for the author, the best reaction came from his mother. "Every time I read that piece," she told him, "it brings him back to me for a while."[17]

***

Two months after the demise of Willie Morris' *Harper's*, Larry L. King's book, *Confessions of a White Racist*, was published by Viking Press. An autobiography told with an eye on race, *White Racist* seeks to explain King's "condition as it related to the most explosive social issue of my day." Looking back at his life, King recalls his earliest views of blacks; the unthinking use of "nigger" in childhood games; how strongly prejudices were formed by the hugely popular radio show, *Amos 'n' Andy*; how his inferior education neglected the eloquent abolitionist Frederick Douglass but made *Gone with the Wind* required reading.[18]

Though King's account is personal, the portrait of Texas that emerges in its pages is far from flattering. King chronicles how the "Texas Rangers swooped in to raid every NAACP chapter in the state"; how "Texas newspapers reacted to our home-grown McCarthys with cheers and accolades"; how Texas Governor Allan Shivers defied federal desegregation orders [in Mansfield] and President Eisenhower refused to intervene; how a young black man attempting to enroll in the local community college was harassed out of town by the police; how Louis Armstrong, dressed in a tuxedo, was told to enter through the back door of the swanky hotel where he was scheduled to play a concert in Dallas.[19]

King also describes the verbal clashes with his family and friends in West Texas. During one whiskey-soaked evening, tired of listening to racist comments, King suddenly interrupted: "Goddamn you, Elder, I've known black people smarter than both of us." The response was chilling: "Elder blew out of his chair, enraged, sloshing whiskey over a wide perimeter. 'They may be smarter than you, you sonnuvabitch, but you don't know any goddamn niggers smarter than I am.' He flailed his long pale skinny arms and screeched profanities, an altogether wild bird, and for the first time I realized just how easy it might be to call up a lynch mob from among my old friends."[20]

Part of King's aim is to make white Americans understand something that they often take for granted—how their lives are made easier by the color of their skin. He describes many of the painful realities of black life that whites don't often recognize. One friend tells him that when driving across the country, "black people key their kidneys to gasoline tanks. We know there are more mean bastards than not; we don't assume anything good. So when we pull up to the gas tanks when we get nature's urge, but before we ask the man to fill 'er up we inquire if his rest room is open. If we get turned down, we drive on to the next station." Later, King quotes a black Vietnam veteran who was outraged by his treatment in the military. Blacks were reprimanded for using the Black Power salute, "but yet Whitey can fly his fucking Confederate flag, man, and nobody says shit. Well, to hell with that flag. That flag means slavery to me."[21]

But King's primary aim is to explore his own acquiescence in the racist world of America. He confesses boldly, sometimes shockingly, his own failings. King tells how, early in his writing career, he became friendly with a well-known writer, who was extremely bigoted in private. King notes that "I occasionally found myself (for what I then assumed to be 'professional reasons') pandering to his bigotry by responding in kind." Other confidences are even more incriminating. At one point King tells how he

> "was piously lecturing my relatives on the insanities of racial exclusions when my mother laughed and said, 'Lawrence, do you remember when some niggers set down by you the first day you got up to New Jersey? And what a fuss you made?'"

"Whatever do you mean?" I asked.

Mother returned from rummaging in an old trunk, bringing a letter I barely recognized to be in my own hand:

Dear Folks. Got here Thursday on the train from Ft. Sam. We no more than set down in the depot to eat than some niggers plopped down next to us and I can tell you they didn't stay long. We told them we were from Texas and we didn't go for that stuff, and believe-you-me they cleared out in a hurry. . . .

"It is interesting to speculate why this fiction was composed," King writes, "for we had actually eaten our hamburgers in a choked and humble silence."[22]

King's candor is so striking that readers sense not only the depth of his thoughtfulness on the subject but the fervor of his commitment. Yet King's book, in its denunciation of racism, is virtually blind to sexism. In the beginning of the book he provides an overview of slavery and writes, "we should remember that 'peculiar institution' for the hard bitch she was, a mean old crone who killed, maimed, and wore out millions of black humans for profit and fun. . . . The old whore lived long and died fighting, leaving white racism as a legacy."[23] Those words pricked the ears of alert female readers, and in the years to come King would be subjected to a withering critique by Celia Morris, ex-wife of Willie Morris and a longtime friend.

Yet those who could overlook King's failings in regard to women saw an unflinching portrait of race relations. As his book progresses, it is revealed that King finds himself becoming alienated from a new generation of militant blacks, who are interested more in separatism than his old dream, integration. King tells of becoming a "whitey," a target: "[W]here I had once walked the streets in confidence, I came to look ahead like a soldier advancing into enemy territory, alert for unfriendly blacks or side-street dangers, vulnerable, tense, and marked—at last—by my white skin. Yes, the world was being turned around."[24] King's conclusion is bleak and chilling, as he notes the increasing distance between the races:

I am judged by blacks as arbitrarily as I once judged them; while there may be more than a little justice in this, there is too much discomfort in it to court. So I have joined my countrymen in becoming more suspicious, more ingrown, more tribal, more cautious, more fearful. On nights when the ghettos swelter I sometimes hear a siren off in the distance, and more than once I have wondered if it is the final signal that certain old white racist chickens are coming home to roost on my personal doorstep.[25]

The reviews for *White Racist* were effusive—the sort that inspired "handsprings and visions of riches." *The New Yorker, Book World, Book Week, Life, The New York Times,* and the nation's newspapers raved about King's "important and disturbing book." One reviewer praised King's "bitingly angry truths . . . in a gut-rending, excruciatingly honest account of one white man's attempt to confront and overcome within himself the sickness which afflicts us all. . . . King hides nothing, obscures nothing, fuzzes nothing over—and thereby helps the more timid of us do the same for ourselves." Another reviewer commented on King's "remarkable personal journey [that can] serve as an eloquent companion piece to Eldridge Cleaver's *Soul on Ice.* it is a confirming report, quite as discerning and deeply dimensioned as Cleaver's, from the other side of the tragic divide of race."[26]

Several reviews took note that King's friend and editor at *Harper's,* Willie Morris, had just published his own book on race matters, *Yazoo: Integration in a Deep-Southern Town.* But while Morris' account seemed optimistic, many reviewers pointed out that King's work was not. "Southern Discomfort" was the title of one review. In *The New York Review of Books,* King was faulted for his "great self-contempt—the worst possible defect in a man who is trying to evoke respect for the humanity of others." Even those who admired King's book conceded, "There is little that is loving or tender about *Confessions of a White Racist.*"[27]

One of the most treasured reactions King received came from Maya Angelou, who had published her memoir, *I Know Why the Caged Bird Sings*, in 1969. She wrote to him, "I've just finished 'Confessions of a White Racist' and I applaud you. I had read 'and other dirty stories' and sensed your perception, but had no idea of your startling courage. I applaud you, man. And pray you stay alive."[28]

Flush with the critical success, Viking dispatched King on a cross-country publicity tour that "we felt certain would culminate in spectacular sales." But the public's uneasiness with King's subject matter quickly made itself apparent. King recalled, "During television interviews conducted before live studio audiences, people began coughing, sighing and shifting in their seats the moment I started to talk of racism in America; after years of racial turmoil and upheavals, they simply didn't want to hear it anymore." King began checking the sales reports from Viking—they were dismal. He complained about the publisher's advertising strategy, but he knew the problem ran deeper than that. There was also the problem of the title, which was misleading to the book-buying public. As Walker Percy had noted in *The New York Times Book Review*, those unfamiliar with King's sympathetic perspective might think that the book was indeed the ranting of a notorious white racist.[29]

While King's title put off potential liberal readers, America's overt racists were angered. On his tour through Texas, King was accused several times of "betraying the southern cause." During a phone-in radio show in Dallas, one caller warned him, "Don't ride in any bubbletops. . . . Remember JFK." In Houston, a man who claimed to belong to the Ku Klux Klan made ominous threats. "Others called in such messages as 'State whether or not you are a Communist,' and 'You goddamned traitor, I hope you turn black.'"[30]

King's book tour continued to flounder all the way to his last stop in San Francisco. There, the publicity agent contracted by Viking openly mocked him. After seeing that a bookstore had plenty of copies of *White Racist* in stock, she chortled to the bookstore manager, "And I'll bet you haven't sold a goddam one!" *White Racist*, trumpeted with such fanfare and praised so highly by the critics, looked to be a complete commercial failure for Viking Press and its author. The book sold so poorly that when fellow writer Joe McGinnis spotted King in a Washington, D.C., restaurant, McGinnis told him, "You know, there's only one book I can think of offhand that's done worse than mine: Yours."[31]

But then something unusual happened to Larry L. King and *White Racist* on its way to oblivion. It was nominated for a National Book Award.

24.

OUTLAWS

By 1970, Bud Shrake, now thirty-nine years old, was at last ready to write his novel about Dallas in the years leading up to the Kennedy assassination. The book would be called *Strange Peaches*. The first editor to see a section of the manuscript was Herman Gollub at Harper's Press. Gollub had despised Shrake's Petronius satire the year before, but he liked what he saw of *Strange Peaches*, and he quickly signed Shrake to a contract. Shrake's previous novels had been written in odd moments between journalism assignments. For this novel, he wanted a large block of free time. He asked *Sports Illustrated* editor André Laguerre for a leave of absence. Laguerre agreed to four months, and in January 1971 Bud and Doatsy Shrake flew to London. "I went there to be free of distractions," Shrake said later. "Nobody in London cared about what I was doing and I wouldn't be interrupted."[1]

Before leaving for London, Shrake sent the movie screenplay he had crafted, *Dime Box*, to his agent. Soon after his arrival in England, Shrake received some welcome news. Daryl Zanuck, head of Twentieth Century Fox, purchased *Dime Box*, hired a producer, and put the film into production—all in one afternoon. "I was pleased," Shrake said later, "but not especially surprised. I assumed that was the way things worked. Only later did I realize, as someone else has said, that I had just leapt over a big pile of shit without knowing it."[2]

A few weeks later, producer Marvin Schwartz arrived in London. He congratulated Shrake on writing "the first hip Western" but also warned him that the studio would probably change the film's title. Shrake wrote to King, "I am quietly and powerfully struggling to keep the title, as I regard it as magical and wonderful and full of symbols." Shrake also told King that the screenwriting itself was easy, but "everybody connected with movies thinks he's a writer, and you got to fight thru the thickets of their minds constantly, and it may take more patience than I have to do this for a living."[3]

After Schwartz returned to the States, another visitor arrived. This was Peter Gent, who had come over unannounced. "I am on page 304 of the Dallas novel," Shrake wrote to King. But with Gent's arrival, "It ain't going to be easy to hit page 305." Shrake did not want to be slowed down because he was in the midst of a creative frenzy. From 1969 to 1971, he wrote two novels, two screenplays, and his *Harper's* article—all while continuing his employment at *Sports Illustrated* and cofounding Mad Dog, Inc., in Austin. His friends could never figure out Shrake's "uncanny ability to somehow manage to get his writing accomplished even when he was staying up all night, every night, with the rest of us."[4]

Shrake developed a seasonal pattern to help him remain productive. During the late summer and throughout the football season, he and Doatsy would rent an apartment in New York. Then they'd return to Austin to live for the rest of the year. "I really liked going back and forth," Shrake said. "I'd come to Austin and it was great at first, getting so laid back. People in Austin really weren't doing much of anything—a lot of them didn't even have jobs. But I'd get so lazy here that I had to go back to New York to recharge my batteries. In New York it was always work, work, accomplish, accomplish."[5]

Bud Shrake produced an exceptional amount of work while retaining his Mad Dog credentials, but Gary Cartwright was struggling. Aside from the *J. W. Coop* script, there was little that Cartwright could point to. He had published occasional articles in the *New York Times Magazine* and in *Life,* but regular work eluded him. He continued to write for *Sport,* even though he had famously kissed off sportswriting in "Confessions of a Washed-Up Sportswriter." For two years, he had been working on his second novel, *Great Issues Debate,* which was set at a newspaper much like *The Dallas Morning News.* But Cartwright had still not found his writing voice, and, as it turned out, his arrest and subsequent trial had affected him far more deeply than he had first realized.

"I was pretty paranoid and pretty bitter," Cartwright said later. "And that attitude caused me to fuck up the book I was writing. On the first one, everything came so easily. . . . With the second book, I thought I knew what I was doing, but it just wouldn't work. I finally ended up writing a book called *The Cave of Delicious Desire,* just spewing out my bitterness towards society in it." Much of Cartwright's anger in the novel was directed at Dallas, a city he described as having "the heart of a rodent."[6]

The Cave of Delicious Desire was about, as one Dallas newspaper columnist later reported, "a group of revolutionary kids living in a cave outside New Dynamo City [Dallas] who were conspiring to destroy the place." Cartwright knew that bats, "in reduced temperatures, go into a state of hibernation. The kids would cool the bats, arm them with incendiary bombs, and then warm them up and unleash them on New Dynamo City."[7]

The novel was a total failure. The publisher rejected it outright, and Cartwright's own writer friends were shocked by how awful it was. That realization dawned on him as he read passages aloud to them and they laughed uproariously. The problem was, the passages weren't intended to be funny.

Cartwright continued to chase magazine work, even accepting assignments from *Harper's* after Willie Morris was fired. That in itself did not cause tension between Cartwright and Larry L. King, but relations between the two freelance writers became less friendly as King's literary stature continued to bloom and Cartwright struggled just to survive. At times King was put off by Cartwright's barbed jibes, which seemed to him excessively mean-spirited.[8]

Cartwright's sense of family responsibilities also seemed to be adrift. When he and his ten-year-old son Mark visited New York, Cartwright, on his way to another engagement, dropped off the boy with a twenty dollar bill at Times Square. "My cab hadn't gone a block when the stupidity of what I'd done slapped me upside the head: I'd deposited my ten-year-old son in the geographical center of the evilest, most sinister square mile in America! I threw open the door and raced back into oncoming traffic, but by then he'd been swallowed up in the crowd. For the next few hours I was nearly sick with fear, imagining what had happened." Fortunately, the plucky boy did just fine.[9]

Back in Austin, Cartwright's friend Bill Wittliff was becoming an integral part of the Texas Institute of Letters, which had long been dominated by academics. Along with his wife, Sally, Wittliff had founded the Encino Press, which produced handsome editions of regionally oriented books and won numerous design awards. In just a few years, the Encino Press made a strong impact on Texas letters, particularly with its 1968 publication of Larry McMurtry's provocative collection of essays, In a Narrow Grave. As Wittliff became more involved in the TIL leadership, he envisioned wresting control away from the academic crowd and reshaping it as an organization for working writers. In 1971 he encouraged Gary Cartwright to apply for the TIL's Dobie Paisano Fellowship, which awarded writers a modest stipend and a six-month stay on the old Dobie ranch southwest of Austin.

In his application for the fellowship, Cartwright called himself "a serious, sworn, full-time, starving writer, born in Texas, living in Texas, and writing about Texas. I have published one novel (copy enclosed), one screenplay and numerous magazine articles, and my shelves sag with other manuscripts—including a finished novel— which haven't been published because they are not good enough. I have known some success and a lot of failure, and I am blithely ignorant of other forms of work. I am at the moment embarrassingly destitute, in great need of the physical and spiritual benefits of this fellowship. I need to lean against Dobie's rock."[10]

Cartwright suggested that he would use his time at the ranch to do a "Villains of the Southwest" book, a series of character studies done in the New Journalism style. He concluded, "Maybe I will discover something about the nature of villainy, maybe not. But I ask you to consider my case. Otherwise, I may have to rob a bank, thus becoming the subject rather than the author of this concept."[11]

***

When Billy Lee Brammer returned to Dallas from Bowling Green, Jay Milner maneuvered to get him back on the SMU faculty for another shot at teaching. But as the spring 1971 semester opened, it became evident that, despite his promises, Brammer's interests lay elsewhere. He resumed his practice of missing classes, and his rental house near the SMU campus became a popular hangout for hippie students. Drugs were in plentiful supply.

Brammer's increasing absentmindedness became a source of concern and, occasionally, amusement to his friends. Soon after the semester began, a local filmmaker made plans to show his new documentary at Brammer's house. Brammer was very interested, because the subject was something he was intimately familiar with—Ken Kesey and the Merry Pranksters.

On the evening of the screening, the filmmaker set up a screen and projector in Brammer's living room, and people began filtering in. Soon the house was packed. But Brammer was nowhere to be seen. The movie started without him. After a while, Brammer appeared, wondering "who the hell was showing movies in his living room." As it turned out, Brammer had not remembered agreeing to host the film. As the evening wore on, it became apparent that Brammer never even realized that it was the Kesey documentary playing in his living room.[12]

A few weeks later, on February 23, 1971, Willie Morris' *Harper's* was breaking up, and Bud Shrake was in London working on his new novel. In Dallas, police officers raided forty-one-year-old Billy Lee Brammer's house. Larry L. King, who learned of the news from Jay Milner, sent word to Shrake that "one B. Brammer was busted in the company of exotic plants and spices, syringes, et al. He has not yet gone before a grand jury, so the tale is not yet public knowledge."[13]

Hard jail time was often mandatory for possession of drugs, yet Brammer seemed oblivious to the seriousness of the charges against him. His friends, led by Larry L. King, had raised money to free him on bail. Lawyer Warren Burnett, who had successfully defended Gary Cartwright, was in Dallas and learned of Brammer's situation. He called to offer his legal services, but Brammer responded that "he was sorry but he had not been given enough notice and had big plans that night and could not see him. [Burnett] was alternately wryly amused and properly horrified."[14]

As Brammer's friends raised money for his defense fund, Brammer gleefully accepted their donations. Soon the contributors began worrying about how the money was being spent. After noting that Brammer had recently received $500 from Shrake and another $500 from Dallas banker David Simmons, Jay Milner reported to King, "Billie has found him a thing nearly as lucrative as *Gay Place*—nobody wants the little bastard to have to go to jail, of course, so. . . ."[15]

Brammer's career as an instructor at SMU was over, and he began drifting while awaiting his court date. After Bud Shrake returned to Texas, he reported to Jay Milner that "Billy Lee stayed at our house in Austin for a while before driving off in the direction of San Francisco. Information about his trial was a little vague. So was he." Eventually, represented by a Dallas attorney, Brammer's charges were reduced to a single count of marijuana possession. In November he agreed to plead guilty in exchange for five years probation.[16]

Unlike Gary Cartwright's high-profile trial, no news of Brammer's legal troubles appeared in newspapers. Though his writer friends had contributed money, none of them was present when Brammer's probation was handed down in court. Instead, they had gone to Durango, Mexico, to help make Bud Shrake's film.

The studio had big expectations for *Kid Blue*, as Shrake's *Dime Box* had been retitled. Dennis Hopper, who had become a huge star in the wake of 1969's *Easy Rider*, was hired to play the lead. Hopper's stardom had quickly gone to his head, and his ranting ego trips became excessive, even by Hollywood standards. Just before filming on *Kid Blue* began, Hopper's long-awaited follow-up to *Easy Rider*, *The*

Last Movie, flopped spectacularly. Many in Hollywood cheered the failure.

The producer, Marvin Schwartz, had already been inducted into Mad Dog, Inc. He invited Shrake, Cartwright, Peter Gent, and their families to Durango for the filming. Shrake was slated for a small role in the film as the town drunk. Everyone else would appear as extras. Shrake, who had earlier arranged for a leave of absence from *Sports Illustrated* to work on his Dallas novel, asked André Laguerre for another three months off. Laguerre, sighing, agreed, though Shrake wondered if he would still have a job when he returned.

The Mad Dog convoy from Texas consisted of a Winnebago driven by Pete Gent and a van driven by Shrake. Each was emblazoned with signs reading "Mad Dog Production Company." Shrake, Gent, and Cartwright all had big plans for Durango. Shrake and Cartwright had been hired by Schwartz to work on a new screenplay. Peter Gent, much to his friends' astonishment, had begun writing his own book, which would be about his experiences as a Dallas Cowboy. The Mad Dogs also planned to make their own movie while *Kid Blue* was being filmed. Shrake and Gent each brought Super 8 cameras for the purpose.

Durango represented the peak of Mad Dog debauchery. As Gary Cartwright's memorable account in *Heartwise Guy* attests, "More than two dozen hallucinogenic plants grow wild in the states of Chihuahua and Torreón, and most of them appeared at one time or another in the Mad Dog Winnebago." Cartwright describes pureed mushrooms served on crackers, vanilla-flavored LSD taken by the spoonful, and "two tanks of nitrous oxide [ordered] from Mexico City."[17]

Dennis Hopper quickly caught on to the spirit of Mad Dog and became an official member. His egotism still ran rampant at times, but Cartwright proved to be the perfect antidote. One night when Hopper wouldn't stop talking, Cartwright said, "Goddammit, I'm not going to stand around here while you dominate the conversation with a bunch of pure bullshit." Cartwright walked away, and Hopper came after him, ordering him to stay. "So Jap pushed him against the wall and got nose to nose and said, lissen, you prick, writers are more important than actors and I'm a better writer than you are an actor, so don't pull that star shit on me!" After Cartwright left, Hopper began crying a bit, "a little strung out anyhow by then. He asked Pete [Gent] to walk around with him and cried and said, goddam I really like Jap."[18]

In addition to Hopper, *Kid Blue* featured Ben Johnson, Peter Boyle, Warren Oates, and Howard Hesseman. Johnson remained straight, but the other actors became full-fledged Mad Dogs. Before long, the Mad Dog mentality began taking over the entire production. Plans were made to disrupt the filming by restaging the action without telling the director or camera operators. As Gary Cartwright recalled, "The longer we were in Durango, the crazier it got—until there was virtually no separation between the movie that Schwarz was producing and the one we were living."[19]

Gary Cartwright had a small role as a congressional assistant, and he prepared for the filming by joining Shrake, Gent, and Warren Oates in the Winnebago. He helped himself to some crushed-up Dexedrine flambéed in brandy, followed by spoonfuls of the vanilla-flavored LSD. By the time Cartwright was due for his first appearance on camera, he was babbling "about needing to catch a train for Cleveland." Howard Hesseman "looked at me, then at Shrake and Gent, who were filming each other from the underside of a wagon, understanding, perhaps for the first time, the true and mean depths of Mad Dog." Later, Cartwright abandoned most of his clothing and retreated to a nearby hill to drink beer. There, he was "sweating like a pig, and under the impression that I was Charles Dickens and this was London during a siege of the black plague." In the meantime, his absence threatened a "scene that had already cost the production company thousands of dollars."[20]

Not everyone enjoyed the antics. Doatsy Shrake in particular had seen enough. She left Durango and returned to Austin alone. Though the Shrakes would remain married a few more years, Cartwright observed later that this was when their "marriage began to fall apart."[21]

Despite the madness, real work was accomplished in Durango. Shrake and Cartwright completed most of their script, and Peter Gent spent much of his time in Durango writing furiously. "He'd take speed and smoke joints and turn out fifty pages a day," Cartwright remembered. "He was writing prolifically, like a demon. "I had no idea then that it would even get published, much less do so well. But I did know that he would finish it. He was very determined." One day a gust of wind caught Gent's papers and scattered them across the compound. Cartwright helped Gent gather them, and as he did so he noticed that none of the pages had been numbered. "That turned out to be the only literary advice I ever gave him," Cartwright later said. "I told him, 'Pete, be sure to number your pages.'"[22]

25.

HACK

OBSERVATIONS

AND LITERARY

FEUDS

The National Book Award nomination for Larry L. King's *Confessions of a White Racist* revived the book's commercial prospects, and it went through several paperback printings. *White Racist* also became a standard text in the new "black studies" courses cropping up on college campuses. While King basked in his critical acclaim and modest sales success, the fact remained that his other writing projects were in deep trouble. He abandoned his *Lost Places* book in favor of a novel called *Growing Old.* Viking, which had already given him an advance for *Lost Places*, agreed to accept the novel instead. The story began well but quickly lost momentum. King described it to Billy Lee Brammer as a "plagued novel" involving "three generations of Texans who bear a strange likeness to the King family, they having lots of clod-hoppers and Baptist fanatics and abortions and divorcements and red necks in their midst. I have thought on this novel a whole lot and have claimed in weak moments to have wrote much of it, but I ain't really wrote much."[1]

King also got sidetracked when he agreed to ghost write, for a decent sum and a percentage of the sales, the "autobiography" of Congressman Paul McCloskey, an antiwar Republican who planned to challenge President Nixon for the 1972 presidential nomination. McCloskey's book was published the same day that Nixon trounced him in the New Hampshire primary. The congressman immediately withdrew from the race, giving "his book a shelf life of about forty-five minutes." King recalled that he spent the next day getting "solitary drunk while thinking dark thoughts about sinking to the level of hack work as a book doctor. What had happened to my grand, innocent dreams of producing memorable literature?"[2]

He would not have to wait long to find out. The reading public was still awaiting the definitive biography of Lyndon B. Johnson. Billy Lee Brammer had given up, and no one else had stepped forward. King's friend and former *Harper's* colleague, David Halberstam, suggested to his own publisher, Random House, that King was the perfect person to write Johnson's biography. Random House agreed and offered King an $80,000 advance to write it. By now, King was wise to the ways of the publishing world. He waited for Sterling Lord to approach Viking, which, in turn, offered King $100,000 for the same book.[3]

A critical darling, National Book Award nominee, recipient of a Harvard Nieman Fellowship, and now contracted to write a "big book," King was leaving Texas behind to join the top ranks of American writers. In 1971 he was inducted into PEN, the nation's leading organization for writers. While King earned national praise and attention, he felt somewhat let down by the folks back in Texas. The Texas Institute of Letters had pointedly ignored *Confessions of a White Racist*, which was not even a finalist for any of the state literary awards. On King's publicity tour through Texas in 1971, he was angry to learn that the *Houston Chronicle* titled its story on him, "A Hick from West Texas." The *Texas Observer*, too, had carried only lukewarm praise for *White Racist*. In its pages, Steve Barthelme viewed Larry L. King's "facile insights" as only "occasionally enlightening." In contrast to others who had lauded King as a "Texas Mark Twain," Barthelme saw only "single-framed humor [which] encourage a negative judgment." In the same review, Barthelme also mocked *Harper's* for running Bud Shrake's essay "heroically describing driving through Texas with long hair." Though Barthelme eventually admitted that *White Racist* had merit, the review's petulant tone was difficult to ignore.[4]

The *Texas Observer*, while still a fierce and eloquent advocate for progressive politics, proved inadequate to the challenge of addressing the state's burgeoning cultural arts. Assigning an amateur historian to slash Bud Shrake's *Blessed McGill* for four small errors of fact was not only inept, it was embarrassing to the *Observer*'s arts coverage. In the 1960s, the *Observer* had boasted a young, thoroughly talented critic named Dave Hickey. The insular world of Texas letters has always needed challenging criticism, and for a few years Dave Hickey provided it in the pages of the *Observer*. But when Hickey moved on, the *Observer*'s reviews increasingly fell to those who expressed only contempt for writers from Texas.

Part of the problem was a standard affliction among hack reviewers —jealousy at the success of others. That was exacerbated by the fact that the *Observer*'s new generation of reviewers, Steve Barthelme and Roxy Gordon, were frustrated writers who had yet to publish their own books. But a deeper rage also fueled the negative tone. A political chasm had arisen with the emergence of the "New Left" in the sixties. The New Left's student leaders wanted a revolution, not reform. The older generation of "liberals" was derided as sellouts, and the *Observer*'s young critics were eager to score political points against older writers like King, Shrake, Cartwright, and Larry McMurtry. Much of the negativity, Larry L. King believed, also emanated from publisher Ronnie Dugger, who had never forgotten how Billy Lee Brammer had betrayed the *Observer*'s cause by lampooning liberals in *The Gay Place*.

In 1971, Dugger confirmed this sense of unease when he published an essay on Texas writers in the *Observer*. Dugger expressed admiration for pastoralists such as John Graves, whom he complimented on his "gentle, granitic temperament." But Dugger was condescending toward the younger generation. Of Larry McMurtry's work, he wrote, "I find something tiresome in it, something linear, really shapeless." He also reminded readers that Brammer had skewered liberals in *The Gay Place* and had made Lyndon Johnson only colorful, instead of true. Dugger dismissed Cartwright, ignored Larry L. King entirely, and of Bud Shrake he wrote, "What [he has] made is there to read, but not to love." Dugger was not among those impressed by *Blessed McGill*. Shrake's major failing, according to

Dugger, was that he "lacked the confidence of the universal artist . . . . Real confidence takes more time than most of us admit."[5]

In 1971, Larry McMurtry became the *Observer*'s main target. McMurtry had emerged as one of Texas' most highly regarded writers in the 1960s, but national recognition largely eluded him, and he took to wearing a T-shirt that contained an ironic comment on his status. It read, "Minor Regional Novelist." In 1971 he published *Moving On*, his first novel since *The Last Picture Show*. While its critical reception was generally positive, the *Texas Observer* had a different view. Steve Barthelme, in a blistering review that spilled across several pages, issued the *Observer*'s most ferocious attack to date. "*Moving On*," Barthelme warned, "is quite simply ugly and dull and occasionally, false." Barthelme jabbed repeatedly at McMurtry for offenses more imagined than real—and almost all of them trivial in the wake of a 794-page novel. Twice, Barthelme condemned McMurtry for representing the graduate students in the novel as too brilliant. Barthelme also focused on a specific sentence: "he poked Davey in the ribs with one finger, and Davey giggled and writhed in his high chair." Barthelme complained, "The number of fingers is irrelevant. It tends to locate interest in the number of fingers and what the other nine fingers are doing, neither of which is ever disclosed."[6]

Larry McMurtry responded in print to Barthelme's review, which he called "a delightful and bracing surprise. To my knowledge, nothing of comparable brashness has occurred on the Texas literary scene since a young turk of my acquaintance purposely stepped on [an older writer's] toe at a cocktail party, eight or so years ago." McMurtry continued:

> I'm aware, of course, that it's a grave breach of taste to reply to hostile critics, but I just can't resist. I've been pining for years for a hostile critic to reply to. . . . If we could develop a taste for literary controversy we might someday even develop a literature. The literary life in Texas is as polite as Sunday school—and about as passionless. Surely a passion for letters ought to engender the same things other passions

engender: malice, jealousy, wit, attacks, insult. The English have it. The New Yorkers have it. Now that I've finally got me a hostile critic, I mean to make the most of him.[7]

From there McMurtry wrote a rollicking admission of his failures. Of Barthelme's charge that the female protagonist is "boring," McMurtry responded, "Bored women are God's gift to novelists—about His only gift, I might add. . . . I like writing about them and don't intend to stop. Mr. Barthelme will just have to read somebody else." In response to the charge that he had been unnecessarily exact in describing a character poking Davey with one finger, McMurtry writes, "Such nit-picking is almost sublime. Next time I'll have the young man poke the kid with a fork."[8]

By the time Barthelme's attack appeared, Larry McMurtry was no longer living in Texas. He had moved to Washington, D.C., and opened a bookstore not far from Larry L. King's apartment. The two expatriate Texas writers soon became friends. They often had lunch together, and as Larry L. King wrote to Billy Lee Brammer, "We drive down to rural Virginia and eat at a place where you can get hot biscuits and red-eye gravy and listen to Ernest Tubb on the juke box and play like you are back home again. . . . He is one of the most enjoyable persons I ever been around not to drink much whiskey or smoke no dope." But King found the relationship difficult to extend to others in the circle. When he learned that Dan Jenkins was coming to town, he suggested that Jenkins stop in and introduce himself to McMurtry. Jenkins did so but was offended by what he saw as McMurtry's condescending air. He and McMurtry would not become friends.[9]

* * *

Undoubtedly Larry McMurtry was somewhat cool to Dan Jenkins because Jenkins was a loud, breezy, self-confident sportswriter. But Jenkins was also on his way to becoming a real author. In 1966 his series for *Sports Illustrated* on the best eighteen golf holes in America was published in book form by Delacorte. In 1970, a collection of his golf writing, *The Dogged Victims of Inexorable Fate,* was published by Little, Brown. In October of that that same year Jenkins published *Saturday's America,* a collection of his articles about college football. Larry L. King was among the reviewers who praised Jenkins' book. King called his friend "perhaps the best sportswriter in America," and added, "There is social commentary in Jenkins' work, delightful airings of the latest cultural absurdities, some of the funniest one-liners since Mel Brooks or Woody Allen sat down to tickle their typewriters."[10]

The praise helped solidify the friendship between Jenkins and King, and with Bud Shrake spending much of the year in Austin, Jenkins and King became closer. During King's visits to New York, he and Jenkins often shared tables at Elaine's, and they enjoyed trading stories about Elaine's growing snobbishness.[11]

As King involved himself in the East Coast literary scene, he retained a high value on his friendships with the other Texas writers. "There is so much jealousy and malice in this goddamn business. That's one of the reasons it was nice to have friends you could count on." As King's stature rose, he became involved in several literary feuds, some of which were capped by savage fistfights. At a *Playboy* writers convention in Chicago, he and James Dickey were drinking together at the hotel bar when they clashed in what King later described as "mutual insufficient praise." The two men were separated by others before the violence got out of hand. But a short time later King walked into a room where Dickey was beating up a terrified Michael Crichton. "Dickey was a bully," King said. "So I went up and put a chokehold on him and brought him down to the floor and held him there until the *Playboy* people came."[12]

King's friendship with William Styron evaporated after King wrote unsparingly of a negative experience Styron had while visiting King at Harvard. King also wrote about Norman Mailer's visit to campus, and he expected that Mailer would also break off their relationship, since Mailer had refused to cooperate with King's earlier desire to write a profile of him. Instead, Mailer wrote to King, "maybe I'm getting modest in my old age but I sure did like your two pieces in the

Crimson. I don't know about Styron but you're all too accurate about me. Anyway it made me miss you, you old prick."[13]

The breakup of Willie Morris' *Harper's* resulted in King's longest-running literary feud, which is now entering its fourth decade. When the *Harper's* staff walked out, the one person who remained behind was Lewis Lapham, who had earlier sworn fealty to the group. Lapham, as it turned out, saw an opportunity to become editor by siding with the ownership. He continues as *Harper's* editor to this day. But Lapham's former colleagues consider him a traitor, and public encounters between them have been unpleasant. David Halberstam cursed Lapham and forbade him ever to speak to him again. King's own confrontations with Lapham have taken a more physical turn. One evening Lapham came into Elaine's and tried to join a table where King was sitting. "I told him, 'Don't sit there, you cocksucker,'" King recalled. When Lapham protested, King raised up from his seat and slapped the man across the cheek. "I didn't want to punch him," King said. "He's not worth fighting. He's a sissy." From then on, King made it a point to slap Lapham every time they met in public.[14]

One of King's most unfortunate fallings-out occurred with Willie Morris. Both men were experiencing a great amount of emotional pain at the time. Morris had largely retreated from the world after losing his wife, family, and his prized editorship at *Harper's*. He seldom communicated with his old friends. Meanwhile, Larry King's wife, Rosemarie, continued to deteriorate from the cancer that ravaged her body. King recalled that by January 1972, her "pain was such that her doctors taught me to shoot her with morphine, every four hours, around the clock." King stopped writing. "Life became a blur of cat-naps, cries in the dark, those accursed morphine shots. . . . In that hard time I grew a new appreciation for the true meaning of the word 'misery.'" Rosemarie was eventually hospitalized, and twice in April her doctors thought she was dying. That month the announcement came that her husband's book had been nominated for a National Book Award, and it seemed to revive her spirits. She told King, "I'm going to those awards ceremonies in New York." But making the trip was impossible, and by May she was down to sixty-four pounds.[15]

As King prepared for the ceremony, he assessed his potential for winning. A three-judge panel had been assembled to make the final decisions, and as luck would have it, one of the panelists was Digby Diehl, a friend of King's who had already effusively praised *White Racist* in print. Another nominee was *The Whole Earth Catalog,* which was not really a book but rather a compendium of articles and products aimed at the counterculture. Few took it seriously, and one of the judges, in fact, had resigned in protest at the catalog's inclusion. Yet as it turned out, *The Whole Earth Catalog* became the surprise winner of the 1972 National Book Award, creating a mini-controversy within literary circles. King said later, "I don't mind losing, but to the goddamn *Yellow Pages?*" For a writer who had claimed that just being nominated was honor enough, King didn't realize until later "how strongly my heart had counted on winning."[16]

***

After the ceremony King returned to Washington, D.C. He visited Rosemarie in the hospital every day, often bringing their friend, writer Barbara Howar, who had earlier been dating Willie Morris. Rosemarie, who knew that she was dying, told a friend, "Barbara is obviously waiting around for Lar, and I guess he could do a lot worse." By June, it was clear that Rosie was down to her last few days. King was there on June 8 when she woke up from sedation and whispered to him before turning her head and dying.[17]

Willie Morris came out of seclusion to attend Rosemarie's funeral in Washington. He met King and the two went out drinking the night before the funeral. Late in the evening, as they walked through D.C.'s Georgetown district, Morris suddenly realized that King and Barbara Howar had become close. "Though Willie was the one who t h r e w Barbara over, he was made furious somehow," King said. "I didn't want to have a fight the night before my wife's funeral over another woman, but I had to, and I whipped his ass pretty good. He's too good a fellow to be a good fighter." The angry confrontation occurred, "right in front of Jackie Kennedy's momma's house." King's friend

Warren Burnett, witnessing the fight, observed, "King, you and Willie Morris managed to bring the cultures of Odessa and Yazoo City to the very heart of Georgetown."[18]

26.

REDNECK

HIPPIES

Back in Austin, the city's mix of hippie and cowboy cultures continued to swell under the aegis of the Armadillo World Headquarters. In 1971, two prominent musicians moved to Austin, remaking themselves in the image of their newly adopted hometown.

Jerry Jeff Walker had long appreciated the warm reception Austin audiences gave him, and he had developed several local friendships. One was with Hondo Crouch, the Hill Country raconteur who managed to purchase his own town in 1971—Luckenbach, Texas. As Walker grew increasingly tired of his drifting way of life, he decided to buy a home in Austin.

That same year, Willie Nelson left Nashville, where he had lived since the late 1950s. Willie had become a successful songwriter, and several country stars had scored big hits with his songs, most notably Patsy Cline's rendition of "Crazy." Willie longed to perform on his own, but an industry town like Nashville specialized in a division of labor, and few executives saw commercial promise in Nelson's distinctive vocal phrasings and understated style. He was earning $100,000 annually from songwriting royalties, but his own albums didn't sell well. "In Nashville, I was looked upon as a loser singer. They wouldn't let me record with my own band. They would cover me up with horns and strings. It was depressing."[1]

After signing a new recording contract that offered him more creative control, Willie returned to Texas, where he felt he could better develop a fan base. He originally planned to move to Houston and even put a deposit down on an apartment in the city. But he kept hearing about Austin. One friend, University of Texas football coach Darrell Royal, advised him that "Austin had a lot of people like me."[2]

Once Willie arrived in Austin, Darrell Royal made it a point to get him and Bud Shrake together. "We hit it off immediately," Shrake said, "and we hung out together quite a bit." One place Shrake made sure Willie visited was the Armadillo World Headquarters. Willie still had short hair and was clean-shaven. But he liked what he saw. "Rednecks and hippies who had thought they were natural enemies began mixing at the Armadillo without too much bloodshed. . . . Pretty soon you saw a long-hair cowboy wearing hippie beads and a bronc rider's belt, and you were seeing a new type of person."[3]

Willie understood what to do. "Being a natural leader, I saw which direction this movement was going and threw myself in front of it."[4]

***

Meanwhile, *J. W. Coop* was on the verge of being released by United Artists, and Shrake and Cartwright's case against Cliff Robertson had taken some strange twists on the road to justice. Robertson had been so unnerved by his experiences with the pair that he claimed to his lawyer "that he had gotten caught up in a Manson-type gang." Part of the problem, undoubtedly, was the communiqué Robertson's lawyer received from Bud Shrake on Mad Dog, Inc., stationery. "The letter chastised Robertson for his perceived misdealings with Shrake and Cartwright, and attached to it was a newspaper clipping bearing the screaming headline: 'Police Believe Frozen Dog Weapon in Beating Death.' To ensure the message was clear, a scrawled warning read, 'Mad Dog on Prowl.'"[5]

Robertson, in response to questions from the press about the lawsuit, portrayed Shrake and Cartwright as two sinister redneck con men, bolstering his argument by pointing out Cartwright's arrest for marijuana. "He said something about Cartwright being a convict on *The Tonight Show,*" Shrake recalled. "He described Jap as a man who had just stepped out of the shadow of the prison walls. It was ridiculous. We should have sued him for libel, but instead we just wanted credit for our writing."[6]

The Screenwriters Guild had ruled that Shrake and Cartwright should receive writing credit along with Robertson. As a result, a "settlement offer was made that seemed to satisfy the contract claim," attorney David Richards later wrote. "[B]ut my guys were having none of it." A lawsuit was filed against Robertson in Travis County. "The Mad Dog view," Richards recalled, "was that Robertson would be too afraid to show his face in Austin again, and at the last minute a big settlement offer would appear."[7]

Instead, Cliff Robertson came to court fully prepared to defend himself. "Dressed in a bush jacket, he looked every bit the movie idol." In contrast, Richards' own clients "looked like street people, with coats and ties that didn't fit and a distinct aura of seediness. The jury panel embodied middle-class Austin—no freaks and no allies." As the trial opened, Shrake began to realize how difficult it would be to make a case against a popular star. "Robertson had been in that movie *Charly* a couple years earlier. So one of the first things a juror says when seeing Robertson in the courtroom is 'Love you, Charly.' Then Cliff and the judge got to talking about movies together. I couldn't believe it."[8]

A commotion interrupted the proceedings, and David Richards "noticed the jurors looking with some fascination toward the gallery. Larry L. King had walked in with two or three young chicks in miniskirts and had plopped down in the first row. King, by now a well-known writer, had come to lend moral support to our duo; he was in a full beard and flamboyant costume. At the break, King and the dolls surrounded and hugged our clients as the jurors filed by open-mouthed. What little rapport we might have had with the jury dissolved at that moment."[9]

After the conclusion of the first day of testimony, Richards told Shrake and Cartwright that the trial would resume the next morning at 8:00. "The look on their faces was utter disbelief. It apparently had never occurred to them that they might have to sit there and behave for several days." A short time later, the pair agreed to accept Robertson's original settlement offer, with the added proviso that neither of them could ever write anything about their relationship with him. "Sure, we each got a share of the screenwriting credit, along with Cliff," Shrake said later. "And the movie poster did have me and Jap's names on it. But our names were printed in yellow—against a field of sunflowers."[10]

***

After his conviction in Dallas, Billy Lee Brammer moved back to Austin. He fell back in with his old comrades but made little pretense about writing. Instead, satisfying his drug addiction became his primary focus, and he became increasingly known as "a legendary junkie, a man who knew the *Physicians Desk Reference* almost by rote, who could seemingly identify every pill ever minted and recount its effects." Jay Milner recalled that Brammer was "far ahead of everyone else I knew. . . . Not the protests and demonstrations, but the experimentation with hallucinogens." Once, the nearsighted Brammer accidentally took his dog's epilepsy medicine. This inspired further stories. Al Reinert later wrote in *Texas Monthly*, "He even copped [his dog's] pills and kept refilling her prescription for three years until she finally died."[11]

While Brammer's writing career seemed to be reaching a dead end, Gary Cartwright received some very welcome news. His application to become a Dobie Paisano fellow was approved, and he and Mary Jo moved to the Dobie ranch southwest of Austin in the spring of 1972. They were joined for much of the six-month stay by Pete and Jody Gent, and the ranch became the new home base for Mad Dog partying. Jay Milner, in *Confessions of a Maddog*, describes a ranch "packed with writers, musicians, several fairly well-known actors . . . various strays, and no telling who all. The soiree went on for several days and nights."[12]

During one of the parties, Bud Shrake and movie producer Marvin Schwartz began to pay close attention to Billy Lee Brammer's behavior. They "furtively followed [him] around and every time he struck up a conversation, they would put a stop watch on him to time how long it would take him to hit up whoever he was chatting with for [speed] pills. Best I recall, the longest interval they noted was twenty-three seconds."[13]

As the Armadillo World Headquarters celebrated its second anniversary on August 7, 1972, many in Austin were amazed that the club was still in operation. Income was meager, and the staff often went unpaid during lean stretches. An ever-present concern was the landlord, who might pull the plug if civic worries about the hippie-oriented joint grew too vocal. But in other ways, the Armadillo seemed to be leading a charmed existence. Even the Austin police, who were as hostile toward hippies as any other police department in Texas, seemed to slacken up. Despite the thick haze of marijuana smoke hanging in the air, the club was largely left alone. "I never figured out how we avoided getting busted," Eddie Wilson later said. "I guess we were just too big. The cops would have had to drop a huge net over the whole place with helicopters."[14]

The week after the Armadillo's second anniversary party, Willie Nelson played his first-ever concert there. It was a rousing success. Soon, Willie began reaching a crossover market, booking shows at college campuses in addition to the usual honky-tonks. "A new audience was opening up for me," he said. "I phoned Waylon [Jennings] in Nashville and told him he ought to come play the Armadillo. Waylon walked into that big hall and saw all those redneck hippies boogying to the opening act, Commander Cody, and he turned to me and said, 'What the shit have you got me into, Willie?'"[15]

* * *

As Gary Cartwright's stay at Dobie's Paisano Ranch drew to a close, he realized that he had done very little writing. "I did publish a piece in an underground magazine, *Rip-Off Review,* under the name M. D. Shafter," he said. But other than that, there was little to show for the six months. His career as a freelance writer was still adrift. He was simply too far away from the New York editors to cultivate many of the necessary contacts, and of course the constant revelry trimmed back the amount of work he was able to accomplish.

In the summer of 1972, Cartwright received a visit from an intense twenty-five-year-old lawyer named Michael Levy, who was touring the state and speaking to writers and editors. Levy had recently interned with *Philadelphia* magazine and saw great potential in Texas for an upscale publication along the lines of city magazines like *Philadelphia* and Clay Felker's heralded *New York*. Texas' newspapers had done little to keep up with the growing professional class in the state, and Levy predicted that Texas could support an upscale, literate, city-type magazine. The working name was *Texas Cities*. "I told him it was a great idea," Cartwright said later. "But that it was also doomed to fail." Levy also visited Bud Shrake. "I thought he was nuts and told him it didn't have a chance," Shrake said. Shrake turned down a request to write for the magazine but did recommend that Levy hire Billy Lee Brammer as the editor.[16]

Levy interviewed some three hundred potential editors before choosing William Broyles Jr., a twenty-seven-year-old Vietnam veteran and a former Rhodes Scholar with almost no experience in journalism. "I hired him on gut instinct," Levy said later, "because of his knowledge of the language and ability to handle people."[17] Broyles had studied creative writing at Rice University under Larry McMurtry. Broyles promptly hired Gregory Curtis, his old college roommate, also a student of McMurtry's, as his assistant. Broyles' second hire was Billy Lee Brammer, whom he brought aboard as an associate editor.

Texas Cities, which was renamed *Texas Monthly*, established its home base in Austin. Broyles invited Cartwright to the Scholz Garten to discuss possible writing assignments. Cartwright was intrigued— until he learned how little the magazine would pay—just $250 for a feature-length story. National magazines paid five times as much. Larry L. King often received close to ten times as much for his work. After some discussion, the offer was increased to $400.[18] The cost of living in Austin was still low, and, after some hesitation, thirty-eight-year-old Gary Cartwright accepted his first assignment. His story would run in *Texas Monthly*'s first issue, scheduled for publication in January 1973.

* * *

Soon after the Mad Dogs returned from Durango, Peter Gent completed the first draft of his autobiographical novel about the Dallas Cowboys. He brought the hefty, messy manuscript to his friend Bud Shrake. "It sat on the floor in the corner of my office for a long time," Shrake said later. "None of us had any inkling that Pete was capable of writing a real novel. I know it was rude to not look at his manuscript for so long, but I wasn't eager to get to it."[19]

After several weeks, Shrake finally picked up Gent's manuscript. It was difficult reading, as there was little punctuation or even form to the narrative. But Gent's account was compelling, and it was surprisingly well told. Shrake realized that his friend was on to something. He and Gent got together and went over the manuscript as Shrake offered advice. "My main contribution, other than explaining punctuation to him, was suggesting how he could structure the story. I told him it might work to break it down into one week—the week between games. Then he took it away and that's what he did." From there, Gent rewrote furiously, with his wife Jody retyping for him. Shrake put Gent in touch with his agent, Sterling Lord, who was as impressed as Shrake had been. Within three weeks, Lord sold the book to William Morrow, Inc. Gent received a large advance, and the novel, titled *North Dallas Forty,* was scheduled for release in 1973.[20]

27.

STRANGE

PEACHES

Bud Shrake's Dallas novel, a full-throttle roar through the months leading up to the Kennedy assassination, was published in May 1972. The dust jacket describes *Strange Peaches* as "a novel about the making of a modern outlaw," and the cover portrays a peach—with a marijuana plant rising from the stem. The novel is set in the early 1960s and opens as John Lee Wallace, the long-haired star of the hit TV series *Six Guns Across Texas*, returns to Dallas. On the flight home, John Lee sits beside a former colonel who has become a lobbyist. The colonel rants about Kennedy "giving this country away to the devil," and he growls that Cuban leader Fidel Castro should be shot for nationalizing prized property once held by Dallas millionaires. Communist threats to U.S. order and prosperity are popping up everywhere, the colonel says, even in Vietnam, where, "little yellow bald-headed Buddhist sons of bitches, they kneel down in public and burn theirselfs up with gasoline. What the hell kind of a way is that to act?" The man finally begins to relax as the plane lands. He turns to John Lee and smiles. "Dallas," he says. "My favorite city."[1]

John Lee, modeled on Shrake, moves into an apartment with his best friend, Buster Gregory, modeled on Gary Cartwright. Together, the two set out to make an uncompromising documentary that will show what Texas is *really* like. Along the way, their lives intersect with an array of Dallas figures—prankstering millionaires, rabid right-wing businessmen, an aged billionaire based on H. L. Hunt, cheap hoods, Jack Ruby, and "Jingo"—the star stripper at Ruby's nightclub.

Shrake's publisher had little confidence in the book. His original editor, Herman Gollob, had moved on to a new publisher and did not offer to take Shrake's novel with him. Instead, *Strange Peaches* was turned over to a new editor, Larry Freundlich, who not only hated Shrake's title, he also "disliked the book, which is a profound disadvantage."[2] *Strange Peaches* was released with little fanfare or publicity. Unlike his friend Larry L. King, Bud Shrake went on no promotional tour. Little advertising was expended on the novel, not even in core markets such as Texas.

Still, reviews of *Strange Peaches* crept into national publications. *The New York Times* wrote, "this big novel, two parts anger to one part humor, is fast and surefire. And Edwin Shrake's narrative technique has been amply dosed with Dexedrine. There's not an ounce of fat on it." *Time* magazine hailed Shrake's "amphetamine apocalypse" that "captures superbly the feeling of combustible chaos that climaxed in the Kennedy assassination." *Book World* wrote that Shrake "records scene after memorable scene, some touched with manic humor, all hurtling towards the fateful explosion. . . . there is not a dull page, not even a dull paragraph, in this book." A reviewer for United Press International called *Strange Peaches* "one of the best-written American novels since World War II."[3]

But the "good reviews didn't mean shit to *Harper's* or Freundlich," Shrake said.[4] The publisher refused to purchase advertising to capitalize on the book's critical support. And back in Texas, Bud Shrake found an entirely different reception for his book.

Most newspapers simply ignored Shrake's book. No mention ever appeared in the anemic book sections of the *Houston Post* and the *San Antonio Express*. Those that did review the novel had little kind to say. In the *Houston Chronicle*, the headline read, "A Sports Writer Takes a Crack at Politics." In Austin, the *American-Statesman* asked, "Is This Texas?" and concluded that Shrake's "puzzling" novel about "sex bums and dope fiends" reflected only a small portion of the state. *The Dallas Times Herald,* noting that "the protagonist's view of Dallas and Texas is not a pleasant one," judged that "the cleverness of it all is a matter of viewpoint." Surprisingly, it was *The Dallas Morning News* that stood out, running an effusive review. *Strange Peaches* "could well be the novel that gains [Shrake] overdue recognition in serious literary circles. It is an ironic, sensitive, sometimes brutally realistic, humorous and sexy account of criss-crossing lives in Dallas in the fall of 1963." There was a good reason for the positive tone—the review was written by Shrake's friend Jay Milner.[5]

The most contemptuous response ran in the *Texas Observer,* where Shrake, Cartwright, Brammer, and King were still listed as contributing editors. Book reviewer Roxy Gordon described *Strange Peaches* as "a long book and a lot of stuff happens between the first of the book and the last." Gordon's main aesthetic objection, it turned out, was that *Strange Peaches* "gets the real and the unreal mixed up." The satire seemed offensive to Gordon, who refused to believe that right-wing millionaires would machine-gun tame rabbits at a private shooting club. The novel, Gordon decided, is nothing more than "a combination rich-Texan joke/liberal horror story."[6]

Despite *Strange Peaches'* praise in the national media, sales were dismal. The book sold even less than *Blessed McGill. Harper's* refused to publish a paperback edition, and *Strange Peaches* quickly went out of print.

In the years since its publication, *Strange Peaches* has retained a devoted following among the Texas literati. In 1987 *Texas Monthly Press* reissued the novel as the third title in its contemporary fiction series. Academicians continue to cite *Strange Peaches* as one of the state's significant novels. Tom Pilkington, in *State of Mind: Texas Literature and Culture,* calls *Strange Peaches* "an exceptionally powerful evocation of urban life in modern Texas." Don Graham, writing in the November 2000 issue of *Texas Monthly,* concluded, "When anybody asks me what Dallas was like during the time of the Kennedy assassination, I always refer them to one book: Edwin 'Bud' Shrake's *Strange Peaches.*"[7]

Strange Peaches adds a unique perspective to the many histories written on the Dallas of that era. In this way it is a marked example of what could be termed "eyewitness fiction." Stories written by first-hand observers, however fictionalized they may seem, often contain truths and perspectives ignored or underplayed by "fact-based" sources, such as newspapers. This is especially true in Texas, where the state's newspapers have been notoriously poor. Yet, traditionally, Texas historians have relied heavily on newspaper accounts. As a result, Texas literature is replete with examples of eyewitness fiction outstripping history, from Elmer Kelton's account of the 1950-1957 drought in West Texas—*The Time It Never Rained*—to Américo Paredes' novel about Texas Mexicans resisting Anglo encroachment in the lower Rio Grande valley—*George Washington Gómez*. For that matter, there's also Billy Lee Brammer's *The Gay Place*, which provides an unparalleled social history of Austin's political culture in the 1950s.

In *Strange Peaches*, Shrake blends his personal history into the larger historical canvas. In this sense, the novel parallels what the narrator, John Lee Wallace, is attempting. Wallace says, "I want to make this into a fictional documentary, using actual people when we can, inventing a few things to help it stick together, re-shooting some parts to show myself in all these places involved. . . . Let this be one good, true, fair thing we can do."[8]

Shrake's previous novel, *Blessed McGill*, focused on transcendence. *Strange Peaches*, in contrast, is a work of resistance. It evokes the themes of the sixties counterculture—with a decidedly Texas twist. Shrake's portrait reveals a Dallas dominated by materialistic greed and sanctimonious racism. We get views of cornpone ostentatiousness ranging from solid gold toilets to extravagant boasts of financial might. John Lee zeroes in on the source of the nouveau riche's buffoonery as he observes a gathering of Dallas elite at a party: "Many of them had leaped from the farm or . . . the Depression shack into the country club and the opera league without a metamorphosis." Though not many of the rich cared for the arts, they cared about status, and the "coarse-faced lout in the corner might be a multimillionaire with a collection of Remingtons and French Impressionists."[9]

In *Strange Peaches,* Dallas police dispense frontier justice as they enforce the establishment's rule. This is most clearly seen in the experience of Hector, a friend of John Lee's who owns a small Mexican restaurant. When Hector is cleaning up outside at closing time, two Dallas cops stop and accost him. "Hey, you damn greaser, what are you trying to steal?" When Hector explains that he is the owner, the response is "You're still a damn greaser." The harassment quickly escalates into physical violence, and the encounter leaves Hector nursing sore ribs, a bloody face, and a long-standing grudge.[10]

The establishment's control of the city also extends to the news media. As John Lee recounts his early experiences as a police reporter, he acknowledges, "Newspapers, radio, and television did not report violence involving blacks unless it was against whites. They did not report much of anything at all involving blacks . . . unless it was humorous, like watermelon stealing. But if a black man killed a white man or raped a white woman, you would see detectives in the hall with shotguns, and you had a story."[11]

One of John Lee's final news stories involves a civil rights sit-in at a drugstore near the SMU campus. "The drugstore doors were locked and a fumigating company was called to spray the inside of the building with insecticide. The demonstrators withstood the white smoke for fifteen minutes or so. Then they came to the glass doors and begged to be let out. Police and firemen dragged out several who were unconscious." John Lee interviews demonstrators, police, and the drugstore owner, who claimed that the demonstrators "had ruined the goods on his shelves." But John Lee's story is not used. "The incident was never mentioned on the air or in the newspapers. If such a thing should be reported, I was told, it would encourage other radicals to cause trouble in a peaceful city."[12]

The undercurrent of resistance churns throughout the novel and assumes forms ranging from small-time hoods with gun-running ambitions to Buster Gregory's self-cultivated marijuana plant, "Baby Giant," which grows peacefully in the closet of his apartment home. One man John Lee meets at Jack Ruby's nightclub explains his own trouble with the law in terms of resistance: "I might of done some stealing a few years ago, but that was mostly just from churches and beer distributors and big chain drugstores, redividing the wealth, you understand."[13]

John Lee drifts through much of his life, often stoned or hung over and vaguely dissatisfied. He is convinced at a visceral level that the documentary he is making—his art—will provide him with the meaning he's seeking. The focus becomes more clear after Kennedy is assassinated. His friend Buster tells him, "I don't like this movie, John Lee, but we've got to see the end of it. . . . It's the movie we've been making."[14] By the end of the book, reality has overtaken the documentary. John Lee finds himself in Zihuatanejo, Mexico, and his television persona takes a surreal turn as he becomes, at last, "a modern outlaw."

28.

SEMI-
TOUGH

Bud Shrake was disappointed by *Strange Peaches'* collapse in the marketplace, but commercial failure was hardly new to him, and he began to take a certain pride in being a cult favorite—a stranger to the best-seller lists but well respected among a small coterie of peers and critics. Shrake's friend Dan Jenkins, however, had different ambitions. By the early 1970s, Jenkins had clearly established himself as *Sports Illustrated*'s most popular writer. The magazine's "big-game collector," he was assigned to cover the most important contests and events. Yet despite his wide following, Jenkins' nonfiction collections—each based on previously published articles in *Sports Illustrated*—had sold very little. Jenkins believed that he could translate his millions of *Sports Illustrated* readers into book buyers—if he could write the right book.

"For years, Jenkins had been toying with the idea of a novel, partly because he realized that he'd never get rich on the nonfiction anthologies," according to Michael MacCambridge. All of his Texas writer friends—Shrake, Cartwright, Brammer, and King—had published a novel, though none had seen much commercial success. In the summer of 1971, Dan Jenkins decided that it was his turn to try. All he had in the beginning was a title, *Semi-Tough,* and a "vague notion that it would be a story about football."[1]

Once Jenkins began writing, the story quickly came together. From his early days at the *Fort Worth Press*, he had created fictional characters in his columns. These often served as alter egos, allowing him to make sardonic commentary while maintaining a journalistic cover. One such creation was a sportswriter named Jim Tom Pinch. With his colleagues Bud Shrake and Dick Growald, Jenkins even put together a faux scrapbook, *The Pinch Papers*.[2] Another creation from those days was a good-old-boy athlete named Billy Clyde Puckett.

In *Semi-Tough*, Billy Clyde becomes an all-star running back for the New York Giants. He's a national celebrity, and his team has made the Super Bowl. The week before the big game, he begins dictating his life story to Jim Tom Pinch, who will in turn publish the account as an "as-told-to biography." Naturally, with the easygoing Billy Clyde as the narrator, Jenkins would enjoy a great deal of latitude to talk about whatever was on his mind, be it sex, football, drinking "young scotches," or listening to country music. "I just sat down and wrote it," Jenkins said later. "It was the only thing I knew how to write, doing it the only way I knew how to do it. Just put yourself in first person, and let Billy Clyde start talking."[3]

Billy Clyde, as it turned out, speaks very frankly about what's on his mind. Women are "wool." African Americans are "niggers." Billy Clyde admits, "I also use a few words like hebe and spick and some other things which might not necessarily flatter a person's name and address." He defends the usage by explaining, "actually this is how a lot of studs talk in the National Football League. We're fairly honest. We might call a spook a spook, unless he's a spick."[4]

Billy Clyde's lifelong friend, also from Fort Worth, is Marvin "Shake" Tiller, who shares several character traits with Bud Shrake. Shake, too, is a star player for the New York Giants. Billy Clyde and Shake both love Barbara Jane Bookman, a Fort Worth girl who has become a top model, complete with breasts that "are certainly very large, but they are also firm and nicely shaped, and they have the good nips. Which is to say that Barb's nips are not big and dark but sort of rose-tinted and they perfectly set off her plenty large, nicely shaped lungs like a gold money clip can set off a roll of green whip-out."[5] Billy Clyde and Shake share a New York apartment known as

"Sperm City." There, they are joined by groups of attractive women for "all-skates," sometimes referred to as the "Eastern Regional Eat-Off."

Dan Jenkins, it seemed, had found his hook. While his writing in the pages of *Sports Illustrated* was funny and satirical, it was also in a form acceptable for families and young readers. In his fiction, Jenkins would retain much of his narrative voice, yet now, unfettered, his writing would become "R" rated.

Jenkins had the same literary agent as the other Texas writers. Sterling Lord showed a section of the manuscript to Herman Gollob, the same editor who had earlier signed Shrake's *Strange Peaches* for *Harper's*. Gollob, now at Atheneum, was excited about the commercial potential of Jenkins' football novel and immediately signed him to a contract.

Jenkins took a copy of his finished manuscript to Bud Shrake in the spring of 1972, looking for helpful comments. "I read it, and I advised him to tone it down," said Shrake, "to take out all the ethnic jokes, or at least to cut 'em way back, and to take out some of the needless profanity. And if he had listened to me, nobody would have read the book, probably. Cause then Dan went to his editor, Herman Gollob, and Gollob said, 'Bud doesn't know shit about it. Instead of doing what he told you to do, put in more profanity, more ethnic jokes.'"[6]

Atheneum was thrilled with the results. "It was a revelation, that goddamn book," Herman Gollob said later. "It revolutionized sports novels."[7] Atheneum began promoting *Semi-Tough* as its lead book for the fall. It would be released to coincide with the opening of the 1972 football season, and the advance notice was generating a marketing buzz. *Semi-Tough* promised to be an "inside" look at America's most popular sport, written by one of the country's best-known sportswriters. Added to that were assurances of vulgar language, groundbreaking humor, and graphic descriptions of sex orgies.

In July, even before the book was published, *Semi-Tough*'s paperback rights sold for $250,000. Dan Jenkins was suddenly semi-rich. Two book clubs announced that they were picking up the novel, and a major studio bought the film rights. *Playboy* ran an excerpt, illustrating the story with comic-strip drawings featuring studly football players and buxom women. Nothing remotely like this had ever happened to any of the famous arthurs. Dan Jenkins, publishing his first novel at the age of forty-three, was on his way to becoming a star.

Semi-Tough roared onto the best-seller lists. The novel, as it turned out, evidences little of the gritty violence of professional football. In fact, Jenkins paid scant attention to the elements normally associated with successful fiction—character, plot, conflict, and motivation. Jenkins simply adapted his well-honed sportswriting technique to fiction. The "story" itself—just as in the sporting events—is merely a point of departure for Jenkins' commentary: an assortment of quick takes, breezy opinions and acrobatic one-liners. Each topic is exhausted within a few lines, allowing Jenkins to move on to his next target. The effect, though hardly deep or profound, proved to be very entertaining, thanks to Jenkins' supple and outrageous humor.

Jenkins' bawdy satire takes on everything imaginable, from Texas oilmen and the manic extravagance of halftime shows to the "striped-tie, Ivy League, midtown, semi-lockjaw, Eastern motherfuckers you run into." Most daringly, Jenkins aims at the sensibilities of women and minorities. The "wool," with the exception of Barbara Jane Bookman, are admired solely for their physical attributes. Those found lacking are treated with contempt. Billy Clyde describes Jim Tom Pinch's wife as "one of those bitches who couldn't wait to get fat right after she got married." Billy Clyde also tramples over polite discussions on race. "One of the big troubles with the world of modern times," he says, "is that somebody is always getting hot because somebody else says nigger instead of nee-grow."[8]

Larry L. King had learned the year before, in *Confessions of a White Racist*, that white America was largely uninterested in examining deeply held racial attitudes. People were tired of the turmoil of the sixties and men, in particular, felt threatened by the rising tide of the feminist movement. Dan Jenkins, in *Semi-Tough*, provided an antidote to both with his comic touch. Billy Clyde Puckett spoke in a language that was shocking but also charming in its directness. "I said nigger just now to get your attention," Billy Clyde says at the outset of *Semi-*

Tough. "But I don't think nigger in my heart." He goes on to explain, "Nobody can help being what he is, whether it turns out to be black as a cup of coffee at a truck stop, or a white Southern dumb-ass like most of our parents."[9]

Jenkins' racial discourse was just as blunt as Larry L. King's in *Confessions of a White Racist.* The major difference was that King examined race matters with depth and sensitivity, while Jenkins—from a white male's perspective—spoofed race and gender. Jenkins' boldness won him admirers among those who could have been offended. Alex Haley, the author of *Roots,* sent Jenkins a letter assuring him that he understood he wasn't a racist. Carolyn Banks wrote, "even a feminist can love Billy Clyde, who, if he were real, would have to be served with an apple in his mouth."[10]

Not everyone agreed. Some reviewers believed that Jenkins was far too gleeful in making sexist and racist jokes. One noted, "The first time that sort of justification comes around in the book, it's fairly plausible in context, but after 20 or 30 references . . . they hit you in the face." *The New Republic* pointed out, "Women are sex objects out of *Playboy* (and don't seem to mind), niggers is niggers (and don't seem to mind either)." Some critics, having hoped for a serious satire of the game, felt let down. "When you mix sports-desk humor with locker-room guffaws," one reviewer wrote, "you get . . . sex jokes, race jokes and flatulence jokes." *The Saturday Review* found that Jenkins' "jokes are more pubescent than adolescent—a lot of mileage is given to the flatulent abilities of lineman T. J. Lambert. . . . *Semi-Tough* takes a subject ripe for satire and treats it all with the humor of a towel slap in the locker room—without the sting."[11]

But other writers lauded Jenkins as a fresh new voice in American literature. Most prominently, Jenkins' friend David Halberstam, writing in *The New York Times Book Review,* hailed *Semi-Tough* as "a marvelous book. I loved it. I read it aloud to my wife, who does not like football one bit, and she loved it. It is outrageous; it mocks contemporary American mores; it mocks Madison Avenue; it mocks racial attitudes; it mocks writers like me; and it even mocks sportswriters for *Sports Illustrated* like Dan Jenkins." Pete Axthelm, writing in

Newsweek, called *Semi-Tough* "an outrageously funny novel and a devastating satire on jocks and jock journalism." Jenkins' friend Larry L. King contributed two glowing reviews—one in *Life* magazine and one in *Publishers Weekly.*[12]

Semi-Tough became a publishing sensation and a cultural phenomenon. It remained on the best-seller lists for several months, eventually selling over 100,000 copies in hardback. The paperback edition sold over two million copies. The prefix "semi" entered the nation's lexicon. When Gary Cartwright visited Jenkins in New York City, he observed that, thanks to Jenkins, "Texas was already becoming a formidable cultural presence . . . execs from the suburbs were patting each other on the back and saying they were semithirsty, then hailing the bartender to order a young scotch. It was a good time to be Dan Jenkins."[13]

PART THREE:

TEXAS. . .

CHIC?

29.

A New

View

of

Texas

On January 22, 1973, four years after leaving office, sixty-four-year-old Lyndon Johnson died at his ranch in the Texas Hill Country. That same month, the first issue of *Texas Monthly* hit newsstands, swaggering with attitude. "We're not a mass medium like a newspaper," publisher Michael Levy wrote. "We're not competing with the vapid Sunday supplements with bluebonnets on their covers, with the promotional magazines with their prostitutional story-for-an-ad format, or with the chamber of commerce magazines with their Babbitt perspectives." William Broyles Jr. added, "If our readers have ever finished the daily paper or the six o'clock news and felt there was more than what they were told, then they know why we started *Texas Monthly*. We designed it as an intelligent, entertaining, and useful publication for Texans whose culture, sophistication, and interests are largely unrecognized by existing media."[1]

The inaugural issue, at eighty-four pages and just six pages of advertising, was hardly the stuff of groundbreaking journalism. The cover featured Don Meredith, who had become a media celebrity as a *Monday Night Football* broadcaster. The by-the-numbers profile of Meredith was accompanied by an article about the rivalry between upscale department stores Sakowitz and Neiman Marcus. Another profile focused on Houston's "Consumer Lawman" Marvin Zindler, who would later gain widespread notoriety for closing down a brothel in La Grange. The *Monthly* also featured sections on travel, books, and film. A "Briar Patch" department functioned much like *The New Yorker's* "Talk of the Town."

Largely following the "city" magazine formula established earlier by Clay Felker at *New York, Texas Monthly* freely borrowed ideas from successful East Coast magazines. As such, the New Journalism found in its pages wasn't particularly innovative. But what was new was that it was happening in Texas, a state where such a thing had never occurred before. The best article by far, and one that showed the magazine's great potential, was Gary Cartwright's story on Dallas Cowboys running back Duane Thomas. More interested in contemplating "The Great Cosmos" than talking to his teammates, Thomas had led the Cowboys to their first-ever Super Bowl victory. But he mocked the aura of hype surrounding the event. If the Super Bowl is the "Ultimate Game," Thomas asked, "why are they playing it again next year?"[2]

Though a supremely talented player, Thomas could never acclimate himself to the Cowboys' organization. He called coach Tom Landry a "a plastic man." At team meetings he refused to answer during roll call, figuring that "anyone could see that he was there."[3] After he was busted for possession of marijuana—an arrest that his wife claimed was orchestrated by the Cowboys—Thomas was traded away to another team. Cartwright's story, though ostensibly about sports, provided exactly what *Texas Monthly* had promised its readers: personal, literate journalism with depth and insight. Through Cartwright's lens, Duane Thomas' story became more than just a tragedy. As Cartwright described it, Thomas' fall also revealed much about Dallas itself, both its people and the hard-edged Cowboy organization.

While Cartwright was only a freelancer, Billy Lee Brammer had been hired on staff, and Brammer was clearly inspired by this journalistic experiment. Many of the younger writers had grown up viewing him as something of a legend, both for *The Gay Place* and for his consumption of drugs. The forty-three-year-old Brammer relished mentoring a new generation of writers, though Jan Reid recalled that his "raconteuring could be quite a distraction to writers trying to push a paragraph along." Reid remembered that Brammer "came in one day strung so tight he hummed like a telephone wire. He sat down, leaned back, clasped his hands behind his head, and soon had the staffers hanging on every word. Suddenly he stopped and looked at his desk with real alarm. 'My hands!' he cried. 'What happened to my hands?'"[4]

Broyles described a Brammer who "helped with story ideas and all the nuts and bolts of getting out a magazine, from writing headlines and captions to rewriting stories." But more than his editorial work, Brammer's real contribution was his very presence, which "made us take our work seriously." Broyles recalled, "He could sit for an hour reading a story, squinting through his cataracts, munching Tom's Peanut Patties and swilling endless Dr Peppers, and we would almost forget he was there; then, very patiently and politely, looking like a benign Mel Brooks, he would tell us in brilliantly succinct fashion just what the article needed. We already knew what was good enough; he taught us what was truly good, and that is the crucial difference."[5]

Brammer's association with the magazine inspired his most substantial writing in a decade. Reverting to his serious journalistic appellation, "Bill Brammer," he contributed a short piece on Larry L. King and Larry McMurtry for the first issue's "Briar Patch." *Texas Monthly's* second issue featured a cover story by Brammer on "Border Radio." Clearly delighted by the primitive huckstering heard over high-powered airwaves, Brammer cited numerous examples that, at the very least, served to assure *Texas Monthly* readers of their own cultural sophistication.

Two months later, Brammer published a provocative article on "Sex and Politics." This, for the first time in Texas journalism, described in some detail this aspect of Texas' political culture. Brammer began with a telling anecdote from his days on LBJ's staff. In 1956, House Speaker Sam Rayburn stared in amazement at the attractive young women clustered around senators John Kennedy and Estes Kefauver. "Goddam," Rayburn said, "Ever'body screws!" Brammer's article also commented on the private life of his former boss, Lyndon B. Johnson, though he avoided explicit details. Still, the innuendoes are obvious, particularly when Brammer noted that, as Senate majority leader, LBJ was known to have retired to a private, guarded cloakroom where he took "an improbable number of naps."[6]

"Sex and Politics" also focused attention on the state legislature, relating overheard gossip with unabashed delight. Though no names were revealed, the stories were titillating enough, ranging from representatives caught in the act to secretaries with the ambition to sleep with every man in the state house.

Brammer's portrait of the state capitol as a sexual place was shocking to many, and his story contributed substantially to the "buzz" generated by *Texas Monthly* in its early days. Brammer also proved to be prescient. Just three months after his article appeared, the "Chicken Ranch," a brothel in La Grange that had long enjoyed special dispensations from Texas politicians, was shut down after a much-publicized crusade led by Houston's Marvin Zindler. Larry L. King would later follow up on this connection between sex and politics in *The Best Little Whorehouse in Texas*.

Brammer's work for *Texas Monthly* offered hope that this comeback would be for good. But there was no escaping the fact that it was the drugs, not the writing, that fueled his life. "We tried to salvage Billy Lee Brammer," Mike Levy said later. But it wasn't working. Brammer made a number of editorial suggestions to Bill Broyles, and almost every one involved some aspect of freak culture. Brammer pitched stories on hippies, underground newspapers, former Students for a Democratic Society activists, "hip investment advisors," police informants, and Armadillo artist Jim Franklin.[7] Those topics, however, were not exactly what a magazine designed for upscale readers was looking for.

After a few months Brammer began to drift away from the *Texas Monthly* offices, thus "sparing admirers the pain of letting him go." His article on sex and politics became his last work published in the magazine. Broyles later made the best of Brammer's departure. "I sometimes thought he had it in his mind that he had shown us all he could, and we had to do the rest ourselves."[8]

Texas Monthly itself, under Broyles' guidance, improved with every issue. "Broyles was a great idea guy," Jan Reid said later, "who could match this idea with that writer and know what particular chemistry would work."[9] Broyles also excelled at making *Texas Monthly* known as "a writer's magazine." Though the pay rates were laughable by national standards, writers understood that their words were cared for, and readers recognized the quality of writing that appeared in the magazine's pages.

As the magazine's literate, irreverent style began to catch on, it soon developed a number of regular must-read features, including "The Best and Worst Legislators." TM also broke several hard-hitting investigative stories that illuminated shadowy areas of the Texas establishment. The daring reporting resulted in lawsuits, threats, and pressure from advertisers. But publisher Mike Levy fiercely backed his editorial staff—again reinforcing the notion that *Texas Monthly* was a writers' magazine. Levy also publicized the controversies whenever possible, taking his case to the state's newspapers. This in turn brought even more attention to *Texas Monthly*, imbuing it with an aura of journalistic integrity.

While many establishment Texans condemned *Texas Monthly* for being too liberal and arrogant, readers were proving to be, just as Mike Levy had forecast, hungry for the coverage it provided. The magazine's circulation increased from twenty thousand to almost fifty thousand in its first year.[10] Then, in April 1974 an announcement was made that stunned the New York-based publishing world. *Texas Monthly* won a National Magazine Award—the industry equivalent of the Pulitzer Prize—for "the entire body of its work" after only one year of publication. This was an unprecedented accomplishment for any magazine in publishing history. For the award to go to a regional magazine far from either coast was even more shocking. Suddenly, people in New York were talking about *Texas Monthly*.

30.

THE

COWBOY

PROFESSOR

A fter his wife's death in June 1972, forty-three-year-old Larry L. King "wandered the country like a gypsy minstrel, singing sad songs, pointlessly roaring, creating havoc, carrying my own chaos along. There was anger in it and self-pity and real grief and not a little guilt." His work suffered as he "mainly got drunk and became involved in witless, fruitless personal entanglements." King continued to produce occasional articles, but his pace dropped off sharply, and his income fell as a result. He was still getting by financially, thanks to his monthly checks from Viking for his biography-in-progress of Lyndon Johnson. King began the project with high expectations. Former LBJ press secretary Bill Moyers offered King complete cooperation, including access to his private journals kept during his years as a Johnson advisor. Billy Lee Brammer offered to sell King, for the modest sum of $500, the research he had collected on Johnson for his own aborted biography. King also had years of contacts built up among the Texas congressional delegation and LBJ confidants, and he planned to conduct extensive interviews to help piece together his portrait.[1]

But it was difficult to gain momentum. Moyers was the first to put King off, resisting interview sessions and questions about access to his journals. He eventually confessed that he had decided not to cooperate because he wanted to write a book about LBJ himself. King waited for several weeks to receive Brammer's research files, for which he had paid in advance. Finally, he wrote to his friend: "You rat fink bastard. What about your pledge to send me all that Lyndon material you compiled, assembled, wrote up, and what not? I hustled my ass and got you your bail and dope money and you drop me like Texas politicians do when one does a favor for them. Get your ass in gear." Finally, Brammer's materials arrived in the mail. When King opened the package, he saw that Brammer's "treasure trove" contained only old newspaper clippings and magazine articles, most of which could have been found at the local library.[2]

In his talks with political insiders, King ran into many of the same obstacles that Billy Lee Brammer had faced. Several of LBJ's former associates "refused interviews because I was not exactly in good odor with the Johnson crowd." Other Texas political figures, both in and out of office, worried about reprisals from the Johnsons—not just from Lyndon when he was alive, but also from Lady Bird. LBJ himself, from his ranch outside of Johnson City, never even bothered to answer King's letters requesting an interview.[3]

King found the "cool receptions discouraging and intimidating. They helped dry me up, along with my own lassitude and, yes, fear of failure." Work on the biography began to slow down. Nevertheless King continued to receive checks from his publisher, and he claimed to his editors, friends, and colleagues that he was making great progress. When King learned of Johnson's death in January 1973, he wrote to a friend, "I felt an amazing loss for the old bugger, more than the usual pious hypocritical beargrease brought forward by death. Not surprising, I guess, when you realize that for most of my life he has loomed in it—for good or ill—like the Pyramids."[4]

Soon King's fortunes began improving. In February 1973 he learned that the Texas Institute of Letters, which had ignored *Confessions of a White Racist* the year before, awarded him the Stanley Walker Journalism Award for his story in *Life* on West Texas. He declined to attend the ceremony, but he did donate the $500 prize in support of the Dobie Paisano Fellowship.[5] By March 1973 he and

Willie Morris began the process of reconciliation. Though it would be several years before the two men regained a close friendship, they did begin to exchange occasional phone calls and letters. Then, something even more remarkable happened. King received a proposal from another Ivy League school: Princeton University asked King to become its visiting professor of journalism.

"Bird nest on the ground," he wrote to his cousin Lanvil and his wife Glenda. "Shameful. Sinful. Ought not to be allowed." The position, which paid very well, required only that King appear on campus twice a week to teach two courses. The prospect of a somewhat leisurely life as a part-time professor offered King a chance to get off the magazine treadmill and devote some real time to his LBJ book. "On paper," King wrote, "it had the look of a grand plan."[6]

Princeton began stunningly well. Several newspapers sent reporters to cover the story of the "Cowboy Professor," and King played the role to the hilt. "This school teachin' is the easiest thing I ever seen," he wrote one friend.

> Had I but knew it was so easy, I would have went to school to learn it. Apparently it don't take much practice. All you do is have a captive audience to bullshit three hours on a Monday afternoon, and make them call you Professor and Sir and all, and write papers which you mark red marks on and saying things like "This ain't done good enuff" and "horseshit to such statements" and "what are you doing after class, Little Girl, and would you like a A plus?" To think I spent all them years carrying letter routes and pissanting pipe and digging sump-pits when I could have been professin' for money.[7]

In truth, King took his role very seriously. He brought several guest lecturers to his classes, including David Halberstam, Morris Udall, Norman Mailer, Larry McMurtry, and Nora Ephron. He also brought a panel of editors, critics, and a literary agent for a seminar on how these professionals deal with journalists. King's classes were popular, but he soon began to feel the strain of university life. The workload was larger than he had expected. Preparing lectures and writing assignments, keeping office hours, grading papers, and "writing comments on 35,000 student words each week" began to take its toll. At the same time, he felt little kinship with the other faculty, most of whom "had three degrees [and] either numbers behind his name or parted it in the middle." King also viewed many of the students as spoiled rich kids, and life in the college town began to bore him.[8] Then, Bud Shrake and Jerry Jeff Walker made a surprise visit.

King was hosting a cocktail party when Jerry Jeff, "dressed like a buffalo hunter," crashed the party. Jerry Jeff began "imitating the walks and lisps of sherry-sipping academicians; he crashed about, stepping on long gowns and howling for Lone Star beer. He asked a highly placed faculty wife her relative expertise in the cocksucking discipline." After the party, Shrake and Walker disappeared with King's rental car. Nothing was heard from either man for several days. With the rental company pestering him about the overdue car, King finally tracked the two men down. It took some prodding for them to recall that they had even visited him at Princeton, and neither could remember having borrowed his car. The vehicle was eventually located two weeks later, abandoned in midtown Manhattan, "Long on traffic tickets and short on operable parts."[9]

While teaching at Princeton, King had to confront the fact that he was making little progress on his LBJ book. In November 1973 he received a letter from David Halberstam. "I am worried to death about the status of the Lyndon book," Halberstam wrote. "It is more than a year since you were supposed to start serious work on the book and you are still not working on it . . . we are talking about your life my friend. A big book is the only security for people like you and me; we can never get ahead of the sheriff on small magazine pieces. . . . Besides we get older and magazine writers get younger and hungrier." Halberstam ended his plea, "You have intelligence and strength and the rarest thing of all—talent, and I know dear God that you did not come all the way from Midland Texas to piss it all away."[10]

31.

LIVE

MUSIC

CAPITAL

By early 1973, Austin's music scene, fueled largely by the appreciative crowds at the Armadillo World Headquarters, was taking off. Willie Nelson and Jerry Jeff Walker were joined in Austin by dozens of musicians bridging the divide between country and rock. Willie Nelson's 1973 album, *Shotgun Willie,* was produced without Nashville's interference. It became his breakout record, winning rave reviews and selling more than any of his previous albums. For the first time, Willie was pictured on an album cover with long hair and a beard. His music began to appeal to a new, younger audience.

Willie's successful flaunting of Nashville conventions, both musically and in his appearance, did not go unnoticed by the press. Some termed this new style "Outlaw Country." Austin journalist Jan Reid began working on a book about what he referred to as "Redneck Rock." Other observers, noting the tinge of mysticism emanating from performers like Michael Murphy, called the musicians "Cosmic Cowboys." Still another term was waiting in the wings. Austin radio station KOKE was the first to feature the new music on its playlist and called it "Progressive Country."[1] People began to speculate that Austin's music scene could even develop into a viable industry, complete with recording studios, record labels, and dozens of clubs featuring live music.

Billy Lee Brammer selling souvenir programs at the first-ever Willie Nelson Fourth of July Picnic, July 4, 1973. *Billy Lee Brammer Archives, Southwestern Writers Collection, Texas State University-San Marcos.*

Natural alliances existed between the musicians and the writers who had made Austin their home. Both groups had essentially rejected far-flung corporate controls, preferring instead the relaxed atmosphere of a "real" place where they could nurture homegrown artistic visions. Shrake, Cartwright, and Brammer could often be found at clubs listening to their favorite musicians. After the clubs closed and the serious partying began, Bud Shrake and Jerry Jeff Walker proved to be the most enduring. Speed became supplanted by cocaine, and the "benders," as Gary Cartwright later wrote, "commonly lasted several days and nights, and sometimes the better part of a week." Jerry Jeff Walker was not only a Mad Dog in good standing, he joined Shrake and Cartwright as the third member of the Flying Punzars.[2]

On one occasion Hunter S. Thompson, author of *Fear and Loathing in Las Vegas*, came to town. Thompson had pioneered what he called "gonzo journalism"—essentially drug-fueled participatory journalism. Thompson's book had made him a celebrity among the counterculture, and his seemingly inexhaustible intake of drugs gave him a legendary aura among partyers. Thompson's influence extended to Austin, and Jerry Jeff Walker's sidekicks began calling themselves "The Lost Gonzo Band." Yet when he came to Austin, "the reputedly insatiable Dr. Thompson folded" about forty hours into the bender. Bud Shrake and Jerry Jeff Walker, however, "were still on the town the morning of the fourth day."[3]

Jerry Jeff Walker hated the sterility of recording studios, and he had long looked for a way to capture the easygoing feel of his live performances. In 1972 he became the first major musician to record an album in Austin, at the city's newly opened Odyssey studio. The following year he decided to get even closer to the authentic feel he was looking for. He decided to make a live album out in Luckenbach, the little Hill Country town Hondo Crouch had remade in his own image. A group of Walker's Austin friends and fans, including Bud Shrake, came out for the recording session. The resulting effort, *Viva Terlingua*, was described by Jan Reid as "emphatically Austin. The album was marked by momentary instrumental brilliance, more than a few bad licks . . . a happy revolt against the established procedures of Los Angeles rock and Nashville country."[4] Among the great songs on the album, the last track in particular stands out. It's Gary P. Nunn's "London Homesick Blues," with its memorable lament, "I want to go home with the Armadillo. . . ." It took a while for *Viva Terlingua* to catch on commercially, but once it did, Jerry Jeff became a bona fide star, finally eclipsing his "Mr. Bojangles" persona.

Willie Nelson, riding high on the success of *Shotgun Willie*, began thinking about staging an open-air concert in the Hill Country outside Austin. He called on his friends and got commitments from Kris

Kristofferson, Rita Coolidge, Waylon Jennings, Leon Russell, and several others. Radio advertisements blanketed the state, and rumors spread that Bob Dylan would appear. Finally the date arrived, and Willie Nelson's first Fourth of July picnic got underway. Some forty thousand fans descended on the area, few of them prepared for the huge traffic jams, suffocating heat, lack of food and water, and inadequate restroom facilities. Eddie Wilson's Armadillo World Headquarters crew was hired to provide security, but they were quickly overrun by counterfeit ticket holders, gate crashers, and those holding forged press passes. Bud Shrake, Jay Milner, and Gary Cartwright were in attendance, hanging out in the air-conditioned Winnebagos with the performers. Outside, caught in the crush of the crowd was a short, middle-aged man selling souvenir programs. His hat and clothes came from the Salvation Army. He sweated with a quiet dignity under the sun. Some recognized him as Austin's one-time famous writer. It was Billy Lee Brammer, trying to make a few extra bucks.

32.

NORTH

DALLAS

FORTY

I n early 1973, Peter Gent left Texas and returned to his
native Michigan along with his wife Jody and their children.
The Gents moved into a house in a quiet wooded area overlooking a lake. With his book contract in hand, Gent had decided to
become a full-time writer. He concentrated mostly on fiction but also
wrote occasional articles for *Sport* magazine.[1] Gent's former employer,
the Dallas Cowboys, had appeared in the 1971 and 1972 Super Bowls.
The Cowboys' disciplined organization allowed them to field high-
caliber teams year after year, even as individual players were injured,
retired, traded, or otherwise replaced. A constant presence on nationally televised games, the Cowboys soon became known as "America's
Team." In Dallas, they were objects of adoration, as many understood
that the city's proud football team, more than any other single civic
initiative, had finally helped erase their stigma as "the city that killed
John F. Kennedy."

The Cowboys' immense popularity made Peter Gent's forthcoming book a hot commodity. Gent's publisher planned a huge promotional campaign, and the football player-turned-author was booked
for a coast-to-coast tour of TV talk shows. In March 1973, advance
copies of *North Dallas Forty* were sent to select readers for review
comments. Among those who responded were Larry L. King, Dan

Jenkins, and Bud Shrake. Quotes from each appeared on the book's dust jacket. Publication was scheduled for the fall to coincide with the start of the football season, and a groundswell of anticipation was growing.

While the previous year's *Semi-Tough* was a fun read, few took it seriously as an "inside" look at the game. Peter Gent's novel, on the other hand, promised to be a riveting behind-the-scenes look at the nation's most popular spectator sport. Gent was highly critical of his experiences as a pro football player, and he was very public in his judgments, particularly as the marketing campaign heated up. If NFL commissioner Pete Rozelle had been worried about the salacious content of Dan Jenkins' novel, the prospect of Peter Gent's more incisive criticism was making many in the NFL nervous—particularly those within the Cowboys organization.

In September 1973 *North Dallas Forty* hit the bookstores and generated immediate controversy for its depiction of football players as drug- and alcohol-crazed psychopaths. Yet the most revelatory aspect of the book was what a fine writer Gent had turned out to be. Though the ending is wildly overwrought and the witty dialogue can be too smart at times, Gent's writing is clear, vivid, and tightly controlled. As Larry L. King wrote, "Reading *North Dallas Forty* convinces me that Peter Gent is not a former football player who happened to write a book, but a writer of real talent who happened to have played pro football." Dick Schaap, in *The New York Times Book Review,* concurred. "[Gent] has demonstrated that he is a far better writer than he ever was a pass catcher . . . and he wasn't a bad pass catcher."[2]

North Dallas Forty is narrated by Phil Elliot, a wide receiver for a professional football team based in Dallas. Gent's relentless hyper-documentarian prose style is reminiscent of Bud Shrake's *Strange Peaches*—fueled by anger and distilled with cool irony. Both books, critical as they are of the world around them, are also subversively humorous. In *North Dallas Forty,* Phil Elliot takes stock of his wounded body's need for constant medication. "I may have ten more years in me," he confides to a teammate, "if I can just master the chemistry of this game."[3]

Though Gent has changed the names, his novel is an unabashed roman à clef, targeting prominent members of the Dallas Cowboys organization. The head coach, portrayed as a pious Christian hypocrite, is easily recognizable as Tom Landry. The general manager, universally reviled by players as a man "totally without honor or integrity," is based on Dallas Cowboys general manager Tex Schramm. Phil Elliot's best friend is Seth Maxwell, the team's star quarterback. Maxwell enjoys singing "Turn out the lights, the party's over. . . ." Gent's old teammate Don Meredith, then a star announcer on *Monday Night Football*, sang those very same lyrics into millions of American homes every week.

Phil Elliot and Seth Maxwell are two of the most injured players in the club and they "marvel at each other's ability to withstand pain." They also have a shared fondness for marijuana. Characters with echoes of Billy Lee Brammer, Gary Cartwright, and Bud Shrake also appear in the narrative. While Elliot himself is based on Gent, there is some obvious self-aggrandizement. As Don Meredith was later reported to say of Gent's depiction of himself, "If I'd known Pete had been that damn good, I'd have thrown him a lot more passes."[4]

Gent's novel succeeds in laying bare the primal forces that motivate the football players. He describes men who are not only physically powerful and mean but have also been made extremely edgy by all the free amphetamines handed out by the club. Players explode into violence with little provocation. They grab and grope women, and anyone who complains is beaten into submission. At one after-game party, a player slaps a woman, forces her face to his crotch, and repeatedly tosses her into a swimming pool. This, apparently, is some sort of game. After a while, Elliot notices that the woman is gone. He decides, "She either had escaped from Joe Bob or was at the bottom of the pool." A current of homoeroticism also runs through the players' ranks, with ass slapping, ball grabbing, and forced mock fellatio. Two players begin wrestling during a party and conclude their match with a ten-second-long French kiss. Elliot, smaller than many of the others, is marginally protected only because of his friendship with Seth Maxwell. He makes no pretense of being friendly with his teammates. "They disliked me," he says, "and I was terrified of them."[5]

If Elliot is often uncomfortable in the presence of the players, at least he understands that they're only coping as best they can with the fear and violence that rule their lives. Much of the real anger in Gent's novel is instead directed at the nerve center of the Dallas organization—the coach and general manager. There is no room for individuality, or even humanity, within the structure. "We're just the fucking equipment to be listed along with the shoulder pads and headgear and jockstraps," Elliot tells Seth Maxwell. Even a horrifying injury to a key player evokes no emotion from coach B. A. Quinlan, who simply sends in a substitute as though the wounded man is "merely a damaged part being replaced."[6]

The long-term health and welfare of the players is not a consideration of the management, and the medical treatment provided is unconscionable. Players who should be reporting for surgery instead line up for novocaine shots to mask their pain. Elliot himself has suffered numerous injuries, but the team's "doctor" warns him to keep playing. "I don't think there's anything bad wrong with your leg," the doctor says. "I know it hurts you but there ain't nothing worse you can do to it by playin' on it. . . . I overheard the coaches talkin' and they're beginning to think that you're doggin' it. Now you and I know better, but that's what they're saying, so go out and show 'em something today."[7]

The organization does whatever it can to gain an edge over its labor costs, and the players are cheated in a variety of ways from large to small. They receive a dime each for autographing footballs that the club sells for an exorbitant profit. During a road game to New York City, they're given $12 in meal money for the two-day stay. Dallas pays its players far less than the league average, and in the absence of free agency, the players have little bargaining power. In contract negotiations, general manager Clinton Foote preys on their insecurities. "Teammates have to fight each other for their piece of the pie," Elliot realizes. Even poorly educated rednecks like O. B. Meadows recognize how the operation works. At one point he attacks an assistant coach, screaming at him, "Every time I try and call it a business you say it's a game and every time I say it should be a game you call it a business."[8]

Hypocrisy rules the team and is mostly expressed through coach B. A. Quinlan, who adeptly blames his players for losses, even in obvious cases where his own coaching decisions are at fault. Though the coach ostensibly relies on computerized data to determine which players are performing best, playing time is often determined by other factors. A case in point is Delma Huddle, a black receiver who "was a perennial All-Pro" even as "B. A. and Clinton Foote had attempted several times to squelch his nomination. They hoped to correct his 'severe attitude problems and outrageous contract demands.'"At one point Huddle is benched in favor a younger white player. Only after the team loses four straight games does the coach notice a "sudden improvement" in Huddle's performance and reinstate him into the starting lineup.[9]

In Elliot's view, the city of Dallas and its corrupt football team are inextricably linked. One of the core elements he sees in that hegemony is enforced segregation. The blacks are largely confined to the south side of Dallas, while North Dallas is reserved for the city's Anglo population. Black players must commute across town to the team's practice facility on the north side. One black player repeatedly asked the team for help in finding a home near his place of employment, but he was always refused "with an explanation that the club shouldn't interfere in community matters." The player eventually files an unfair-housing suit against a North Dallas real estate agent. After that, he is "severely reprimanded by [the coach] for doing something that might distract the team's preparation for the coming Sunday."[10]

Though he tries to remain aloof from politics, Elliot finds it impossible to escape Dallas' right-wing society. A friend of the team owner invites him to a party, and when Elliot arrives, he discovers that the gathering is in fact a meeting of the John Birch Society. Everyone is given a blank sheet of paper and asked to "list people they thought might be Communists, use drugs, or otherwise act suspicious." Later, Elliot goes to an exclusive Dallas club that belongs to the team owner. There he meets a man who enthuses at the great job Francisco Franco is doing in Spain. "Yessir, you can say what you want about a dictatorship, but there's no crime in the streets." This brings up talk of administering the death penalty to dopers. When Elliot blurts out that the idea reminds him of Hitler, "The man's eyes brightened, pleased with Hitler for supporting his philosophy."[11]

Gent's stinging novel created a sensation, and the book received strong praise from reviewers across the country. The reception in Dallas, however, was much cooler. The *Morning News* rebuked the work, calling it "heavy-handed" and "one-sided" while predicting that the book would "shock a few, delight some, and infuriate most." Though other critics had pointed out the real-life inspirations for Gent's fictional creation, the *Morning News* was far more circumspect, never once mentioning coach Tom Landry by name.[12]

The Cowboys organization retained a stony silence about the book, refusing to comment even as the novel climbed up the bestseller lists and speculation mounted over the accuracy of Gent's exposé. Finally, on December 8, 1973, the Dallas Cowboys responded publicly for the first time to Gent's novel. General manager Tex Schramm charged that Gent "has a sick approach to life [and] has indicted the whole NFL and the Dallas Cowboy organization." *North Dallas Forty*, Schramm said, is "a total lie. . . . ninety-five per cent of the people in the National Football League are decent human beings who in no way resemble the degenerate characters depicted in Gent's book."[13] Newspapers across the country carried news of Schramm's first public comments on the book. But in Dallas, neither *The Dallas Morning News* nor the *The Dallas Times Herald* chose to print any stories on this new development.

Though debates continued to rage over the accuracy of Gent's portrayals, *North Dallas Forty* represented a maturing of how America understood its most popular spectator sport. No longer was football seen simply as "a game." Gent's book, more than anything else, made it clear that the sport was a business. In the years since its publication, *North Dallas Forty* has endured in the public's consciousness, aided by the successful 1978 film adaptation starring Nick Nolte and Mac Davis. The novel was reprinted several times during the 1970s and 1980s. In 2000 it was reissued with a new foreword by Gent. In Texas, Gent's novel is viewed as a milestone in the state's literature. Tom

Pilkington, in *State of Mind: Texas Literature and Culture*, writes knowingly of the extensive literature on Texas football. Assessing the merits of books ranging from Don DeLillo's *End Zone* to Dan Jenkins' *Semi-Tough*, Pilkington concludes, "The best of all Texas novels about professional football is Peter Gent's *North Dallas Forty*."[14]

Gent's challenging social portrait of Dallas, like his friend Bud Shrake's *Strange Peaches*, provides a personal, alternative history of the city. While Shrake covers the early 1960s, Gent writes of the end years of the decade. Taken together, the two novels—complementary in style and subject matter both—form bookend views of a turbulent era in Texas' second-largest city.

33.

THE

REGENERATOR

ERECTION

LABORATORY

A s his film *Kid Blue* geared up for release, Bud Shrake became increasingly interested in screenwriting. "I always thought that movie writers were hacks, the bottom of the barrel," Shrake said. "But I'd gotten more satisfaction out of seeing *Kid Blue* get made than anything I've done. The whole adventure of making a movie . . . was a lot more exciting than being holed up for ten hours with the phone turned off and writing."[1]

Kid Blue became one of three U.S. movies to premiere at the New York Film Festival in September 1973. Like Shrake's novel *Blessed McGill*, *Kid Blue* eschews romanticized notions of the West. The town of Dime Box is not a picturesque Old West village. Instead, it is dominated by a smoke-spewing factory. The train robbers who botch a robbery attempt at the film's outset don't wear the dandy clothes of the popular imagination. Instead, they're outfitted in patched-together overalls. The townspeople are racist, hypocritical, and sanctimonious. The outlaw hero, Kid Blue, played by Dennis Hopper, attempts to go straight and takes a series of demeaning jobs, including work as a shoeshine boy and a chicken plucker. His chicken plucking brings him to the attention of the town's leading capitalist, who tells him, "You're making a very worthwhile contribution to this community, young man."[2]

Kid Blue meets some Comanches who have been forced off their tribal lands. They introduce him to hemp smoking, and they soon become friends, brought together by their common status as outcasts. Eventually, Kid Blue and the Indians team up to stage a raid on their main source of irritation—the smoke-belching factory. "It's gonna be like the old days for you boys," he tells the Comanches as they prepare for the raid.

Kid Blue's critical reception was less than stellar. The venerable Vincent Canby, reviewing the film in *The New York Times,* concluded, "*Kid Blue* is the sort of movie that is likely to sound a lot better than it really is . . . *Kid Blue* is never very funny or provocative. It tries too hard. It's too insistent."[3] As Canby suggested, Shrake's script, written in 1969 as the sixties were peaking, has a far too didactic view on the issues of the day—conformity, racism, evil sheriffs, free love, and intergenerational conflict. In the movie, as in the times, it seems too easy to separate the good from the bad, and the script lacks the subtlety and thoughtfulness of Shrake's best novels. By 1973, many of the issues addressed in *Kid Blue* had become clichés.

Kid Blue did not become the hit for which Shrake and the studio had hoped. The movie made some money, but it did not linger in the public's imagination. Though friends in Texas have steadfastly maintained over the years that *Kid Blue* is a cult classic, in truth the film has all but disappeared. It has never been released on video or DVD, and it only rarely appears on American television. Still, the payoff from scriptwriting was gratifying for Shrake. Far more people watched Dennis Hopper acting in *Kid Blue* than had ever read Shrake's novels.

***

Because his first two screenplays were made into films, Bud Shrake was seen by Hollywood as a hot commodity. Screenwriting offers came pouring in. In the meantime, there was the matter of his unpublished novel, the *Satyricon*-inspired comic romp through Texas that he'd written back in 1969. After the chilly reception among New York editors, Shrake set the manuscript aside.

But in Austin, his friend, Bill Wittliff, owner of the Encino Press, suggested that he could publish the book. "I knew that Bill did really nice, beautiful books," Shrake said later. "So I said, 'sure.'"[4] Released in 1973 as *Peter Arbiter*, the limited-edition book was indeed gorgeous to behold, designed by Wittliff and illustrated throughout with woodcuts by artist Barbara Whitehead.

Peter Arbiter's picaresque tales are narrated by Peter, the modern incarnation of Encolpius, the rakish, profligate bisexual who narrates *The Satyricon*. While Petronius served the Emperor Nero's court as an arbiter of taste and elegance, *Peter Arbiter* is a long-haired, bisexual interior designer for the Texas Big Rich. Peter and his longtime companion, Albert, split violently over their shared passions for Guy-Guy, a teenage boy. The events and characters in Peter Arbiter closely parallel Petronius' classic work. The crude, wealthy businessman, Lichas, becomes "Big Luke" in Shrake's retelling. His nymphomaniacal lady friend, Tryphaena, is "Thelma." In some ways, Shrake's novel can be seen as a mere literary exercise, an opportunity to flex his narrative skill. But the adaptation is so inspired and the scope of the satire is so audacious that *Peter Arbiter* outpaces even Terry Southern's *The Magic Christian* as black comedy.

Peter, like Encolpius, is an unapologetic aesthete with a talent for finding trouble. His misadventures across Texas' cultural landscape open at the scene of a campus demonstration, where students are protesting the price of black-eyed peas. Peter wishes that the speaker "could address the crowd with eloquence rather than bombast," and he mourns "the passing of elegance, a demise brought on by the ambition of parents who shoved all these assembled young people into the university for no better purpose than to enter or keep hold in the middle class, a parody of the ideals of wisdom and beauty and pain to the sensibilities of my own self."[5]

From there, Peter visits a whorehouse and attends a party where he comes to the attention of Big Luke and Thelma. They promptly fly Peter and Guy-Guy to their ranch house with the promise of kinky sex. Big Luke also plans to introduce Peter to the local priest. "You'll like him, Petey," Big Luke tells him.

Illustration from *Peter Arbiter* by Barbara Whitehead published by Encino Press.
Courtesy Barbara Mathews Whitehead

The Father's not one of your Red-lining atheistic fakes but a real man of God. He can drink like a shrimp boat captain. Wine, gin, vodka, beer, it's the same to him. Down the hole and bless your ass. That's the kind of religion we need in this country. Your damn sissy black-robed Reds with all their hollering about Jesus, why they don't do nothing but make people unhappy. The Father, though, he makes them happy. That's what God wants, ain't it? If it ain't, then I learned my Bible wrong.[6]

Peter has numerous sexual encounters throughout the chronicle, yet they are far fewer and more heterosexually oriented than those of Encolpius in the original *Satyricon*. At one point, Peter, like Encolpius, suffers from a prolonged bout of impotence despite the most enticing sexual opportunities. While Encolpius seeks a cure from a priestess, Peter visits a Regenerator Erection Laboratory.

Peter also meets up with a poet, Sidney Hulme, who poses as a billionaire and targets the Texas Big Rich with an absurd scam. Sidney enlists the aid of Peter and Guy-Guy. As the money comes pouring in, Peter begins to worry about the seriousness of their crime, but Sidney reassures him, "Frankly, dear Peter, this has worked even better than I had expected. There's no limit to the avariciousness of the local citizens! Tease them with the lure of fast money earned by the sweat of

distant peasants, and it's like pouring pudding in a swine trough!" Indeed, the coarse wealthy class is becoming increasingly sycophantic toward Sidney and his friends, even to the point that they begin to express admiration for their long hair.[9]

At the height of his huge prank, Sidney completes his epic poem, *The Grubiad,* and reads it to the assembled businessmen. The prospect of poetry causes some grumbling at first. "If he wasn't rich I'd think he was a damn communist," complains one man. Nevertheless, the reading begins, and the businessmen are forced to listen. The reading of *The Grubiad,* a parody of T. S. Eliot's *The Wasteland,* is one of the few events in *Peter Arbiter* not based on *The Satyricon.* The poem itself, wretched in its excesses, was a collaborative effort, with contributions from Shrake's friends Gary Cartwright, Billy Lee Brammer, Jay Milner, David Simmons, and John Sullivan. After reading the poem, Sidney's scheme begins to fall apart, and an unruly mob turns on him. But Sidney doesn't mind. For him, the grand plan was never about money. Instead it was about poetry, and forcing the louts to hear it. "I did it! I did it!" he says with immense satisfaction as his death looms. "I made those bastards listen."[10]

Despite the reach, depth, elegance, and inventiveness of Shrake's satire, *Peter Arbiter* would not find a national audience. It was published by a small regional press and few reviews ever appeared. Even the *Texas Observer,* which had criticized Shrake's earlier work with glee, ignored the book. Yet not all was lost in Texas. The new statewide magazine, *Texas Monthly,* carried rave review written by senior editor Gregory Curtis. The novel has "some of the funniest writing about sex since *Candy,*" Curtis exulted, "yet told in a fluid, deadpan prose that seduces you into Peter's bizarre world." The book is "ribald, visceral, excessive . . . [creating] a Texas even more extreme than Texas at its most extreme. If Shrake hadn't done it," Curtis concluded, "that mightn't have seemed possible."[11]

34.

CHALLENGING

TEXAS

On the heels of Shrake's and Gent's novels, Larry L. King had his own book coming out, *The Old Man and Lesser Mortals*. Published in January 1974, this was the second of King's collected magazine pieces. In addition to his portrait of Clyde King, it contains "Blowing My Mind at Harvard," a profile of lawyer Warren Burnett, his TIL award-winning story on West Texas, and a critical look at the "blood and thunder" of Texas junior high school football. Also present is a satiric review of a Jacqueline Susann novel and a reminiscence, newly written for the collection, about his days at *Harper's* with Willie Morris.

As usual, King pulls no punches in his writing. He confesses to his fight with Willie Morris even as he's embarrassed to admit to it. King also lays bare his journalistic methodology. "Despite a whisky tendency to aggressively claim attention," he concedes, "I tend to shrink inside and stammer when faced with interviewing people." As a result, he often works slowly, "preferring to observe for two weeks rather than interview for two hours. My goal becomes, simply, to wear the other fellow down: to hang around until he forgets my purpose and carelessly begins to consider me a part of the scenery worth rapping to." The technique, King admits, does not always work, and he lists some of the subjects, such as Nelson Rockefeller and Jane Fonda, who never let down their guard.[1]

King's critical reputation had been in ascendancy ever since the publication of . . . *and other dirty stories* five and a half years earlier, and the reviews for this new book were his best ever. He was hailed nationwide as a signature figure in the New Journalism. King could not only capture the essence of people and events, he was seen as a writer whose disparate pieces come to function as "chapters in an autobiography that continues to unfold as the reporter keeps writing"[2]

King declined to go on another publicity tour, as he had few hopes that the collection would sell well. Viking agreed, "perhaps burned by the expensive, nonproductive tour on behalf of *Confessions of a White Racist.*" But in light of the good reviews, King's publisher began to believe that that this new book might prove to be King's long-anticipated commercial breakthrough. Viking purchased more advertising and ordered a second printing of seventy-five hundred copies. Paperback rights were sold to Dell, which planned to bring out two editions—one for college bookstores and the other a mass-market paperback. As King wrote in a letter, "It's rare that a non-fiction collection makes the 'popular' paperback market, and so I'm delighted."[3]

Yet once again, despite the effusive praise for King's book among critics and the new push from his publisher, the book failed to catch on. Sales figures were disappointing. Many publishers and editors had long viewed Larry L. King as a good investment—a writer so talented and engaging that he surely would provide a huge commercial payoff at some point. But as the moderate sales figures remained in place for book after book, doubts about King's commercial viability began to creep into the picture. Writers can't subsist on great reviews forever.

***

After finishing his spring semester at Princeton, Larry L. King spent the summer of 1974 in Austin, where he planned to research and work on his LBJ book. King arrived in a state of unusual sobriety. In January, during a physical accompanying his forty-fifth birthday, he learned that his liver functions were beginning to fail. His doctor warned him that he needed to give up alcohol for at least a year to allow the tissue to begin healing. By April King decided to quit drinking. He did fine for several weeks. But once he arrived in Austin, he "fell off the wagon with a great thud."[4]

Despite his health worries, King's writing continued, and he found a new home for his magazine work. During the previous year, he had become friendly with Bill Broyles, the editor of *Texas Monthly*, and Broyles often suggested that King's work was a natural fit in the magazine. The problem, however, was that *TM* paid only $250 per story. Broyles offered to double the amount, but his main pitch was that King would find a natural audience in the pages of the magazine, which might in turn draw attention to his books.

King's first *Texas Monthly* article appeared in March 1974, and his name joined the masthead as a contributing editor. The article, "Leaving McMurtry," had originally been commissioned by *Life*, but that magazine folded before it could be published. The story recounted the hapless attempts of New Yorkers to adapt McMurtry's second novel, *Leaving Cheyenne*, to film. Larry L. King was the biggest name yet to appear in *Texas Monthly*, and Broyles was proud of his coup. Announcing King's presence in his editor's column, Broyles described him as having "carved out a substantial niche as a major American writer." He also told readers, "It has always been one of our goals, along with providing an outlet for promising young writers, to furnish a forum for the best Texas writers to publish in *Texas*. We all gain when a writer of the sensibility and talent of a Larry King turns his hand to the home soil, for the home folks."[5]

Soon King had two other articles in the works for *Texas Monthly*. Each would appear as a cover story. Both pieces also challenged the ban on obscene language imposed by publisher Michael Levy, who did not want his magazine to be too vulgar for Texas tastes. In one story, King had quoted a person saying "Fuck you." After some debate, Broyles was forced to print the dialogue as "F--- you." Broyles also explained to readers in his editorial column that normally such language "is not appropriate in this magazine because when used loosely it gives a tone to the language with which we do not usually feel comfortable."[6]

King, accustomed to writing for magazines where there were no such restrictions, found the censorship hilarious. He pointed out to Broyles that any person in Texas who read the article could surely supply the missing three letters in the phrase "F--- you." He also sent Broyles a letter that read:

Dear Brer Broyles,

I've been working this morning on using the four banned words—fuck, cunt, balls, and dick—in one sentence, in a way they would *have* to be published. But I am having a little trouble with it. The first part is easy: "Four balls," cried Dick, "take your base." But the fuck and cunt, now, they're giving me a lot of trouble. . . .

It does seem to me that the morality of Texas might be more effectively improved if we spent our time catching thieves in public office than in censoring writer's words but, then, it is well-knew that I am a Godless Communist Eastern Ivy League Motherfucker so what do I know. But to apply the New Rule to my sentence of the first paren, I guess it would read, "Four gentials," cried Penis, "take your base." . . . Gotta run. Doing 'Goodbye Penis Nixon" piece for *New Times*, with deadline 48 hours away.[7]

King's writing, aside from its challenging language, provided an immediate jolt to *Texas Monthly*. His August 1974 story on rednecks, which described them as America's "white niggers" and peaked with a fictionalized drama, drew the most mail the magazine had ever received. In September 1974, King's story "Coming of Age in the Locker Room" chronicled his love-hate relationship with football. The sport was in his blood, he knew, yet at the same time he despised its "root poisons," which crippled bodies and psyches and even whole communities that came to believe that their sense of honor rested with the success or failure of their local football team. King quoted two prominent University of Texas figures. One was Darrell Royal, who said, "A coach likes to have a lot of those old trained pigs who'll grin and jump right in the slop for him." The other was Frank Erwin, chairman of UT's Board of Regents, who was reported to say, "When it comes to sports and education, I want a university the football team can be proud of."[8]

Picking up on the themes introduced by Peter Gent in *North Dallas Forty*, King noted how "Locker room references to women are base. They are exclusively represented as pigs, bitches, sex objects. Tales begin, 'I made her do such-and-so,' or 'I grabbed her head' or 'I *forced* that bitchin' dolly to. . . .' It is the language of violence, of hostility, of sex crimes." This article also drew a strong response. Among those upset was Darrell Royal's family. His wife wrote to *TM*, canceling her subscription and demanding a refund. The magazine chose not to print Edith Royal's letter, but it was quickly learning that King's uncompromising journalism could be problematic. In the months ahead, King would also issue a tough criticism to editor Bill Broyles, challenging the magazine's very conception of Texas.[9]

35.

CHANGES

AT

SPORTS

ILLUSTRATED

While Bud Shrake's interest turned toward screen-plays, he continued his employment at *Sports Illustrated*. Shrake's work for the magazine was steady and competent, but a real dichotomy existed between his sports reporting and his "serious" writing. Editor André Laguerre, who much admired Shrake's narrative technique, increasingly pulled Shrake off the football beat, assigning him long, heavily researched feature articles. Shrake wrote profiles of Dallas Cowboys coach Tom Landry, running back O. J. Simpson, rodeo star Larry Mahan, and others. In his 1972 article on Landry, Shrake became the first journalist to address criticisms of the coach's handling of his team. Focusing on Landry's intense devotion to Christianity, Shrake also posed one of the more provocative questions to appear in the sports-oriented magazine: "Could Jesus have been a fan of a game that is so violent and mercenary?"[1]

Shrake also wrote several stories only marginally related to the sports world, and here his writing blossomed as his reporting became filled with his observant, subversive, and playful eye. By the early 1970s, he was contributing memorable pieces on diverse subjects such as the Kilgore Rangerettes drill team, a canoe trip through the canyons of Big Bend National Park, and the resurgence of alligators in Louisiana and Florida. His story on alligators began with a lead that would make even Dan Jenkins jealous: "It could be the twang of an ancient danger signal going off in the stomach or it could be no more than a paranoid hangover from *Tarzan* movies, but the sight of an alligator oozing down a mudbank into dark water invariably makes one think: that big lizard is looking for lunch and I'm the fattest thing he sees."[2]

The main area in which Shrake's reporting evolved was in the direction of film and television. He wrote on the founding of *Monday Night Football*, of Burt Reynolds' football movie *The Longest Yard*, and an article titled "The Film-Flam Men," about portrayals of sports in Hollywood's film industry. As Shrake's reporting for *Sports Illustrated* evolved in the early 1970s, both in style and substance, his work brought a larger measure of the New Journalism to *Sports Illustrated*'s pages. Though Shrake's magazine writing, mostly buried in old issues of *Sports Illustrated*, has never been anthologized or collected, it's clear in retrospect that, like his friend Larry L. King, Shrake became a first-rate writer of magazine journalism, and much of his work in *Sports Illustrated* far transcended the world of sports.

***

Sports Illustrated was one of America's premier magazines by the early 1970s. It boasted more full-color pages than any other publication in the country; its circulation rose to well over two million, and advertising revenues increased sixfold. It continued to publish cutting-edge sports journalism that overlapped into literary terrain and social commentary. Its 1973 story on unequal opportunities for women in athletics won *SI* its first National Magazine Award. The article also helped create the groundswell that led to the eventual passage of Title IX, which equalized funding between male and female collegiate athletes.

Though the magazine was peaking in terms of prestige and success, André Laguerre's reign as editor became increasingly precarious. For years, Laguerre had retreated to the friendly neighborhood bar for long drinking lunches where story ideas were tossed around. But as the drinking became more important than the ideas, staffers began to sense that Laguerre was losing his edge. Though still a brilliant editor, Laguerre was often in no shape to run the magazine's affairs after returning from his extended lunches. Several times he would sleep off the liquor in his office. One writer recalled, "You wouldn't exactly go into his office at 3:30 and suggest a five-part series."[3]

Laguerre's idiosyncratic style had often resulted in clashes with Time-Life's upper echelon. As *Sports Illustrated* came to occupy an increasingly important place in the Time-Life empire, management decided that a more businesslike approach was in order. The fact that Laguerre's drinking interfered with his work made their decision to fire him much easier. *Sports Illustrated* staffers were informed of the change in February 1974, and Bud Shrake was among those upset by the move. "But what I didn't realize yet was how different the magazine would become. That's when it changed from a writers' magazine to an ad salesmans' magazine. It was no longer any fun."[4]

The new editor was Roy Terrell, who had long chafed under Laguerre's command. Terrell had been the one to bring Jenkins and Shrake on board at *Sports Illustrated,* but over the years relations became frosty. "I think he resented the impact they made, the attention they received," another staffer said. "He did [his job] quietly, efficiently, effectively, and then here came these extrovert newcomers. People noticed them. They hung around the right joints, were big hello guys." Relations became so strained that when Time-Life was considering whom to name as its next editor, Dan Jenkins openly backed Ray Cave, Terrell's rival for the position.[5]

With Terrell's ascension into the post, "almost instantly, the culture of the magazine changed." In contrast to many of the magazine's cynical writers, Terrell remained a devoted, even idealistic admirer of professional sports. He had no use for the drinking and socializing that marked Laguerre's tenure. "Alcoholism, long accepted as a matter of fact throughout the company, was finally being viewed as a problem." Terrell surrounded himself with assistants who felt the same way. Meanwhile, many of *Sports Illustrated*'s best-known writers, Dan Jenkins and Bud Shrake among them, were far more comfortable in the bars than they were in the offices at Time-Life, Inc. Inevitably, new antagonisms were developing between *SI*'s writers and editors.[6]

Terrell and his superiors believed that things had been too loose during the Laguerre era, and the first order of business was to crack down on expense accounts. In April 1974, two months into his tenure, Terrell issued a memo titled "Expense Account Abuse." There was little question at whom the memo was aimed. Two weeks before, Dan Jenkins had run up a $2,200 tab at a restaurant and billed *SI* for the dinner. Soon thereafter, Jenkins was summoned into Terrell's office. Jenkins was told, "If you're going to live like King Farouk, you're going to have to pay for half of it yourself." Jenkins stared back at the editor. "Roy, what's that got to do with journalism?" he asked. "Shouldn't you be thinking about what's gonna be on the cover? I did my expense accounts the same way I've always fuckin' done 'em." Later, Jenkins recalled, "That's when I realized that Roy was more concerned about being a CPA than he was about putting out a good magazine."[7]

Jenkins was in a strong position to confront the editor. He was the magazine's star writer even before publishing *Semi-Tough,* and the novel's phenomenal success only reinforced his status. But several staffers were noticing a change in Jenkins' approach to sportswriting. No longer did he seem as devoted to providing memorable coverage of the week's most important sporting events. Instead, he appeared to spend more time luxuriating in his role as a rich and famous novelist. Jenkins had quickly gained a contract for a follow-up novel, and less than two years after *Semi-Tough* was published it was complete.

Realizing that he had tapped into a lucrative formula, Jenkins' biggest challenge in *Dead Solid Perfect* was how to keep Billy Clyde Puckett in it. As Larry L. King wrote to Peter Gent, "I reckon we are gonna have to suffer a whole spate of Billy Clyde books. I sure do hope Jenkins writes one about him bowling or shooting skeet. And he probably will. So would I, if I owned that money-making Puckett boy."[8]

The new novel essentially placed Billy Clyde Puckett on the pro golf tour. Since it was a bit of a stretch to have Billy Clyde function as an all-star football player and a professional golfer, the protagonist became Kenny Puckett, Billy Clyde's uncle. Kenny Puckett, just like Billy Clyde, is a wisecracking, laid-back narrator who serves up semi-funny one-liners every few sentences. The book's subject is, basically, in the words of Kenny, "golf and cunt." Just as Billy Clyde had won the Super Bowl for his team, Kenny wins a clutch victory at the U.S. Open, holding off none other than Jack Nicklaus in the final round.

Dead Solid Perfect is little more than *Semi-Tough* goes golfing and was hardly the cultural phenomenon that Jenkins' first novel was. Some reviewers sniffed that Jenkins "is making no bones about trying to repeat the super-successful formula of *Semi-Tough*." Others, such as Barry Hannah, writing in *The New York Times Book Review,* went even further. There are "some minor tickles in the book," he wrote, "But you've got refried beans here in comparison to the voluptuous sirloin of *Semi-Tough* . . . Kenny Puckett is as narrow and brainless a creep as I've ever seen in a book. I believe Jenkins thinks Kenny is also sort of cute. Kenny is forever recalling his own clever lines." Hannah concluded, "It may be the intent of the author to elevate self-conscious banality into an art form, but I thought the whole affair came off tacky."[9]

Still, Jenkins had plenty of admirers. Even those who derided his storyline as "soap opera, jock style . . . pure formula" conceded that "he's a fantastic gag writer." Pete Axthelm, writing in *Newsweek,* described the book as "vintage Jenkins—profane, outrageous and sharp-eyed in its parody of the overblown world of big-time golf. . . . But for aficionados, the real joy is still in the one-liners."[10] And it was those one-liners that connected with Jenkins' readers. People didn't pick up his books looking for insight or wisdom into the human condition. They simply wanted to be entertained. Jenkins understood that perfectly, and his raunchy, easygoing sarcasm went over well with readers. *Dead Solid Perfect* became his second consecutive best-seller. Dan Jenkins, it seemed, had the golden touch.

Jenkins had always looked after his old friend Bud Shrake—getting him on at the *Fort Worth Press,* recommending him for hire at *Sports Illustrated.* Now, as a successful novelist, Jenkins began to wonder how he could help his obviously talented, critically heralded friend become a best-selling novelist, too. Then the idea struck: What if they collaborated on a novel?

36.

TEXAS'

GONZO

JOURNALIST

With Dan Jenkins and Peter Gent on the best-seller lists, Texas letters suddenly boasted two bona fide literary superstars. Texas culture was becoming a force at the national level, not just in fiction but in music and journalism. Willie Nelson and Jerry Jeff Walker were storming their way up the music charts, and *Texas Monthly* magazine was creating a stir. Even those who remained derisive of Texas' newfound cultural relevance could not deny the state's economic prominence. The 1973 Arab oil embargo quadrupled domestic oil prices, and Texas, rich in oil reserves, was primed to take advantage. The state's economy boomed, and new residents flooded in by the tens of thousands, many fleeing the "Rust Belt" states of the upper Midwest. Texas boosters, with characteristic immodesty, began crowing that perhaps the state should secede from the rest of the Union. For much of its history Texas had enjoyed an exaggerated sense of its own importance. Now, with unprecedented success in the cultural arts and formidable economic muscle, Texas' reality seemed to be closing in on its rhetoric.

The rise of Texas in the national consciousness triggered massive media attention, and in March 1975 *Atlantic Monthly* published a special issue on the state. Included were articles by Larry McMurtry, Barbara Jordan, John Graves, Molly Ivins, and Katherine Anne

Gary Cartwright modeling his specially-tailored "Jap" boots. *Courtesy of Gary and Phyllis Cartwright.*

Porter. Bill Broyles and *Texas Monthly* staffers contributed several stories and sidebars. Larry L. King published two pieces in the issue, including one of his trademark personal essays, "Playing Cowboy."

King had suggested to *Atlantic Monthly*'s editor that Gary Cartwright could write about Texas football for the special issue.[1] Instead, the Atlantic went with Cartwright's *Texas Monthly* colleague Al Reinert for the story. In truth, Cartwright's reputation among editors was much the same as it had been back in 1968. He was capable of producing brilliant stories that rivaled King's finest efforts. But more often he brought forth clunkers, most of which died, unmourned, prior to publication. His friends, Bud Shrake, Dan Jenkins, and Larry L. King, had seen nearly every magazine article they ever wrote accepted for publication. Cartwright's own journalism, however, was littered with failures. Screenwriting had seemed like a potential option for him at one point, but unlike Shrake, Cartwright was unable to sell his subsequent work to studios.

Though Cartwright published more work in *Texas Monthly* than any other freelancer, he often seemed to follow in the wake of his better-known peers. Just as Shrake had profiled Tom Landry and Larry Mahan, Cartwright, too, produced stories on both men. A few years earlier, Larry L. King had made criminal defense lawyer Warren Burnett nationally famous in a memorable *Harper's* profile. Cartwright prepared his own story on Burnett for *Texas Monthly* in 1974, but editors were dissatisfied with it and reworked the manuscript substantially prior to publication. Bill Broyles even called upon Larry L. King for assistance in revising it. Cartwright, insulted, quit writing for *Texas Monthly*. He began making contacts at *Rolling Stone* and told others that he would soon be moving away from Austin.

During this time, Cartwright's second marriage crumbled. As his fortieth birthday approached in August 1974, he was sitting outside his apartment drinking beer with Bud Shrake and Jerry Jeff Walker. His wife of eleven years, Mary Jo, "came down the stairs carrying all of my earthly possessions bundled in her arms. She dropped them at my feet and walked away without a word. I remember thinking: Damn, is that pitiful little pile everything I own?" The formal divorce followed soon after. Cartwright moved to New York, deciding to reestablish himself there.[2]

A new opportunity arose with Fawcett Publications, a paperback house based in Connecticut. The editor was familiar with *The Hundred Yard War*, particularly the paperback edition that featured a football player flanked by two aroused women. Cartwright was offered a deal to write a paperback novel about pro hockey. "I didn't know the first thing about hockey," Cartwright said later. "But I figured if I could set the book in Texas I might have a shot at it."[3]

Thin Ice was published in 1975 as an original paperback. Marketed at bus stations and drugstores, the book had a cover depicting a topless woman, in a locker room, hugging a half-dressed hockey player. The only cover blurb came from Dan Jenkins, who effused: "Penetrating, haunting, hilarious, original. . . . Cartwright tells a story with brilliant humor, insight, and outrage." Despite his friend's testimonial, formal reviews of *Thin Ice* were lacking.

"*Thin Ice* came and went in a second," Cartwright said later. "I wish in retrospect that I'd spent more time on it, rewritten it a time or two. It might've turned out pretty good." In truth, *Thin Ice* has more to recommend it than *The Hundred Yard War*. Though Cartwright still had not found his voice as a novelist, the work is clearly that of a talented writer—though one still in search of a storyline. While the plot and dialogue are ludicrous at times, Cartwright's set pieces and local color are often superbly rendered, providing hilarious and insightful commentary on Texas' cultural foibles. Based mostly in Houston, the novel nicely captures the city's sweaty, earnest capitalism. In a reclaimed swamp outside of Houston stands "Jesusland," a Disneyland-like theme park for the devout. Jesusland's developer "was not necessarily a religious man," Cartwright wrote, "unless worship of the almighty dollar was the over-riding qualification."[4]

Thin Ice boasts a number of eccentric secondary characters, including a morose astronaut who makes claims to a UFO cover-up conspiracy. Other characters are takeoffs on Cartwright's Mad Dog friends, and some, such as Peter Gent, appear as themselves in the novel. True to the promise of the cover art, the sex is abundant, graphic, and kinky. For those who were later shocked by Cartwright's detailed and intimate confessional of his experiences with Viagra in a 1998 issue of *Texas Monthly,* the encounters between "Frenchy" and "Monique" in those passages have clear antecedents in *Thin Ice.*

Cartwright's dashed-off novel helped pay the bills, but it hardly threatened the best-seller lists, nor did publishing an original paperback do much to enhance his literary stature. His output as a freelancer had also declined during the book's writing, but he gained a toehold in *Rolling Stone*. In early 1975 the magazine commissioned a new article. Cartwright was asked to write an exposé of the illegal sport of dogfighting, which often pitted dogs in matches to the death.

The article was not one for delicate sensibilities. The first draft began with a view of a live cat being dropped into the pit. "The cat number is traditional at dog fights," Cartwright wrote, "much like clowns at a circus or halftime bands at football games."[5] The story concluded with a savage recounting of a final grudge match staged between two dogs—a father and his son. Both dogs died. The editorial staff at *Rolling Stone* was split. Half of them loved it; the other half hated it. After some debate, the article was handed back to Cartwright. He was free to peddle it elsewhere.

Several other magazines rejected the story for being too intense, including *Esquire, Playboy,* and *Sports Illustrated.* As Cartwright noted later, people had a real problem with the notion of animals being killed. "It was okay to write stories about humans being murdered, but animals, well, that was going too far."[6] Finally, he found a magazine willing to publish his article. It was *Texas Monthly.* This was not the first time that *Texas Monthly* would prove its loyalty to its writers, nor would it be the last. Cartwright's article appeared in the August 1975 issue, marking his first appearance in the magazine in nearly a year.

Cartwright also decided to move back to the much cheaper Austin from New York City. In Austin he married Phyllis McCallie Sickles, whom he had met at a Willie Nelson picnic. The ceremony was performed by a minister from the "Universal Life Church." That was Bud Shrake, who had earlier sent $100 to a mail-order house in New Jersey and became an "ordained doctor of metaphysics."[7]

Cartwright returned to Austin with a new perspective on his writing. Completing his novel and seeing the visceral reactions his dogfighting article evoked gave him more confidence than he'd had in years. As he matured, with Phyllis at his side, he also gained greater control over his work. Cartwright, in the best New Journalism fashion, began to successfully incorporate himself into his narratives. The bulk of his life and experience had been lived in Texas. Of all the publications in the country, *Texas Monthly,* he realized, was best suited for his writing voice and sense of perspective.

In November 1975 *Texas Monthly* published another Cartwright article. This one was a cover story on Jack Ruby, featuring the famous photograph of Ruby plugging a bullet into Oswald. Cartwright provided a stark insider's view of Ruby and reviewed his own history in Dallas. In taut, hardboiled prose, he convincingly dismissed the various conspiracy theories, concluding that Ruby, never a stable person to begin with, was probably mentally ill and was certainly beset by brain tumors when he jumped out from the crowd and shot Oswald. "If there is a tear left," Cartwright wrote, "shed it for Jack Ruby. He didn't make history; he only stepped in front of it. When he emerged from obscurity into that inextricable freeze-frame that joins all of our minds to Dallas, Jack Ruby, a bald-headed little man who wanted above all else to make it big, had his back to the camera."[8]

Cartwright's story was compelling as an elaboration of history, but his larger success was in bridging his personal experience with the historical event. His reporting style made him as prominent a character in the story as Jack Ruby. This technique of immersing himself into the fabric of stories was hardly new—it was after all a major element of the New Journalism, and Tom Wolfe, Joan Didion, Hunter S. Thompson, and Larry L. King had been doing it for years. But in Texas, Gary Cartwright had a reservoir of real-life experience that few other journalists could match. As he noted later, "Every writer should have a Jack Ruby and a Dallas." Recalling his and Shrake's friendship with Jada, the star stripper at Ruby's Carousel Club, Cartwright wrote, "Every writer has a Jada in his life, or should."[9]

In 1976, Gary Cartwright published just three articles in *Texas Monthly*, but each was a sensation. He solidly debunked Jay J. Armes, an El Paso detective who claimed to be the world's greatest private eye. Another story, "The Ultimate Game," was a backstage look at the Dallas Cowboys' participation in that year's Super Bowl. Willie Nelson and Jerry Jeff Walker played at the pregame parties, and Peter Gent covered the event for *Sport*. Cartwright zeroed in on Gent's portrayal of "the Cowboys as a seething mutation of dope fiends, paranoiacs, fruits, cretins, and homicidal maniacs—managed by direct descendants of Daddy Warbucks and Genghis C. Khan." Tom

Landry's response to Gent's novel was to claim, "that he doesn't read that sort of book, but is halfway through *The Rise and Fall of Richard Nixon.*"[10] Nearly missing from the account is any mention of the football game itself, though few seemed to mind. Gary Cartwright was delivering Texas-styled gonzo journalism.

The December 1976 issue contained another Cartwright cover story, this one on Dallas stripper Candy Barr. That cover, one of the magazine's most famous ever, featured the young, blonde Barr outfitted in scanty cowgirl getup and firing a prop pistol from between her legs. Candy Barr, aka Juanita Dale Slusher, was a teenage runaway who arrived in Dallas in the early 1950s. She was almost immediately induced to star in a porno film, *Smart Aleck*, that became one of the country's most notorious of the time. Later, she became a star stripper at Dallas' premier men's joint, the Colony Club. Much of Dallas' business establishment became well-acquainted with Candy Barr during after-hours gatherings. In 1957 she was arrested for marijuana possession and, in a widely publicized trial, received a fifteen-year prison sentence.

After her parole, the forty-one-year-old Barr became a recluse, living a quiet life in Brownwood, Texas. She remained an object of curiosity but refused reporters' requests for interviews. She eventually agreed to talk to Cartwright, in part because she had seen his Jack Ruby story and was impressed. After several delays and postponements, Cartwright finally received an invitation to her home. Once he arrived, he was kept waiting in the front room for two hours. Finally, Candy Barr emerged from her bedroom. Cartwright's description of her entrance has taken on an aura of legend among other journalists of the era:

> Her blonde hair was in curlers. She had scrubbed her face until it was blank and bleached as driftwood. Her green eyes collapsed like seedless grapes too long on the shelf. She wore a poor white trash housedress that ended just below the crotch, and no panties.
> "Don't think I dressed up just for you," she told me.[11]

By the time he published the Candy Barr story, Cartwright was recognized as one of the state's top journalists. He was aided immeasurably by *Texas Monthly*'s own formidable presence, as the magazine's circulation had increased tenfold from twenty thousand in 1973 to nearly two hundred thousand by 1976. In 1977 Cartwright had his most prolific year for TM ever, writing six feature stories. One of them, "The Endless Odyssey of Patrick Henry Polk," won him his first major award as a freelance writer—the Texas Institute of Letters Stanley Walker Award. Savoring the acclaim was sweet, and Cartwright's friends and writing colleagues considered the honor well deserved. But even as his magazine journalism was in ascendancy, Cartwright was discovering what Larry L. King had learned before him—a good reputation doesn't guarantee a freelance writer enough money to be comfortable.

Like his friends, Cartwright worked on novels between magazine assignments in the hope that a novel would bring him a big score, just as it had done for Jenkins and Gent. Jenkins' editor at Atheneum, Herman Gollob, suggested that Cartwright write a detective novel set in Houston. Cartwright complied, but Gollob was unimpressed with the effort. So were other publishers. Cartwright also attempted to write a novel set in Fort Worth, but that effort, too, failed.

Cartwright's finances were often stretched thin. Despite his growing acclaim as a journalist, he was sometimes reduced to taking on physical labor to help pay his child support and other bills. He even spent one summer digging ditches for a living. Many times his friend Bud Shrake, still employed at *Sports Illustrated*, helped Cartwright out with small "loans" that never required repayment. Shrake provided similar services for Billy Lee Brammer and gained a reputation for generosity among his friends. When the subject came up years later, Shrake shrugged it off, saying, "I was the only one then who had a job."[12]

Cartwright's financial prospects improved dramatically on August 2, 1976. On that day a masked gunman broke into a hilltop mansion in Fort Worth and shot three people at close range. Two of the victims died, but one, Priscilla Davis, survived. She was the estranged wife of

Cullen Davis, the multimillionaire who owned the mansion. Soon Cullen Davis became the richest man in America ever to be charged with murder. The publicity was enormous. For Gary Cartwright, the old police reporter from Fort Worth, this case was exactly what his writing career had been waiting for. He had deep experience and contacts in the city; his prose style had been honed by years of experience; and he was ready for the challenge of a nonfiction book.

True-life crime stories had become popular since Truman Capote's 1965 best-seller, *In Cold Blood*. Texas had already seen one sensational high-society murder case turned into a hit book, Tommy Thompson's *Blood and Money*. Gary Cartwright knew that if he handled the Cullen Davis case well, he might have the same opportunity for success.

37.

TEXAS

BRAIN

FRY

After spending the summer of 1974 in Texas, ostensibly researching his LBJ book, Larry L. King returned east to resume his teaching duties at Princeton. But he found it difficult to return to the academic life. He decided instead to take an apartment in New York City and commute to campus. As the semester got underway King worried that another year of teaching would slow his writing career, allowing younger and hungrier writers to gain ground. When a new administrator demanded that he spend more time on campus, King had enough. He announced his resignation effective at the end of the semester.

King emerged from Princeton focused not on his LBJ book but on his magazine journalism. He began writing a twice-monthly column for *New Times,* an upstart weekly designed to appeal to *Harper's* and *Atlantic* readers. Though he sorely missed having *Harper's* as his base, King did find work in *The Atlantic* and *Playboy.*

After leaving Princeton, King's involvement in politics notched up several degrees when his friend, Congressman Morris Udall of Arizona, decided to run for president. King had been close to Udall for several years—his late wife Rosemarie and Udall's wife Ella had been best friends, and the two couples had often vacationed together. King had written about Udall in *Harper's,* and he'd often volunteered his political acumen and writing skill on Udall's behalf. With a presidential campaign in the works, King became serious. He wrote speeches for Udall, helped script his television appearances, and arranged fund-raisers. He counseled Ella Udall on how to handle media interviews, and he organized other writers in support of Udall's candidacy.[1]

King's interest in politics remained acute, and, at one point, he nearly moved back to Texas to run for Congress. Not to win but to write a book about the experience. His connections with Texas and politics made him a top choice for certain assignments. *The Atlantic* sent him to cover the criminal trial of John Connally, who had been charged with taking bribes. As Texas itself became more prominent in the media, offers to write about his home state increased. King accepted them, even though he began to worry about being typecast as *only* a Texas writer. In 1973 *Playboy* had sent him to cover the closing of the Chicken Ranch in La Grange. King's resulting article would eventually inspire the Broadway hit *The Best Little Whorehouse in Texas*.

Playboy also commissioned King to write about Willie Nelson's Fourth of July picnic. His article, "The Great Willie Nelson Commando Hoo-Ha and Texas Brain Fry," is one of King's most playful works ever—a countrified takeoff on Hunter S. Thompson's gonzo journalism. King recounted a demented journey through the blistering heat, crazed violence, and mind-numbing drugs. He and his sidekick, Bud Shrake, arrive at the picnic only to find that their press passes are deemed irrelevant. Trapped out in the Texas sun with some seventy thousand "writhing human forms as far as the eye could see," King and Shrake go several hours without food, drink, or shade—though drugs are in plentiful supply. King reported to *Playboy* readers that he snorted "a hog tranquilizer," mistakenly believing it to be cocaine.[2]

As King and Shrake weave their way through the crowds, they are confronted with guns and King is beaten by a three-hundred-pound "Samoan" security guard. They eventually crash the small trailer reserved for the Pointer Sisters, and there King, fighting off attempts to restrain him, eats the Pointer Sisters' dinner. As chaos and madness descends over Willie's picnic, Willie himself remains comfortably sequestered in a secret hideaway, far removed from the broiling masses.[3]

After the concert, King's story turns more serious. Willie's promoter explains that, despite the overflow crowd and distinct lack of amenities, Willie will probably lose money on the show. The promoter takes great pains to portray Willie as "a goodhearted raggedy-ass who might have to sell his horses or find his wife a part-time job." King is almost convinced, until two pistol-packing cowboys walk in and dump several sacks onto a table. One tells the promoter, "This here's the $40,000 from advance ticket sales in San Antonio."[4]

At a post-picnic party, people hang out in an Austin apartment, listening to a stereo play Willie's songs of "how cold it is sleeping in the ground, of life's rough and rocky traveling." By then, King had learned that Willie had jetted out to Hawaii immediately after the picnic. "I'd been a Willie Nelson fan for years," King wrote, and "his mournful, melancholy music never had failed to reach me. But now all I could think of was Willie picking up the phone in the Waikiki Hilton to call room service, he and God grinning together at the irony of his poor-boy songs."[5]

King also continued to produce articles for *Texas Monthly*. In June 1975 he wrote of the rivalry between two cities he knew well— Midland and Odessa. In December he profiled Blackie Sherrod, the sportswriter who had trained Jenkins, Shrake, and Cartwright. King's story was largely endearing, spiced with funny quotes and reminiscences from Jenkins and Shrake. But inspired by Bill Broyles' editing suggestions, King also addressed lapses in Sherrod's coverage, as the sportswriter failed to "aggressively go after the soft underbelly of sports, or write of its darker side."[6] King's stories on Sherrod and Willie Nelson made it clear how uncompromising his writing was. Despite the fact that both subjects were close friends of King's own good friends, and he was marginally friendly with both men himself, King chose to raise difficult, yet valid, points that challenged the popular conceptions of both men.

Larry L. King at the Encino Press, 1976. *Photo by Bill Wittliff. Bill Wittliff Archives, Southwestern Writers Collection, Texas State University-San Marcos.*

King worked well with Bill Broyles and soon he and Broyles began discussing the possibility that he would accept a monthly salary from *Texas Monthly* in exchange for producing a handful of stories each year. King would also be expected to help lure some well-known non-Texan writers to its pages. King's increased presence in Texas also led to his involvement in other state matters. He helped organize, along with David Halberstam, a fund-raising appeal on behalf of the *Texas Observer.* King also agreed to take a more active role in the Texas Institute of Letters after Bill Wittliff became president of the organization in 1974. Wittliff made a concerted effort to include the newer generation of Texas writers in the TIL and he got King to agree to deliver the keynote address at the organization's 1975 meeting. King also served on a judging committee. There, he voted to award the TIL prize for journalism to Gary Cartwright for a *Rolling Stone* story on drug dealing in Austin. But the majority of the committee judged otherwise, and Cartwright lost that year to Griffin Smith's rural-themed story in *Texas Monthly* on the state's "Forgotten Places."

King enjoyed writing for *Texas Monthly* and, just as he accepted editorial advice from *TM*, he in turn offered his own suggestions for the magazine. In early 1976 he sent a letter to Bill Broyles, identifying a weakness that would become the magazine's Achilles heel in the years ahead. King wrote, "The *Monthly's* one shortcoming, I think, has been a lack of covering "'the other Texas'—the poor, the blacks, the chicanos, etc. I do not mean to say that you should become a bleeding heart magazine, but it does appear to me that a vital part of what Texas constitutes is being missed there."[7]

Though Broyles contested King's assertion, the editor did in fact significantly broaden *TM*'s coverage soon after receiving King's letter. The magazine ran a photo essay on "The Other Texas," and minorities were incorporated into feature stories. Broyles himself wrote an incisive examination of Barbara Jordan that went far beyond the easy stereotypes about her politics and leadership. Gary Cartwright wrote about a family on welfare, and it was this story that won him the Texas Institute of Letters award in 1977. In 1979, *Texas Monthly* won another TIL award for Richard West's cover story on African Americans' retaining a sense of family and community in a rough-edged Houston neighborhood. From 1976 to 1979, *Texas Monthly* featured African Americans on its cover five times. After Broyles left the magazine in 1980 and Gregory Curtis took over as editor, it would be another fifteen years before a black person appeared on the cover of *Texas Monthly*.

***

In January 1976 *Texas Monthly* published an article by King on Lyndon Johnson. Titled "Bringing Up Lyndon," it examined Johnson's complex relationship with his parents and the importance of LBJ's

Texas childhood in his psychological makeup. The article might have served as a preview of King's forthcoming book on LBJ, had there been one. It had now been over four years since King had signed his contract, but other than this magazine article, there was little to show for his efforts. The lack of cooperation from LBJ confidants had made his challenge difficult, but King conceded later that there was a larger problem. "I was petrified at thoughts of producing an inferior book, and so produced none."[8]

King finally began to confess to others that he was postponing the book indefinitely. He also had to come to terms with the fact that he had spent every penny of his $100,000 advance. There were no more monthly payments. Unfortunately, King had not been good at handling money, as his lifestyle had been predicated on making "merry until I dropped in my tracks."[9] For a couple of years, he had earned excellent money with his magazine work, Princeton salary, and Viking payments. Now, his income was dwindling at the same time his debt was rising. A financial noose was tightening.

King continued to "whoopee away" money at Elaine's, running up tremendous tabs. "I couldn't have kept hanging out there if Elaine hadn't carried me like she did," he said later. "At times I owed her several hundred to several thousand dollars, and I just paid it whenever I could. She never called anything in."[10]

Elaine was far more easygoing than King's other creditors. The financial pressures made him less picky about accepting assignments. Instead of hanging out with subjects for weeks at a time and publishing thoughtful, heavily researched, and well-crafted stories in magazines like *The Atlantic,* King began churning out articles for *Sport, True, Classic,* "and other publications that did not demand Faulknerian prose, but wanted a lot of it, and had the virtue of paying promptly."[11]

It became harder for King to stay ahead of the game, especially after IRS auditors determined that he owed substantial back taxes. King's fading writing prospects, his massive debt, and the high cost of living in New York prompted him to look toward Texas in the hope of renewal. He had often imagined returning to the state, though it had been more than thirty years since he'd left. Texas had changed significantly in recent years, and it seemed a more hospitable place for him. Austin boasted a flourishing writers' colony, and *Texas Monthly*'s editorial and commercial success seemed ripe with opportunity. King renewed his conversations with Bill Broyles about signing on with the magazine. He asked about the possibility of becoming a full-time *TM* staffer. By this time, however, it seemed to King that the magazine was less enthusiastic about him. "I somehow never got as much encouragement as I'd hoped or expected from Broyles," King said later.[12] Once the discussions with *Texas Monthly* fell through, King abandoned his plans to move to Austin, and his work for the magazine soon dried up. After an August 1976 article on country music, it would be almost ten years before his byline appeared in *Texas Monthly* again.

38.

LBJ,

SPEED,

AND

PARANOIA

After he drifted away from *Texas Monthly* in the spring of 1973, Billy Lee Brammer was back to scrambling for money to see him through his days and nights. As always, his many friends helped however they could. Still, it was tough to get by, and that's how Brammer found himself selling souvenir programs at Willie Nelson's first-ever Fourth of July picnic.

A few weeks later, Brammer was flipping through the Austin newspaper when he noticed a photograph of an attractive performer starring at the Country Dinner Playhouse. It was an old friend, Diana de Vegh, the New York socialite who had bailed him out in Europe eleven years earlier. Now an actress, she had starred in the original version of the ABC television soap opera *All My Children*. Brammer went to the club, and before long the two resumed their relationship. After de Vegh's run in Austin ended in mid-August, Brammer returned with her to New York. The man who a short time earlier had been outfitted in clothes from the Salvation Army would now be living in an upscale apartment overlooking Central Park.

In New York, Brammer found renewed opportunities for his writing. *Rolling Stone* commissioned an article on Don Meredith, who had recently announced that he was leaving *Monday Night Football*. Brammer visited Meredith and got a good interview, but the article itself never took shape. Another opportunity came from filmmaker Robert Benton, who suggested that Brammer write a screenplay for him. Benton promised that he would either direct the movie or, at least, help sell the screenplay. Brammer took on a writing partner, his friend and former *Texas Monthly* colleague, Al Reinert. A few months later, a thirty-nine-page film treatment, written mostly by Reinert, was completed. The project never advanced beyond that.[1]

Brammer remained in New York for much of 1974, and he experienced an epiphany of sorts while attending a seminar at the Lehrman Institute. There, he heard Doris Kearns, a historian at Harvard, talk about her experiences with Lyndon Johnson. A few years earlier, Kearns had caused something of a scandal in the Johnson camp. She was young and pretty and had become a favorite of LBJ's after his retirement. She stayed several months at the LBJ Ranch and helped Johnson draft his memoir, *The Vantage Point*. Though Kearns denied that she and Johnson had ever had a physical relationship, she did tell reporters that he had once proposed to her. Johnson's confidants were not amused, nor were they impressed. "Hell," Bill Moyers was reported to say, "he would have asked me to marry him too if he thought it would have helped get something done. That's just how he was." In 1974, when Brammer saw her, Kearns was finishing her own book on Johnson, and she described it as an "intimate history" that would go into detail about LBJ's personality.[2]

Throughout 1974, much of the nation was consumed by the drama of Watergate and Richard Nixon's eventual resignation. For Brammer, hearing Kearns talk about Lyndon Johnson brought back vivid memories of his own experiences. By this time, his view of LBJ had soured. In light of Nixon's conduct, Brammer judged that Lyndon Johnson was at least as bad, and he believed that the last two presidencies were disgraceful.[3]

Brammer spoke to Doris Kearns after the conference, and, as they talked, an idea for a magazine article came into his head. He would write about Kearns and her book, and, in the best New Journalism style, he would also inform the piece by drawing on his own experience with Johnson. Brammer quickly wrote a seventeen-page

Bud Shrake, left, and Billy Lee Brammer in New York City, ca. 1973.
(Brammer has his eyes closed because he was recovering from cataract
surgery.) *Photo by Jody Gent. Bud Shrake Archives, Southwestern Writers
Collection, Texas State University-San Marcos.*

prospectus for the article. The prose, emotionally taut and lucid, was
his most coherent writing in many, many years. If *The Gay Place* had
largely ignored LBJ's "dark side," Brammer was determined to set the
record straight now. Brammer described Johnson as a raving egoma-
niac and a venomous, cruel, hateful, charlatan.[4]

Brammer's prospectus promised to expose Johnson's social and
sexual transgressions in detail. He described how Johnson relentlessly pursued women—including employees and friends' wives—and
how Johnson's heavy drinking made for many terrible evenings among
those who were part of his circle.[5] Brammer also described unsavory
aspects of LBJ, such as his fondness for showing off his penis and talking to it affectionately, that would appear in print only twenty-eight

years later with the publication of Robert Caro's third volume of his Johnson biography.

Brammer advanced a theory about Johnson's failed leadership that paralleled much of what Doris Kearns would argue in her own book. Johnson's refusal to accept reality, Brammer wrote, was evidenced by his creation of self-serving lies—such as his claim that he had been born in a log cabin and his grandfather had died at the Alamo. In addition, Johnson had crippled his understanding of his own country by disregarding popular culture. This created a stagnant and self-delusional view of America, Brammer concluded, that destroyed his presidency because he could no longer understand the people he was governing.[6]

Brammer's proposed article, especially with its revelations of Johnson's sexual predatorship, was a daring publishing gamble in the mid-1970s. *Playboy* expressed interest and wanted to see more. Yet as the months went by, it became clear that Brammer's prospectus itself, written in a blaze of outrage, indignation, and, possibly, interest in Doris Kearns, would become his final word on the subject.

Brammer did complete one article for publication in 1974. One of the young *Texas Monthly* writers he had befriended, Jan Reid, had finished his book on the Austin music scene, *The Improbable Rise of Redneck Rock.* Brammer agreed to write a review essay for the premiere issue of the *Austin Sun,* the city's new alternative newspaper. The review would be something of a coup for the *Sun,* having a writer of Brammer's stature in its first issue. Brammer missed several deadlines but gave repeated assurances that he would finish the piece. Finally, on the eve of publication, with a blank space where Brammer's article would be, a staffer was dispatched to check on Brammer's progress. The writer's apartment door was wide open and music could be heard from the street. Inside, Brammer was sitting in front of his typewriter, beating a tambourine against his thigh in time to the music, and poking out his article one finger at a time.[7]

Brammer's review appeared under the title, "Austin's Musical History Explored." His fitful digressions strained connections to the topic at hand, but he faithfully reprinted some of the book's best lines, and asked for "a little whoop of appreciation for the effort put forth by Jan Reid."[8] Though he would live another three and a half years, this became the last prose ever published by Billy Lee Brammer.

By early 1975, Brammer, now forty-five years old, moved back to Austin. He stayed in a garage apartment behind the home of *Texas Monthly* staffer Richard West. Hopes that Brammer might recover his writing voice soon faded. Yet he continued to make a deep impression on those around him. "Over the years Billy had followed his curiosity wherever it wandered, and he always discovered friends," Al Reinert wrote later. "No matter who you were or what your story, when Billy was with you he gave you his full attention, and that was a lot of attention to have."[9]

Brammer's friends usually found it easy to forgive him whenever he stole from them, and jokes about him being a kleptomaniac became common. In 1975 he was arrested for shoplifting. More serious trouble developed in January 1976. Brammer was a passenger in a car driven by a friend, "who proved to be the subject of a statewide police alert." A police car attempted to pull them over, and soon the chase was on, with several cops in hot pursuit. "Following the inevitable smash-up, there was a bit of a shoot-out, Billy huddling all the while on the floor of the back seat groping for the plate-glass bifocals he needed to see with." Brammer "looked so incredibly harmless," his friend Al Reinert later wrote in *Texas Monthly*, that it "was two hours before [the police] bothered to search him." When they did, Brammer had over an ounce of pure crystal methedrine in his pocket. He could have easily left it in the car or ditched it at any time, but it had been a long time since he'd had that much speed in his hands, "and he just couldn't bring himself to throw it away."[10]

This new arrest brought another outpouring of help from friends. "Sympathetic journalists censored news of his arrests, several lawyers offered to defend him, bail money was gathered." For his release on bond, Brammer listed Edwin Shrake, Bill Broyles, and his ex-wife Dorothy as his permanent contacts. As his case moved through the legal system, Brammer's lawyer moved to suppress the evidence on the grounds that he had been searched without probable cause. The motion failed, and on November 22, 1976, the thirteenth anniversary of the Kennedy assassination, Brammer had his day in court. He pled guilty in exchange for five more years' probation.[11]

In late 1976, Brammer moved back to his parents' home outside of Dallas. There, he "inaugurated the ongoing garage sale that so baffled and amused his friends all winter." Brammer was selling off anything he could from the house—old table lamps, photographs of his grandparents, his high school baseball uniform. Cash was accepted for the transactions, but drugs were preferred. He seemed entirely unworried about his legal problems, and he continued to greet acquaintances with his trademark query, "Hidy, got any speed?"[12]

* * *

Peter Gent made over $500,000 on *North Dallas Forty*, became a media star, and earned "a lasting place in the mythology of football." But as Gary Cartwright wrote, Gent "didn't always handle fame and fortune as well as friends wished." Soon after Gent's novel was published, the Dallas Cowboys played on *Monday Night Football*, and Don Meredith broadcast the game for ABC. Gent planned to meet Meredith before the contest but arrived at the stadium under the influence of psychedelic drugs. Gent recalled, "I just hallucinated. I kept seeing Texas Stadium as a big transmitter to God." Instead of walking through the entrance, he tried to climb a fence. A security guard spotted him and a chase ensued, with Gent running through the parking lot, jumping from roof to roof of cars. Corralled by several guards, Gent began ranting uncontrollably. He was taken to a holding tank and locked up while the police were called. It was at that point that Gent decided to leave the cell. "I actually felt I could disassemble and reassemble my molecules to the other side of the bars," he said later. As he approached the iron bars, he thought to himself, "Now here comes the hard part." But instead of dematerializing, he just clanged into the bars. At that point, his captors began talking about sending him to a mental institution.[13]

Gent was rescued by Don Meredith, who strolled in wearing his yellow ABC blazer. Meredith called a friend in stadium security, explained that Gent was very tired, and arranged for him to be sent to a local hospital instead of jail or asylum. Meanwhile, the game started without Meredith in the broadcasting booth. After rejoining his colleagues Frank Gifford and Howard Cosell, Meredith grinned and explained his tardiness by saying, "I have to weewee just like everyone else."[14]

Gent's drug use was making him increasingly paranoid. He became certain that the NFL was spying on him, looking for opportunities to destroy him. As his paranoia grew, the imagined conspiracy widened. Cartwright noted that Gent "carried several loaded guns and believed that the CIA and the Mafia were neck and neck in the race to bring about his end."[15]

At times, Gent would recover and go through periods of extreme lucidity. Gary Cartwright recalled that when he saw Gent at Super Bowl X, he looked "trim, confident, and comfortable." But the paranoia could strike quickly. A few months after the Super Bowl, Larry L. King saw Gent at Bud Shrake's house. King mentioned that he was going to fly to Odessa the next day to visit lawyer Warren Burnett. Gent suggested that he could drive King there, and, the next morning, King hopped into Gent's car. He quickly realized that he had made a big mistake. Gent, who had been awake for several days, outfitted himself with a large quantity of marijuana and cocaine for the drive. He also kept two pistols on the front seat next to him in case of trouble. Six rifles were packed in the trunk.

Other than Gent stopping to shoot at a cow, the trip to Odessa was largely uneventful. In Odessa, the two met Warren Burnett in a bar. King recalled, "Gent took one look at Burnett and decided that he is a CIA man in cahoots with the FBI, who he's sure is chasing his ass. I found out later that the whole reason Gent had gone with me to Odessa in the first place was to give the FBI in Austin the slip." Gent's paranoia caused him to believe that Larry L. King had cleverly led him into a trap. After some threats of gunplay, Gent announced very loudly to everyone in the bar that he was driving back to Austin. No one was sorry to see him go.

A few months later Gent apologized to King. He also told him that he had only *pretended* to drive back to Austin. Instead, he drove in the opposite direction—to El Paso. This way, Gent thought at the time, he would finally give his tormentors the slip. King and Gent

Peter Gent outside of Wimberley, Texas, early 1980s. *Photo by Jody Gent. Courtesy of Jody Gent.*

continued to be friends, but King felt that their relationship changed after the trip. "Ever since that time, I had much less to do with him socially," King said.[16]

During his periods of lucidity Gent continued working on his follow-up novel, *The Texas Celebrity Turkey Trot.* The new book would look at the life of a Dallas football player after retirement. Gent's friendship with Bud Shrake remained the most stable of any of his relationships with other writers, and by 1977 Gent decided to move back to Texas, purchasing a small spread in the hamlet of Wimberley, thirty miles southwest of Austin in the Hill Country.

39.

HOLLYWOOD

VS.

SPORTS

ILLUSTRATED

By mid-1975, Austin was abuzz with talk of Willie Nelson's new record, a concept album that told a story of betrayal, murder, and redemption. For the first time, Willie made the recording in Texas, using his own band instead of studio musicians. Willie's Austin fans were excited, but Columbia Records was worried that the unconventional record would prove to be a flop. To their eyes the album's saving grace was that it had cost only $20,000 to produce. But any doubts about the record's viability vanished as it met with overwhelming critical and popular acclaim. *Red Headed Stranger* became Willie's biggest album ever, selling millions of copies and winning a Grammy award. It spawned a huge crossover hit, "Blue Eyes Crying in the Rain." Willie was becoming one of America's biggest music stars.

Austin, Texas, was no longer a well-kept secret. The success of its music scene and favorable press accounts were attracting more and more newcomers. The tremendous growth worried established residents, and Bud Shrake made his feelings known in a rare article for the *Texas Observer*, "The Screwing Up of Austin." "Austin is engaged in a death-grope with real estate developers," Shrake warned, "and there is nothing less hip than that." Forget about Austin, he told readers. "Stay home or go to Indiana. If you move here, Austin won't happen."[1]

Austin was experiencing other changes as well. Women were becoming increasingly active in Texas politics, and Frances "Sissy" Farenthold made a breathtaking run at governor in 1972. That same year, Austin elected a new state representative—Sarah Weddington, the lawyer who successfully argued *Roe v. Wade* before the U.S. Supreme Court. Weddington's campaign manager was Ann Richards, who became Weddington's administrative assistant. In 1975, Richards decided to run for elective office herself and entered the Democratic primary for Travis County commissioner. She beat the incumbent, and in November 1976 she won the general election handily, becoming Travis County's first woman commissioner.

As Richards became a public figure, she found it necessary to leave her "Mad Dog" persona behind, though she never gave up her raucous sense of humor. But the Mad Dogs didn't always choose to leave her alone. One morning Richards woke to discover Bud Shrake, Gary Cartwright, and Jerry Jeff Walker in her bedroom. Outfitted in black tights, green capes, and red-and-yellow caps, they grinned maniacally. No introductions were needed. The Flying Punzars were set to attempt, once again, their vaunted "Triple Flip."[2]

***

In 1975, forty-four-year-old Bud Shrake received an invitation to stay with Dan Jenkins at his elegant beach home in Hawaii. The two old friends would do more than visit. They would also begin work on a collaborative novel.

"We knew that it would be about TV, but not much other than that," Shrake said. "We flipped a coin to see who would write the first sentence and Dan won." The sentence was one Jenkins recalled from their old days of hanging out together in Fort Worth, when the young writers imagined the first lines of their future novels: "It was a hot sticky night in Barcelona and all the good whores had the summer flu." From there Shrake wrote the second sentence and passed the manuscript back to Jenkins. Then the men took turns writing entire chapters, exchanging the manuscript for revisions. "We knew each other's styles so well it wasn't hard to do," Shrake said. "By the time the book was published I could no longer remember who had written what except for Dan's first sentence."[3]

Limo, published in 1976, recounts the escapades of Frank Mallory, a network executive from Fort Worth who rides to work every morning in a silver Rolls Royce equipped with four televisions and a bar. Mallory sounds much like a typical Dan Jenkins protagonist as he ruthlessly satirizes everything around him, particularly the vapidity of television and Hollywood. Mallory, though very successful, has a life complicated by an estranged wife, an angry girlfriend, a rebellious daughter, a down-home buddy, and crazed colleagues. A quote from Willie Nelson prefaces the novel: "Sometimes I take it as far as I can. . . . Sometimes I don't even go."

Limo, "light, fast, and funny," attracted mixed reviews. Most agreed that the novel had plenty of laughs in it, even as some cringed that Jenkins and Shrake "are sure making a last ditch stand for what has come to be called male chauvinism." A reviewer in *Texas Monthly* summed up much of the critical reaction: "Dan Jenkins and Bud Shrake may not be breaking new ground with this novel but they are sure to break the funny bones of their fans in Texas and elsewhere."[4]

Limo sold far better than Shrake's *Blessed McGill* and *Strange Peaches*. In that sense, it was a success. But the book also sold worse than any of Dan Jenkins' previous novels. Still, *Limo* generated momentum, and Jenkins and Shrake were hired by Hollywood to write a screenplay adaptation. The paperback edition announced: "Soon to be a major motion picture!" At one point, a director was hired and casting was only weeks away. But then the studio hesitated. The director was fired, and a new screenwriter was brought aboard for a rewrite. From there, the *Limo* project took a familiar route. The movie was never made.[5]

Limo was the latest in a string of Hollywood disappointments for Shrake. He and Cartwright failed to get a production for *Rip*, the screenplay they wrote in Durango. Shrake went on to write *Pancho Villa* and *Ambrose Bierce*, a script focusing on the historical meeting between Villa and the aged American author, who disappeared in Mexico at the height of the revolution. This is the same terrain that Carlos Fuentes would later explore in a novel, *The Old Gringo*. Shrake teamed up with Dennis Hopper to produce the film, and the two men, representing themselves as Mad Dog, Inc., tried to raise $500,000 from investors. But after some tantalizing leads, that project, too, collapsed.[6]

After his early success, cracking the film industry was proving to be much more difficult than Shrake initially thought. But by Hollywood's standards, he was still a success. This was a different world from that of New York publishing. In New York, Shrake had once been viewed as a talented young writer with good commercial potential. But as the years went by and each of his books sold less than the one before, Shrake's career as a novelist was in decline. His experiences in Hollywood appeared similar on the surface. *Kid Blue* had not done as well as hoped, and he had fought with Cliff Robertson over *J. W. Coop*. His subsequent screenplays were not getting productions. But screenwriting in Hollywood operated by a different standard than publishing books in New York. Movie studios buy hundreds of screenplays for every film that ever gets made, and many screenwriters earn a nice living without having a single movie produced. As one screenwriter noted, "It's funny because success is determined by how well you write the script, and that's what gets you your next job, not necessarily by how many things you get made. It seems like an incredible waste of money, but when you think of it as [research and development] costs, well, it's not so egregious."[7] Studio heads saw that Bud Shrake wrote good scripts, particularly about the Southwest, and as such he remained in demand. It was just a matter of time, it seemed, before a Shrake screenplay scored a big hit.

* * *

Willie Nelson's popular success soon brought him to the attention of Hollywood. The storytelling aspect of *Red Headed Stranger* seemed to lend itself naturally to a film adaptation, and Shrake helped broker an agreement between Willie and Universal Studios. Willie wanted Shrake to write the screenplay, but Shrake claimed "he didn't know how to write a story where the hero shoots a woman to death for stealing his horse." Instead, Shrake introduced Willie Nelson to another friend, Bill Wittliff.[8]

Wittliff, who would come to be known as a Texas Renaissance man, was already branching out from the Encino Press. In 1972 his photographic series on Mexican vaqueros became a traveling exhibit. In 1973 he showed his first-ever screenplay to Bud Shrake, who helped Wittliff obtain an agent in Hollywood. Remarkably, three of Wittliff's first four screenplays would be made into feature films. By 1978, when he met with Willie to discuss a screenplay adaptation for *Red Headed Stranger*, Wittliff had joined Shrake as the second Austin-based screenwriter to make a name for himself in Hollywood.

Bud Shrake's own screenwriting fortunes seemed to take a turn for the better when Columbia Pictures hired him to adapt Martin Cruz Smith's best-selling novel *Nightwing*. On the surface, the novel's plot seemed like high camp, as a colony of vampire bats threatens a small Hopi town in the Southwest. But Cruz's book was an intricately layered exposition that brings to life the tribe's myths and challenges. The bats themselves, while an element of psychological horror, were intended to be as symbolic as they are real.

The studio began making noises about a new big-budget block-buster. Shrake would write "a really high class thriller that dealt with important issues like the clash between the Hopis and the Navajos . . . the ecology of the area and the strip mining. . . . I didn't want [to] bring the bats in until the end, like the shark in *Jaws*." Columbia treated Shrake lavishly, putting him up at the Beverly Hills Wilshire for several weeks, and providing a generous stipend for expenses.[9]

Sports Illustrated, in contrast, was becoming increasingly tiresome. With the loss of André Laguerre, "it just wasn't as much fun as it was before," said Shrake. The new editor, Roy Terrell, installed assistants who shared his conservative mindset, and the cultural rift between writers and editors continued to grow. When one writer made a reference to reggae star Bob Marley in a basketball story, an editor examining the copy asked, "What in hell does this have to do with Charles Dickens?"[10]

The magazine's transformation became clear when a memo was issued demanding that writers contribute to the spirit of the enterprise. Many staffers, the memo accused, "never have even the slightest notion what stories will appear in the magazine each week . . . and couldn't care less about it." Among the complaints ticked off were writers who "spend much of their *working* time at home . . . dreaming up ways to augment their incomes with outside jobs." Also problematic were writers who "drag out over weeks feature-writing assignments that should be accomplished in days." Finally, the directive warned, management was growing tired of writers who "consider their expense accounts the ideal vehicle to adjust their salaries to the level they feel they deserve."[11]

The memo was quickly leaked to the press and caused a stir in New York media circles. Shrake himself was so bemused by its tone that he framed his copy and hung it in his home office. But there was no escaping the fact that, as his prospects in Hollywood expanded, his role at the magazine was shrinking. In 1978, he contributed far fewer stories than he ever had before. A few weeks before Christmas 1978, Shrake received an assignment to cover the National Junior Rodeo Finals. "I said no. Never in my life would I have told André [Laguerre] no." He responded by requesting a year's leave of absence. When that was turned down, he quit. His fourteen-year tenure at *Sports Illustrated* was over. At the age of forty-eight, the man who had once longed to become a full-time novelist was going to make a new career for himself—as a screenwriter.[12]

40.

WHOREHOUSE

After his hope of moving to Texas collapsed in 1976, forty-seven-year-old Larry L. King decided to quit writing about the state once and for all. He began "a painfully autobiographical novel about a middle-aged writer who drank too much [and] was ass-over-elbows in debt." As King explained it, "the novel would be confined to my New York period . . . the word Texas would nowhere appear in it, [and] my protagonist would be a rootless urbanite with no personal history beyond the moment he lived in."[1]

The novel, *Emmerich Descending*, began as a sharp burst and grew in fits and starts thereafter. Reminiscent of the dark, self-loathing humor found in Frederick Exley's *A Fan's Notes*, King paints a bleak picture of a once-proud writer. Emmerich's career is floundering and his agent begins hinting that he might drop him. Emmerich latches on to any writing assignment, no matter how degrading. Heavy drinking takes an ominous toll:

> He often has come awake to find improbable items, objects he could not have explained under penalty of death: stray hats, strange gloves, books foreign to his library, telephone numbers scrawled in unfamiliar hands beside the names of utter strangers, indecipherable messages in his own

hand appearing to read, *Fotz toom ungantly bisserso Tuesday* or *Simaleon guris thumper agais txd 6p.m.* Sometimes such codes had been thrice underlined, as if stressing their importance or urgency."[2]

Though exaggerated, there was raw truth in King's account. "It didn't quite get as bad in real life as how I wrote it," King said later. "But it could've gotten there before much longer." As the writer took stock of his twelve-year career, there was precious little to celebrate. Despite great reviews, none of his books had sold particularly well. His much-ballyhooed "big" book, the LBJ biography, was dead. His past was littered with failed novels, ranging from a few pages to a few dozen pages. He wasn't just tired of writing about Texas, he was tired of magazine journalism itself. Moreover, King felt inadequate to the challenge of long projects. "I seem not to have enough inner resources to stay the course," he wrote. "It is rather like facing a five-mile run while knowing I haven't enough in the legs and lungs to last past one hundred yards."[3]

As he sat down at his typewriter, the words no longer flowed as easily as they once did, and he began drinking more in the hope of jumpstarting the circuitry. Like Billy Lee Brammer, Larry L. King was losing his inspiration. "I am often blocked these days," King wrote in September 1976. "The longer I sit and stare at blank paper the greater the desperation and the growing conviction I'll never be able to get back on track."[4]

Complicating matters were the constant phone calls and letters from creditors. By this time, King's only guaranteed salary came from his column for *New Times*, which paid $900 monthly. Then, in October 1976, the magazine fired him. "For the next few days I did my wild-man act," King wrote, "hooting and dancing in a frenzy against *New Times*." He attempted to persuade writer friends to boycott the magazine but realized later that it "was terribly selfish, as well as wasteful of my energies."[5]

King's friends maintained that he had always landed on his feet, and, sure enough, two new prospects quickly opened up for him. King was contacted by Bobby Baker, once "a Lyndon Johnson intimate and powerful Capitol Hill wheeler-dealer."[6] In the early 1960s, Baker was targeted by Attorney General Robert Kennedy. After a well-publicized trial that briefly made him a household name, Baker was convicted of several felonies and sent to prison.

Now free on parole, Baker suggested that he and King could co-write his memoir. King "doubted whether many Americans remembered Bobby Baker or gave a hoot about his story." The project also seemed to be "the literary equivalent of shoveling shit in somebody else's barnyard."[7] King accepted for one reason only: It was his best hope for earning some decent money.

Shortly after his conversation with Bobby Baker, King received a phone call about his dashed off story on "The Best Little Whorehouse in Texas," which had appeared in *Playboy* a couple of years earlier. An expatriate Texan actor, Peter Masterson, had come across the old issue in a Broadway dressing room. He saw the whorehouse story and "read along, enjoying it, laughing, and then it hit me: *Goddamn, this is a musical!*"[8]

Masterson wanted to direct the show and help King write the play. Another expatriate Texan, Carol Hall, would write the songs. King was not impressed, nor did he like the idea of a musical, because, "as a writer it irritates me when the story comes to a screeching halt so a bunch of bank clerks in candy-striped coats and carrying matching umbrellas can break into a silly tap dance while singing about the sidewalks of New York."[9]

Because the *Whorehouse* project offered no advance money, King had little interest. He suggested that they simply pay him for the rights to his article. But Masterson and Hall were persistent, and King finally agreed to give it a shot. He still didn't believe that the project had any chance of success. But by this time, he had decided that the play's failure would make a good magazine article.

Masterson suggested that King could begin by writing a scene where two new girls arrive at the Chicken Ranch for a job interview. Thus challenged, King retreated to his typewriter to see what would happen. He began writing the dialogue and suddenly the "characters became people my mind's eye could see; they talked as they might in real life. I knew what they were going to say or do—what they *should* say or do." King had known for years that dialogue came easily to him, but it wasn't until he began writing scenes for this play that he realized that his gift for dialogue might make him a natural dramatist. He became consumed that first evening and a voice cackled inside, *"Shit, this ain't so fucking tough! I can do this! I'm a goddamn playwright!"*[10]

As much as King enjoyed writing for drama, the collaborative nature of the project drove him crazy. He rebelled against the revisions Peter Masterson suggested, and he feuded constantly with composer Carol Hall, believing that she wanted too many songs. "Simply put, I was always maddest at the unreasonable person or persons who in any given moment would not permit me to have my way." Still, after months of hard work and much wrangling, King thought that the play had reached a good place. It had well-developed characters, and it "contained generous amounts of dialogue; we had no dancing; songs, while plentiful, were not stuffed in willy-nilly at the expense of the book."[11]

By the fall of 1977 Peter Masterson worked out an arrangement to present the play at the Actors Studio in New York. The performances were a success, and a number of production companies expressed interest, including Universal Studios in Hollywood. Universal's plan was to develop an off-Broadway production, take it to Broadway, and then eventually make a film if the play succeeded. Once Universal became involved, hopes for *Whorehouse* began to rise dramatically. But the company also demanded changes that crushed King's original vision, the most dramatic of which was the decision to incorporate dancing. Another Texas expatriate, Tommy Tune, was hired as choreographer and codirector.

"Each time a song or dance number was added, I lost precious dialogue and pieces of my mind," King wrote. "I began to think of my book portion of the production as a mere skeleton on which to hang greatcoats of song and dance. Naturally, I howled and hooted— loudly accusing all hands of ruining my play, and predicting just as loudly that the 'cartoon version' emerging would close quicker than a switchblade." King's hostility toward Tune and King's ugly remarks about "fags" created even more tension. At one point Peter Masterson pulled King aside and cautioned, "You're gonna have to ease off Tommy. He tells me he's afraid you might 'strike' him." Tune himself told King, "Your negative attitude has taken all the fun out of it . . . all I can see when I close my eyes is your angry face!"[12]

Though King didn't realize it at the time, the changes were crucial to the play's success. King had greatly admired Preston Jones' *A Texas Trilogy*, a series of interrelated plays, rich in character, setting, and dialogue that warmly evoked life in small-town West Texas. Jones' plays had won great acclaim when they premiered at the Dallas Theatre Center. They also became a big hit at the Kennedy Center in Washington, D.C. In September 1976, *A Texas Trilogy* opened on Broadway with great fanfare. But the crowds stayed away in droves, and the plays closed after three weeks.

Whorehouse's bawdy nature already gave it an inherent advantage over the sometimes saccharine sweetness of *A Texas Trilogy*. But *Whorehouse* would also need more than well-developed characters, funny dialogue, and a strong sense of place to succeed. Universal Studios understood that Broadway audiences were looking for a dazzling spectacle, with singing, dancing, outsized performances, and glitzy costumes. They weren't looking for the real Texas; they wanted a caricature. King's original story was stripped away, and his characters became archetypes. But in the process the concept of Texas as Entertainment became amplified.

As much as he railed against the changes, several components of King's work survived the transition and even flourished in the new setting. *The Best Little Whorehouse in Texas* fired a powerful shot in the ongoing culture wars, and King and Masterson's script made no pretense about which side it was on. Miss Mona and her whores are the heroes. They are morally superior to the cowardly hypocrites who seek to shut them down. Just as in King's magazine article, *Whorehouse* aims at Texas politicians. The governor, who dances a sidestep, ignorantly babbles that "it behooves both the Jews and the A-rabs to settle their differences in a Christian manner."[13] A state senator, who is among the whorehouse's best customers, ends up joining a mob when the tide turns against the Chicken Ranch. King's script also contains some sly names. The play-by-play of the Aggies' football game mentions quarterback "Bubba Schrake." The Aggie running back who scores the winning touchdown is "Gary Cartwright."

By 1978, as *The Best Little Whorehouse in Texas* geared up for its opening, controversy erupted over the word "Whorehouse" in the title. *The New York Times* and several other newspapers steadfastly refused to print "Whorehouse" in paid advertisements, and television reviewers were told that they could not say the word on the air. Universal dispatched a series of executives to New York to come up with a cleaner title. Though King "had originally dashed off the title because I couldn't think of a good one," he now understood how bankable it was, and how the controversy would only help ticket sales. "Fixing each new Universal crusader with my meanest beer-joint glare, I would snarl, 'Are you willing to be the guy who throws away a million-dollar title?'" Universal decided to keep "whorehouse" and eventually most of the media caved in, with the exception of *The New York Times*.[14]

In retrospect, the timing for a Broadway musical titled *The Best Little Whorehouse in Texas* couldn't have been better. The 1970s had become a decade of sexual libertinism, and the play took full advantage, with double entendres and provocative choreography. Mainstream audiences were ready for material that was sexual without being explicit. "Texas Chic," which had been flowering since the early 1970s, was now in full bloom. The film version of *Semi-Tough*, starring Burt Reynolds and Kris Kristofferson, appeared in 1977 and was a box office hit. Willie Nelson's album *Stardust*, released in 1978, became a pop sensation and turned the singer into a national icon. Boots, cowboy hats, and jeans were popular, even in big cities on the East Coast. *Esquire* ran a cover story on "The Ballad of the Urban Cowboy." A prime-time soap opera called *Dallas* became a worldwide phenomenon. The Dallas Cowboys, "America's Team," won their second Super Bowl in 1978. Perhaps even more important, the scantily clad Dallas Cowboys cheerleaders became a national industry, starring in TV specials, commercials, and a poster that sold in the millions. With a little imagination, it was easy enough to conjure up images of those same cheerleaders starring in *The Best Little Whorehouse in Texas*.

The play opened on Broadway in June 1978 and became a smash hit. Its 1,584 performances over nearly four years made it one of the longest-running Broadway shows in history. For Larry L. King, life was doubly sweet. While *Whorehouse* was taking off, his book with Bobby Baker, *Wheeling and Dealing: Confessions of a Capitol Hill Operator*, astonished him by sailing up the best-seller lists.

Whorehouse received several Tony Award nominations, and Larry L. King, who had once been a finalist for the National Book Award, also received a Tony nomination. Better than anything was the money. The IRS claimed most of King's *Whorehouse* proceeds until his $13,000 back tax obligation was satisfied. After that, the weekly checks sailed King's way, and each one brought a new sense of wonder. One week he received a check for $46,000, an incredible sum for a man once on the verge of declaring bankruptcy. As the Broadway run continued and plans were made to stage the musical across the country and around the world, Larry L. King could declare, with some satisfaction, that he was now "two-thirds rich."[15]

41.

A
FRACTION
OF HIS
TALENT

I n late 1977, while his friend Larry L. King was inching closer toward success with his stage play, Billy Lee Brammer's health, finances, and prospects continued their marked decline. Though he remained listed on *Texas Monthly*'s masthead as a contributing editor, few took Brammer seriously as a writer anymore. He could still discourse brilliantly on a vast number of topics, depending on how the drugs and the spirit moved him at the time. Austin's younger generation continued to view him as a hero, even as the ravages of speed addiction wore his body down and made him appear much older than his forty-eight years. His friend Jan Reid recalled, "I'm sure he had dark nights of the soul. But socially, he didn't have that tortured writer sense about him. I think he was doing what he wanted to. He was embarrassed that he didn't have more money. But he was happy."[1]

Brammer worked a variety of menial jobs, accepting his circumstances with a calm equanimity that his friends found admirable. One season he might be washing dishes, another he would be a chef's assistant. The occupations themselves meant little to him, other than the opportunities they provided for graft. As Al Reinert recalled, Brammer's work in the kitchen meant that "his friends' refrigerators [became] swollen with stolen hams, huge buckets of shrimp Newburg, and occasional champagne magnums. Billy himself never wavered in his preference for cake frosting and Pepsi; rather he used his booty to barter for drugs."[2]

It was easy for Brammer's friends to take pity on him, but "he sure didn't take much pity on himself, and while he may have viewed his situation as uncomfortable, or unbecoming, he certainly never thought of it as tragic."[3] Despite his second felony conviction for drugs, Brammer's appetite for speed only expanded. He became increasingly involved in the drug trade, using the proceeds to finance his own habit.

On February 11, 1978, Billy Lee Brammer was flush from a big score on a drug deal. Sitting in his apartment near the Austin airport, he had a large cache of crystal meth and $3,000 tucked away inside a coat pocket. He reached for his needle. A short time later, his roommate discovered him gasping for breath and attempted mouth-to-mouth resuscitation. An ambulance was called but it was too late. Billy Lee Brammer was pronounced dead within an hour. The cause of death was ruled acute methamphetamine intoxication.[4]

Bud Shrake was in New York when he heard the news. He rushed to find Larry L. King. "Shrake was truly shaken," King recalled. "I think he was also stung by my reaction: 'Well, hell, Billie Lee has been looking for it a long time. I guess he finally found it.'"[5]

Over the years, Brammer had maintained a close emotional relationship with his three children, even as he found himself unwilling or unable to provide child support. Now that his children were grown, Brammer often spoke of making up his financial failure to them in some way. His daughter, Sidney, was living in Austin, attending classes at the University of Texas. She knew that her father had $3,000, because he told her that he wanted to use it to help his kids buy a house. Instead, the children used the money to bury him.[6]

Hundreds of people turned out for the funeral, including "veteran legislators, dope dealers, musicians, innumerable married women who came alone, and anyone in Austin who claimed to be a writer." Bud Shrake was there, along with Gary Cartwright, Ann and David Richards, Bill Broyles, Peter Gent, Ronnie Dugger, Jay Milner, Dorothy Brammer, Celia Morris Dugger, and Nadine Brammer Eckhardt. An old colleague of Brammer's from LBJ's staff in the 1950s also made an appearance. Sam Houston Johnson, Lyndon's brother, took a long, mournful look into the casket.[7]

In death, Brammer's best qualities were remembered by his friends. He was viewed not as a tragic figure, but as a fearless cultural avatar. Brammer had helped turn Austin into a cultural mecca, and as such he was canonized as a secular saint. In the *Texas Observer*, editor Kaye Northcott wrote that Brammer was as "important to the Austin underground as Ginsberg was to the Beats. They were both mentors, teaching the impatient how to cope with an imperfect world. . . . Back when we weren't trusting anybody over thirty, Brammer was a shining exception, an ally." At the funeral service Marge Hershey said, "He was a teacher all of us learned from. . . . He was civilized and he helped us all be a little more civilized when we were in his presence." Al Reinert, in *Texas Monthly*, judged that "In his own way, Billy died singing, like William Blake."[8]

Even Brammer's drug use and his subsequent inability to write became romanticized as part of his legend. Kaye Northcott, setting aside the question of Brammer's negligible literary production, wrote, "During his last decade, Brammer's gift to Texas culture was his own sweet, droll, eloquent, paradoxical, lascivious self." Gary Cartwright, in his own tribute, depicted a Brammer who willfully rejected his art. "Billy Lee was always ahead of the game. Instead of writing, he was cueing the rest of us on what to expect. . . . He went to the edge and stayed there. Some people thought it was a great loss to literature, and I suppose it was, but everyone who knew the man profited. . . . We won't likely meet his kind again."[9]

These sorts of accolades did not sit well with Larry L. King. "I was fond of Billy Lee, too, but I got awfully tired of him having all that talent and not producing," King said. "I got even more tired of hearing people make excuses for him all the time."[10]

* * *

In the years ahead, Brammer's literary reputation, fortified by its sense of tragedy, would remain secure in Texas. *The Gay Place* became one of five books chosen to represent the state during its 1986 sesqui-centennial. The novel itself has remained in print over the years, with new editions appearing at regular intervals. Interest in Brammer has remained acute. Occasional attempts at a biography have been launched, including one in the 1980s by Mark McKinnon, who would later gain fame as George W. Bush's media advisor during the 2000 presidential campaign. Several prominent essays and magazine articles have appeared, including stories in *Texas Monthly* by Al Reinert and Jan Reid, and a *Texas Observer* essay by Sidney Brammer. In 1995, the state's leading literary critic, Don Graham, wrote the introduction to the newest edition of *The Gay Place*.

Over the years, three major theories have emerged to explain how Brammer's writing disintegrated. The first, proposed by Al Reinert in 1979, essentially blamed Lyndon Johnson for Brammer's undoing. When Johnson publicly rebuked him, it caused Brammer to lose faith in himself, and, subsequently, in his writing. As Reinert put it, "in the moment of truth [Brammer] believed in his hero more than in himself." From that point on, Reinert argued, Brammer was never able to write well again. The second theory is less dramatic but more plausible. Larry L. King has written, "I've long wondered if Brammer received too much praise too soon from the literary critics. Something threw him off—frightened him, changed him—and I suspect that was it." King recalled Brammer's reaction upon hearing a rave review of *The Gay Place*: "Oh, Jesus, now they'll be waiting to pin my ears back if I can't do it again." This follow-up anxiety has also been cited by other friends of Brammer's, including Bud Shrake. The third theory, which appears in Don Graham's introduction to the 1995 reprint of *The Gay Place*, is less charitable. Graham wrote, "Brammer's decline and death have more to do with the stark and indisputable fact of pro-longed drug addiction than with the anxiety of achievement."[11]

The emotional dissipation that occurs with drug use reinforced Brammer's basic equanimity, making him appear to be ever more non-judgmental. To the sixties generation, this was seen as a philosophical breakthrough, and Brammer was credited for having "rejected wisdom." Others had a different view. Some who knew Brammer prior to his drug addiction were not impressed by the changes in his personality. They didn't believe that Brammer was transcending human emotion. Instead, he appeared to be escaping from it. The apathy was not attractive, no matter how hip it may have appeared to some at the time. As Brammer became detached from the conflict that governs most human emotions, he found himself at the forefront of what the sixties generation was trying to accomplish: a rebellion against the oppression of the self. Yet Brammer's method—the drugs—exacted their own toll of tyranny over him.

Brammer's death left a community of writers enriched by his mind and spirit, yet deflated by his lost literary vision and wasted potential. As Larry L. King wrote, "I felt, too, a quick surge of irrational anger. But even as I recognized it as such, a part of me began yelling at my old friend's ghost: *Goddammit, Billie Lee, why'd you get yourself so screwed up you left the world a fraction of your talent?"*[12]

42.

MEASURES

OF

SUCCESS

The high-pitched squeaks grow closer. Dark flutters appear and then suddenly, fangs slashing, a colony of vampire bats tears into its evening meal—shrieking human beings. Titters of laughter break out across the audience. *Nightwing*, as it turned out, became substantially different from Bud Shrake's initial conception. "It didn't take long before the studio heads decided that they wanted bats, bats, and more bats," Shrake said. "They had long meetings where they did nothing but talk about the bats." A prop specialist was hired to engineer robot bats that flew like remote-controlled airplanes, but then the finished models were far larger than any bat known to humankind. Shrake was present when the producer yelled at the designer, "Goddam you, you built our fucking bats too big." Shrake said later, "If I ever write a Hollywood novel I'm going to call it *You Built Our Bats Too Big*." The studio eventually fired Shrake from the project and ordered a rewrite. He retains a share of the screenwriting credit on the finished film, but it's not one he's proud of. "I've never been able to watch that movie all the way through," he said.[1] *Nightwing* was panned by critics, performed poorly at the box office, and did little to advance human-bat relations.

Despite his troubles on *Nightwing*, Shrake remained in demand. In 1979 Steve McQueen asked to meet with him to talk about a film on legendary Old West figure Tom Horn. The original script by

Thomas McGuane was unwieldy, and McQueen was looking for someone to rewrite it. Shrake flew to Los Angeles and arrived wearing old Levis and a cowboy hat. McQueen, who also preferred jeans, was reading a copy of *Blessed McGill.* He looked up approvingly as Shrake walked in. "I could tell when he looked at me that I had the job, because I looked worse than he did," Shrake said.[2]

Tom Horn, ambitiously conceived, did decent box office business, but it failed to reach the blockbuster status of McQueen's previous films. "I thought it was a real good movie, myself," Shrake said later. "Except for the last 15 minutes. And that was all Steve McQueen's fault. Warner Brothers was trying to talk him into letting Tom Horn live at the end. But McQueen wouldn't go for that, he wanted to get hanged onscreen." The producers had argued that people didn't want to pay to see Steve McQueen die. "And they were right," Shrake said.[3] As it turned out, McQueen may have had his own reasons for being preoccupied with death while working on *Tom Horn.* The actor was suffering from terminal lung cancer. He died later that year, just a few months after the film was released.

Following *Tom Horn,* Shrake returned to work on an idea he and Willie Nelson had been discussing for several years—a feature film loosely based on Willie's own life. "The story involved a country songwriter getting fucked by Nashville who moves home to Texas and figures out how to fuck Nashville back and come out on top. The movie was going to be about greed and power and loyalty and love. A musical." By 1979, Shrake completed the script and called it *Songwriter.* His agent sold it immediately to Tri-Star, which envisioned Willie starring in the film along with his friend Kris Kristofferson. Waylon Jennings was also suggested as a possible costar. Several times *Songwriter* was on the brink of production yet each time got canceled at the last moment. In the meantime, Willie Nelson became a movie star. He appeared in a cameo in *The Electric Horseman* in 1979. In 1980 Willie was signed for *Honeysuckle Rose,* his first starring role. *Honeysuckle Rose* "killed *Songwriter* for the next three or four years," Bud Shrake said later. "It took that long before anybody would touch a movie with the same subject."[4]

Screenwriting made for a nice living, but as the frustrations mounted Shrake grew eager to return to fiction. In 1979 he started a new book. Returning to a historical setting, he focused on the Comanche Indians' daring raids across the new Republic of Texas in 1842—a trail of death and destruction precipitated by President Mirabeau Lamar's aggressive exterminationist policy toward Native Americans. The climactic battle occurred outside the new capitol of Austin along Plum Creek, and Shrake's novel would be titled *Plum Creek*. In his book he would explore Comanche customs and lifestyles even more intimately than he had in *Blessed McGill*. In 1979 Shrake discussed the project with the editor in chief of Delacorte in a New York restaurant. The editor signed him to write the novel, based "on the two-word idea, written on a napkin: 'Comanche Sex.'"[5]

Screenplay assignments kept him busy, and work on the novel progressed slowly. At one point Shrake's editor wondered, only half in jest, "if I am really going to finish that book, or if I was just kidding." By late 1980, Shrake completed some three hundred pages of the manuscript. He had also substantially expanded his original concept. Instead of focusing exclusively on the Comanches, the novel now centered on the struggles of the young Texas republic. Actual historical personages became characters in the book, including Sam Houston and Texas Ranger Captain Matthew Caldwell. Just as in *Blessed McGill*, the novel included vibrant detail, bringing a sense of immediacy to the historical setting. Yet by the time Shrake submitted the draft, Delacorte's editor-in-chief had resigned and left publishing. The new editor had no interest in the book and rejected it out of hand. Shrake put the novel away and went back to screenwriting.[6]

* * *

While Bud Shrake's career as a novelist appeared to be over, his friend Gary Cartwright was engaged in what promised to be his breakthrough work. Murder defendant Cullen Davis spent an estimated twelve million dollars on his defense, and his murder trial drew national publicity. Gary Cartwright was not the only one writing a book on the case. The trial became a referendum on Davis' estranged wife, Priscilla, who had survived the shooting and was the prosecution's star witness. With her platinum-blonde hair and silicone breasts, Priscilla was no match for the parade of "character" witnesses who testified that she was a drug and sex-crazed floozy. Cullen Davis himself never took the stand. The jury concluded that reasonable doubt existed and found Davis innocent. Cartwright, like most observers, was disgusted. "Rich people can buy their way out," he later told a reporter. "If this had been a black poor guy . . . there's no question he would have been on death row."[7]

In the spring of 1979, David Atlee Phillips' *The Great Texas Murder Trials* was issued. Cartwright's own *Blood Will Tell* followed soon after. It would be joined by a third, and then, eventually, a fourth book on the Davis case. But Cartwright's work successfully "brought together a great cast of characters and a plot any novelist would envy." He made full use of Truman Capote's New Journalism crime reportage. Like Capote, Cartwright re-created conversations and detail from episodes he had not observed firsthand. The fictional effect is supported by the information Cartwright managed to uncover. He spent days and weeks hanging out with key figures in the case—becoming as much of a part of the scenery as the lawyers themselves. On one occasion he left his notebook behind in the courtroom. It was found by Cullen Davis' girlfriend. "She called me and said, 'Tee, hee, hee, guess what I've got?'" She agreed to return it after Cartwright promised to take her out for drinks.[8]

In *Blood Will Tell*, Cartwright successfully interpreted the events through a prism of Texas culture. "Like a masterly archeologist sinking his shovel into a midden heap," Robert Sherrill wrote in *The New York Times*, "Mr. Cartwright delicately uncovers one layer of trash only to lay bare the mysteries of a second layer of trash, which, being uncovered, reveals still a third layer of trash, and so on. Sometimes amiable, sometimes bloodthirsty, sometimes raunchy, sometimes pious, but trashy through and through: here is a society whose various strata are delineated only by differences in income."[9]

Blood Will Tell became a best-seller. After his long struggle as a freelancer, Gary Cartwright was thrilled to learn that he would make at least $50,000. Then Pocket Books purchased the paperback rights for $150,000. "Lord did we sing and dance," Cartwright wrote. He went out and immediately bought a new sports car because, "What the hell—you only feel like a king once!"[10]

***

The Best Little Whorehouse in Texas won only two of the seven Tony Awards for which it was nominated. Larry L. King and Peter Masterson's script lost, but King didn't particularly care. Instead, he relished the financial comfort *Whorehouse* brought him—and the changes it augured for his writing. "I can be more independent in my career, not having to approach editors like a blind beggar rattling a cup in his hand. I can say 'no,' after years of not daring to or feeling uncomfortable when I did."[11]

Whorehouse's resounding commercial success generated tremendous publicity, and King received the lion's share of the attention. His collaborators, naturally, took offense. Carol Hall kept complaining, "It is not 'Larry King's musical.'" Peter Masterson's friends sent letters to *Texas Monthly* and the *Texas Observer* with similar observations. As production for the film version of *Whorehouse* geared up, Universal Studios hired King and Masterson to work on the screenplay. Talk was that the movie would feature Paul Newman and Shirley MacLaine in the starring roles.[12]

King's life had also undergone a change in addition to his Broadway success. In May 1978, shortly before *Whorehouse* debuted on Broadway, King married Barbara Blaine, a lawyer who had been in the first female class admitted to Yale University. He had to borrow money from his new wife for their honeymoon. Blaine worked for a prestigious Washington law firm and soon began studying entertainment law. She would replace Sterling Lord as Larry L. King's literary agent.

The Best Little Whorehouse in Texas transformed King from a journalist into a playwright. He wrote a new play, *The Kingfish*, about Louisiana politician Huey P. Long, with Ben Z. Grant. In the 1930s, Huey Long built a political empire, railing against bankers and big business, and calling for the redistribution of wealth. His slogan, "Every Man a King," found many adherents during the Great Depression, and Long was seen as a serious challenger to Franklin Roosevelt's reelection in 1936. He was shot in Louisiana at the state capitol in 1935. Before dying, he was said to have pleaded, "God, don't let me die! I have so much to do!"

In writing a "one-man play about a dead Southern politician," King knew that *The Kingfish* would "not possibly have the firepower and dazzle and box-office clout of a musical such as *Whorehouse*." But then King was after more than money this time. He was also looking for "the assurance that you are not a one-play author." He found it. *The Kingfish* is a sparkling play that showcases two of King's best strengths—dialogue and politics. Long comes back from the grave and comments on scenes from his life, including his assassination. The technique is compelling, and the politician's dialogue crackles with energy. "They accused me of raisin' taxes," the Kingfish says. "And I stand guilty as charged. When you want ham, by God, you go to the smokehouse. The Kingfish went in that smokehouse and reached up high on the hog . . . and cut off a few good slices of the very sweetest meat. And then he tossed it out to the poor ol' hungry yard dogs. And it was the first time in Louisiana's history they'd been tossed more'n table scraps or a dry bone."[13]

Barbara Blaine produced a showcase run in Washington, D.C., and several investors expressed interest. An attempt to turn it into a musical failed, and *The Kingfish* remained unproduced for several more years. But the play's initial run had struck a chord with southerners, who "kept it fitfully alive through occasional one-night stands at conventions or other gatherings." In 1991, a group of Louisiana investors raised $400,000 and took *The Kingfish* to New York with actor John McConnell. In a familiar turn of events for King, the play was praised by critics but failed commercially. In 1992, SMU Press issued a print edition of the play, and *The Kingfish* continues to receive productions to this day. King himself has come to view *The Kingfish*, with some justification, as "the little play that refused to die."[14]

King's publisher, Viking Press, sought to recoup its $100,000 investment by capitalizing on King's *Whorehouse* success. He obligingly began work on a memoir, *The Whorehouse Papers*. Viking also rushed into print a new anthology of King's work, *Of Outlaws, Con Men, Whores, Politicians and Other Artists*. King grudgingly agreed to go on a short promotional tour for his new collection, and his visit to Texas in April 1980 was the subject of a feature story in *The Dallas Morning News*. The reporter chronicled King's alcohol consumption with evident awe. At an Austin book signing, King "swigged enough [beer] to irrigate a cotton field." King then went to the airport, "downing a couple of Bloody Marys." Though King didn't tell the reporter, his health was an increasing concern, as new tests had revealed extensive liver damage. On the airplane for a short ride to Dallas, King obliquely referred to his health problems. While "belting down a Scotch," he wondered, "when you have so many things you want to write [why] do you insist on slow suicide with whiskey and cigarettes?"[15]

43.

HITTING

THE

WALL

Peter Gent's second novel, *The Texas Celebrity Turkey Trot*, was published to lavish media attention in 1978. Following closely in the wake of Gent's own life, *Turkey Trot* functions as a sequel of sorts to *North Dallas Forty*—though without the inherent appeal of being an exposé on America's most popular spectator sport. Gent's protagonist snorts a lot of cocaine, has an affair with a rich married woman, and pals around with an outlaw country musician named Willy Roy Rogers. The novel tackles the ironies of "celebrity" and contains funny moments, but much of the work is disjointed, and the numerous subplots never manage to connect. An undercurrent of paranoia runs through the narrative, with vast conspiracy theories playing out across the book's pages. Reviews were lukewarm, and interest in Gent's follow-up quickly dissipated.

Shortly after his novel appeared, Gent went to Hollywood, where he helped fashion the screenplay for the film version of *North Dallas Forty*. His old Cowboy teammate, Don Meredith, was living in a Beverly Hills mansion and acting in several television projects. Meredith was offered a chance to play the hard-partying quarterback of Gent's novel, but he declined. Later, Meredith was sharing a table with Bud Shrake and Frank Gifford at Elaine's when the subject of the movie came up. Meredith told them he turned down the part because

"I just don't want others to think that's me." Gifford replied, "Well, it is you." Gent's friendship with Meredith faded after the release of the film. "The book didn't seem to bother [Meredith,]" Gent said later. "He was sort of glad to see it. But when it came out as a movie, his attitude changed about it."[1]

After his sojourn in Hollywood, Gent returned to Wimberley, Texas, to begin work on a new novel. This one would return to a setting with which his readers were familiar—professional football. Life in Wimberley seemed tranquil. Bud Shrake was a frequent visitor and bought some hilltop land nearby on Buttercup Mountain. Peter and Jody Gent got a wooden swing for him to hang from an old oak tree, and Shrake later told *Texas Monthly* that he liked to enjoy a view "that is open to rich sunsets with hawks cruising in the clouds above the valley. It is a place to go when the world is too much with me."[2]

***

Larry L. King's new wife, Barbara Blaine, tried to help her husband come to terms with his drinking. She made only limited progress, and by July 1980 King arrived in Texas in the midst of a two-week partying binge. He came to attend Willie Nelson's eighth annual Fourth of July Picnic, and he celebrated his return to Austin by drinking and doping even more. At some point, King "went a little bit crazy," as he later described it. He became paranoid and ended up on the roof of a friend's house. It took a while to talk him down. For a writer who relied on sharp powers of observation and keen judgment, the fissure in his sanity was a disabling experience. King returned to Washington and, in consultation with Barbara, agreed to check himself into Melwood Farm, "a plush drunk tank for rich folks" in rural Maryland.[3]

King scored a perfect hundred on the test Melwood's counselors gave for determining whether or not one is an alcoholic. He received intense therapy and was placed on valium and lithium because of fears he would turn violent. "I was not a good patient," he said later.

"It was a dismal experience, very painful, and I hated it." He received letters of support and encouragement from friends such as Norman Mailer and David Halberstam. Another friend, Congressman Charlie Wilson from Texas, made regular visits to cheer up King. Cartoonist Pat Oliphant created a special comic strip, titled "Larry of Melwood." The comic opened with a view of a hostile King trapped behind an electrified barbwire fence. It ended a few panels later with a newspaper headline that read "87 Slain, One Missing. Police Seek Playwright."[4]

King also received letters from Texas. Bud Shrake reported that when Peter Gent learned about King "going bonkers," Gent became very happy. "I have passed the baton on!" he cried. Shrake also sent King a number of requests. "[Jody Gent] said she hoped you would crochet her a purse while you are locked up. Pete said he would like you to make him anything in leather, but preferably a shoulder holster. . . . I'm not asking for much for myself—just a paper doll every now and then, maybe a nice crayon drawing."[5]

In a more serious vein, Shrake confided to King that he'd gone on the wagon himself since King left town. "I do know I've been drinking way too much," Shrake wrote, "I don't get cute so much any more as I get stupid and red-faced and hollow-eyed." King wrote Shrake back a "serious letter" and included the alcoholism test. Shrake replied that he, too, had scored disturbingly high on it, and he confided that his hangovers were getting worse. "I know I'm heading for real trouble if I don't lighten up some with the whiskey and the dope—and I swear I will in no way contribute to any backsliding on your part if I can help it. If you notice me doing so, slap my face. But not hard, please."[6]

Ann Richards was another friend of Shrake's who was experiencing a crisis with alcoholism in 1980. Richards had become a remarkable success as a county commissioner, transforming her precinct and winning respect from her mostly male employees. Her constituents also approved of her performance, and she ran unopposed for reelection in 1980. But David Richards began to believe that "Ann's involvement with alcohol suddenly seemed totally out of hand. . . . It struck me that Ann had fallen victim to the perennial risk of successful politicians—beginning to think they are bulletproof." Several of Ann Richards' closest friends became increasingly concerned about her drinking. One Sunday morning in September 1980, just weeks before the general election, they staged an intervention, confronting her with detailed stories about her ugly behavior while drinking. "It was overwhelming. Unbelievable," Richards wrote later. At the end of the session, "I was sitting there crying and so were they."[7]

Richards emerged from treatment a changed person. "I had seen the very bottom of life. There was no one worse than I had been." She became a recovering alcoholic and called the interventionists together to thank them. The entire affair was kept private, and no mention of Richards' troubles appeared in the press. In November, she was reelected to the commissioner's court. By early 1981, Ann and David Richards separated after almost twenty-eight years of marriage. The formal divorce came a few years later.[8]

If Ann Richards had been an attractive and successful politician while she was drinking, her newfound sobriety made her even more so. In January 1982 a number of prominent Democrats began urging the forty-eight-year-old Richards to challenge the incumbent state treasurer, who was tainted by scandal. Richards was a tireless and appealing campaigner, and volunteers flocked to her aid. "No woman had won statewide office in fifty years, and I was hell-bent on breaking that string," she recalled. An opponent in the primary raised her alcoholism, and she was besieged with questions. She admitted that, "yes, I certainly was an alcoholic and I had received treatment and was in recovery, and felt very positive about that." A backlash soon swelled against her attacker, who was depicted as a slug in an editorial cartoon in the *Austin American-Statesman*.[9]

The 1982 Democratic primary proved to be an election that Texas liberals had long dreamt about. Ann Richards prevailed, as did consumer advocate Jim Mattox, who won the nomination for attorney general. Garry Mauro became the land commissioner nominee. Most surprising of all was former *Texas Observer* editor Jim Hightower's win over conservative incumbent Reagan Brown for agriculture commissioner. As David Richards later recalled, "Granted, Jim's race had been aided somewhat when [Reagan Brown] thrust his hand into a fire ant mound to demonstrate for the press the harmless nature of the pests. There were memorable photos of Brown wringing his hand after the full pain of the stings began to take hold."[10]

There remained the problem of defeating Republicans in November, and Texas had become an increasingly Republican state. But at the top of the Democratic ticket was popular incumbent senator Lloyd Bentsen—the conservative Democrat who had unseated Ralph Yarborough twelve years before. Bentsen's top-notch organization boasted a stellar get-out-the-vote ability, and, ironically, it was Bentsen who helped sweep into office the new generation of "Yarborough Democrats," including Ann Richards.

***

In December 1979 forty-six-year-old Gary Cartwright went in for a routine checkup—which revealed that his blood pressure was an astonishing 235/180. Within an hour he was in the hospital "being pumped full of stuff to bring my blood pressure down to acceptable levels." Cartwright's doctor asked him if he'd taken any drugs the previous day. "I'll never forget the look of amazement in his eyes as I began to itemize them. 'Let's see, I had a few drinks, maybe ten double scotches, maybe more. And some beer. And some wine. And some tequila. Then . . . oh, right . . . I remember now, we smoked some pot, a lot of pot. Then . . . oh, yeah, about two in the morning somebody passed out some speed.'" When Cartwright checked out three days later the doctor warned him, "Remember now, no more speed!"[11]

After that day Cartwright stopped taking speed. "But since the doctor had not said specifically that I was to avoid whiskey, pot, cigarettes, or other specific stimulants, I permitted myself to believe that anything except speed was acceptable." Nevertheless, Cartwright did begin to take blood pressure medication in an attempt to regulate his condition.[12]

After the success of *Blood Will Tell*, Cartwright had his eyes on another high-profile true-crime story—the assassination of federal judge John Wood. Known as "Maximum John" for the stiff sentences he imposed on drug offenders, Wood was murdered as he left his home in San Antonio. El Paso's Chagra family was implicated in the murder-for-hire, and Charles Harrelson, father of actor Woody Harrelson, confessed to being the hit man. Some were calling it "The Crime of the Century." For Gary Cartwright, this would be his sequel to *Blood Will Tell*.

Feeling stagnant in Austin's "fur-lined trap," Cartwright now had the money to act on a long-held dream—living in northern New Mexico. In the summer of 1980, he and Phyllis moved into an old adobe house near Taos. From there, he would have relative quiet, a fresh perspective, and he would still be close enough to El Paso to follow the developments in the murder case.[13]

True to his style of personal involvement, Cartwright soon transcended mere reportage. "I really got close to the Chagra family and the people who knew the Chagras," he said. When Joe Chagra, younger brother of the defendant, was charged in the murder conspiracy, Gary Cartwright appeared as a character witness on his behalf. Cartwright came to the FBI's attention when his name "reportedly surfaced on an FBI tape of a conversation between [two defendants.]" At Charles Harrelson's murder trial, Harrelson's lawyer "announced at the outset [that] he might put Cartwright on the stand."[14]

Cartwright's work on his book "put me in constant communication with drug users and dealers, and gradually I went from using cocaine on rare occasions to using it fairly often." He and Phyllis began having increasingly angry arguments. After a year in Taos, Cartwright's "marriage was about to break up because of my love of coke."[15] He'd stopped doing magazine work, his book was not finished, and he was running out of money.

Once again, *Texas Monthly* came calling. In 1978, the magazine launched a new venture, the *Texas Monthly* Press, which published a number of significant titles including a reprint of *The Gay Place*. For years, the idea of an anthology of Cartwright's magazine work had been kicked around. In 1980, *The New York Review of Books* asked selected writers what they most wanted to read over the summer. Roy Blount Jr. answered, "A collection of Gary Cartwright's *Texas Monthly* pieces." *Texas Monthly* agreed, and in 1982 the press published *Confessions of a Washed-Up Sportswriter, Including Various Digressions About Sex, Crime, and Other Hobbies.* The majority of articles are from *Texas Monthly,* though work from *Harper's, Rolling Stone,* and the *Texas Observer* also appears. Just as Larry L. King had contributed revealing postscripts in his own previous collections, so too does Cartwright. The collection, aimed primarily at a Texas audience, received generous reviews in newspapers across the state. And they were deserved. After his long struggle as a freelance writer, Gary Cartwright had finally assembled a collection of stories that rivaled the best magazine work of Larry L. King. King himself concurred, telling an interviewer, "I think he's damn good. [In] the last, oh, five to six years, Jap's been doing some of the best magazine stuff *Texas Monthly's* ever done. I liked him twenty years ago . . . and he's done nothing but get better."[16]

Texas Monthly was interested in more than publishing Cartwright's anthology. The magazine also wanted him to join the staff as an associate editor. In early 1982, Cartwright accepted. His nearly fifteen years as a freelance writer came to an end, and he and Phyllis returned to Austin.

44.

A

RECOVERY

When Larry L. King emerged from treatment at Melwood, he had no conception of how to write as a sober person. "I had been so used to smoking dope and drinking, all those crutches, while I worked. Without them, I couldn't stay at the typewriter long. I just felt so fidgety." For three or four months King struggled. His writing felt mechanical and uninspired. Then, in December 1980, he agreed to write a Christmas piece for the *Washington Post*. King reached back deep, telling a story about Christmas 1933. His family was broke, and King was a four-year-old who desperately believed that Santa Claus would bring him something. King's father, uncharacteristically, decided to make a purchase on credit. He trudged off through the woods, unaware that a severe winter storm was approaching. The resulting story, "That Terrible Night Santa Got Lost in the Woods," brought King back. "I recovered my voice writing that story," King said, "and haven't had any problems ever since. In fact, I soon discovered that I was much more productive without all the doping and drinking."[1] In 1981 Bill Wittliff's Encino Press published a book version of the story, illustrated by Pat Oliphant.

King also completed a screenplay for the movie version of *Whorehouse*. For one who resented the Broadway maneuvers that had transformed his stage play into an outsized cartoon, King found Hollywood's treatment even more maddening. Soon it became obvious that Universal Studios had no interest in signing Shirley MacLaine to play Miss Mona. Instead, the studio wanted Dolly Parton. "Jesus Christ," King cracked to a gossip columnist when he heard the news. "She looks too much like she really runs a whorehouse." King's comment was widely reported and soon he received a letter from Dolly Parton, informing him that, despite what he thought of her, she would try her best. King quickly issued the most gracious apology he could manage under the circumstances.[2]

Then a feud erupted over Universal's choice for Sheriff Dodd. Paul Newman was no longer a consideration, and King lobbied for Willie Nelson. But Universal signed Burt Reynolds, at that time the world's top male box office star. King's public complaints began again. "Great," he said, "now we'll have 'Smokey and the Bandit go to the Whorehouse.'" Reynolds reportedly wanted more fistfights, car chases, and "wants to play it real macho. The sheriff [who is sixty-two in the play] can't be older than about thirty-five, and all the whores must be in love with him."[3]

Universal soon dumped King from the project, and the writer was not shy about expressing his displeasure over the film. He began referring to Burt Reynolds as "the alleged actor Burt Reynolds." He told one gossip columnist, "I see only a tenuous connection between *Whorehouse* as we did it and the mess they're concocting in Hollywood. I doubt whether I'll even go see the film version of the sonovabitch." In response to a question about whether Dolly Parton would wear one of her outlandish wigs in the film, King responded, "I suppose she will, and probably Burt will wear his, too. I understand that they're both bald."[4]

King's comments drew an angry letter from Reynolds, who threatened to take King "behind the barn" to settle their differences. King, in turn, was reported to have drafted a response to Reynolds that began, "You Turd." As the publicity mounted, a feeding frenzy erupted among gossip columnists. Eventually, even King became tired of it all and expressed a desire to move on. This brought a rebuke from an old

Texas friend, columnist Liz Smith. "You did want to be rich and famous, didn't you," she wrote to King. "Now you are, and I fear my column is the penalty."[5]

***

In May 1981 Larry L. King and Barbara Blaine purchased an elegant home in an upscale D.C. neighborhood. Next door is an embassy and nearby is the vice-president's residence. King took special pride in the fact that he and Barbara managed to win out over another interested party for the home—Republican senator John Tower of Texas. King remained sober for almost a year after graduating from "Whiskey Tech," as he called Melwood. He decided that he could probably handle a glass of wine or two during social occasions. But as he later wrote to Norman Mailer, "I've tried, shortly graduated myself to stronger gargle, and wound up in strange precincts at 3 A.M. singing 'Hinky Dinky Parley Voo.' I knoweth moderation not."[6] Abstinence, it seemed, would continue to be won one day at a time.

In 1981, King agreed to CBS television's proposal to write and narrate a documentary about the Texas legislature. He spent several weeks in Austin, interviewing politicians and conducting extensive debriefing sessions. At the end, he and his producer compiled some fifty hours of film footage, and King was pleased with the results. "I think I held several important feet to the fire," he wrote to his cousin. "I believe we'll have a good film."[7]

The Best Little Statehouse in Texas, as the documentary was called, aired August 26, 1981. King, appearing on camera as the narrator and chief inquisitor, humorously and cogently interpreted the legislative processes at work. He took great pleasure in exposing the hypocrisy and corruption, and he concluded by telling viewers, "Perhaps my Texans are a bit more colorful, a bit rawer, but the process, alas, is the same in your state."[8]

The program received great reviews, but CBS judged the telecast a failure, telling King that "only" some twelve million people had tuned in. "Only twelve million? Jesus fucking Christ," King said later.

"Even with *Whorehouse* it takes an awful lot of performances to rack up twelve million people. And when you're writing books that sell three thousand copies. . . .Well, twelve million sounds like a whole lot of folks to me. But they took great pride in telling me that it was the lowest-rated edition ever of 'CBS Reports.'" Yet King felt vindicated when the Emmy Award nominations were announced and his name was among those honored.[9]

King's friends found it remarkable—here was a man who became the only person ever nominated for a National Book Award, a Tony Award, and an Emmy. "Yeah, I thought about that, too," King said. "But there was no way I was going to that ceremony. "I'd already gotten my hopes up for those other awards and nothing happened. So when this came up I just said 'fuck it.' I knew there was no way I was going to win."[10] Then, the morning after the awards program, King woke up to some remarkable news. He had, in fact, won the Emmy for best writer of a television documentary.

45.

"EVER

A

BRIDEGROOM"

B y the late 1970s, Ronnie Dugger's *Texas Observer*, always on the brink of financial collapse, was facing a different kind of crisis: editorial turmoil. Over the years the *Observer* had weathered transitions in its editors well, each succession bringing forth new young talent. From Willie Morris to Molly Ivins, Kaye Northcott, and Jim Hightower, the *Observer* had a memorable run of editors from the early 1960s to the late 1970s.

In 1979, Hightower resigned to run for public office, and his departure exposed a weakness that was beginning to afflict the venerable *Observer* in its twenty-fifth year. Because the magazine's wages were so low, its editors were often young journalists in the early stages of their careers. Yet as Ronnie Dugger grew older, a distance developed between him and younger generations. After Hightower left, Dugger had no one to turn to, and he issued a public appeal for applicants. Finally, after a seven-month search, he hired Rod Davis. Within a year Davis announced his resignation, citing "an irreconcilable conflict with the publisher and owner, Ronnie Dugger, concerning editorial direction, policy and control." The search for another new editor consumed several more months, and in the meantime Dugger had to reassume editorial duties even as he was in the process of moving away from Texas to New York. "I began to feel unwelcome in Texas," Dugger told a reporter later. "I began to feel I was staying on too long in one place. I was happy to get out. . . . There's a mean-ness that's taken over."[1]

Dugger was between editors in the summer of 1981 when he paid a visit to Larry McMurtry's bookstore in Washington, D.C. The two men began discussing Texas and its literature. McMurtry had become increasingly distant from the state in recent years. He had rarely returned after moving away twelve years earlier, and he explained some of his feelings about Texas in the *Atlantic Monthly*'s special issue in 1975. "For people with active intellectual needs, the state becomes increasingly less habitable as they mature and these needs increase. Informed conversation is simply too hard to get; those who could give it are spread thin."[2]

Initially, McMurtry's move to the D.C. area gave him a fresh per-spective that helped his writing. He produced the novels that have since become known as his "Houston Trilogy": *Moving On, All My Friends Are Going to be Strangers,* and *Terms of Endearment.* The film made from his earlier novel, *The Last Picture Show,* had been a big hit, and many assumed that the movie had made McMurtry rich. Yet he had accepted only an up-front fee, signing away rights to the film's enormous profits. But his experience working with director Peter Bogdanovich and actress Cybil Shepard drew him into Hollywood's orbit. McMurtry took work script-doctoring, and he also wrote origi-nal screenplays, though none was ever produced. He became a con-tributing essayist to *American Film* magazine. Like Bud Shrake, McMurtry began to collect Hollywood material with an eye toward writing a novel.

McMurtry allowed his former student at Rice, Bill Broyles, to lure him into occasionally writing for *Texas Monthly.* McMurtry also agreed to be listed as a contributing editor for the magazine. But his rela-tionship with *Texas Monthly* was always prickly. McMurtry complained to Broyles because his first article in the magazine appeared under a different headline than he had given the piece. A year later, *Texas Monthly* commissioned a book review from him but then chose not to run it. McMurtry again fired back, arguing that the magazine had no reason to reject the review. This time, McMurtry's complaints jabbed deeper, as he criticized Broyles' editing of the magazine. He told Broyles that the magazine seemed designed to make all writers sound like Gary Cartwright. And that, McMurtry tersely pointed out, was not a model he wanted.[3]

In 1978, Larry McMurtry published a new novel that underscored his distance from his home state. *Somebody's Darling,* McMurtry's Hollywood opus, was his first book with a non-Texas setting. It also was the first of three substandard novels that critics later referred to as McMurtry's "Trash Trilogy." Among the poor reviews *Somebody's Darling* generated was a notice in *Texas Monthly.* Gene Lyons wrote that McMurtry's effort had joined a long list of failed books on Hollywood, as it is difficult to capture "the crudity and the almost unimaginable pettiness of the movie-making world without writing a book that itself partakes of those same sleazy values."[4] This dilemma, in fact, is why Bud Shrake eventually decided against writing his own Hollywood novel.

McMurtry himself was quick to recognize his book's weaknesses after publication. "I didn't have much business writing about Los Angeles," he told an interviewer. "[M]y grasp was superficial. I had been there a lot, but I hadn't lived there like I've lived in Texas. I was on very thin ground, and I ultimately wrote a rather thin book as a result." McMurtry, unlike many writers, could display remarkable equanimity about his work, even agreeing with negative critical judgments. Certainly, intellectually, he might have accepted Gene Lyons' criticism of his work in the pages of *Texas Monthly.* But what McMurtry could not easily forgive was how *Texas Monthly* capsulized the review in its table of contents. *Texas Monthly* tagged it: "Sleazy Hollywood inspires a book that is even sleazier."[5]

After that, McMurtry broke off relations with the magazine and demanded that his name be removed from the list of contributing editors. The coolness persisted for some years, though Broyles anxiously sought to mend relations. In the 1980 "Bum Steer Awards" issue, *Texas Monthly* ran a photo of McMurtry with the caption, "People it would be nice to hear from again."[6]

When Ronnie Dugger and Larry McMurtry met at McMurtry's bookstore in the summer of 1981, Texas writer and critic A. C. Greene had just published an essay in *Texas Monthly* on "The Fifty Best Texas Books." Greene had compiled his list with the thought that Texas "has needed more positive criticism, more outspokenness from within, with regard to its own culture."[7]

Greene's essay only found room to discuss twelve of the fifty books. The other thirty-eight were listed by title and author only. The appended list included Larry McMurtry's first two novels, *Horseman, Pass By* and *Leaving Cheyenne*. But in Greene's essay itself, it was Bud Shrake's *Blessed McGill* that appeared prominently. Shrake, in fact, was the only living writer Greene discussed. Greene's high praise of Shrake would not go unnoticed by Larry McMurtry. Green wrote that *Blessed McGill*

> combines the best of Shrake's talents: an appreciation for the absurdities of existence, a recognition of irony's major role in the world, highly suggestive humor, and a decent amount of historical and anthropological research. . . . Shrake does not sacrifice truth or wisdom for sheer entertainment, and when McGill—by a sequence of inevitabilities—moves toward sainthood in Taos, it is not merely an absurd plot twist but a subtle study of what spiritual deliverance really is.[8]

McMurtry found the very idea of Greene's "positive" view of Texas literature ludicrous, as the state's insular literary society was already "a pond full of satisfied frogs." Many of the books Greene listed, McMurtry believed, were "soft, thin, and sentimental—not to mention dull, portentous, stylistically impoverished, and intellectually empty." Though McMurtry had told an interviewer two years earlier that he had read "Not a whole lot" of Texas literature, he readily accepted a suggestion offered by Ronnie Dugger. He would write an essay that would "expound on the sorry state of Texas letters."[9]

"Ever a Bridegroom: Reflections on the Failure of Texas Literature," appeared in the October 23, 1981, issue of the *Texas*

Observer and sent shock waves through the world of Texas letters that reverberate to this day. The essay inspired heated debates, subsequent essays, at least one literary conference, and two books. It also revitalized the flagging *Texas Observer*. Twenty years later, McMurtry's essay remains an important touchstone in discussions of Texas literature, and it is referred to in recent books by the state's most prominent critics, Don Graham and Tom Pilkington.

McMurtry surveyed a broad expanse of Texas literature, though he also made startling omissions indicating that his distance from the state had not just been physical—it was also intellectual. Among the writers he neglected even to mention were Tomás Rivera and Rolando Hinojosa, both of whom were already garnering significant national attention and prestigious literary awards.

McMurtry's major complaint was that Texas writers have been unwilling to discard the state's rural ethos. Though the "vast majority of Texas writers have been urbanites for decades," writers seem content to offer up "an endless stream of what might be called Country-and-Western literature. . . . Easier to write about the home-folks, the old folks, cowboys, or the small town than to deal with the more immediate and frequently less simplistic experience of city life." This is the reason, McMurtry concluded, that Texas has produced only "a limited, shallow, self-repetitious literature that has so far failed completely to do justice to the complexities of life in the state."[10]

McMurtry had attacked Texas letters once before, in his memorable 1968 essay "Southwestern Literature?" There, McMurtry stomped a big hole in the reputation of J. Frank Dobie, the state's dominant writer for most of the century. In his new essay, McMurtry returned to the subject of Dobie, noting that the writer's reputation had declined even more swiftly than anyone could have imagined. This is because his books "are a congealed mass of virtually undifferentiated anecdotages: endlessly repetitious, thematically empty, structureless, and carelessly written."[11]

McMurtry moved on to debunk another well-known writer from Texas, Katherine Anne Porter, who died the year before. Porter was the most distinguished of all writers to have hailed from Texas.

Considered a major American writer, she won a Pulitzer Prize and a National Book Award and has long been the subject of extensive literary scholarship. Porter was an exceptional stylist, yet to McMurtry this signified that "she was genteel to the core." He found her work "fragile, powdery, and frequently just plain boring. . . . The plumage is beautiful, but plumage, after all, is only feathers."[12]

Because of McMurtry's harsh condemnation of the state's best-known writers and his caustic comments on the overall state of Texas letters, his essay has come to be seen as a spirited attack on other Texas writers. In fact, it wasn't. McMurtry, as it turned out, was surprisingly mild with most of his contemporaries. John Graves, for example, seemed to be someone who represented exactly what McMurtry was condemning. Graves had published his earliest fiction in the *New Yorker* and had traveled widely, only to return to Texas and settle on a small farm. True, in 1960 he had published the classic *Goodbye to a River,* but since then he seemed content to write introspective essays on such rural matters as goats, beekeeping, and dirt. Yet McMurtry could find little to criticize about Graves. Instead he judged that Graves' "work seems to me to be a good deal more complicated than it is popularly thought to be."[13] McMurtry's main objection to Graves, as it turned out, was disappointment that the dedicated pastoralist had not published more books over the years.

McMurtry was equally deferential to other contemporary writers. Donald Barthelme is "a brilliant, high-risk modernist," whose most recent book is "an impressive achievement." William Humphrey and William Goyen also drew complimentary remarks, as did Terry Southern, James Crumley, Max Crawford, and John Irsfeld. McMurtry also had a soft spot for his old friend Billy Lee Brammer. "Bill Brammer is not the first writer to lose control of his life before gaining full control of his art," McMurtry wrote, "but his loss is the one Texas readers might justly lament the most." Brammer "brought to our letters an easy and natural urbanity then almost unknown in these parts. . . . He was alert, curious, and witty, happy to use the absurdities which lay so abundantly to hand; and, in the end, just romantic enough to make it all seem more charming and less destructive than it really was."[14]

Once one gets beyond McMurtry's scornful remarks about Texas literature as a whole, his pointed jabs at dead literary heroes, and his largely generous view of many contemporary writers, there remains one major target—his peers, the "Mad Dog" writers. It is in this section of the essay that McMurtry issues his strongest denunciations aside from his attacks on Dobie and Porter.

Bud Shrake is the only writer McMurtry discusses in two separate parts of his essay. The first comes in McMurtry's response to A. C. Greene's initial *Texas Monthly* article. McMurtry had reviewed *Blessed McGill* favorably after it first appeared, but he gave no indication that he recognized the novel's philosophical dimension. Responding to *Blessed McGill* anew, McMurtry still views it as simply a black-humor western. The "overpraised" novel, McMurtry writes, was "an interesting tour de force that seemed to work when published—our *Sot-Weed Factor*, as it were. Now, like *The Sot-weed Factor* itself, it seems alternately grandiloquent and stilted."[15]

Four pages later, McMurtry returns to Shrake, whom he calls "an intriguing talent, far superior to most of his drinking buddies." The problem with these journalists-turned-novelists, McMurtry writes, is that they "all are insecure in relation to readers. Trained to write columns that can be read in a few seconds, or articles that take at most a few minutes, in their novels, they seem desperate to *affect* the reader every few seconds, or at least every minute or two." This "seems to be a holdover from sportswriting" and it results in a "rat-a-tat-tat effect, with a joke, an aperçu, or a dazzling rhetorical move every few lines, [that] quickly becomes intolerable in a novel."[16]

McMurtry makes a perceptive criticism here—one that points to a major flaw in Dan Jenkins' fiction, as well as the early fictional efforts of Gary Cartwright and Larry L. King. But these writers, Shrake's "drinking buddies," are small game. McMurtry is after Shrake himself. "This tendency," he writes, "is particularly noticeable in the work of Edwin Shrake. . . . All of his books begin well, and yet all are difficult to finish. . . . In a novel, trying to keep the reader alert every single second is the one sure way to insure that the reader will go to sleep."[17] Shrake's novels sometimes generated controversy or were misunderstood, but reviewers over the years consistently praised his spare, clear, fast-paced narrative technique. In "Ever a Bridegroom," Larry McMurtry became the only person ever to advance a countervailing argument—that Shrake's narrative style induces slumber.

McMurtry took one last rhetorical swipe at Shrake. In the next section of his essay he pointedly excluded Shrake from the "only four Texas writers who have been able to reverse the tendency towards nostalgia, sentiment, and small-town mythicization."[18] Considering that Shrake's work in *Strange Peaches, Blessed McGill, But Not for Love,* and *Peter Arbiter* represents a vital opposition to nostalgia and pastoralism, McMurtry's misreading of Shrake's fiction seems deliberate.

Though he had not yet published a blockbuster, McMurtry was well recognized as Texas' most important contemporary novelist. If McMurtry had any competition in the state at the time for critical praise, it was from Bud Shrake. The heady write-up of Shrake's *Blessed McGill* in the pages of *Texas Monthly,* along with the absence of any similar commentary on McMurtry's own work, was obviously threatening. McMurtry's essay, brilliant and provocative as it was, apparently sprang from ulterior motives.

In retrospect, perhaps the most astonishing aspect of McMurtry's "Ever a Bridegroom" essay was the fact that he went on to ignore his own advice. After stating in the most forceful way possible that Texas writers need to leave the rural past behind, McMurtry began work on an epic novel about, of all things, a cattle drive. *Lonesome Dove,* of course, would win him the Pulitzer Prize, turn McMurtry into a bestselling author, and establish his dominance in Texas letters once and for all. But in the years after *Lonesome Dove,* McMurtry began churning out sloppy, mediocre sequels and even a "prequel" to *Lonesome Dove.* As he did so, Texas letters found itself coming full circle. McMurtry became exposed to the same criticism he had once leveled at J. Frank Dobie: producing books that are "repetitious, thematically suspect, structureless, and above all, carelessly written."

***

In contrast to Shrake, Jenkins, and Cartwright, Larry L. King emerged relatively unscathed by McMurtry. King "has a strong, vivid style," McMurtry wrote, though "he tends to splash the same colors and repeat certain characteristic verbal devices a good deal too often." McMurtry found that, "Unfortunately, very little of this work has made any demands on his emotions." But when King is engaged emotionally, as in his essay "The Old Man," "the effect is wonderful and makes us wish it weren't so uncommon." McMurtry concluded by expressing hope that because "*Whorehouse* has freed him from journalism . . . more of that kind of work will result."[19]

Twenty years later, Larry L. King chuckled at the memory of McMurtry's essay. "Bud Shrake said McMurtry eased up on me because we just lived a few blocks apart from each other in D.C. He said that McMurtry must've been worried that I'd go over to his bookstore and whoop his ass." King paused for a moment. "Hell, I might well have done it at the time."[20]

46.

THIRD

COAST

Austin-based screenwriters Bud Shrake and Bill Wittliff were advised repeatedly to move to Los Angeles. "Everybody you talked to out there said you can't live in Austin, Texas, and write movies that are gonna be made in Hollywood," Wittliff recalled later. "And that's just not so. And I was lucky, I was really ignorant. I didn't know that could be true, so I just didn't pay any attention to it and just kept writing." Bud Shrake had already established the precedent of living in Austin and writing for New York-based *Sports Illustrated,* so he shrugged off suggestions that he needed to move to California. "Sure, I spent a lot of time out there," he said. "But I never lived there." Wittliff and Shrake both understood that Austin offered a creative base absent in Hollywood. "Out there are multilayered pressures," Wittliff said. "I knew I had a better chance to write well from here than from out there."[1]

The two men shared office space at Wittliff's Encino Press, housed in an old Austin home where short-story writer O. Henry once lived. Wittliff wrote downstairs, and Shrake wrote upstairs. Wittliff said, "When Bud and I would have writer's block, we'd leave a paper and pencil out, hoping [O. Henry] would give us a signal. Alas, he never did. The message seemed to be, 'You guys do it.'"[2]

In 1983, Shrake's *Songwriter* script, which had languished for nearly five years, was suddenly rejuvenated by Tri-Star and went into production. Willie Nelson and Kris Kristofferson agreed to star in it. The movie was shot on location in Austin, and in the years since it has come to be seen as "the genesis of Austin homegrown films. Not only did [it] give the world a taste of local color, lifestyle, and points of view, it gave local crews a chance to prove themselves, to prove that major films could—and should—be made in Austin."[3]

True to its promise, *Songwriter* has a funky, homegrown feel as it mocks Nashville's taste and rebels against the industry's business practices. Tri-Star, however, "missed the entire point of the movie," Shrake said later. "Instead, they saw it as a country music vehicle." Anxious to sell the concept, the studio staged a world premiere in "Country Music U.S.A."—Nashville, Tennessee—over the objections of Shrake and Willie Nelson. Country music insiders were invited to a gala event that culminated in a screening of the film. *Songwriter*'s most memorable scene comes as Willie Nelson flees Nashville and heads for Austin in an open convertible, singing "Write Your Own Songs." Willie's stinging lyrics were aimed directly at Nashville music executives, and the song offended many in the audience. Boos and catcalls echoed throughout the theater, and several guests walked out. "That's when the people at Tri-Star panicked," Shrake said. "They were sure that they had a dog on their hands. After all, if a film about country music was hated in Nashville, what good could it be?" The studio pulled the plug on its advertising campaign. Even the standard press screenings were abandoned.[4]

As it turned out, Tri-Star totally miscalculated the critical reception in store for *Songwriter*. The *Los Angeles Times* lauded it as "fresh, original, blessedly real . . . with absolutely no pretensions about it." In *The New Yorker*, Pauline Kael began her review, "The least publicized of the American movies that have just opened in New York, *Songwriter*, is the freest and funniest of the bunch—the most sophisticated, too." Reviewers in Los Angeles and New York, familiar with industry practices, made pointed comments about Tri-Star's handling of its property. *Songwriter* "has been shrouded in the sort of secrecy and obfuscation that you associate with the Defense Department," sniffed the *Los Angeles Times*. "Its treatment at the hands of Tri-Star is only short of scandalous."[5]

Even subsequent nominations for an Academy Award and Golden Globe Award did nothing to improve the studio's marketing efforts. *Songwriter* died at the box office just a few weeks after release. This became yet another commercial disappointment for Bud Shrake. But *Songwriter* itself represented another artistic breakthrough for Austin. Thanks in large measure to its creative talent, Austin was gaining a reputation as the center of a Texas film colony.

By the early 1980s, Bill Wittliff, negotiating roles for himself as a coproducer, was bringing film productions to Texas, making use of local talent and crews. Soon after *Songwriter*, Wittliff's *Red Headed Stranger* and *Lonesome Dove* were shot in Austin. These were complemented by breakthrough movies from independent filmmakers: the Coen Brothers' *Blood Simple*, Richard Linklater's *Slacker*, and Robert Rodriguez's *El Mariachi*. By the 1990s, Hollywood studios were shooting big-budget features in Austin. Bill Wittliff and Bud Shrake helped mentor former *Texas Monthly* staffers William Broyles Jr. Stephen Harrigan, and Lawrence Wright, who began writing scripts for Hollywood while also maintaining home bases in Austin. Other successful screenwriters included Mike Judge, novelist Sarah Bird, and Texas Film Commission founder Warren Skaaren. Just as Austin had once loosened Nashville's grip on country music, the city was helping to decentralize Hollywood's hold over the film industry. Austin, and Texas, were no longer places artists had to leave in order to pursue their vision. Texas was no longer the "boondock country" described in Billy Lee Brammer's *The Gay Place*. Instead, Texas was becoming "The Third Coast."

47.

FACES

IN THE

FIRE

Membership in Mad Dog, Inc., is not guaranteed for life, and Peter Gent is no longer a Mad Dog. Gent's relationship with the other writers fell apart in the early 1980s, and it all began in the tranquil village of Wimberley. The movie version of *North Dallas Forty* had been a success, and to Gent that meant "the fast lane led right to my door. . . . I had scores of 'new best friends' who drove [in] for their daily feeding on 'fame' like schools of piranhas. They ate me alive." Gent often felt that forces outside his control were battling to undermine his sense of well-being. He later wrote, "In the years I had lived in Texas, I had many guns pulled on me and had been shot at several times."[1]

Others, however, saw Gent as paranoid and delusional. One journalist reported with mock solemnity that when she met with Gent, he was sitting in a darkened living room and "insisted on keeping the lights down so the NFL spies across the street in the Doggie Diner parking lot couldn't see us." Gent claimed to her that "The NFL was following him, and when I left that night they'd be following me, too. . . . They're an insidious lot, the NFL men, with ties to the CIA and Lord knows what else. You can't be too careful." Another reporter noted that Gent had a "penchant for seeing faces in the fire, shapes in the shadows." Gent often warned journalists of various conspiracies, but he refused to be directly quoted. "If I started saying what I know," he warned one reporter, "I'd probably end up sleeping with Jimmy Hoffa."[2]

In his lucid moments, Gent could joke about his anxieties. He advised Larry L. King to keep his hands up at all times if he ever came to visit the Gents in Wimberley. In a series of letters to King, Gent became increasingly fixated on weaponry, describing his guns in great detail. He began patrolling his property every night, telling King that he fired off shots at random as a warning.[3]

Just as his friendship with Don Meredith faded, Gent also believed that his relationship with Bud Shrake went into decline. By the early 1980s, the two men visited far less than they had before, and they seemed to have less to talk about whenever they did. Gent did become involved in the Texas literary scene, however. As an active member of the Texas Institute of Letters, he appeared at a high-profile conference on "The Texas Literary Tradition." As Bud Shrake pointed out in a subsequent letter to King, Gent went to the seminar "packing a gun and not unprepared to add a colorful highlight to the history of Texas letters."[4]

By January 1983 Gent was closing in on the final rewrites for his new novel, and its prospects seemed promising. *The Franchise* would be the lead title in Random House's new hardcover division, Villard Books, and another big promotional campaign was in the works. Three different movie studios had already expressed interest in the book. Larry L. King contributed a review quote that poked fun at Gent's paranoia. King wrote, "Pro football moguls and players may have to put a contract out on Pete Gent if the ex-Dallas Cowboy persists in revealing their habits and Achilles heels."[5]

But just as Gent's novel was gearing up for release, his personal life shattered. His wife of fourteen years, Jody, abruptly left him and told law enforcement officers that she feared Gent would kill her and their six-year-old son. Soon two sheriff's deputies were dispatched to Gent's house to claim the boy. An armed Gent answered the door and a tense standoff ensued, defused only when another deputy who knew Gent arrived on the scene. Later, Gent began to wonder if his wife had artfully staged the entire confrontation with the deputies—in the hope that he would be shot dead.[6]

For Gent, the next three years were consumed by a bitter divorce and child custody battle. He claimed that Jody "took all the cash, book and film contracts, car and house titles, land deeds . . . eleven hundred ounces of silver bars, and two hundred ounces of gold coins . . . certificates of deposit, jewelry, and the safe-deposit box keys." His hostility would simmer for years to come. She "wiped me fucking out," he later complained to an interviewer compiling an oral history of the Dallas Cowboys.[7]

Legal troubles dogged Gent after the divorce, and it seemed to him that the Texas criminal justice system, in cahoots with his ex-wife, was out to get him. At one point, Gent wrote, he was expected to "sign over my life to a lawyer of my wife's choosing or go to jail indefinitely for contempt." Another time he was arrested for "entice-ment of a child," though the charges were later dropped. The year after Jody left, the couple had an angry confrontation, and she later "swore I had grabbed her by the throat, slammed her into the kitchen walls, and tried to kill her." Despite Gent's explanation that he'd only lightly brushed his fingers against the front of Jody's shirt, a "judge found me guilty and sentenced me to a year in jail." Later the sen-tence was suspended "with the proviso that I would be immediately jailed for the full term should my ex-wife notify the court of any mis-behavior on my part."[8]

Gent's battles with Jody created a crisis in his relationships with his Texas writer friends. Gent sought to rally them to his cause but was devastated by their lack of support. "Pete and I were friends for a long time," Bud Shrake said. "And Pete believed that I had to take his side in the divorce. But I liked Jody, too, and so I remained neutral. For Pete, there was no such thing. For me to be neutral meant that I was his enemy, and that's what I became in his eyes. We haven't spoken in years." Larry L. King was initially sympathetic to Gent's claims but quickly backpedaled as he learned more about the breakup. King con-siders Gent unstable and says, "I've avoided him for years now."[9] Jody Gent, after her divorce, eventually went to work as Shrake's assistant, and she has worked for him for the past eighteen years.

Gent wrote later that "although only a few friends stayed the course in Texas, all my friends and family in Michigan put themselves on the line, personally and financially, to keep . . . me from sinking."[10] Gent returned to Michigan in 1985 and moved in with his parents. He eventually gained custody of his son, and he has lived in Michigan ever since. He has continued writing books but has never recaptured the critical and popular success he enjoyed with *North Dallas Forty.*

In 1996 Peter Gent published *The Last Magic Summer: A Season with My Son.* That book, a memoir, received favorable comments for Gent's heartfelt portrayal of his relationship with his teenage son. *The Last Magic Summer* is also notable for Gent's perspective on his final years in Texas, although his narrative is unreliable. Gent tells of having been "traded" by the Dallas Cowboys to the New York Giants when in fact the Cowboys cut him from the team. In describing encounters with his ex-wife, Gent always portrays himself as a model of concern and caring, even as he fumes with hostility. Gent takes great pride in depicting himself as an outpost of lucidity in the midst of an insane society, and his extreme self-righteousness is chilling.

In *The Last Magic Summer,* Gent describes how life in Texas caused him great anxiety, and how his condition eased only after he retreated to Michigan. Back in Texas, many of his former friends felt the same way. They also experienced great anxiety during Gent's final years in Texas, and they, too, were greatly relieved when Peter Gent moved out of their lives. The stressful falling-out with Peter Gent, coming as it did on the heels of Billy Lee Brammer's overdose, coincided with increasing health problems for the remainder of the group. As the writers entered their fifties, a long chapter in their lives was drawing to an inexorable close.

PART FOUR:

HOW TIME

SLIPS

AWAY

48.

JENKINS

After nearly two decades at *Sports Illustrated*, Dan Jenkins had become "a pressbox legend, an idol to a new wave of young, talented, irreverent sportswriters." But Jenkins, who turned fifty in 1979, "was not yet ready to be the Grand Old Man of anybody's games." He still held court at the all-night gatherings of sportswriters, but age was inevitably slowing him down. At one time, Jenkins could boast of close relationships with the athletes and coaches he wrote about. This had been one of his great advantages as a journalist and had intimidated more than a few rival sportswriters. But as Jenkins grew older, he had less in common with younger athletes, and many of his coaching friends had retired. His once-vaunted access was dwindling.[1]

It was also true that the glamour had long since gone out of covering the same events year after year. Jenkins had seen it all, over and over again. As Gary Cartwright had observed in "Confessions of a Washed-Up Sportswriter," after eight or ten years in the profession there is nothing new to say. Dan Jenkins, after some thirty years of sportswriting, was losing his edge. Those in the highly competitive world of Time, Inc., were the first to notice. Still, as one staffer maintained, "Jenkins's routine stuff was a hell of a lot better than most writers' career best." But Jenkins' declining prose ran into a new obstacle—an antagonistic editor.[2]

In 1979 *Sports Illustrated* chose Gil Rogin to replace the retiring Roy Terrell. Though Terrell and Jenkins had feuded over his extravagant expense accounts, Terrell had largely left Jenkins' prose alone. Gil Rogin, on the other hand, had little respect for Jenkins, whom he considered nothing more than a "fucking gag writer." Rogin promptly used his new editorial powers to launch a blitzkrieg on Jenkins' prose. In 1980, Rogin made wholesale changes to Jenkins' write-up of the year's premier sporting event—the Super Bowl. When Jenkins saw how the story came out, he "went into a blind rage." For *SI*'s new editor to treat his star writer in such a cavalier manner became a worrisome sign to other writers at the magazine.[3]

As the 1980 football season geared up, Jenkins informed Rogin that he would no longer cover football for *Sports Illustrated*. Instead, he would concentrate solely on golf. Jenkins explained his plan to Blackie Sherrod. "I'm going to make it to twenty years and I'm fuckin' out of there. And I'm taking the furniture with me—they've got a hell of a retirement plan."[4]

***

Jenkins published a new novel in 1981, *Baja Oklahoma*, that was a marked departure from his earlier work. For the first time, he placed a novel directly in his heart's country—Fort Worth, Texas. Instead of a male-narrated novel about sports, the protagonist, Juanita Hutchins, is a Fort Worth waitress at Herb's Café. Juanita—witty, cynical, and profane—sounds exactly like Jenkins' male narrators. During the course of the novel, she becomes an improbable country music star and even shares the stage with Willie Nelson. *Baja Oklahoma*'s subject matter overlaps a good deal with Bud Shrake's *Songwriter*, which was written at roughly the same time. A major difference, however, is that Dan Jenkins has his protagonist go to Nashville in order to become successful. In *Songwriter*, as in real life, Willie Nelson had to leave Nashville in order to find his musical vision.

Baja Oklahoma showcases a number of Jenkins' strengths. The opening sentence is as vivid as any ever written by him: "The scrub

Dan Jenkins, 1988. *Photo by Bill Wittliff. Bill Wittliff Archives, Southwestern Writers Collection, Texas State University-San Marcos.*

oaks looked like twisted wrought iron, and everybody's front yard had turned the color of a corn tortilla." Jenkins also fully realizes a potential only hinted at in his earlier fiction. Since the storyline doesn't center on a high-profile sports event, Jenkins' characters are free just to hang out at Herb's Café. In that setting, Jenkins adroitly captures the language and rhythms of America's bar culture. In the best of those circumstances, the patrons exchange first-rate stories, opinions, and witticisms. Among the well-known comic riffs in *Baja Oklahoma* is "Mankind's Ten Stages of Drunkenness," which range from "Witty and Charming" to "Patriotic," "Invisible," and then, finally, "Bulletproof."[5]

The one-liners and clever banter, however, come at the expense of character development. The effect is much like watching a TV sitcom as every character steps forward to deliver humorous zingers. Many of the jokes have racist or sexist punch lines, and reviewers raised pointed questions about how closely Jenkins identified with his characters. "All I'm doing is reflecting what's out there in society as I know it," Jenkins said in his own defense. "There are a lot of people like that in Texas. You trip over them everywhere you go. . . . There are all kinds of people that hang around the bar that are exactly like that . . . but they probably talk a lot dirtier in real life."[6] But *Baja Oklahoma* is far from a useful sociological study of marginally educated Anglo Americans in Fort Worth. Nor is it a serious examination of the challenges that a female musician faces in a male-dominated music industry. Instead, *Baja Oklahoma* is a collection of jokes, gags, and one-liners, all distilled by a master collector.

    ***

Jenkins' appearances in *Sports Illustrated* dropped off sharply after he gave up the football beat. Editor Gil Rogin had little interest in golf, but that didn't stop him from harassing Jenkins' prose. The climactic showdown occurred with Jenkins' report on the 1984 British Open. Rogin rewrote the article and informed the fifty-five-year-old Jenkins that he was placing him on probation. He sent Jenkins a memo telling him, "You're concentrating on books and movies and not giving us your best work. I'm going to have to think a long time, long and hard, if I want to keep you on as the golf writer."[7]

Jenkins' reaction was swift and sure. "I told my wife, 'I'm not gonna work for that cocksucker anymore.'" He tendered a short note of resignation: "I'm going to relieve you the worry about what to do with your golf coverage because I shan't be writing that for you anymore."[8]

Jenkins' acrimonious departure from *Sports Illustrated* marked the end of an era. As Michael MacCambridge writes in his history of the magazine, the situation "confirmed what many had long since suspected: that the balance of power had decisively shifted from writers to editors." As one staffer concluded, "That loss was about as staggering, from my point of view, as the magazine has ever suffered. It should never have lost Dan Jenkins. He was synonymous with this magazine."[9]

***

Jenkins' exit from *Sports Illustrated* coincided with the publication of his newest novel, the book everyone had been waiting for since *Semi-Tough*. The sequel, *Life Its Ownself: The Semi-Tougher Adventures of Billy Clyde Puckett & Them,* Jenkins' best-known character has retired from pro football and become a TV sportscaster. The one-liners and comic gags are the novel's chief appeal, and, increasingly, Jenkins' use of race-based humor was becoming a defining element of his work. Though Billy Clyde no longer uses the "n-word," as he did so profusely in *Semi-Tough*, he still defends the right to say it, if he chooses to. "I'd stopped worrying about the way people talked a long time ago. Anyhow, the word wasn't going to disappear, no matter how loud your Eastern liberals hollered at your truck-stop Southerners."[10]

At points during the novel, Jenkins comes to the defense of black athletes, decrying the hypocrisy of their treatment by white coaches. But more often, Jenkins mines the comic possibilities of black vernacular. One black college athlete tells a news conference that he plans to study "Joggaphy," because it "be tellin' you what's Eas' and Wes'. I like to look at pictures of maps and shit."[11]

Passages such as this were increasingly offensive to a certain class of readers. Back in 1972, when *Semi-Tough* was published, Jenkins' pointed jabs at delicate racial sensitivities were viewed as disarming candor. By 1984, a more nuanced discourse was required. Jenkins accepted some measure of this development, as indicated by his restraint in using the word "nigger." But his continued vigorous use of race-inspired humor sent a clear signal that he would refuse to concede the issue. As a result, the largely liberal cultural elite that had once hailed Jenkins as a fresh new literary voice began to express growing uneasiness about the nature of his humor. Yet for another, more conservative class of readers, these sex and race jokes were exactly what they were looking for. Jenkins had once charmed liberal critics while enjoying commercial success. Now, however, a cultural divide was opening up in responses to his work.

***

By the early 1980s, Dan Jenkins' friend Bud Shrake was earning a comfortable living as a Hollywood screenwriter. With Shrake's help, Dan Jenkins learned that he could sell the same one-liners he had once given to *Sports Illustrated* for considerably more at Hollywood studios. From 1983 to 1985, Shrake and Jenkins cowrote five scripts and doctored several others. They sold all of their screenplays, but none of the films was ever made. "I'm sure part of it was our attitude," Shrake said later. "We were sort of arrogant out there. I thought movie writers were the bottom of the barrel, and Dan thought they were total shits. He was out there just for the money, and he let everyone know it. Some people took offense at that."[12]

The pair's most celebrated collaboration came in 1985 when they were signed to write the long-awaited sequel to Eddie Murphy's hit *Beverly Hills Cop*. They set the story in London's Scotland Yard and supplied Eddie Murphy with a plethora of one-liners. But as the power struggles began, Shrake and Jenkins were fired, and the movie went through several more rewrites. When *Beverly Hills Cop II* was finally released, four different writers received screenwriting credit, including Eddie Murphy. Shrake and Jenkins were left out, and therefore denied a share of the film's profits. They sued the studio for eight million dollars and appealed the case, unsuccessfully, all the way to the California Supreme Court. The protracted legal struggle did little to enhance their standing in Hollywood.[13]

Dan Jenkins did pick up a few tricks in the screenwriting trade, however. He came to understand how important plotting and character are to films, and when he returned to fiction, he parlayed these elements into his most ambitious work ever. With his stature as a best-selling novelist seemingly assured, Jenkins decided to write a novel set in Fort Worth in the 1930s. "He wrote it purely for himself," his daughter Sally Jenkins observed. "His readers, his publishers, and his agent urged him to return to the sports novel form. He ignored them and instead wrote the book that I, for one, had always wished he would."[14]

Fast Copy, published in 1988, tells the story of Betsy Throckmorton, a crusading proto-feminist newspaper editor who flees from her job at Time, Inc., where arrogant editors mangle the prose of fine writers. Betsy takes over a paper in a small town outside of Fort Worth. There she seeks to create first-class journalism, even as the locals chafe under her journalistic standards.

Like Jenkins' other protagonists, Betsy chain-smokes, cracks jokes, and loves TCU football. She's also a fearless editor. She demonstrates her gravitas by growling, as Gary Cartwright once did, that "nothing is ever off the record."[15] She also daringly solves a series of murders involving a corrupt Texas Ranger. The book is elaborately plotted, and the developing murder mystery takes some hard turns, including the brutal death of a major character. Steeped in history and local lore, *Fast Copy* integrates a number of real-life figures into the story, including Amon Carter and Texas Ranger Captain Frank Hamer. The climactic scene, fittingly, takes place at Casa Mañana, Fort Worth's alternative spectacle to Dallas' official State Centennial celebration. As dancers from Sally Rand's Nude Ranch cavort on stage, Betsy Throckmorton's quest for justice is finally achieved.

Though *Fast Copy* is serious, there is plenty of comic relief. Much of the humor involves Betsy's attempts to transform the *Claybelle Times-Standard* into a serious newspaper. To do that she must contend with reporters, including a sportswriter named Big 'Un Darly, whose only previous instruction had been, "Don't write me nothin' that rhymes." The earnest amateurism of Texas newspapers is warmly lampooned in several instances. Even an old headline from one of Bud Shrake's stories in the *Fort Worth Press* makes an appearance: "Cops Eat Kid's Pet."[16]

While many literary critics applauded Jenkins' newfound ambition, *Fast Copy* proved that most Jenkins readers preferred the fast-paced humor of his earlier work. The book sold less than any other Jenkins novel. Though it failed to reach a national audience, *Fast Copy* has found an enduring place in Texas. In 2001 TCU Press republished it as part of its Texas Tradition Series. If any Jenkins novel survives over the years ahead, *Fast Copy* will surely be it.

***

Jenkins returned to his best-selling formula for his next novel, *You Gotta Play Hurt*, published in 1991. Covering a year of highlights in the life of sportswriter Jim Tom Pinch, the novel is Jenkins' most personal ever. Jim Tom Pinch is a star writer for *The Sports Magazine*, and is legendary for his brilliant leads and devastating one-liners. Pinch is also renowned for his ability to finesse expense accounts, and he travels across Europe and the United States in grand style.

Jenkins' book offers a decent amount of insight into the world of sports journalism—how major sporting events are staged, the press accommodations, the deadline pressures, and some local flavor. But the novel is hardly an exposé of big-time magazine journalism. Instead, Jenkins' focus is on lambasting the idiotic magazine editors who ruin the work of great writers like Jim Tom Pinch. The book is pointedly dedicated to "the memory of André Laguerre, last of a breed—a writer's Managing Editor."

Jenkins' frustrations from his final years at *Sports Illustrated* are expressed throughout. The very first sentence sets the tone: "Here's how I want the phony little conniving, no-talent, preppiewad asshole of an editor to die: I lace his decaf with Seconal and strap him down in such a way that his head is fastened to my desk and I thump him at cheery intervals with the carriage on my Olympia standard." The opening paragraph concludes, "Yeah, it would be slow, but death by typewriter is what the fuckhead deserves."[17]

A new development in *You Gotta Play Hurt* is the undisguised aging of Jenkins' protagonist. Jim Tom Pinch, in his early fifties, is the oldest of any Jenkins narrator. (Dan Jenkins himself was sixty-two at the time of publication.) For the first time, humor based on aging appears, including a much-quoted list of "three rules that senior citizens must live by." Age is clearly evident, too, in the decline of Jenkins' humor. Pinch spends a lot of his time complaining. In addition to the numerous jabs at editors, Pinch targets the sports themselves. "Most baseball players," he tells us, "are a sorry lot, as I had known them, basically the dumbest and lowest-rent collection of athletes I had ever encountered." Pinch had once enjoyed professional football, but that was a long time ago. "In the past several years," he says, "pro football had been doing everything within its power to encourage intelligent people to ignore it." Pinch lists several things wrong with the sport, including indoor stadiums and "head coaches you had never heard of."[18]

Though a number of Jenkins' barbs hit their targets, many of the jokes fall flat. At one point Jim Tom Pinch is ushered into the ostentatious office of the magazine's CEO. Pinch tells us, somewhat vaguely, that there are "many paintings that hung on the walls." Of them the wisecracking Pinch can only offer, "I gathered all of the paintings were notoriously expensive, or why else would they have been so large, ugly, and stupid?"[19] In *You Gotta Play Hurt,* Dan Jenkins' vaunted humor was, for the first time, becoming more grouchy than funny.

***

Dan Jenkins' friends Bud Shrake, Gary Cartwright, and Larry L. King had well-known liberal political leanings. Jenkins always considered himself middle of the road. His cynicism about politics seemed to transcend ideology. In fact, it could be argued that cynicism *was* his ideology. Yet it was also increasingly clear that Jenkins' characters were becoming more conservative as the author himself aged. Still, the idea that Dan Jenkins could be an active Republican seemed ludicrous to those who knew him best.

All that changed in June 1990 when Jenkins received a friendly call from President George Herbert Walker Bush. Soon Jenkins met with Bush at the White House, and the president told him how much he enjoyed his books. The two played a round of golf at a country club, and then went to dinner and took in a baseball game. Soon gossip columns were buzzing with the news of a friendship between Jenkins and Bush.

More presidential invitations came Jenkins' way. He and June spent nights at the White House and were invited to Camp David for weekend visits. Luxury power trips on *Air Force One* were part of the package. Through his personal relationship with Bush, Jenkins finally found a political expression for his own increasing conservatism. By the time the 1992 election rolled around, Dan and June Jenkins were fervent George Bush backers.

Many Republicans found it difficult to accept Bill Clinton's victory over George Bush in 1992, and Dan and June Jenkins were among them. The loss immediately negated their White House access and political prestige. Clinton's inauguration also marked the usual quadrennial speculation about who was "in" and who was "out." Soon, Dan Jenkins, a man who helped make lists famous, found himself on one. *Dallas Morning News* reporter Anne Reifenberg, in an article syndicated across the country, speculated on "what's going to be cool in '93, and what's not." With Clinton in office, Reifenberg observed, Tony Hillerman was "cool." Dan Jenkins, she reported, was not.[20]

***

Jenkins' fall from political favor coincided with increasing health problems. In 1993, sixty-four-year-old Jenkins experienced deep chest pains and was rushed to the hospital. Though it was not a heart attack, tests revealed extensive blockage in his arteries. This was not Jenkins' first serious health encounter, but for years he'd shown a flippant disregard for commonly accepted notions of health. In addition to drinking and smoking heavily, he was notorious for eating nothing "except 'browns and whites,' meaning meat, potatoes, cream gravy, white bread, chocolate cake."[21]

Jenkins underwent two separate angioplasties and eventually received a triple bypass. After recovering, he reported to Gary Cartwright on the changes in his life. "I walk three miles a day and watch my diet. I started having one or two J&Bs and water instead of thirty and gave up the three or four packs of Winstons a day I had smoked for forty-five years. The hardest part was trying to write without a cigarette. That's the hardest thing I've ever tried to do. I still cheat now and then." Two years after his bypass, Jenkins was still struggling to come to terms with the changes. At a dinner with an old *SI* colleague, Jenkins "began grousing about all the things he couldn't eat, drink, or smoke anymore." He summed up his complaints by conceding that they are "Dues—for all the good times I had."[22]

***

Younger sportswriters often cited Jenkins as a major influence, but it was also true that they often went on to transcend his style of reportage. Jenkins himself rarely deviated from the formula he had learned from Blackie Sherrod: Hook the reader with a great opening line, adopt a strong point of view, talk about anything you want but remain detached from the games themselves. Above all, feed the reader plenty of one liners. This style—long on commentary, short on reporting—is well suited for short newspaper columns. It can also be entertaining in longer magazine stories when a writer is as funny as Dan Jenkins is. But the approach is limited: There's little serious analysis and the reporting often lacks depth. Jenkins was notorious among other journalists, in fact, for his disinclination to engage in reporting. Roy Blount Jr. was among those who marveled at how Jenkins "would sit there in the bar drinking and wait for the golf players to come in and tell him what they did." George Plimpton observed, "I've never seen [Jenkins] actually cover a story . . . . I think he gets most of it by osmosis."[23]

Despite his popularity among readers, Jenkins' reputation has not endured as well among his peers. By 1976 he was eligible for the National Sportscasters and Sportswriters Hall of Fame. Admission is granted through votes among colleagues. Years went by and several of Jenkins' lesser-known peers on daily newspapers were admitted. Only in 1996, after a disquieting interlude of twenty years, was Jenkins himself finally inducted.

An even sharper rebuke occurred with the publication of *The Best American Sports Writing of the 20th Century*. The anthology was edited by Pulitzer Prize-winning journalist (and Jenkins friend) David Halberstam, who gave *Semi-Tough* a rave review back in 1972. The 776-page book is replete with examples from noted writers, including those Jenkins admired, such as Damon Runyon and Ring Lardner. But conspicuously absent from the book is Dan Jenkins. For Halberstam, a serious reporter who prided himself on intensive research, thoroughness, and explication, Jenkins' breezy opinions proved to be of insufficient caliber for inclusion.[24]

* * *

In 1998, the sixty-nine-year-old Jenkins returned with a new novel guaranteed to attract attention. It was *Rude Behavior*—the third installment of what was now a *Semi-Tough* trilogy. Billy Clyde Puckett has helped found an expansion NFL team, the West Texas Tornadoes. As one might expect in a Dan Jenkins' novel, Billy Clyde's team manages to win the Super Bowl in its very first season. But long gone is Billy Clyde's warm, easygoing jocularity. Though the character is ostensibly only in his late forties, he has become a full-fledged grumpy old man.

Billy Clyde rails against political correctness, insolent service workers, baseball caps worn backward, antismoking ordinances, government regulations, and a host of other social ills. As *Publisher's Weekly* observed, Billy Clyde has slipped "from redneck obstreperousness to fundamentally racist and misogynist stupidity." Back in *Semi-Tough*, Billy Clyde had said "nigger" with disarming intent, explaining that he doesn't think the word in his heart. What seems clear in *Rude Behavior* is that Billy Clyde now does think "nigger," even as he refrains from using the word itself. By page two he is complaining about "those end-zone celebrations [where] they dance all the way to Mozambique and back."[25]

Rude Behavior was followed in 2001 by a new golf novel, *The Money-Whipped Steer-Job Three-Jack Give-Up Artist.* The narrator, Bobby Joe Grooves, is less sour than Billy Clyde Puckett, but he remains more caustic than funny. Bobby Joe is impatient on the golf course, impatient at home, and impatient in the checkout line at the grocery store, where a particular peeve is the women who take too long to conclude their transactions. "About then," Jenkins writes in Bobby Joe's voice, "it's all I can do to keep from telling the clerk, 'Yo, Conchita, just put all that on my bill so I can get the fuck outta here.'"[26]

In *The Money-Whipped Steer-Job,* Jenkins' right-wing commentary becomes his most intense yet. As the political perspectives harden, his jokes lose their suppleness. When Bobby Joe sees a Broadway play, he reacts with an outrage guaranteed to raise cheers from the talk radio crowd: "We only know we spent two hours listening to a group of fags and lesbians brutally ridicule every straight, hardworking, law-abiding, God-fearing, Christian in the United States of America."[27]

The cultural divide that gradually developed in Jenkins' fiction came to redefine his core audience. Although Jenkins was once among the funniest of American writers, readers increasingly responded to him based on their political perspectives. As such, Jenkins' appeal became strongest among the "angry white men." These readers shared a distaste for minorities, feminists, liberals, homosexuals, and anyone or anything else they believed was responsible for eroding the once-dominant position of white males in American society.

Jenkins' novels provide the perfect antidote for the insecurity inherent in these prejudices. Rather than deeply examining issues, as Jenkins' literary compadres have often done, Jenkins has been largely content to write entertainment. His male protagonists are always comfortably rich. They receive lavish attention from sexy, beautiful women. They can immediately spot pretentious phonies, and they have the status to speak their minds. In the end, Dan Jenkins' heroes always come out on top, winning life's Super Bowls.

This formula has gained Dan Jenkins a devoted following, but it is one far removed from his early days as a mainstream cultural phenomenon. In the long arc of Jenkins' fiction, he has come to occupy a lucrative, though hardly prestigious, niche market in American letters—white male fantasy fiction.

49.

KING

As he settled into his post-*Whorehouse* life, Larry L. King's writing career entered a second, distinct phase that has remained poorly understood. He continued to struggle with alcoholism, but by 1983, at fifty-four years old, he finally kicked the drinking habit for good. King also became a father again when he and Barbara had two children. This time around, he would become a much more active and involved parent. King's literary production during this period was immense. From 1982 to 1999 he wrote six stage plays, eight books, several magazine articles, short stories, and film screenplays. King's mature work included significant achievements—most notably the best of his stage plays, *The Night Hank Williams Died* and *The Dead Presidents' Club*. This output was, if anything, even more prolific and substantive than in the first half of his career. As he wrote to Bud Shrake in 1984, "Since I quit layin' around drunk and healing from drinking, I sure get a lot of typing accomplished."[1]

Yet the typical view, as expressed by critics such as Tom Pilkington, is that King had accomplished little since *Whorehouse*. "It is somewhat shocking to survey the corpus of King's work," Pilkington wrote in the mid-1990s, "and note how slight and evanescent it is: a less than-mediocre novel . . . a few plays . . . a handful of magazine pieces." King complained in a letter to Bud Shrake about Pilkington's comments. He added, "I believe Dr. Pilkington teaches over at John Tarleton, so next time you are in Stephenville I shall expect you as a loyal friend to drop by the campus and kill him for me. Let me know when this has been did, so I can send flowers like Mafia hitmen do to the funerals of their victims."[2]

Another criticism came King's way from an old friend, Celia Morris, and this one couldn't be laughed off as easily. Celia Morris, the ex-wife of Willie Morris, represented, as well as anyone, the frustrations of the intelligent, talented women linked to the Texas writers. She eventually earned a Ph.D., and her first book, *Fanny Wright: Rebel in America,* was published in 1984 by Harvard University Press. Morris' book won that year's Texas Institute of Letters nonfiction prize. "I took an unholy relish in that award," she wrote later. "My former husband and several men whose friendship had graced my twenties and thirties had won it earlier, and during our years together, neither they nor I had ever dreamed I might aspire to the prize, much less grasp it."[3]

Celia Morris' main memory of spending time in the company of the men was their "self-absorbed jousting" and their disinclination to include women in the conversation. "For me, being around them was rather like living with a cyclone—often dramatic and exciting, but you had to watch out for the funnel and no matter how expertly you dodged, you were stuck with the clean-up."[4] In the mid-1980s, Morris wrote a striking personal essay on the role of women in Texas literature. She first offered the article to *Texas Monthly,* which declined to publish it. The essay eventually appeared in *Range Wars,* an anthology of critical writings on Texas literature.

In her essay, Celia Morris saw an "overwhelmingly masculine" mythos in Texas letters, and the writer she pinpoints as symptomatic of that limitation is Larry L. King. Morris recalled how King had published an account in the *Texas Observer* about the "Southern Dogwood Party" she and Willie Morris had hosted several years earlier. That was the party where King met Robert Penn Warren. In King's write-up of the event, his list of notable attendees included only the men. Celia Morris wondered why King had overlooked the illustrious women who were also present. "As I recall," she wrote, "one of them had won a National Book Award, another was an accomplished jour-nalist and writer of children's stories, still another a translator of Russian poetry."[5]

Though Morris considered herself "a great admirer of Larry King's," she bluntly addressed a basic truth about his work. "The important fact is that a writer so gifted, so experienced, so ambitious, and so primarily identified with Texas neither sees women nor describes a social world in which they matter." *The Best Little Whorehouse,* one could argue, was about women. But as Celia Morris wryly noted, "Larry, that's not quite what I had in mind."[6]

***

Larry L. King's once-sterling literary reputation also suffered in the wake of *The Best Little Whorehouse.* Once the play became a commercial blockbuster, King observed that, "critics took a second look—and re-evaluated it sharply downward." King's own account of the musical, *The Whorehouse Papers,* was published in 1982 to coincide with the Burt Reynolds/Dolly Parton movie. The disap-pointing film was panned by critics, and King shared in the blame. *Texas Monthly* reviewed the *Whorehouse* movie and King's *Whorehouse* memoir together, asserting, "What *Hee Haw* is to coun-try music, *The Best Little Whorehouse* is to Texas Pride. A self-fancy-ing, light-headed giggle." King's book was viewed as an "ungracious, grudge-settling account" that is "full of the same button-popping bluster that bedevils *Whorehouse,* as he recounts every bitchy remark he's ever made behind an actress's back. From its inception, *The Best Little Whorehouse in Texas* was a parade of wind-swollen ego."[7]

Despite also receiving some good reviews, *The Whorehouse Papers* did not sell as well as hoped. Whereas *Confessions of a White Racist* had proved that King could expand a magazine essay into a superb book-length treatment, *The Whorehouse Papers* demonstrated the opposite—commercial instincts inflated the material beyond its natu-ral boundaries. In truth, a story about the making of the *Whorehouse* play was better suited to King's initial notion—a magazine article.

Larry L. King, 1995. *Photo by Bill Wittliff. Bill Wittliff Archives,
Southwestern Writers Collection, Texas State University-San Marcos.*

Back in the 1960s, King's stature resulted in large part from his
regular byline in *Harper's*. But by the 1980s, King rarely appeared in
the nation's most respected magazines. Instead, he wrote for the
nation's best-paying magazines. *TV Guide* carried his review essays on
political coverage and TV movies. He accepted $15,000 from
National Geographic to write about Anchorage, Alaska. *Parade*, the
weekly supplement that appears in Sunday newspapers across
America, boasted a number of King cover stories. The topics were a

far cry from his cutting-edge *Harper's* journalism. King wrote of being an older father, of returning home to Texas for a visit with his children, of his inspirational high school football coach, Aubra Nooncaster.

None of King's writing friends could blame him for taking the *Parade* assignments. After all, they had been in the writing game long enough to appreciate the pay scale. King's *Parade* articles were, in fact, thoughtfully crafted, always artfully transcending the sentiment and cliché that burden most such efforts. But wrapped around advertisements for cuckoo clocks and Norman Rockwell-themed plates, King's *Parade* work did little to enhance his literary reputation. He recounted to a friend, "I had a twenty-year-old journalism student ask me recently had I ever written anything other than the two articles she had read in *Parade*. I said, 'Naw, not much,' and went off and cried."[8]

Indications of his diminished stature were becoming more apparent. In 1984 *Playboy* declined to publish an article it had commissioned from him. King wrote to Willie Morris, "First time that has happened to me in a long time. Well, screw 'em." An increasing problem was the presence of the *other* Larry King—at the time America's best-known radio talk show host. Both men lived in Washington, D.C., and both frequented the same social gatherings. Acquaintances began to distinguish them as "Radio" King and "Whorehouse" King. "It's not very subtle," one said, "but it works." When Larry L. King was introduced to people at parties, he was more likely than ever to hear, "I never miss one of your broadcasts."[9] But as the "Radio" King made a successful move to television, his fame soon eclipsed that of the writer.

King still owed Viking two books to compensate for the $130,000 he had been advanced for his LBJ biography and "Lost Places" book. King had two ideas in mind. One promised to be his life's definitive work—an autobiographical novel set in West Texas, of the time and place where he grew up. The book was inside of him, he knew. It was just a matter of drawing it out. The other project was more straightforward, and easier to finish. In 1983, *Writer's Digest* had published King's essay on surviving as a freelance writer. With Viking's permission, King expanded the piece into a book-length work. *None But a*

Blockhead: On Being a Writer was published in 1985 as King turned fifty-seven years old. Taking its title from Samuel Johnson's observation that "no man but a blockhead ever wrote except for money," King's memoir-as-instruction manual is unorthodox—but it works. Just as *Confessions of a White Racist* had been an autobiography told through the prism of race, *None But a Blockhead* is an autobiography of a self-conscious writer.

One of the most pleasing aspects of *None But a Blockhead* is seeing how King's writing, mature and sober, became, if anything, richer and deeper than ever before. As Christopher Lehmann-Haupt noted in *The New York Times,* King's voice "reads as easy as molasses, but has the sound in it of whiskey and cigarettes and many years of contemplating Mark Twain." The stories are compelling, insightful, and, as always with King, candid and self-piercing. King even acknowledges Celia Morris' criticism of his sexism, and he issues a public apology. This is even more remarkable considering that her essay was unpublished at the time. All he knew of it was what she had read to him over the telephone.[10]

King would do more than simply apologize for his previous chauvinism. He went on to create strong, complex female characters in his stage plays. This new emphasis is seen throughout his later work and is most notable in *The Golden Shadows Old West Museum,* where the majority of roles belong to women. Celia Morris is among those who became aware of King's evolution, and she wrote to him in 2003 to tell him that he had long since invalidated her earlier criticism.[11]

***

King's writing also evolved in a new direction as a result of his closeness to his children. After his son came home worried about a neighborhood bully, King wrote a story for the boy in which a mean-looking bigger kid turns out to be a friend. On an impulse, he sent the story to his publisher, who liked it. *Because of Lozo Brown* was published by Viking's children's book division, but even that brought a humiliating reminder of just how far his stock had fallen with his publisher. In the galley proofs for the book, Viking listed his name as "Larry King" rather than "Larry L. King." The proposed biographical blurb read, "Larry King, a former Texan, has a radio talk show out of Washington, D.C. where he now lives."[12]

As King's national stature eroded, he could find solace in the fact that, back in Texas, he was still considered one of the state's most important writers. In 1985, TCU Press published *Warning: Writer at Work: The Best Collectibles of Larry L. King*. There were few surprises in the collection, as most of it consisted of previously anthologized pieces. But this time, the stories were selected largely for their Texas themes. King's friend Bud Shrake wrote the foreword, solidifying a bond between the two writers that would grow even closer in the years ahead.

Shrake and King would come to represent something of an anomaly among the Mad Dogs. Generally, as the Mad Dogs aged, they settled into separate routines and tended to drift apart, though they took care to keep in touch with one another. Shrake and King, in contrast, developed an active espistolary relationship that brought them much closer together than they had ever been before. As the years passed, their letters began to transcend the playful, boasting jocularity. They began to exchange personal confidences, offer serious literary advice, and give each other critical feedback on works-in-progress.

***

King often maintained over the years that he had given up on fiction after the failure of his first novel. But in truth, the form remained a tantalizing lure to him. The few glimpses available from his never-completed "Man Down," an autobiographical tale of a New York-based writer in decline, showcase some of the most compelling work of his career. His short story, "Something Went with Daddy," published in *Story* magazine, also revealed a vivid fictional presence. King had already proved himself an accomplished journalist and playwright at the national level. His intriguing forays into fiction seemed deeper, darker, more profound. If he could harness this talent, he was capable of writing a great novel—a final emphatic stamp on an illustrious career.

In 1987, he thought he was there. For a couple of years, he had been toying with the idea of "War Movies," an autobiographical novel set on the "home front" of West Texas during World War II. Finally, with other obligations completed, King devoted more time to the book. The project quickly gained momentum. Soon King was writing ten, twelve, and then fourteen hours a day, totally consumed. This intensive writing spell came to an end in May 1987, leaving him with a 633-page manuscript. He believed that he had "never worked on anything so hard for so long."[13]

King told friends that Viking would soon publish the book, but there was a long silence from his editor. Finally, after two months, a verdict was announced: The book was too long, there was not enough plot, the protagonist was unsympathetic, and the work seemed "confused." Viking, as it turned out, would not publish the book after all. Larry L. King, for the first time since he broke into the business, had been flatly rejected by his publisher.[14]

King would have much more success interpreting West Texas in drama. His play, *The Night Hank Williams Died*, offers a single, compressed chapter highlighting King's view of his homeland. Set in 1952, it tells of a young man's longing to escape his bleak hometown. The protagonist, twenty-seven-year-old Thurmond Stottle, pumps gas at a local service station and dreams of going to Nashville to become the new Hank Williams. But he possesses little talent, drinks too much, and clings pathetically to fading memories of high school football glories. As King told one reporter, "Losers make better stories than winners."[15] When Stottle's old high school sweetheart returns to town, he is pressed into action. The results, predictably, are tragic. Earlier, playwright Preston Jones had poked fun at West Texas culture in *A Texas Trilogy*. King's own view, despite the humorous asides, is a significantly darker take on the same subject. Though few elements in the drama are surprising, the story and characters reverberate deep in the bones.

The Night Hank Williams Died premiered in Washington, D.C., in 1988. It received glowing reviews, performed well commercially, and won the Helen Hayes Award for Outstanding New Play. From there, it moved to New York City for an off-Broadway run. Again, the play was warmly received by critics, and King earned a nomination for Outstanding New Play from the New York Outer Critics Circle. But New York audiences proved to be less enthusiastic than those in Washington, D.C. *The Night Hank Williams Died* fell short of Broadway, and investors lost some $300,000.

The Night Hank Williams Died never fulfilled King's large ambitions, but he was somewhat consoled by the fact that regional theater groups across the country would continue to stage productions. For a man who had earlier told Bud Shrake that he needed a second Broadway hit "before I am ready to die," Larry L. King still had much to live for.[16]

Despite his tremendous output from 1981 to 1987, King felt disappointed by the limited payoff. He wrote to a friend:

> I feel written out, burned out. Problem is if I'm not writing something I'm miserable. It was easier to avoid work when I doped and drank, but now that I've reformed there's nothing to do but work. At age 58-1/2 I hear the old Grim Reaper rustling his black robe and sharpening his scythe and I have this foolish egotistical notion the world demands that I produce a certain amount of work before I'm dispatched to Jesus. In truth, as you know and as I know in my honest moments, the world ain't thinking of me at all, much less trembling in fear I'll check out before I've written a bunch more books.[17]

***

By the late 1980s, King began donating his writing archives to the Southwestern Writers Collection, established by his friends Bill and Sally Wittliff in 1986 at Texas State University-San Marcos. Among the dozens of major donors are Bud Shrake, Gary Cartwright, and the family of Billy Lee Brammer. King's papers are among the collection's most extensive. He saved nearly everything over the years and, as a prolific correspondent, kept carbon copies of the thousands of letters he'd typed, as well as all those he'd received. Founding Curator Richard Holland estimated that King's correspondence weighed some 240 pounds and contained over fifteen thousand letters. King, in his typical fashion, placed no restrictions on scholarly access, allowing researchers to make full use of the material. The files offer an unabashed, uncensored look at the full range of King's life, from personal exchanges with senators and congressmen to his relationships with other writers, family, and friends. King often spun out as many as ten or twelve letters a day, and correspondence was clearly the form of writing that brought him the most joy. His spirited letters are marked by playful humor and disarming candor, and from his earliest days as a writer, those in the literary business recognized "a future day when his letters would be collected and published."[18]

Placing his writing archives at Texas State University brought King, in a roundabout way, back into Lyndon Johnson's orbit. The school is LBJ's alma mater, and the president's spirit still presides over much of the campus. In 1991, much to the delight of King's irony-minded friends, Texas State invited the sixty-two-year-old author to deliver its annual "Lyndon Baines Johnson Distinguished Lecture." After eleven years of Reagan and Bush presidencies, King was ready to reassess Johnson. "The poor, the homeless, the minorities, the have-nots, the rotting cities, our fouled planet have largely been ignored," King told the audience. "LBJ at least tried to use his presidential power . . . to strike the chains and bonds of racial, economic and civil slavery from the underclass citizens of the United States."[19]

King was among the first of former LBJ critics who came to hold a more magnanimous view of the president. Having made his peace with LBJ's historical legacy, King was also ready to return to the subject of Johnson in his work. But this time, instead of a biography, he began to envision how he could feature LBJ in a stage play.

But first, more pressing matters interceded. Twelve years is a long time between hit Broadway musicals, and in 1990 King met in New

York with original *Whorehouse* producer, Stevie Phillips, along with collaborators Peter Masterson and Carol Hall. The IRS had recently confiscated a Nevada brothel, and the situation seemed ripe for exploitation as a sequel. King wrote to Bill Wittliff, "I don't know whether to be excited or ashamed! Perhaps, if we live long enough, our entire lives are reduced to sequels."[20] Tommy Tune came back aboard as choreographer and codirector, and for the next three and a half years King and his cohorts worked on the new production, *The Best Little Whorehouse Goes Public.*

The critical mutterings could be heard even before the play opened, as some wondered about the appropriateness of a whorehouse play in an age of AIDS and safe sex. One journalist, noting the absence of characters from the original *Whorehouse*, asked, "Why is anyone doing this?" A grinning Larry L. King supplied the answer. "For the money," he said. "Why else do these things happen?" Compounding the critical reception was an advertising campaign that seemed as vulgar as the musical's Las Vegas setting. A thirty-minute infomercial costing nearly $500,000 aired on New York-area TV stations, asking viewers to call 1-800-BROTHEL for tickets. As dark hints of a critical backlash loomed, Tommy Tune began to make a remark that became his mantra: "I've never had a Broadway flop and certainly don't intend to begin now." Larry L. King recalled, "I flinched every time I heard him say that. He was just daring them to kill the play."[21]

The Best Little Whorehouse Goes Public opened in May 1994 and "received as vicious a pounding as any Broadway play has taken in recent years." *The New York Post* headline read, "Oh, Brother! This is Awful!" *New York Newsday* chimed in, "A moronic catastrophe." One of Broadway's most extravagant spectacles ever closed after just three weeks, and the creators slunk out of town. Larry L. King, as was his custom, had saved his correspondence, manuscripts, notes, and memos from the play. He sent the archives to the Southwestern Writers Collection. He attached a note suggesting that the materials could be exhibited "under the heading of 'How to Craft an Abject Failure.'"[22]

* * *

The collapse of the *Whorehouse* sequel sent the sixty-five-year-old King into a funk lasting several months. Health was also an increasing concern for the two-packs-a-day smoker, and more old friends were dying off. King's publishing prospects continued to decline, and many of the editors he had once known were no longer around. In fact, publishing itself was changing, and not to King's benefit. In 1995 he wrote an article about his experience as a juror in Washington, D.C., in which he and a mixed-race jury debated the fate of a ghetto man charged with rape. The piece was exactly the sort of closely observed, thoughtfully nuanced essay that he had once published to great acclaim. But now there was little demand for this sort of work in the marketplace—unless the trial involved a celebrity or one was a "name" writer. The article, criticized for its lack of a "celebrity" angle, was rejected by the *Atlantic Monthly, Vanity Fair,* and *Esquire.* As King wrote to his cousin, "hardly a decent magazine exists in America any more. . . . I think that the Celebrity horseshit has been the ruination of magazine journalism."[23]

King still ostensibly owed Viking Press one last book, but when his wife/agent Barbara Blaine contacted the publisher, she learned that the press no longer even had a clear idea of who King was, nor were they familiar with the details of his contract from the early 1970s. Blaine quickly extricated her husband from any remaining obligation, freeing King to approach other publishers with his work. One promising prospect was another novel. This one, too, sprang from West Texas, drawing from King's experiences covering the bush-league Midland Indians baseball team. Several editors expressed interest in the book, and by 1997 King completed the manuscript. Yet again, his finished effort was rejected. He wrote to Bud Shrake:

Wal, Hail, when you come down to it I guess I've gotta conclude that I have proved—once again—that I ain't no novelist . . . Bah humbug. Don't know why Jesus don't want me to write novels. What is embarrassing about my novels is that I think they're good and got potential until about twenty folks tell me they ain't. Rap my knuckles if I ever say I am gonna write another 'un.[24]

By this time, King had also compiled another batch of stories for an anthology, yet not a single New York publisher expressed interest. It seemed that King's career as a national writer was, at long last, over. Yet back in Texas, King was considered a cultural treasure. University presses had eagerly published his work during the 1990s. In 1997, the University of Texas Press, as part of its Southwestern Writers Collection Series, agreed to publish King's new anthology, *True Facts, Tall Tales, and Pure Fiction*. The collection is less consistent overall than King's other works—at least a third of the stories are substandard compared with his previous anthologies. Another third are merely average. But also included among the nineteen pieces are a half-dozen works that, by any standard, measure up to King's best work—that is, work that ranks with the best writing in America, whether it is currently in favor or not. King's collection begins with "Taking Justice," his story about D.C. jury duty that was rejected by every magazine he approached. The inclusion of this first-rate, unpublished article serves, as much as any piece of writing ever could, as an indictment of the current state of American magazine journalism. Another of King's stories, "Happy Birthday to a Fine Boy," is a gripping account of a King family tragedy that displays a heretofore unknown range in King's writing technique.

Most revelatory in the collection, as noted by several reviewers, is the inclusion, for the first time, of King's short fiction. Though King had yet to write a successful novel, his fictional voice brims with so much potential it is easy to understand why he continued to be lured by the novelistic form. Tom Pilkington observed, "For me, one of the unexpected outcomes of reading this volume was that it made me wish Mr. King had not more or less abandoned the writing of fiction at the start of his career. . . . The 'Pure Fiction' segment of his new book contains four short stories . . . I think three of the four are excellent."[25]

* * *

In 1999, as he turned seventy years old, TCU Press published Larry L. King's long-awaited book of letters, *Larry L. King: A Writer's Life in Letters, Or, Reflections in a Bloodshot Eye.* Coming in at just over four hundred pages, the book serves as an epistolary autobiography, with representative letters from the entire spectrum of his writing career. King's rollicking missives, directed to friends, family, politicians, critics, and fellow writers, are funny, angry, boastful, irreverent, self-pitying—sometimes all at once. They track his brash, self-confident rise during the *Harper's* days, turning more serious near the end as he comes to terms with his career's "slippage." Reviews of King's book, largely relegated to Texas, were uniformly excellent and enthusiastic. In the absence of a West Texas novel, this book of letters would do just fine as a career-crowning work.

But King was not done. By 1995 he had completed his new play, *The Dead Presidents' Club.* Set in a celestial purgatory, Lyndon Johnson, Harry Truman, and Calvin Coolidge have been awaiting their judgment at the hands of an "Evaluation Committee"— described by LBJ as "a buncha narrow-minded goddamned Saints!"[26] With the arrival of the freshly dead Richard Nixon, the intrigues begin, as Nixon and LBJ conspire to circumvent the Evaluation Committee and deal directly with God. She, as it turns out, is not at all what they expect.

The Dead Presidents' Club premiered in 1996 at the Live Oak Theatre in Austin, where it was enthusiastically received by critics and audiences, breaking all attendance records. A successful production was also staged in Fort Worth in 2000. For several years King has been engaged in negotiations to bring the play to Washington, D.C., where its commercial possibilities seem ripe with potential. This play, perhaps King's best, may come to be seen as his life's masterpiece if it ever receives wider productions.

King's health deteriorated markedly in 2001, leaving the seventy-two-year-old hooked up to an oxygen machine and sharply limiting his travel outside the home. Still, the work continued. He produced a nineteen-thousand-word profile on Willie Morris—who died in 1999—for *Texas Monthly*. The magazine's editors, citing space limitations and readers' short attention spans, cut the article by almost two-thirds prior to publication, leaving King fuming to Shrake about the "Dick-and-Jane" editing that stripped away the context. "Goddamn. I ain't writing another magazine piece ever, for anybody, on a subject I truly CARE ABOUT," King wrote.[27] Still, the article was warmly received, and it earned King a second Texas Institute of Letters Award for Best Magazine Journalism. King began work on expanding the piece into a full-length biography of Willie Morris.

Now, near the end of his career, it has been largely forgotten that King was once considered among America's best and most vital writers. Back in 1973, Tom Wolfe edited an anthology titled *New Journalism* that failed to include any of King's work. That omission drew a rebuke from a reviewer who groused that King's absence was the major flaw in the book. King's work has appeared in some anthologies over the years, such as *Roy Blount's Book of Southern Humor*. But more often, King has been left out of publications that, by all rights, should have included him. One in particular is the 1993 anthology, *Voices in Black and White: Writings on Race in America from Harper's Magazine*. King's "Confessions of a White Racist"—one of *Harper's* most celebrated articles ever on the subject of race—is as natural a fit as one can conceive of for that anthology.

What has remained remarkable about King is that, as his literary stock went into decline, his writing itself continued to develop, becoming ever more complex and substantive. Aside from a few magazine puff pieces and the *Whorehouse* sequel, the long trajectory of King's career has indicated, above all, a dedication to the principles of his craft. At the beginning of the 1980s, King was regarded as an excellent magazine journalist, a failed fiction writer, and the untested author of a fluke Broadway hit. By the end of his career, he still had not succeeded as a novelist, but King proved that he can write compelling, absorbing fiction. He also proved that he can write plays that, while they may not challenge Tennessee Williams or Arthur Miller, are well-regarded works that have succeeded in multiple productions across the country. Some, such as *The Dead Presidents' Club,* have only begun to test their potential. Stylistically, King continued to develop his writing voice, surprising and delighting long-time readers and critics with fresh new works published while the author was in his late sixties. Versatility, more than ever, became a byword for his work. In addition to drama, fiction, and journalism, King wrote a TV documentary, film screenplays, a children's book, and songs for his stage plays.[28]

Aside from the unlikely event that future literary scholars will resurrect King as a major American writer, his literary legacy will be largely limited to Texas. For one who lived away from the state for nearly fifty years and harbored strong ambitions to become a national figure, this seems a heavy blow. Yet surprisingly, King has accepted the judgment with a remarkable equanimity. He wrote to a friend, "my consolation is that in Texas, at least, I am still both socially and professionally accepted as a writer and even, maybe, a little bit venerated. And there is no way to say how important that is to me, from the standpoint of personal ego and my 'writerness' and my feeling of worth."[28] King's willing acceptance of the mantle attests to how much Texas' own literary environment has matured in recent decades.

50.

CARTWRIGHT

By the time *Texas Monthly* celebrated its tenth birthday in 1983, the magazine had become the most successful journalistic experiment ever launched in the state. Circulation stood at nearly three hundred thousand. Annual advertising pages had climbed from 176 to more than sixteen hundred, and annual ad revenues reached $16 million. In addition to its financial success, TM continued to receive the prestigious National Magazine Award. Other regional magazines were debuting across the country, with varying degrees of success. *Texas Monthly*, however, has remained the archetype.[1]

As a major influence in the literary, journalistic, and cultural life of Texas, *Texas Monthly* has introduced new generations of writers to the state's readers. In this role, TM's arrogance has become a thorny problem. It has failed the state's ethnic communities, both in its hiring practices and in its coverage. As a result, those groups have become, as Jan Reid noted, "alienated and contemptuous."[2] Yet the magazine has also boasted enormous successes. Three staff writers—Mimi Swartz, Nicolas Lemann, and Lawrence Wright—later moved on to prominent roles at the *New Yorker*. Another former staffer, James Fallows, now writes for the *Atlantic Monthly*. All are considered major American journalists, and each has written widely heralded books. TM also boasts Stephen Harrigan, now a successful novelist and screenwriter. Founding editor William Broyles Jr. became editor of *Newsweek* and later cocreated the hit television series *China Beach.* Broyles' subsequent screenwriting credits include *Apollo 13* and *Cast Away.* TM also introduced Texas to new generations of influential journalists including Jan Reid, Dick Reavis, Prudence Mackintosh, Joe Nick Patoski, Robert Draper, Kaye Northcott, and dozens more.

Gary Cartwright, upon returning to Texas and joining TM's staff in 1982, immediately became—and has remained—the magazine's signature writer. Older, wiser, and more settled, he eschewed the temptations to move on to national publications, though he continued to receive national acclaim—his 1986 *Texas Monthly* story, "The Last Roundup," was a finalist for a National Magazine Award. In his work for *Texas Monthly,* Cartwright has become the state's foremost practitioner of the New Journalism. As one admirer noted, he is Texas' "droll daredevil, our literary loose cannon who [views] the world from strange and wondrous angles out there in orbit, but with the precision and resolution of the better satellite cameras."[3]

Though Cartwright's work is often extravagantly bizarre or sensational, it is hardly superficial. His stories usually go through a dozen rewrites before an editor ever sees them, and he has honed his talent to a fine, sharp edge, resulting in consistently excellent prose. His sentences are as tightly coiled and carefully calibrated as those of magazine's most careful stylists—Stephen Harrigan and Jan Reid. Cartwright often wraps his stories up too neatly, but his freewheeling gonzo style, bolstered by his careful attention to language and form, creates a formidable journalistic presence. His former *Texas Monthly* colleague Robert Draper has written that Cartwright combines the "omnipresence of a tough-ass intellect, a free spirit, and a deeply empathetic heart. To read Cartwright's work was, for this boy, to recognize that journalism could be affecting, lastingly so . . . calling Gary Cartwright a regional writer is like calling Joe DiMaggio a regional hitter."[4]

But considering his lifestyle, the wonder is that Cartwright survived at all. As he admitted later, "There is a ten-year period in my life, from roughly the early seventies to the early eighties, when my

Gary Cartwright, 1988. *Photo by Bill Wittliff. Bill Wittliff Archives, Southwestern Writers Collection, Texas State University-San Marcos.*

Austin memories come in streaks and blurs. I'm told that others who lived here at the time have the same problem . . . I'm sure I must have been around . . . because I see my name on books, screenplays, and magazine articles. But it's as though someone mailed them to me in a box with no return address."[5]

After being diagnosed with high blood pressure in 1979, Cartwright made some attempts to moderate his drinking, but he continued to eat poorly and exercised little. Two years later, he was hospitalized with hypertension, and doctors feared that he'd suffered a heart attack. Still, Cartwright maintained his habitual disregard for consequences. He even wrote a story for *Texas Monthly*, "I Am the Greatest Cook in the World," which showed him preparing "to fry the bejesus out of buttermilked and battered up chicken."[6]

As Cartwright turned fifty in 1984, he reflected, "there was a definite sense of aging, of having witnessed—Good Lord, could it be a half century—of debauchery." He saw that, "One by one, my old pals were hitting the wall, sometimes not too hard, sometimes permanently." Cartwright was inevitably slowing down, and he began incorporating references to his advancing age into his stories. In 1988, as *Texas Monthly* celebrated its fifteenth anniversary, he published an "An Old Five and Dimer," his most direct look yet at aging. Cartwright wrote, "Things I used to ridicule now seem indispensable—God, country, home, harmony, hard work, and family. It took me five decades to figure out that the values that truly matter are the ones I learned before I ever left home." Though he was only fifty-three, the article was underscored by an elegiac tone. Reviewing the course of his life, Cartwright came to the realization that "What matters now is harmony." He concluded the essay with a vision of his own death: "Writers don't retire, but their clocks stop like everyone else's. When that happens, I expect some weeping and wailing, but I want to hear belly laughs, too. . . . In case I forget, let me post my epithet right here. Just write, 'Okay, Pops, what's the score?' Only don't wait around for an answer."[7]

The article proved nearly prophetic. A few months later, Cartwright hit the wall, and the collision was nearly fatal. The heart attack and subsequent quintuple bypass created permanent changes in his life. "Having my chest ripped open encouraged in me two virtues that had never been my strong suits—patience and humility," he wrote. Cartwright recovered fairly quickly, and worries about losing his writing voice proved to be short-lived. He even learned to write without cigarettes. Though he paid closer attention to his health, he began to drift back into his old habits. Two years later, he blacked out while on assignment for *Texas Monthly*. A pacemaker was installed. Another blow struck in 1992 when he learned that he suffered from a rare kidney disease.[8]

Finally, in 1993, after a bleak medical evaluation, Cartwright resolved to change. He reformed his eating habits and began working out regularly in an Austin gym—"a discipline that in my wildest dreams I never imagined I would practice, especially at age fifty-nine."

His wife Phyllis joined him on this new path. Before long, he was look-ing and feeling better than he had in years. As he realized the extent of his improvement, Gary Cartwright became a convert. His new atti-tude was about more than just health—it was about spirit, too. Cartwright became a man who prays instead of parties. The transfor-mation stunned many long-time observers, and as one reporter noted in evident amazement, "There are even scattered reports of his turn-ing up in the pews of Austin churches." Cartwright himself saw little remarkable in the situation. "It is easy, fashionable, and even fun to deny the existence of God when you are young," he wrote, "but athe-ism in anyone of advancing years seems to me the ultimate conceit."[9]

Once considered a "kamikaze on auto-pilot," Cartwright success-fully retooled his journalism in the face of his personal transformation, retaining his distinctive gonzo edge. In 1998 he wrote "How to Have Great Sex Forever," recounting his adventures with Viagra for *Texas Monthly* readers. This—the most explicit article ever published by the magazine on the subject of sex—came from its oldest writer. Cartwright described in great detail the sexual relationship he and Phyllis enjoy, including the fantasy games staged by "Frenchy" and "Monique." He addressed his problems with erectile dysfunction and described the scene as he took his first dose of Caverject behind a closed door. Phyllis, waiting in the bedroom, asked, "How's it going?" The author stepped out proudly, showcasing himself. He asked, "Does the term Louisville Slugger ring a bell?"[10]

Cartwright's positive approach to aging seemed validated by the trajectory of his career in the 1990s. The decade began with the film-ing of the old screenplay, *Rip*, that he and Bud Shrake had cowritten nearly twenty years earlier in Durango. Starring Willie Nelson and Kris Kristofferson, the movie, retitled *A Pair of Aces*, appeared on net-work TV to high ratings and excellent reviews. The next year saw a sequel, *Another Pair of Aces*, coproduced by Cartwright and Shrake. In 1995 a TV miniseries, *Texas Justice*, was made from Cartwright's Cullen Davis book, and *Blood Will Tell* was reissued in a new paper-back edition to coincide with the event. In 1998, Cinco Puntos Press published a new edition of *Dirty Dealing*, Cartwright's account of the Judge John Wood murder case. Also in 1998, TCU Press issued a reprint of Cartwright's *Galveston: A History of the Island*. This engaging popular history was originally published by New York-based Atheneum in 1990 but had quickly gone out of print. Now, with new editions available of three of his last four books, Gary Cartwright was enjoying the most sustained attention of his career. He also had a new book in the works. St. Martin's Press signed him to write a part memoir, part instruction manual on how to "lead the good life after a heart attack."

Coming to terms with one's past, particularly when embarrassing behavior is involved, is not an easy thing to do. The most successful memoirs are brutally—often painfully—honest. Larry L. King had always succeeded, thanks in large measure to his refusal to obscure his personal failings or his frustrations about his career. But even King had his limits. In 1998, old friend Jay Milner finally, after years of struggle, managed to publish another book. This was *Confessions of a Maddog: A Romp Through the High-Flying Texas Music and Literary Era of the Fifties to the Seventies*. King agreed to write the foreword for Milner, provided that Milner delete a section of his manuscript. Milner acquiesced. King, in the foreword, obliquely refers to the episode, telling readers, "And, believe me, I am *equally* grateful for certain things [Milner] left out. . . ."[11]

As Cartwright prepared to address his own years of debauchery head-on, old friends were understandably nervous about some of the stories that might surface. Bud Shrake wrote to King: "Jap has just turned in his manuscript of his book on how he spent 40 years as a drunk and doper and scoundrel, but has recovered to become a combination of Superman and Buddha." Shrake continued, "He let me read part of an early version in which I noticed he was led into being a drunken doping scoundrel by me and you and Jenke [Dan Jenkins] and even Guv Ann [Ann Richards], and seeing that this part made me nervous, he didn't let me read any more of it."[12]

Heartwiseguy: How to Live the Good Life After a Heart Attack, was published in 1998. A smiling Gary Cartwright appears on the front cover, sitting with his back to a tombstone. Ann Richards contributed the foreword, though she warns readers, "Be aware that all the rest of us have a different version that makes Gary look worse and us look better." Richards also pays heed to Cartwright's major theme: "Sobriety and sanity are better, and so is growing older. Gary Cartwright is a living, breathing example."[13]

Heartwiseguy, as one would expect from Cartwright, is a thoroughly readable and informative overview of bypass surgery and also a revealing account of the excesses that led to the situation. As Cartwright told one reporter, "I don't regret anything. That's who I was, and those were the times."[14] The writer's lessons on aging are simple and direct; the key, he maintains, is attitude. Cartwright smoothly bridges his past and present lives, sharing his new lessons while refusing to agonize over past mistakes. A hint of sanctimony hangs over the preachments, but Cartwright's self-awareness of this tendency and his enthusiasm for his subject make it easier to forgive. What is clear from *Heartwiseguy* is that Cartwright has emerged stronger and better than ever, and he has aged with grace and élan.

In 2000, the University of Texas Press, as part of its Southwestern Writers Collection Series, issued a new collection of Cartwright's magazine journalism. *Turn Out the Lights: Chronicles of Texas during the 80s and 90s* contains seventeen of the nearly one hundred articles Cartwright had written for *Texas Monthly* since joining the staff in 1982. Featured in the book is a new essay, "1963: My Most Unforgettable Year," that returns to the subject of Dallas and the Kennedy assassination. While nostalgia is at work in many of the pieces, his senses remain sharp. Gary Cartwright, in his many years as a Texas-based journalist, has proven inspiring to new generations of reporters, not just because of how well he writes, but in how he uses his hard-won experience as the foundation of his work.

Bud Shrake, 1999. *Photo by Bill Wittliff. Bill Wittliff Archives, Southwestern Writers Collection, Texas State University-San Marcos.*

51.

SHRAKE

Bud Shrake hit the wall at fifty-two in 1984 after being diagnosed with diabetes and liver damage. A doctor gave him a year to live unless he quit drinking and doping. "Even then," Shrake admitted, "I actually had to think about it. I thought I needed the speed for energy and the whiskey for dreaming. Now I realize that's what a good night's sleep is for." Like his friends, Shrake discovered that sobriety made him even more productive. "In a way I wish I'd changed sooner," he said. "But on the other hand, maybe I wouldn't have been ready for it sooner. . . . I think I had to hit the wall pretty hard to make me change."[1]

Shrake's health crisis coincided with the Austin premiere of his stage play, *Pancho Villa's Wedding Day,* adapted from his unproduced screenplay. While not without flaws, the play received generally positive notices. Yet once again the *Texas Observer* offered a contrasting view, issuing yet another fierce attack on Shrake's work. *Observer* critic Ray Reece, writing a month after the play ended its run, speculated that Shrake's intention was to win "himself a bit of unearned grandeur by riding the myth of Pancho Villa across the willing minds of a friendly, hometown theatre audience." But Shrake's sleazy ego trip failed, Reece contended, because of "the play's insipidness." Shrake was angered by the review, but the attack was not entirely unexpected, coming from the *Observer*. What really upset him was the subsequent letter he received from the critic, "apologizing for the extreme nastiness of his review. He said he had been so drunk at the play that he hardly remembered seeing it at all, and he took out his personal frustrations—and jealousy—on me in print." Shrake sent a copy of the letter to Ronnie Dugger and suggested that it should be printed to set the record straight. Dugger refused, and Shrake said, "since then I have had nothing to do with the *Observer,* including reading it."[2]

Pancho Villa's Wedding Day became the only screenplay Shrake adapted for theater, although he has plenty of unproduced scripts to choose from should he ever decide to try again. From the late 1970s to the mid-1980s, Shrake sold several screenplays to Hollywood, including the three—*Nightwing, Tom Horn,* and *Songwriter*—that were turned into films. Shrake conceded that many of the unproduced scripts were written solely for the money—the same reason he kept writing for *Sports Illustrated* all those years. But just as selected *Sports Illustrated* articles transcended their unexceptional setting, so, too, do some of Shrake's screenplays. Those written for love were intended to be works of art.

Several of Shrake's screenplays are intriguing, and the finest of them all is *The Big Mamoo.* Rivaling his best novels, this "gonzo portrait of Los Alamos" during the Manhattan project is a clever and substantive work, exquisitely plotted, deadpan funny, and stuffed with rich characters. *The Big Mamoo* is as chillingly funny as Terry Southern's *Dr. Strangelove,* yet is "reality unvarnished but told with a point of view that favors the absurdness of real events and real people."[3]

Shrake's fictional characters interact easily with real-life figures Robert Oppenheimer and Edward Teller. The world's most brilliant scientists have gathered in the remote mountain community, and spirits are kept up with dances, drag shows, lab alcohol, and, as one article termed it: "bored exhibitionist wives who look for sex in public places." Prowling about are FBI agents, Communist spies, and possible Nazi saboteurs.[4]

The scientists conduct their work well aware that it may lead to the extinction of humanity, yet they are unable to contain their enthusiasm for the scientific challenge. After "Fat Man" is assembled, no one is quite sure what the extent of the blast will be, or even if the bomb will work. The scientists discuss the upcoming Trinity Test with the army's chief public relations officer when the general in command interrupts. "You eggheads don't understand the public mind," he tells them.

Enrico Fermi—an Italian physicist who learned English from reading Jack London novels—fires back: "I can dictate your press release." He pauses for a moment, then intones, "a huge meteor struck New Mexico this morning and blasted the shit out of the whole state and all its citizens. Hunters and skiiers planning to vacation in New Mexico, be advised it is now a crater and too hot to touch."

The public relations officer counters: "I do have a press release describing a celestial body smashing into New Mexico. I have prepared press releases to explain a total fizzle, a small embarrassing flop, a major explosion such as we hope for, the destruction of the State of New Mexico, the destruction of the Western United States . . . if the atomic bomb goes off bigger than that, the hell with the p.r. game, frankly."

Edward Teller, deeply serious, says, "I'd make it 35 to one we don't blow up New Mexico. A thousand to one we don't blow up the whole world."

After a disquieting pause, Robert Oppenheimer speaks up: "The press release could say: 'Even though the odds were 1,000 to one against them, the most brilliant men in history managed to obliterate the planet Earth today.'"[5]

***

Director Jonathan Demme, who considered *The Big Mamoo* his "dream project," labored for nearly a decade to bring Shrake's script to the screen. In 1988 Demme told *Premiere* magazine that "studio executives admire the script [but] are baffled by its tone. . . . It is just too far out there for them." Shrake explained the failure by pointing out, "the studio did not want to make a black comedy. My argument that real life is a black comedy only made things worse. It's human beings who decide what movies to make, and the wrong human beings for *Mamoo* were in power at the time."[6]

By the 1990s, Demme gave up on trying to direct the film, though he did promise to continue serving "as its godfather and help get it made." Producer Ed Pressman, who once put up his own money to pay for a studio-demanded rewrite, sent Shrake a note telling him, "I will make *The Big Mamoo* into a movie if it's the last thing I do." As Shrake noted wryly in 2002, Pressman is still in business.[7]

The Big Mamoo became the most painful of Shrake's many frustrations in Hollywood. His talent was widely recognized within the film industry, and many anticipated the day when a Shrake script would become a big hit. Dennis Hopper told an interviewer that Shrake has "more good screenplays that *haven't* been done than most people *ever* write." Esther Newberg, representing a major Hollywood agency, said, "There are two heads of major studios now who think the great American western is one Bud will write." But for Shrake, as the years passed by, the disappointments took their toll. By the end of the 1980s he drifted away from screenwriting. "The only time you can be absolutely sure your movie will make it to the screen," he said, "is when you go to the theatre and watch it."[8]

By 1985 it had been ten years since Shrake had published a novel. He decided to "set himself a test: to write a novel without a cigarette or a drink—or a single mention of Texas."[9] *Night Never Falls*, published in 1987 by Random House, is a swashbuckling adventure story starring Harry Sparrow, a hard-drinking, world-renowned foreign correspondent. Sparrow travels to Vietnam in 1954 and becomes trapped with the French in the siege at Dien Bien Phu. After a miraculous escape, he heads to Algeria in pursuit of the Nazi war criminals and Arab terrorists who have kidnapped his wife and child. Sparrow's bravado is complemented by his sense of style, and he emerges at the end as victorious and jaundiced as any Dan Jenkins hero.

Like Dan Jenkins' *Fast Copy*, published the next year, *Night Never Falls* is an appreciative look at "vintage" journalism. However, the book was not a success. As Jan Reid noted in *Texas Monthly*, it "works from the outline of a superb plot, but the book reads like a screenplay. . . . Shrake leaves nuance and character development to actors who don't show up. The scenes in Vietnam . . . are vivid and spooky. His belief and interest in his characters, however, seems fitful, and the reader has the same problem."[10] *Night Never Falls* became Shrake's first pedestrian novel since his first, *Blood Reckoning.*

Over the next three years, Shrake, closing in on his sixtieth birthday, took a different tack. He began cowriting "as-told-to" autobiographies of celebrity friends. The first was a collaboration with Willie Nelson, a project that had been jelling for at least a decade. In addition to Willie's own words, the book includes contributions from "The Chorus"—an assortment of Willie's friends—and their recollections don't always coincide with the singer's. The result is, as one reviewer noted, "an outrageous, hilarious, yet deeply serious book."[11]

In 1990 *Bootlegger's Boy* appeared, the autobiography of former University of Oklahoma football coach Barry Switzer. Though Switzer had won national championships, his program was beset by scandal, and he gained a reputation as an "outlaw coach." Like the Willie Nelson autobiography, Switzer's tale is marked by great candor in its telling. Both books made the best-seller lists, bringing Shrake income—if not exactly literary prestige—as a credited ghost writer.

By 1989 Bud Shrake and Ann Richards, good friends for some twenty years, began "going steady," in the words of Gary Cartwright. "This is the only relationship I've ever had in my life that was completely guilt-free," Ann Richards said. "Each of us is totally free to live our lives and do the things we want to do without the other feeling that it intrudes or takes up space." Shrake observed, "It makes us better companions that neither of us drink. A lot of our good friends do drink, which makes it easier for us to go off by ourselves."

In 1990, Ann Richards was elected governor, and Bud Shrake, at her side for the parties and receptions, became "The First Gent." Shrake has sidestepped the politics, telling a reporter, "She doesn't ask me for my advice, and I try not to give her any. She has gotten this far without me." The two have maintained their close relationship in the years since, bringing up the inevitable talk of marriage. "Ann and I love each other and enjoy being together," Shrake told Gary Cartwright in 2000. "[B]ut neither of us wants to get married again. We live very different lives. She travels constantly, working, making

445

speeches, taking her kids on holidays to China and Peru. I'm not so keen on traveling anymore, but I go with her now and then. I can imagine that we may live together somewhere down the road, and we intend to grow old together."[12]

***

Since becoming sober, Shrake became a serious golfer, playing nearly every day, often with Willie Nelson and Darrell Royal. "I had to fill up my time doing something else besides drinking," he explained. Constantly attempting to improve his game, Shrake "tried every golf gimmick known to man. . . . . My home is a golf museum and I have at least twenty different drivers." It was this passion for golf that led to his next book project. In 1991 he met with eighty-six-year-old Harvey Penick, a legendary instructor who had taught, among others, professional champions Tom Kite and Ben Crenshaw. Penick had compiled a notebook of his observations and tips from a lifetime of teaching, and he wondered if Shrake could help him publish it. Penick enjoyed something of a reputation as "a mystical holy man," and his golfing advice was "spare and deceptively simple, homespun snippets of wisdom such as 'take dead aim.'" Non-golfers might find such tips "mundane, almost moronic, but every word in the book had, according to Harvey, 'stood the test of time.'"[13]

Once the manuscript was ready, Shrake made several suggestions about the book's marketing, all of which the publisher approved. The volume was small enough to fit into a golf bag, the dust jacket was reminiscent of books published a century earlier, and it sold for around twenty dollars. Shrake believed that, "Everyone who plays golf has twenty dollars and will spend it on anything that he thinks will help his game."[14]

He turned out to be right. *Harvey Penick's Little Red Book* remained on *The New York Times* best-seller list for over a year and became the biggest selling sports book of all time. It spawned a veritable cottage industry, with audio books, videos, newsletters, calendars, and, of course, sequels. Bud Shrake, after years of living from project to project, had finally scored big. He could, at last, recharge his career—this time for himself. "With the money from the Penick books, I could finally become what I had hoped to be twenty years before," Shrake said. "A former newspaperman who writes novels full-time."[15]

Back in the early 1980s, his publisher had rejected Shrake's idea for a "Texas epic," and he kept the manuscript in a trunk. "The only person who continued to believe in the book was his friend [Bill] Wittliff," Gary Cartwright wrote later. "From time to time Wittliff would ask Bud when he planned to finish [it] and Bud would tell him, 'Never!'" Then, in 1996, the novel "began to rewrite itself." Shrake, who had long resented Austin's transformation from a pleasant medium-sized city into an overdeveloped megalopolis, was

> sitting on his balcony, looking across the Colorado [River] to Austin, lamenting the scars and follies of a generation of developers and their monuments to greed and ego. In the days of the Comancheria (Comanche territory), he reminded himself, a chief might have sat in this same location, looking southwest toward Barton Creek, the Comanche's Palm Springs. In 1839 he would have seen hundreds of white people pouring into his valley with mule carts, lumber, and building tools. What would he have thought?[16]

Shrake resurrected his story of the early days of the fledging Texas Republic. Mirabeau Lamar had succeeded Sam Houston as president and pursued a ruthless expansionist policy that provoked bloody confrontations with the state's Indians. Lamar's decision to move the state capital to a new city named Austin was a direct challenge to the Comanches, who controlled the hills west of town. Shrake's epic drama blends historical figures with his own original characters, and all of them seem larger than life. Chief among these is Romulus Swift, a dashing, brilliant, deeply compassionate physician. Swift, who is half-Cherokee, can quote Wordsworth or kill an opponent with equal grace. Swift comes to Austin on a quest for knowledge, having heard of a magical presence in Comancheria that can reveal "The Third Wisdom."

Shrake spent three years immersed in the novel, which became his longest and most ambitious book ever. As in Larry L. King's later work, Shrake's own view of female characters expanded significantly. The women in *The Borderland* inhabit major roles, and, indeed, Shrake's most compelling creation is Hannah Dahlman, a German Jew who emigrates to Texas to marry a Texas Ranger—Captain Matthew Caldwell.

As one would expect from Shrake, the novel brings the time and place alive in a vivid way, moving easily between the Indian camps to the new Anglo towns as he charts the collisions that created Texas. Yet in this new novel, Shrake would also eschew the limitations of the historical fiction, consciously adapting elements of "magical realism" into his tale. This is most pronounced in his creation of a "man-ape," the creature who holds the keys to the spiritual knowledge sought by Romulus Swift.

The Borderland, published by Hyperion in 2000, was Shrake's first novel in thirteen years. The epic was viewed by many as the crowning achievement of his nearly fifty-year writing career. *The Los Angeles Times* cited *The Borderland* as one of the Best Books of 2000, and *The Dallas Morning News* was among those hailing it as equaling "the best of Larry McMurtry." In *Texas Monthly*, Gary Cartwright wrote, "At 68 Bud has hit the literary equivalent of a grand slam. *The Borderland* is the work of a naturally gifted writer who has honed his skills and instincts, marshaled his courage, and scaled the peak of maturity." Cartwright also quoted Bill Wittliff: "*Blessed McGill* was a quartet," Wittliff said. "*The Borderland* is a symphony."[17] The book became a modest commercial success, selling out of its hardback printing of twenty-eight thousand—the most copies ever sold of a Shrake novel in hardback. *The Borderland* has found a sustained audience in Texas, where, of course, epic dramas about the state are most appreciated.

Yet despite the successes and accolades, there remains an aura of disappointment over the book. Friends of Shrake and longtime observers of the literary scene have concluded that, as much as they *want* to like *The Borderland*, in their hearts they know it's not Shrake's best work.[18] The novel suffers from two distinct deficiencies, both of which have been amply commented on by reviewers. The often outlandish characters are, as Shrake acknowledged, "purposely over the top, and bigger than life."[19] Larry McMurtry's protagonists in *Lonesome Dove* were also larger than life, yet they succeed in large part because they emerge organically from the historical context. In *The Borderland,* in contrast, Shrake's characters are imposed on the scene from above, as though from a master puppeteer. For all their spectacular uniqueness, they lack the vital human dimensions that connect them deeply to readers.

Compounding this are the rather condescending metaphysical lessons. In contrast to the subtle spiritual matrix of *Blessed McGill, The Borderland* is too obvious. The man-ape's "final wisdom" is insightful, yes, but it's also a simple precept that left at least one reviewer feeling "as something he needed to know yet already learned in kindergarten."[20] Harvey Penick's short, simple declarations of eternal wisdom in *The Little Red Book* may have won the hearts of millions of golfers, but the approach did not translate successfully to fiction.

Despite the failure of *The Borderland* to fulfill the highest hopes set for it, the novel is an important one in Texas letters. Shrake's failures—the exaggerated characters and pedantic spirituality—are failures of ambition, rather than omission. Like the coyote trickster who provides illumination while singeing his own paws, Shrake's novel offers an instructive vision. Historical fiction, particularly that set in Texas, has been largely limited to a certain methodology in its telling. Shrake, through this "highly evolved tall tale," has broken through to new territory, expanding the genre to encompass other styles, such as magical realism. As Wittliff told Gary Cartwright, Shrake "took some wonderful chances." Time will tell how other writers follow these trails in the years ahead.[21]

***

In 2001, Shrake turned seventy, and despite medical ailments including heart trouble and the loss of a kidney, he has remained intensely engaged. He finished a stage play, *Benchmark,* cowritten with Michael Rudman, that premiered in London in 2002. He also published a new novel, *Billy Boy,* written within a matter of months.

Far different from any previous Shrake book, *Billy Boy* is a warmly told coming-of-age story that incorporates sports into the narrative. Set in 1950s Fort Worth, it poses the question: Is golf a metaphor for life, or is life a metaphor for golf?

Billy Boy is populated by charming oddball characters who mix easily with real-life golf celebrities such as Ben Hogan. Harvey Penick, too, makes an appearance. Most fascinating of all is John Bredemus, the "Father of Texas Golf," who designed many of the state's best courses in the 1920s and 1930s. In contrast to *The Borderland*, Shrake's characters in *Billy Boy* are believable and engaging. They arise out of the seemingly unassuming fictional world being created, and yet there remains a measure of magical realism in the air.

Billy Boy again showed the overlap between the fiction of Bud Shrake and Dan Jenkins. Jenkins also published a golf novel in 2001, *The Money-Whipped Steer-Job Three-Jack Give-Up Artist*. But the two books by the two old friends could hardly be more different. While Jenkins' narrator, Bobby Joe Grooves, spends much of his time complaining, Shrake's book is guided by a quiet Zen sensibility. John Bredemus counsels, "Golf reacts to cheerfulness more than anything else. . . . The man who goes onto a course with good cheer in his heart will soon find himself playing better." As in *The Borderland*, Shrake's Penick-inspired proverbs are less sanguine than overstated. Still, the novel retains a good deal of charm and is largely successful. One can also hardly blame Shrake for his attempts to distill metaphysics into proverbs. After all, the ideas he comunicated in *Blessed McGill* went largely unnoticed by reviewers and readers.[21]

Shrake's return to fiction hasn't brought him to the forefront of American letters. Yet it has earned him a quiet sense of respect, and it has reminded readers in Texas that the writer now publishing new work in his seventies has been a major force in the state's literature for some forty years. Shrake's later fiction does not measure up to his peak works—*Blessed McGill* and *Strange Peaches*. But then few novels do.

52.

"DOING
INDEFINABLE
SERVICES TO
MANKIND"

As mentioned before, J. Frank Dobie dominated Texas letters from the 1920s to the 1960s. In addition to his numerous books and magazine articles, starred on radio shows and penned a syndicated column that appeared in newspapers around the state. His interpretations of Texas culture were sacrosanct, and he was a well-loved celebrity. During his lifetime, Dobie was known, simply, as "Mr. Texas."

Dobie was a singular inspiration to dozens of writers, many of whom also understood that he "exercised considerable control over what was published about Texas."[1] In 1939, when the newly established Texas Institute of Letters inaugurated its annual award for best book, Dobie won out over Katherine Anne Porter. She was an artist of national and international acclaim. He, on the other hand, had Texas in his back pocket.

Dobie cast such extraordinary light in his lifetime—much of it by the dint of his formidable personality—that many of his contemporaries were blind to the limitations of his prose. After his death, the inevitable reappraisals began, and Dobie's literary reputation went into rapid decline.

Dobie remains celebrated for his vigorous spirit. Schools, streets, and buildings are named for him, and rare volumes of his work are still prized by collectors. But his writing is no longer of scholarly consequence. The case of J. Frank Dobie has emerged as a cautionary tale in Texas letters: Beware the writer whose personality overshadows his work.

***

Texas' Literary Outlaws are legendary for their excesses, and their exploits have been recounted in the state's newspapers for decades. Their popular image is of a group of "bad boys" more interested in partying and pulling pranks than in creating lasting literature. Like J. Frank Dobie, their larger-than-life personalities have overshadowed their literary production.

This raises an uncomfortable question. Will their work, like Dobie's, fall into irrelevance once we no longer have the force of their personalities to keep it before the public eye?

Damning evidence abounds. The writers routinely supplied each other with lavish review quotes that far exceeded the merit of the books in question. They've slyly inserted one another's names into their works, often for no other reason than to show off. They actively inflated their own mythology, exaggerating and polishing accounts of their hijinks. They satirized any notion of meaningfulness in their self-proclaimed motto: "Doing Indefinable Services to Mankind." Their best-known works, from *Semi-Tough* to *The Best Little Whore-house* to *Harvey Penick's Little Red Book,* do not stand at the forefront of American letters, or even Texas letters.

The most serious charge of all is that the writers squandered their talent, partying it away, night after night. The writers themselves express regret on this count. Bud Shrake admitted that he thinks "a lot" about the many wasted nights, reporting, "I wake up at three in the morning . . . remembering our drunken adventures. Only now they don't seem funny." Gary Cartwright, in *Heartwiseguy,* conceded, "It's what I don't see that fills me with regret: All the work that was never attempted because my body and brain were pickled in the pursuit of . . . that's the real rub; I can't remember what I was pursuing." Larry L. King, assessing his failure to complete his Lyndon Johnson

Left to right: Gary Cartwright, Larry L. King, Bud Shrake, and Dan Jenkins at the ceremony commemorating their inclusion among the Texas Walk of Stars at 6th Street in Austin. November 1987. *Gary Cartwright Archives, Southwestern Writers Collection, Texas State University-San Marcos.*

biography, concluded, "I now see, in retrospect, that my alcoholism caused me to turn and run. Had I been clear-headed and hungrier, I might have pushed on."[2]

In *Confessions of a Maddog,* Jay Milner points to the case of Bud Shrake as the most heartbreaking. Shrake, according to Milner, had the potential to "leave a permanent mark on the literary world, and I don't mean just the Texas literary world. . . . He's always had the talent and the necessary keen eyes, ears, and philosophical perception to be regarded among the best America had to offer."[3]

***

Of all the writers, Bud Shrake has faced the most obstacles in gaining recognition for his serious work. Much of this is a consequence of circumstances. Despite his efforts to become a full-time novelist, Shrake largely earned his living as a sportswriter, a screenwriter, and an as-told-to biographer. His successes in these areas—rather than as a novelist—have reinforced views that his interests lie in a separate realm from "literature." Compounding the perception is Shrake's well-known friendship with Dan Jenkins, a man who famously derides notions of "profound" literature.

Shrake has often ventured a disarming casualness about his own work, gliding over commercial disappointments by telling reporters, "I have never given any thought to having a career anyway." At a point when all of his novels save *Peter Arbiter* were out of print, Shrake decided that it was probably for the best. "I've tried [to reread them] and I can't stand them," he said. "I'll come to a real clinker, go put the book back on the shelf, and think, Jesus, how can I write this shit?"[4]

Despite Shrake's self-effacement, a closer look reveals subtleties about his work that have largely escaped notice. Though he has lamented the wasted nights, in fact he was extraordinarily productive throughout his career. Even during the height of the Mad Dog craziness, he completed two novels and two screenplays within a two-year period. Though friends such as Jay Milner didn't always recognize it at the time, Shrake did indeed take great pains to isolate himself in order to produce work. He went to London to finish *Strange Peaches*. He completed *Peter Arbiter* while touring Asia for *Sports Illustrated*. He developed a seasonal pattern of escaping from Austin in order to buckle down and work. Shrake also made exceptional use of the opportunities his travel afforded him. His *Sports Illustrated* assignments—such as his story on the Tarahumaras of Mexico—became part of his work in *Blessed McGill*. His journeys through Asia were later incorporated into his novel *Night Never Falls*. Even a vacation in Mexico became part of the fabric of *Strange Peaches*.

The best measure of Shrake's subtle methodology is seen in how he used his occupation as a sportswriter in Dallas in the early 1960s. Dan Jenkins, Gary Cartwright, and Peter Gent all translated their experiences with football teams into novels about football. No surprises there. Shrake's approach was wholly different. Instead of writing about the game, he used the access his sportswriting granted him to observe closely a class of wealthy Texans often shielded from intimate views. The results are on vivid display in *But Not for Love* and *Strange Peaches*.

In 1964, the modest commercial and critical success of *But Not for Love* established Bud Shrake as a chronicler of hip young Texans. His publisher expected to build on what Shrake had begun and assumed that Shrake would write another book in the same vein. Instead, he confounded expectations by creating a totally original work—a densely philosophical absurdist western. After *Blessed McGill*, Shrake again changed course—this time with a searing portrait of Dallas in 1963. *Strange Peaches* was followed by another improbable evolution—the Satyricon-inspired farce, *Peter Arbiter.* Shrake's refusal to be typecast alienated New York publishers because it kept them from building a market for his work. But the artistry apparent in each novel endures.

The relative paucity of critical attention on Bud Shrake has deflected understanding of the sophisticated narrative techniques employed in his best work. *Blessed McGill* is a rare enough accomplishment in American letters—an engaging adventure tale complemented by an integrated, cogently argued philosophical structure. Even more striking is how Shrake's narrative style mimics his protagonist's spiritual transformation. Just as Peter McGill evolves from existentialism toward an interrelated "cosmic consciousness," Shrake's narrative transcends its Beat-inspired "immediacy" to become a carefully calibrated universe in which the interrelated plot, theme, and tone exist in perfect harmony—all this without losing an ounce of the story's energy. In *Strange Peaches*, a very different book, the same care is evident, as the author's work parallels what the narrator, John Lee Wallace, is attempting: "a fictional documentary, using actual people when we can, inventing a few things to help it stick together, re-shooting some parts to show myself in all these places involved."[5] Shrake's elaborate yet subtle narrative techniques aren't the sorts of things that get mapped out on cocktail napkins in hotel bars.

Bud Shrake, in his long-lasting, versatile career, has never achieved the popular success or received the critical attention he deserves. From 1964 to 1973 he produced a remarkable run of four fine novels—*But Not for Love, Blessed McGill, Strange Peaches,* and *Peter Arbiter. But Not for Love* remains a vivid early urban Texas novel, and the satire *Peter Arbiter* is a worthy heir to the more celebrated work of Terry Southern.

Shrake's two best works, *Blessed McGill* and *Strange Peaches,* are singular accomplishments in American literature. *Blessed McGill,* in its scope, ambition, and execution, is as cohesive and powerful a work of the Southwest as Leslie Marmon Silko's *Ceremony.* It is a major regional novel with universal appeal. *Strange Peaches* is a great undiscovered novel of the American sixties, a work that stands easily with Ken Kesey and Kurt Vonnegut. If any measure of justice ever comes to serve the literary canon, Shrake's two best novels will be cherished for generations to come.

***

Bud Shrake's case is the most exceptional example of the dilemma faced by the writers, but it points to a conclusion that can be drawn about much of their work. J. Frank Dobie's larger-than-life personality caused people to take his writing more seriously than it deserved. In the case of the Literary Outlaws the exact opposite is true. Their rambunctious personalities and apparent nonchalance have overshadowed their substantial literary accomplishments.

Larry L. King's work has also been largely misunderstood. His reputation may always be eclipsed by *The Best Little Whorehouse in Texas.* One commentator noted, "King's plight is similar to that of the great English actor Alec Guinness, who trod the boards of the English stage and stood before the cameras of the world for almost 70 years and now lives in popular memory as Obi Wan Kenobi of *Star Wars* . . . thus reducing a lifetime of brilliant work to a trivia answer question." King himself said, "I've long since reconciled myself to *Whorehouse.* It'll always be that way. I don't like it, but it sure beats being poor. But there are a lot of people out there who think it's my best work or only work and, sure, that bothers me."[6]

In assessing King's writing career, his book *Confessions of a White Racist* should not be overlooked. Its power has not diminished over the years, and King's withering insights remain as vital today as they were in 1971. Future historians looking back at white attitudes toward African Americans in the twentieth century will profit immeasurably from a close study of King's soul-baring account.

In *White Racist,* as in much of his other work, Larry L. King makes extensive use of a literary technique that is neither glamorous nor much in favor among writers. He described his approach in a letter to a friend:

> First and foremost, tell all of the truth it is possible to tell. Some of it may not make you feel comfortable or it may not at times make you appear as faultless as you'd prefer: the honest confession may or may not be good for the soul, but it is good for the writing man. Do not worry about your image or what Mama may think. The writer trying to tell all the truth he knows will tell no more than 70%; however, he will be roughly 40% ahead of the average. When you feel yourself about to pull punches, re-think the subject matter and be true to it and to thine own-self. One by one, the little truths will emerge and multiply themselves. Before you know it, you are on the way to an "honest" book—which goes a long way toward crafting a *good* book.[7]

King's prose style already benefits from a rare quality—he is the raconteur who comes across as vividly on paper as he does in person. King's abundant humor and deep insight transcend mere "entertainment," and his talent, fortified by his intense commitment to honesty, creates a compelling voice. *The Washington Post* observed in a perceptive review that his work is "notable for the persistence and consistency with which it explores certain themes. King is a novelist masquerading in journalist's clothing and he has the novelist's sense of thematic unity." The *Post* saw that King's collected magazine pieces "actually complement and strengthen each other. If some of them seemed, when published individually, to be exercises in narcissism, taken as a group they disclose deeper and more abiding concerns."[8] In his journalism, as in his stage plays, Larry L. King's best work has proved to be distinctive, enriching, and enduring.

***

Texas didn't necessarily have a problem producing talented writers in the era before the 1960s. After all, the state gave rise to Katherine Anne Porter, Américo Paredes, Terry Southern, and John Graves. Texas' problem was in nurturing writers. Katherine Anne Porter left the state at an early age and retained a stiff distance for much of her life. Américo Paredes, the dean of Chicano literature, was years ahead of his time, yet he was unable to find a publisher during most of his writing life. Terry Southern and John Graves emigrated to Europe in the 1950s. Graves, after publishing early fiction in *The New Yorker* and *Esquire*, returned to Texas and embraced the rural tradition. Terry Southern stayed away and eventually became a counterculture icon, appearing on the cover of *Sergeant Pepper's Lonely Hearts Club Band.*

Texas' relatively barren literary environment meant that little of the state's culture was documented by writers of fiction. Aside from large-canvas stereotypes like Edna Ferber's *Giant,* the rest of the country had little sense of what the state and its inhabitants were really like. Texas' economy, politics, and culture underwent dramatic transformations after World War II. The state was ripe for chronicling by observant and daring young writers. When the literary outlaws arrived on the scene—and crashed headfirst into the sixties—the reverberations resounded throughout Texas literature.

Literary superstars like Larry McMurtry and Cormac McCarthy draw more attention, but the Literary Outlaws have provided something largely absent from the works of the better-known writers. In their "eyewitness fiction" as in their journalism, they have documented, in vivid detail, significant aspects of Texas' contemporary history. As Larry L. King has pointed out, "My writing has been about, and was meant to be about, the Texas of my time there. I felt it my job to define and record Texas culture as best I knew it, to leave signposts saying to those coming along later, *This is how it was then.*"[9]

More than just eyewitnesses, this group of writers had the unerring instinct to find themselves at the center of the action, time after time. They helped Texas evolve toward a more mature literature, and they helped establish Austin as the state's literary capital. They are among the most talented writers the state has produced. Despite their popular image, they were often deadly serious as they turned their gaze on their home state. Much of their work is engaging, entertaining, and illuminating. In the years ahead, their best work will survive as vibrant social documents—primary texts that tell the story of Texas during one of its most thrilling eras.

NOTES

Preface

1. Sidney Brammer, email to author, 1 September 2003.

Texas Literary Outlaws

1. Gary Cartwright, *Turn out the Lights: Chronicles of Texas in the 80's and 90's.,* n.p.
2. Larry L. King to Leonard Saunders, 24 July 1966, Larry L. King Archives, Southwestern Writers Collection, Alkek Library, Texas State University-San Marcos, (hereafter cited as King Archives, SWWC). Larry L. King, *None But a Blockhead: On Being a Writer* (New York: Viking, 1986), 254.
3. Willie Morris, *New York Days,* 91–92.
4. Gary Cartwright, *Confessions of a Washed-Up Sportswriter, Including Various Digressions About Sex, Crime, and Other Hobbies,* 287.
5. Gary Cartwright, *Heartwiseguy: How to Live the Good Life After a Heart Attack,* 12.
6. George Axelrod, review of *Limo* by Dan Jenkins and Edwin Shrake, *Los Angeles Times Book Review,* 10 October 1976, n.p.

Chapter 1: A Rebel in West Texas

1. Larry L. King, "Hard Times," *Playboy,* March 1975, 140, 178; Larry L. King, Interview by author, Washington, D.C., 19 April 2001 (hereafter cited as King interview).
2. Larry L. King, *None But a Blockhead: On Being a Writer,* 7; Larry L. King, *A Writer's Life in Letters, Or, Reflections in a Bloodshot Eye,* 3–4.
3. King interview; "Hard Times," 178.
4. King interview; http://www.tsha.utexas.edu/handbook/online/articles/view/MM/hdm3.htm, *Handbook of Texas Online,* "Midland."
5. King interview.
6. Clippings file, King Archives, SWWC.
7. King, *Confessions of a White Racist,* 23–24.
8. Larry L. King, "We've Been Ordered to Make This Thing Work," *Parade,* 19 February 1984, 4.
9. Ibid., 6.
10. King, *Confessions of a White Racist,* 53.
11. King interview; Larry L. King, email to author, 17 January 2003.
12. King interview; Larry L. King, email to author, 17 January 2003; King, *Confessions of a White Racist,* 67-69.
13. King interview.

14. King interview; King, *Confessions of a White Racist*, 17.
15. King, interview; King, *Confessions of a White Racist*, 71–72.
16. King, email to author, 11 July 2001.
17. King interview.
18. Ibid.
19. Ibid.
20. Ibid.
21. http://www.tsha.utexas.edu/handbook/online/articles/view/OO/hd01.html, *Handbook of Texas Online*, "Odessa."
22. Editorial, *Odessa* (Texas) *American*, 25 July 1954, n.p.
23. King interview; King, *Confessions of a White Racist*, 73.
24. King, *Confessions of a White Racist*, 79.
25. King, *None But a Blockhead*, 9.
26. Larry L. King, email to author, 12 July 2001.
27. King, *Confessions of a White Racist*, 82.
28. King interview.
29. Larry L. King, "Happy New Year for Batchelors," *Odessa American*, 1 January 1954, 1; King, *Confessions of a White Racist*, 82.
30. Larry L. King, "Negro Vet Feels Eyes of Race On Him," *Odessa American*, 23 May 1954, 1; King, *Confessions of a White Racist*, 82; King interview.
31. King interview.
32. Ibid.
33. Larry L. King, "Border City Scene of Most Politicking," *Odessa American*, 4 July 1954, 4; King interview.
34. King interview.

Chapter 2: A Texas Oasis

1. http://www.tsha.utexas.edu/handbook/online/articles/view/BB/ftbr23.html, *Handbook of Texas Online*, "Brann, William Cowper."
2. George Norris Green, *The Establishment in Texas Politics: The Primitive Years, 1938–1957*, 83–87; Joe B. Frantz, *The Forty Acre Follies*, 71; Ronnie Dugger, *The Invaded Universities*, 45; Jack Lala, "Academic Freedom Under Duress: Political Witch Hunts at the University of Texas, 1939–1952" (unpublished master's thesis, Texas State University-San Marcos, 1994), 19.
3. http://www.tsha.utexas.edu/handbook/online/articles/view/RR/fra54.html, *Handbook of Texas Online*, "Rainey, Homer Price"; Green, *The Establishment in Texas Politics*, 83–89; Frantz, 82.
4. Quoted in Lala, "Academic Freedom," 19.
5. Richard Ray Cole, "A Journal of Free Voices: The History of the *Texas Observer*" (unpublished master's thesis, University of Texas at Austin, 1966), 60–65; Ann Fears Crawford, *Frankie: Mrs. R. D. Randolph and Texas Liberal Politics*, 33–35.
6. Green, 62.
7. Cole, "A Journal," 60–65; Dugger, *The Invaded Universities*, 50; Crawford, *Frankie*, 34.
8. Ronnie Dugger, "Outgoing, Incoming Editors Talk," *Texas Observer*, 16 December 1960, 5; Cole, "A Journal," 75.

9. Ronnie Dugger, "To a Novelist Dying Young," *Washington Post,* 18 June 1978, F9.

10. Al Reinert, "Billy Lee," *Texas Monthly,* February 1979, 79, 81.

11. Reinert, "Billy Lee," 83; Billy Lee Brammer Archives, Southwestern Writers Collection, Alkek Library, Texas State University-San Marcos (hereafter cited as Brammer Archives, SWWC); Dugger, "To a Novelist Dying Young," F2; Reinert, "Billy Lee," 83.

12. "Three AP Awards Won by *American-Statesman*," *Austin American-Statesman,* 10 January 1954, 1.

13. Reinert, "Billy Lee," 83.

14. Paul Cullum, "The Second Act." Typescript, Brammer Archives, SWWC, 7.

15. Willie Morris, "Billy Lee Brammer, 1929–78" *Texas Observer,* 3 March 1978, 20.

16. Dugger, "To a Novelist Dying Young," F2

17. Bill Brammer, "Tom Reagan's Story." *Texas Observer,* 11 April 1955, 6.

18. Bill Brammer, "Hit 'Em Where They Live: The Political Hucksters II." *Texas Observer,* 9 May 1955, 4.

19. Bill Brammer, "Enormous, But Incredible: On Rereading 'Giant.'" *Texas Observer,* 4 July 1955, 7.

20. Bill Brammer, "A Personal Reminiscence." *Texas Observer,* 25 August 1961, 6; Bill Brammer, "A Fragile Subject," *Texas Observer,* 17 August 1955, 2.

21. Bill Brammer, "Unworldly Little Marfa," *Texas Observer,* 27 June 1955, 1; Bill Brammer, "A Circus Breaks Down on the Prairie," *Texas Observer,* 4 July 1955, 4.

22. Dugger, "To a Novelist Dying Young," F2.

23. Clippings file, King Archives, SWWC.

24. Al Reinert, Introduction to *The Gay Place* (Austin: Texas Monthly Press, 1978), viii.

25. Bill Brammer, "Lyndon Comes Home," *Texas Observer,* 30 August 1955, 1; Nadine Brammer to Dear Folks, n.d., Brammer Archives, SWWC.

26. Bill Brammer, "Pow Wow on the Pedernales," *Texas Observer,* 5 October 1955, 1.

27. Bill Brammer, "That Old Depleted Feeling," *Texas Observer,* 12 October 1955, 3.

Chapter 3: *The Gay Place*

1. Reinert, "Billy Lee," 162.

2. Bill Brammer, "Mencken and Minnesota Fats," *Texas Observer,* (18 October 1968), 8; King interview.

3. Bill Brammer to Lyndon Johnson, 11 May 1956, Brammer Archives, SWWC.

4. Dugger, "To a Novelist Dying Young," F2; Reinert, "Billy Lee," 162.

5. Dugger, "To a Novelist Dying Young," F2

6. Clippings file, Brammer Archives, SWWC.

7. Bill Brammer to Nadine Brammer, "Sunday" 1958, Brammer Archives, SWWC; Reid, "Return to the Gay Place," 164.

8. Dugger, "To a Novelist Dying Young," F2; Reinert, "Billy Lee," 164.

9. Reinert, "Billy Lee," 162; Dugger, "To a Novelist Dying Young," F2.

10. Reid, "Return to the Gay Place," 164; Bill Brammer to Mrs. Cannon, 17 November 1959, Brammer Archives, SWWC.

11. Reinert, Introduction to *The Gay Place,* xiii.

12. Ibid., xii.
13. Clippings file, Brammer Archives, SWWC; Cullum, 6.
14. Bill Brammer to Nadine Brammer, n.d., Brammer archives, SWWC; Dugger, "To a Novelist Dying Young," F3.
15. Jay Dunston Milner, *Confessions of a Maddog: A Romp Through the High-flying Texas Music and Literary Era of the Fifties to the Seventies*, 70; Reid, "Return to the Gay Place," 163; Reinert, "Billy Lee," 164.
16. King interview.
17. King interview; King, *None But a Blockhead*, 15.
18. Dorothy de Santillana to Bill Brammer, 25 February 1960, Brammer Archives, SWWC.
19. Dorothy de Santillana to Bill Brammer, 30 June 1960, Brammer Archives, SWWC.
20. Clippings file, Brammer Archives, SWWC.
21. Clippings file, Brammer Archives, SWWC; Billy Lee Brammer, *The Gay Place*, 17.
22. Brammer, *The Gay Place*, 94.
23. Dorothy de Santillana to Elizabeth McKee, 22 March 1962, Brammer Archives, SWWC.
24. Sidney Brammer, "My Old Man," *Texas Observer*, (21 April 1995), 20.
25. Gary Cartwright, "Billy Lee Brammer, 1929-78," *Texas Observer*, (3 March 1978), 21.
26. Cullum, 2-3; Dave McNeeley, "The Courting of Willie Morris," *Austin American-Statesman*, (15 November 1983); Don Graham, Introduction to *The Gay Place* (Austin: University of Texas Press), xxviii.
27. Dugger, "To a Novelist Dying Young," F3.
28. Brammer, *The Gay Place*, 6.
29. Roger Shattuck, "Politics, Its Responsibility and Thrall," *Texas Observer*, (8 April 1961), 6.
30. Reid, "Return to the Gay Place," 164.
31. Brammer, *The Gay Place*, 452.
32. Ibid., 450-451.
33. Clippings file, Brammer Archives, SWWC.
34. Dugger, "To a Novelist Dying Young," F3.
35. Dugger, "Observations," *Texas Observer*, (11 November 1966), 11.
36. Reinert, Al, Introduction to *The Gay Place*, xxv.

Chapter 4: Fort Worth's New Journalism

1. Michael MacCambridge, *The Franchise: A History of Sports Illustrated*, 48.
2. Jerry Flemmons, *Amon: The Texan Who Played Cowboy for America*, 86–88; Cartwright, *Confessions of a Washed-Up Sportswriter*, 355.
3. Flemmons, *Amon*, 86.
4. Bud Shrake, "Cops Eat Kid's Pet," *Texas Observer*, 25 July 1975, 7.
5. Cartwright, *Confessions of a Washed-Up Sportswriter*, 12.
6. MacCambridge, *The Franchise*, 49–50.

7. Ann Arnold, *Gamblers and Gangsters: Fort Worth's Jacksboro Highway in the 1940s & 1950s*, 2.
8. Flemmons, *Amon*, 182.
9. Ibid., 136; Arnold, *Gamblers and Gangsters*, 3–8.
10. MacCambridge, *The Franchise*, 50.
11. Ibid., 51.
12. Ibid., 50; Bud Shrake, Interview by author, Austin, Texas, 15 March 2001 (hereafter cited as Shrake interview).
13. Shrake interview.
14. Ibid.
15. Ibid.
16. Ibid.
17. Clippings file, Gary Cartwright Archives, Southwestern Writers Collection, Alkek Library, Texas State University-San Marcos (hereafter cited as Cartwright Archives, SWWC); Larry L. King, "The Best Sportswriter in Texas," *Texas Monthly*, December 1975, 142.
18. King, "The Best Sportswriter in Texas," 142.
19. Kevin Sherrington, "Still a Prose Pro," *Dallas Morning News*, 7 November 1999, B20.
20. MacCambridge, *The Franchise*, 53.
21. Bud Shrake, email to author, 7 January 2003; Bud Shrake, email to author, 1 September 2001; Shrake interview.
22. Diane Jennings, "High Profile: Bud Shrake," *Dallas Morning News*, 22 January 1989, E1.
23. MacCambridge, *The Franchise*, 57; Shrake interview.
24. Bruce Garrison, with Mark Sabljak, *Sports Reporting*, 25–27, 28–29.
25. Stanley Woodward, *Sports Page*, 47–49, 60–61.
26. King, "The Best Sportswriter in Texas," 94; Sherrington, "Still a Prose Pro"; MacCambridge, *The Franchise*, 55.
27. Sherrington, "Still a Prose Pro."
28. King, "The Best Sportswriter in Texas," 142.
29. MacCambridge, *The Franchise*, 56.
30. Ibid.
31. Cartwright, *Heartwiseguy*, 48.
32. MacCambridge, *The Franchise*, 53
33. Dick Hitt, "Stars of Granite: Four Literary Legends Shine in Austin," *Dallas Times Herald*, 8 November 1987, clipping file, Cartwright archives, SWWC; MacCambridge, *The Franchise*, 57; Dan Jenkins, *Fairways and Greens: The Best Golf Writing of Dan Jenkins*, 169.
34. Cartwright, *Confessions of a Washed-Up Sportswriter*, 343; MacCambridge, *The Franchise*, 54.
35. MacCambridge, *The Franchise*, 119, 120, 54.
36. Shrake interview.
37. MacCambridge, *The Franchise*, 57.

Chapter 5: The Texas Beats

1. Shrake interview.
2. Ibid.
3. Bud Shrake, "Cops Eat Kid's Pet," 7-8.
4. Shrake interview.
5. Ibid.
6. Ibid; Gary Cartwright. Interview by the author, Austin, Texas, 16 October 2001 (hereinafter cited as Cartwright interview).
7. Gary Cartwright, "An Old Five and Dimer," *Texas Monthly,* (February 1988), 58; Cartwright, *Heartwiseguy,* 8.
8. Cartwright interview; Tracie Powell, "Gary Cartwright, Editor/Writer of TM Magazine," *Austin American-Statesman,* (31 December 1999), J4.
9. Cartwright, *Heartwiseguy,* 9; Cartwright interview.
10. Cartwright, *Heartwiseguy,* 9–10; Cartwright interview.
11. Cartwright, *Heartwiseguy,* 11.
12. Cartwright interview.
13. Ibid.
14. Ibid.
15. Ann Charters, Introduction to *The Portable Beat Reader,* edited by Ann Charters, xviii.
16. Shrake interview; Cartwright interview.
17. Cartwright, "An Old Five and Dimer," 92; Cartwright, *Heartwiseguy,* 12; Shrake interview.
18. Cartwright interview.
19. Cartwright interview; Shrake interview.
20. Cartwright, *Confessions of a Washed-Up Sportswriter,* 348.
21. Ibid.
22. http://www.tsha.utexas.edu/handbook/online/articles/view/MM/jcm2.html, "Mansfield School Desegregation Incident."
23. Bud Shrake, email to author, 25 January 2002.
24. Cartwright, *Confessions of a Washed-Up Sportswriter,* 351; Shrake interview.
25. Shrake interview.
26. Cartwright, "An Old Five and Dimer," 58, 92; Cartwright, interview.
27. Cartwright interview.
28. Shrake interview.
29. Clippings file, Cartwright archives, SWWC.
30. Cartwright, *Heartwiseguy,* 12.
31. MacCambridge, *The Franchise,* 60.
32. Cartwright, *Confessions of a Washed-Up Sportswriter,* 12–13.
33. MacCambridge, *The Franchise,* 62.
34. MacCambridge, *The Franchise,* 119–120.

Chapter 6: Big D Meets the Flying Punzars

1. Shrake interview.
2. "Dallas, Texas":
    http://www.tsha.utexas.edu/handbook/online/articles/view/DD/hdd1.html;
    "Federal Reserve Bank of Dallas":
    http://www.tsha.utexas.edu/handbook/online/articles/view/FF/cpf1.html;
    "Texas Centennial":
    http://www.tsha.utexas.edu/handbook/online/articles/view/TT/lkt1.html;
    and "Neiman Marcus":
    http://www.tsha.utexas.edu/handbook/online/articles/view/NN/dhn1.html.
3. "Thunder on the Right: Fear and Frustration Rouse Extremists to Action Across
    the Land," *Newsweek*, 4 December 1961, 30.
4. Lawrence Wright, *In the New World: Growing Up With America, 1960–1984*,
    14–16; Darwin Payne, *Big D: Triumphs and Troubles of an American Supercity in
    the 20th Century*, 285–286.
5. Wright, 36–37.
6. Ibid., 8–9.
7. Ibid., 26; Payne, *Big D*, 306.
8. Wright, *In the New World*, 27.
9. Ibid., 28.
10. Ibid., 18.
11. Ardis Burst, *The Three Families of H. L. Hunt*, 106.
12. Bobby Baker, with Larry L. King, *Wheeling and Dealing: Confessions of a Capitol
    Hill Operator*, 48–49; Peter Golenbock, *Cowboys Have Always Been My Heroes:
    The Definitive Oral History of America's Team*, 24.
13. Cartwright, *Confessions of a Washed-Up Sportswriter*, 28; Cartwright interview.
14. Cartwright interview.
15. Jane Wolfe, *The Murchisons: The Rise and Fall of a Texas Dynasty*, 345–346;
    Golenbock, *Cowboys Have Always Been*, 128.
16. Joe David Brown, "A Big Man Even in Big D," *Sports Illustrated* 21 January
    1963, 63; Golenbock, *Cowboys Have Always Been*, 155–156.
17. Shrake interview.
18. Ibid.
19. Cartwright, *Heartwiseguy*, 14–15.
20. Shrake interview.
21. Ibid.
22. Cartwright, *Heartwiseguy*, 16; Shrake interview.
23. Cartwright, *Heartwiseguy*, 26.
24. Ibid.

Chapter 7: A Gathering Force

1. Shrake interview.
2. Gary Cartwright, "Shrake's Progress," *Texas Monthly*, April 2000,
    SWWC; Shrake, interview.

4. Shrake interview.

5. Clippings file, Shrake Archives, SWWC.

6. Box scores, *Dallas Times Herald,* 8 September 1962 through 24 November 1962.

7. Cartwright, *Heartwiseguy,* 20.

8. Dick Hitt, "Heart Attack Took Many by Surprise," *Dallas Times Herald,* 17 October 1988, clipping in Cartwright archive, SWWC; Gary Cartwright to author, 2 February 2003.

9. http://www.tsha.utexas.edu/handbook/online/articles/view/DD/eed12.html, "Dallas Morning News."

10. Wright, *In the New World,* 30.

11. Shrake interview; Clippings file, Shrake Archives, Austin History Center.

12. Douglas Swanson, "Bud Shrake, Almost Famous," *Pearl,* May 1976, 20.

13. Cartwright, "Shrake's Progress"; Cartwright, interview.

14. Bill Brammer to Larry L. King, n.d.; King Archives, SWWC.

15. Ibid.; Brammer Archives, SWWC.

16. Brammer Archives, SWWC.

17. Carolyn G. Heilbrun, *The Education of a Woman: A Life of Gloria Steinem,* 88-112

18. Brammer Archives, SWWC; Bill Brammer, "A Famous Arthur Returns to Dallas," *Texas Observer,* 27 December 1962, 6.

19. Carolyn Willyoung Stagg to Bud Shrake, 28 March 1961, Shrake Archives, SWWC; Carolyn Willyoung Stagg to Bud Shrake, 29 March 1961, Shrake Archives, SWWC; Carolyn Willyoung Stagg to Bud Shrake, 30 August 1962, Shrake Archives, SWWC.

20. Shrake interview.

21. Ibid.; Ken McCormick to Bud Shrake, n.d., Shrake Archives, Austin History Center.

22. Shrake interview.

Chapter 8: A Long Way from Beaumont

1. Dan Jenkins, "Lockwrists and Cage Cases," *Sports Illustrated,* 16 July 1962, 56; MacCambridge, *The Francgise,* 120–121.

2. MacCambridge, *The Francgise,* 121–123.

3. Ibid., 123, 183; Cartwright, *Heartwiseguy,* 48.

4. Dan Jenkins to Bud Shrake, n.d., Shrake Archives, Austin History Center.

5. Ibid.

6. MacCambridge, *The Franchise,* 123.

7. Dan Jenkins, Saturday's America (Boston: Little, Brown, 1970), 79.

8. Dan Jenkins to Bud Shrake, n.d., Shrake Archives, Austin History Center.

9. Bud Shrake, "In Barcelona, Glitter Can't Conceal Slums," *Dallas Morning News,* 20 April 1963, section 1, p. 16.

10. Gary Cartwright, "Bishop Sheds Its Image," *Dallas Morning News,* 21 February 1963, section 2, p. 1; Gary Cartwright, "The Word on Integration," *Dallas Morning News,* 12 February 1963, Section 2, p. 1.

11. Gary Cartwright to Bud Shrake, n.d., Shrake Archives, Austin History Center; Cartwright, *Confessions of a Washed-Up Sportswriter,* 27.

12. Bud Shrake to Billy Lee Brammer, 10 April 1963, Shrake Archives, SWWC.
13. Shrake Archives, Austin History Center.
14. Cartwright interview; Clippings file, Shrake Archives, SWWC; Shrake interview.
15. Shrake interview.
16. Gary Cartwright, "Jimmy Ling, The Conglomerate King," *Los Angeles Times West Magazine,* 20 October 1968, 14; Shrake, interview.
17. Cartwright, "Jimmy Ling, The Conglomerate King," 11; Shrake, interview; Edwin Shrake, *Strange Peaches* (Austin: Texas Monthly Press, 1987), 49–52.
18. Larry McMurtry, *In a Narrow Grave: Essays on Texas* (Austin: Encino Press, 1968), 134.
19. Reinert, Introduction to *The Gay Place,* xxv.

Chapter 9: Dallas, 1963

1. Cartwright, *Confessions of a Washed-Up Sportswriter,* 38; Shrake interview.
2. Ibid., 40.
3. Cartwright, *Heartwiseguy,* 18; Cartwright, "My Favorite Year," typescript, 11, Cartwright Archives, SWWC.
4. Cartwright, *Confessions of a Washed-Up Sportswriter,* 38, 40–41; Shrake interview.
5. Gary Cartwright, "Who Was Jack Ruby?" *Texas Monthly,* November 1975, http://www.texasmonthly.com/archive/ruby.1.php?3922099095.
6. Cartwright, *Heartwiseguy,* 26; Cartwright interview.
7. Wright, 39.
8. Ann Richards, *Straight from the Heart,* 118–119; Wright, 40.
9. Wright, 41.
10. Ibid.
11. Gary Cartwright, "Who Was Jack Ruby?" typescript, 10, Gary Cartwright Archives, Austin History Center.
12. Cartwright, "Who Was Jack Ruby?" http://www.texasmonthly.com/archive/ruby.1.php?3922099095; Cartwright, *Heartwiseguy,* 19.
13. Shrake interview.
14. Ibid.
15. Gary Cartwright, *Turn Out the Lights: Chronicles of Texas in the 80s and 90s,* 2.
16. Shrake, *Strange Peaches,* 260.

Chapter 10: A New Beginning

1. King interview.
2. Larry L. King, "The Confessions of an American Father," typescript, 1974, 61, King Archives, SWWC.
3. King interview.
4. Ibid.; King, *None But a Blockhead,* 12.
5. King interview.
6. Ibid.; King, *None But a Blockhead,* 13.

7. Larry L. King to Billy Lee Brammer, 24 January 1963, Billy Lee Brammer Archives, SWWC.

8. King, *None But a Blockhead,* 15–16.

9. King, *None But a Blockhead,* 16, 17; King interview.

10. King interview.

11. Larry L. King to *Texas Monthly,* 23 March 2001, King Archives, SWWC; King interview.

12. Larry L. King to Brad King, 3 March 1992, King Archives, SWWC.

13. King interview; King, *None But a Blockhead,* 22.

14. King interview.

15. Ibid.

16. Larry L. King to Billy Lee Brammer, 1 September 1964, Billy Lee Brammer Archives, SWWC.

17. Ibid.; King, *None But a Blockhead,* 27–28, 33.

18. King interview.

19. Ibid.

20. Larry L. King, "Second Banana Politicians," *Harper's,* January 1965, 42.

21. Ibid., 45.

22. John Kenneth Galbraith to Larry L. King, 31 December 1964, King Archives, SWWC.

Chapter 11: The Doors of Perception

1. Shrake interview.

2. Cartwright, *Turn Out the Lights,* 2.

3. Cartwright interview.

4. Shrake interview; Cartwright interview.

5. MacCambridge, *The Franchise,* 127, 130–131.

6. Ibid., 131.

7. Dan Jenkins to Bud Shrake, n.d., Shrake Archives, Austin History Center.

8. Shrake, *But Not for Love,* 298.

9. Clippings file, Shrake Archives, SWWC; Herb Wind to Bud Shrake, n.d., Shrake Archives, SWWC.

10. Bud Shrake, email to author, 30 July 2000.

11. Shrake, *But Not for Love,* 100, 94.

12. Ibid., 186.

13. James Ward Lee, *Classics of Texas Fiction,* 140.

14. James Ward Lee, Afterword to *But Not for Love* (Fort Worth: TCU Press, 2000), 377.

15. MacCambridge, *The Franchise,* 131; Liz Smith, Natural Blonde: A Memoir, 217.

16. MacCambridge, *The Franchise,* 132.

17. Edwin Shrake, "Tough Cookie Marches to His Own Drummer," *Sports Illustrated,* 14 December 1964, 71.

18. Bud Shrake, email to author, 25 January 2002.

19. Shrake interview.

20. Billy Lee Brammer to "Stuart," 8 December 1963, Brammer Archives, SWWC.

21. Al Reinert, Introduction to *The Gay Place,* xxvi; Cullum, "The Second Act," 4.

22. "The Shadow" to Bud Shrake, n.d., Shrake Archives, SWWC; Billy Lee
    Brammer to Bud Shrake, no date, Shrake Archives, SWWC.
23. Billy Lee Brammer to Bud Shrake, no date, Shrake Archives, SWWC; Bud
    Shrake to "All Frens," n.d., Shrake Archives, SWWC; "Larry" to "Sothan,"
    n.d., Shrake Archives, SWWC.
24. Bud Shrake, email to author, 23 February 2002.
25. Ibid.; Cartwright, "Shrake's Progress."

Chapter 12: Literary Comanches

1. King interview.
2. Shrake interview; Willie Morris, *New York Days*, 262.
3. Jay Milner to Bud Shrake, 16 March 1965, Jay Milner Archives, Southwestern
    Writers Collection, Alkek Library, Texas State University-San Marcos (here-
    after referred to as Milner Archives, SWWC).
4. King, *None But a Blockhead*, 42; King interview.
5. King, *None But a Blockhead*, 43.
6. Morris, *New York Days*, 261; A. E. Hotchner, "If You've Been Afraid to Go To
    Elaine's These Past 20 Years, Here's What You've Missed," New York, (2 May
    1983), 34.
7. Hotchner, "If You've Been Afraid," 34
8. King interview.
9. Larry L. King. Introduction to *The One-Eyed Man* (Fort Worth: TCU Press,
    2001), ix.
10. Larry L. King to Charles C. Neighbors, n.d., King Archives, SWWC.
11. King, *None But a Blockhead*, 52.
12. Ibid.

Chapter 13: These Happy Occasions

1. Bud Shrake to "Poolzy Paulzy," 10 April 1965, Shrake Archives, SWWC.
2. Shrake interview.
3. Edwin Shrake, "The Once Forbidding Land," *Sports Illustrated*, 10 May 1965, 83.
4. Shrake interview.
5. Bud Shrake to Sterling Lord, 14 May 1965, Shrake Archives, SWWC.
6. Bud Shrake to Billy Lee Brammer, 20 May 1965, Shrake Archives, SWWC.
7. Bud Shrake to Ken McCormick, 22 May 1965, Shrake Archives, SWWC.
8. Shrake Archives, SWWC.
9. Dan Jenkins, "The Joy of Having a Foe You Know," *Sports Illustrated*, 9
    September 1968, 35.
10. MacCambridge, *The Franchise*, 147.
11. Dan Jenkins, "All the Way With O. J.," *Sports Illustrated*, 27 November 1967, 19.
12. MacCambridge, *The Franchise*, 149.
13. Ibid., 178.
14. Dan Jenkins, "A Glory Day for Gay," *Sports Illustrated*, 7 April 1967, 22; Dan

Jenkins, Dan, "Lee's Fleas Cheer 'Super Mex' to Victory," *Sports Illustrated*, 28 June, 1968, 19.

15. Valk, Garry, "Letter from the Publisher," *Sports Illustrated*, 24 July 1967, 4.

16. MacCambridge, *The Franchise*, 202.

17. Dan Jenkins, "The Sweet Life of Swinging Joe," *Sports Illustrated*, 17 October 1966, 42.

18. Dan Jenkins, "Life With the Jax Pack," *Sports Illustrated*, 10 July 1967, 61.

Chapter 14: *The One-Eyed Man*

1. Larry L. King to Lanvil and Glenda Gilbert, 9 May 1966, Larry L. King Archives, SWWC.

2. Ibid.

3. Ibid.

4. Larry L. King to William Styron, n.d., Larry L. King Archives, SWWC.

5. Larry L. King to Lanvil and Glenda Gilbert, 29 May 1966, Larry L. King Archives, SWWC.

6. King, *None But a Blockhead*, 74, 77.

7. Larry L. King to Ronnie Dugger, 24 July 1966, Larry L. King Archives, SWWC; Ronnie Dugger, "More Thoughts on a Novel," *Texas Observer*, 22 July 1966, 1.

8. Clippings file, Larry L. King Archives, SWWC.

9. Larry L. King, *The One-Eyed Man*, 9.

10. Bud Shrake to Jay Milner, 12 July 1966, Shrake Archives, SWWC.

11. King, *None But a Blockhead*, 77; Larry L. King to David Halberstam, 10 July 1966, King Archives, SWWC; Larry L. King to Bob Gutwillig, 16 July 1966, King Archives, SWWC.

12. Larry L. King, Introduction to *The One-Eyed Man* (Fort Worth: TCU Press, 2001), xii.

Chapter 15: Cowboys and Indians

1. Bud Shrake to "Herky," 28 March 1966; Bud Shrake to "deardickiedickie," 31 March 1966; Bud Shrake to Jim Smitham, 10 November 1966, Shrake Archives, SWWC.

2. Golenbock, *Cowboys Have Always Been*, 269; Cartwright, "An Old Five and Dimer," 92; Bud Shrake to David Simmons, 7 April 1966, Shrake Archives, SWWC.

3. Shrake interview; Cartwright, *Confessions of a Washed-Up Sportswriter*, 23; Gary Cartwright, "The Greening of Cowtown," *Texas Monthly*, August 1977, 160.

4. Bud Shrake to Dick Growald, 16 April 1966, Shrake Archives, SWWC; Shrake interview.

5. Dick Hitt, "Would You Believe . . ." *Dallas Times Herald*, 13 April 1966, clipping, Cartwright archive, SWWC.

6. Ibid.; Valk, "Letter from the Publisher," 4.

7. Cartwright interview.

8. Cartwright, *Confessions of a Washed-Up Sportswriter,* 27.
9. Cartwright interview.
10. Ibid.
11. Golenbock, *Cowboys Have Always Been,* 362.
12. Ibid., 218, 229.
13. Ibid., 369.
14. Cartwright interview; Golenbock, *Cowboys Have Always Been,* 280–281.
15. Golenbock, *Cowboys Have Always Been,* 287–288.
16. Ibid., 287, 227.
17. Larry L. King to Gary Cartwright, 20 December 1966; Gary Cartwright to Larry
    L. King, n.d.; King Archives, SWWC.
18. Golenbock, *Cowboys Have Always Been,* 267–268.
19. Gary Cartwright to author, 2 February 2003; Golenbock. 267–268.
20. Cartwright, *Confessions of a Washed-Up Sportswriter,* 17; Cartwright interview.
21. Golenbock, 267–270; Cartwright, *Confessions of a Washed-Up Sportswriter,* 17.
22. Cartwright interview.
23. Ibid.

Chapter 16: *Harper's* on the Rise

1. King interview; King, *None But a Blockhead,* 81.
2. King, . . . *and other dirty stories,* 81; King, *None But a Blockhead,* 83.
3. Morris, *New York Days,* 91–92.
4. King, . . . *and other dirty stories,* 30.
5. Ibid., 222.
6. King, *None But a Blockhead,* 89.
7. Ibid., 82; Larry L. King, "My Hero LBJ,"*Harper's* October 1966, 54.
8. King, . . . *and other dirty stories,* 44–48.
9. King, *None But a Blockhead,* 78, 82.
10. Ibid., 63.
11. Ibid., 78; King interview.
12. King, *None But a Blockhead,* 64, 95.
13. Ibid., 88.
14. Morris, New York Days, 9.
15. Ibid., 212.

Chapter 17: Obscure Famous Arthurs

1. Larry L. King to Jay Milner, 4 October 1968, King Archives, SWWC.
2. Cartwright, *Heartwiseguy* 21; Cullum, "The Second Act," 10.
3. Shrake interview; Cullum, "The Second Act," 13.
4. Billy Lee Brammer to Bud Shrake, 17 May 1965, Shrake Archives, SWWC.
5. Bud Shrake to Billy Lee Brammer, 20 May 1965; Bud Shrake to Fletcher Boone,
    12 February 1966, Shrake Archives, SWWC.
6. King interview; Cartwright, "Shrake's Progress."

7. Larry L. King to David Halberstam, 10 July 1966, King Archives, SWWC.
8. Billy Lee Brammer to Larry L. King, 23 January 1967; Don Graham, Introduction to *The Gay Place* (Austin: University of Texas Press, 1995), xv.
9. Billy Lee Brammer to Bud Shrake, 23 January 1967, Shrake Archives, SWWC; Reid, "Return to the Gay Place," 167.
10. Larry L. King, "Lyndon Johnson in Literature," *The New Republic* 3 (August 1968): 30.
11. Billy Lee Brammer to Larry L. King, 23 August 1968, King Archives, SWWC.
12. Larry L. King to Billy Lee Brammer, 8 September 1968, King Archives, SWWC.
13. Bud Shrake to Larry L. King, 12 September 1968, King Archives, SWWC.
14. Billy Lee Brammer to Larry L. King, 23 August 1968, King Archives, SWWC.
15. Billy Lee Brammer, review of *. . . and other dirty stories* by Larry L. King, *Texas Observer*, 18 October 1968, 8; Larry L. King to Lanvil and Glenda Gilbert, 18 February 1968, King Archives, SWWC.
16. Larry L. King to Jim Brosnan, 5 October 1968, King Archives, SWWC.
17. King, *None But a Blockhead*, 96–97.
18. King, *. . . and other dirty stories*, xiv.
19. Brammer, review of *. . . and other dirty stories*, 10.
20. Billy Lee Brammer to Larry L. King, 23 August 1968; Larry L. King to Jay Milner, 15 October 1968, King Archives, SWWC.
21. King, *None But a Blockhead*, 121.
22. Ibid.

Chapter 18: Absurdism in the Southwest

1. Edwin Shrake, *Blessed McGill*, d.j.
2. Clippings file, Shrake Archives, SWWC.
3. Bud Shrake to Ken McCormick, 4 October 1967, Shrake Archives, SWWC.
4. Larry L. King to Jay Milner, 24 December 1967, King Archives, SWWC.
5. Shrake interview.
6. Shrake, *Blessed McGill*, Sam Whitten book collection, Southwestern Writers Collection, Alkek Library, Texas State University-San Marcos; King interview.
7. Clippings file, Shrake Archives, SWWC; Shrake interview.
8. Clippings file, Shrake Archives, SWWC.
9. Gaines Kinkaid, "A Very Historical Novel," *Texas Observer*, 15 November 1968, 13–14; Shrake interview.
10. Larry L. King to Bud Shrake, 12 July 1969, King Archives, SWWC.
11. Shrake interview.
12. Shrake, *Blessed McGill*, 25, 30.
13. Ibid., 117–118.
14. Ibid., 105, 227, 3.
15. Ibid., 183–185
16. Ibid., 2.
17. Ibid., 231.

18. Shrake interview; Bud Shrake, "Thoughts on Texas Essay," manuscript, Shrake Archives, Austin History Center.

Chapter 19: Busted in the Oasis

1. Willie Nelson with Bud Shrake, *Willie: An Autobiography,* 170; Cartwright, *Heartwiseguy,* 21.
2. Darrell Royal to Bud Shrake, 12 March 1967, Shrake Archives, SWWC.
3. Billy Lee Brammer, "Apocalypse Now?" *Texas Observer,* 1 November 1968, 8–10.
4. Cartwright, "An Old Five and Dimer," 94.
5. Cartwright, *Confessions of a Washed-Up Sportswriter,* 32.
6. Jay Milner to Larry L. King, 2 September 1968, King Archives, SWWC.
7. Gary Cartwright Archives, SWWC; Cartwright interview.
8. Cartwright interview; Gary Cartwright, "Busted," manuscript, 14, Cartwright Archives, Austin History Center.
9. Cartwright, "Busted," 32.
10. Bud Shrake to David Simmons, 1 April 1968, Shrake Archives, SWWC.
11. Cartwright, "Busted," 34.
12. Gary Cartwright to author, 2 February 2003; Jay Stevens, *Storming Heaven: LSD and the American Dream,* 85–196; Shrake interview.
13. Shrake interview; Bud Shrake to Larry L. King, 1 August 1969, King Archives, SWWC.
14. Gary Cartwright, *The Hundred Yard War,* cover blurb.
15. Tom Pilkington, *State of Mind: Texas Literature and Culture,* 144.
16. Cartwright, *The Hundred Yard War,* 33.
17. Clippings file, Cartwright Archives, SWWC.

Chapter 20: Harvard's "White Racist"

1. Larry L. King, *The Old Man and Lesser Mortals,* 32.
2. King, *None But a Blockhead,* 118.
3. Ibid., 125–126.
4. Ibid., 127.
5. Ibid., 127; John Carr, editor, *Kite Flying and Other Irrational Acts: Conversations with Southern Writers,* 130–131.
6. King, *None But a Blockhead,* 127.
7. Carr, *Kite Flying,* 130–131.
8. Morris, *New York Days,* 91.
9. Larry L. King to Ben Peeler, 19 October 1969, King Archives, SWWC.
10. Larry L. King to Lanvil Gilbert, 19 October 1969, King Archives, SWWC.
11. King, *None But a Blockhead,* 132.

Chapter 21: Land of the Permanent Wave

1. Shrake interview.

2. Shrake interview; Bud Shrake to Larry L. King, 1 August 1969, King Archives, SWWC.
3. Shrake interview.
4. Shrake, Bud, "A Story of Thailand," *Texas Observer*, 12 September 1969, 13.
5. Shrake interview; Edwin Shrake, "The Land of the Permanent Wave," *Harper's*, February 1970, 81.
6. Morris, *New York Days*, 327.
7. Ibid., 326.
8. Cartwright interview; Cullum, "The Second Act," 8.
9. Billy Lee Brammer, "Life After Meth," manuscript, Brammer Archives, SWWC.
10. Reinert, "Billy Lee," 168; Dugger, "To a Novelist Dying Young," F4.
11. Bud Shrake to Larry L. King, 1 August 1969, King Archives, SWWC.
12. Jay Milner to Larry L. King, 11 August 1969, King Archives, SWWC.
13. Golenbock, *Cowboys Have Always Been*, 357.
14. Ibid., 371.
15. Jay Milner to Larry L. King, 13 January 1970, King archive, SWWC; Milner, *Confessions of a Maddog*, 88–89.
16. Milner, *Confessions of a Maddog*, 89–93.

Chapter 22: Mad Dog, Texas

1. Robert Pardun, *Prairie Radical: A Journey Through the Sixties* (Los Gatos, Calif.: Shire Press, 2001), 287–289.
2. Larry L. King to Ralph Yarborough, 4 May 1970, King Archives, SWWC.
3. *The Rag*, Austin, Texas, (27 April 1970), 20.
4. Nightbyrd, Jeffrey, review of Wilson, Burton, *The Austin Music Scene, 1965–1994: Through the Lens of Burton Wilson*, *Texas Observer*, (December 2001), http://www.texasobserver.org/showArticle.asp?ArticleFileName—01221_b1htm
5. Cartwright interview; Shrake Archives, Austin History Center.
6. Cartwright interview; Dugger, Ronnie, "Before the Bar for Pot," *Texas Observer*, 20 March 1970, 1.
7. Dugger, "Before the Bar for Pot," 2.
8. Shrake interview; Cartwright interview.
9. Bud Shrake to David Simmons, 28 May, no year, Shrake Archives, SWWC; Bud Shrake to Larry L. King, 1 August 1969, King Archives, SWWC; Shrake interview.
10. Shrake interview.
11. Ibid.
12. David Richards, *Once Upon a Time in Texas: A Liberal in the Lone Star State* 182–183; Shrake interview.
13. Shrake interview.
14. Ibid.
15. Ibid.; "Playboy After Hours," *Playboy*, November 1970, 19; Shrake Archives, Austin History Center; Richards, *Once Upon a Time in Texas*, 177–178.
16. Shrake Archives, Austin History Center; Cartwright, *Heartwiseguy*, 24.

17. Shrake Archives, Austin History Center.
18. Cartwright, *Heartwiseguy,* 25.
19. Richards, *Once Upon a Time in Texas,* 177; "Playboy After Hours," 19.
20. "Playboy After Hours," 19.
21. Clay Smith, "Notes on Mad Dogs," *Austin Chronicle,* 26 January 2001, http://www.austinchronicle.com/issues/dispatch/2001-01-26/books_feature.html.
22. Brad Buchholz, "Days of the 'Dillo," *Austin American-Statesman,* 10 December 2000, K1.
23. *The Rag,* Austin, Texas, 3 August 1970, 8–9; Shrake interview.
24. Buchholz, "Days of the 'Dillo," K1.
25. Cartwright, *Heartwiseguy,* 26–27; Richards, *Once Upon a Time in Texas,* 185.
26. Cartwright interview.
27. Larry L. King to Billy Lee Brammer, 21 September 1970; Dan Jenkins to Larry L. King, no date, King Archives, SWWC.
28. Larry L. King to Billy Lee Brammer, 21 September 1970, King Archives, SWWC.

Chapter 23: King's Road

1. Morris, *New York Days,* 326.
2. Ibid., 341–342; King, *The Old Man and Lesser Mortals,* 288.
3. King interview; Morris, *New York Days,* 254-255.
4. Carr, 143; Larry L. King to Frank Rich, 15 March 1971, King Archives, SWWC.
5. Morris, *New York Days,* 346; King, *None But a Blockhead,* 140.
6. Morris, *New York Days,* 355.
7. Ibid., 360.
8. Ibid., 362; King, *None But a Blockhead,* 145-146.
9. McMurtry, Larry, "Ever a Bridegroom: Reflections on the Failure of Texas Literature," *Texas Observer,* (23 October 1981), 15.
10. King, *None But a Blockhead,* 135–136.
11. Larry L. King, "The Old Man," *Harper's,* May 1971, 83.
12. King, *The Old Man and Lesser Mortals,* 29.
13. Ibid., 5, 7.
14. Ibid., 15.
15. Ibid., 23.
16. Ibid., 28–29.
17. King, *None But a Blockhead,* 136.
18. King, *Confessions of a White Racist,* xviii.
19. Ibid., 106–107.
20. Ibid., 117.
21. Ibid., 125, 159.
22. Ibid., 138, 36.
23. Ibid., xv.
24. Ibid., 147.
25. Ibid., 167.

26. King, *None But a Blockhead*, 149; Hodding Carter, review of *Confessions of a White Racist* by Larry L. King, *Book World*, 4 July 1971, 3; Marshall Frady, review of *Confessions of a White Racist* by Larry L. King, Life, 11 June 1971, 16; Reviews from clipping files, King Archives, SWWC.

27. Edgar Z. Friedenberg, review of *Confessions of a White Racist* by Larry L. King, *New York Review of Books*, 2 September 1971, 7; Carter review; Reviews from clipping files, King Archives, SWWC.

28. Maya Angelou to Larry L. King, 1 June 1971, King Archives, SWWC.

29. King, *None But a Blockhead*, 149.

30. King interview; Larry L. King to Frank Rich, 25 June 1971, King Archives, SWWC.

31. King, *None But a Blockhead*, 150; Clipping files, King Archives, SWWC.

Chapter 24: Outlaws

1. Shrake interview.
2. Ibid.
3. Bud Shrake to Larry L. King, 7 April 1971, King Archives, SWWC.
4. Bud Shrake to Larry L. King, 19 April 1971, King Archives, SWWC; Milner, *Confessions of a Maddog*, 102.
5. Shrake interview.
6. Cartwright interview; Clippings file, Cartwright Archives, SWWC.
7. Clippings file, Cartwright Archives, SWWC.
8. Correspondence files, King Archives, SWWC; King interview.
9. Cartwright, *Heartwiseguy*, 209.
10. Gary Cartwright, Dobie Paisano application letter, Cartwright Archives, Austin History Center.
11. Ibid.
12. Jay Milner to Larry L. King, 1 February 1971, King Archives, SWWC.
13. Larry L. King to Bud and Doatsy Shrake, 29 March 1971, King Archives, SWWC.
14. Ibid.
15. Jay Milner to Larry L. King, n.d., King Archives, SWWC.
16. Bud Shrake to Jay Milner, 29 August 1971, Milner Archives, SWWC; Criminal District Court Records, Dallas County, Texas, 12 November 1971.
17. Cartwright, *Heartwiseguy*, 28.
18. Jay Milner to Larry L. King, n.d., King Archives, SWWC.
19. Cartwright, *Heartwiseguy*, 28–29.
20. Ibid., 30.
21. Cartwright, "Shrake's Progress."
22. Cartwright interview.

Chapter 25: Hack Observations and Literary Feuds

1. Larry L. King to Billy Lee Brammer, 21 September 1970, King Archives, SWWC; King, *None But a Blockhead*, 150.

2. King, *None But a Blockhead,* 148–149.

3. Ibid., 149.

4. King Archives, SWWC; Barthelme, Steve, "Larry King's Confessions," *Texas Observer,* 30 July 1971, 14.

5. Ronnie Dugger, "Fallow Fields," *Texas Observer,* 5 November 1971, 21.

6. Steve Barthelme, review of *Moving On* by Larry McMurtry, *Texas Observer,* 8 October 1971, 13–15.

7. Larry McMurtry, "Answer from McMurtry," *Texas Observer,* 26 February 1971, 22–24.

8. Ibid.

9. Larry L. King to Billy Lee Brammer, 21 September 1970, King Archives, SWWC; King interview.

10. Larry L. King, review of "Saturday's America" by Dan Jenkins, *Harper's,* January 1971, p. 95.

11. King interview.

12. Ibid.

13. Jay Milner to Larry L. King, 13 November 1970, King Archives, SWWC.

14. King interview.

15. King, *None But a Blockhead,* 152–153.

16. King interview; King, *None But a Blockhead,* 155; Larry L. King, "Confessions of a Black-Hearted Loser," New York, 8 May 1972, 37–38.

17. King interview; Larry L. King, email to author, 1 January 2003; King, *None But a Blockhead,* 156.

18. King interview.

Chapter 26: Redneck Hippies

1. Robert Hilburn, "From the Vaults: A Few Nelson Classics Hidden on His Debut, 'Country Willie,'" *Los Angeles Times,* 28 January 2000, F32.

2. Nelson, *Willie: An Autobiography,* 169.

3. Shrake interview; Nelson, *Willie: An Autobiography,* 171.

4. Nelson, *Willie: An Autobiography,* 171.

5. Richards, *Once Upon a Time in Texas,* 183.

6. Shrake interview.

7. Richards, *Once Upon a Time in Texas,* 183–184.

8. Ibid., 183–184; Shrake interview.

9. Richards, *Once Upon a Time in Texas,* 183–184.

10. Ibid.; Shrake interview.

11. Reinert, "Billy Lee," 168; Milner, *Confessions of a Maddog,* 77.

12. Milner, *Confessions of a Maddog,* 96–97.

13. Ibid., 97.

14. Carol Rust, "Threadgill's Austin has lots of institutions, but only one motto: 'Vegetables you can drink beer with,'" *Houston Chronicle,* 28 August 1994, 2 Star 8.

15. Nelson, *Willie: An Autobiography,* 171.

16. Cartwright interview; Bud Shrake, email to author, 16 May 2002.

17. Mike Shropshire, "The Write Stuff: *Texas Monthly* at 10: A past perfect, a future tense?" *Dallas Morning News*, 20 February 1983, F1.
18. Cartwright interview.
19. Shrake interview.
20. Ibid.

Chapter 27: *Strange Peaches*

1. Shrake, *Strange Peaches*, 17, 18, 21.
2. Bud Shrake, email to author, 16 May 2002.
3. Clippings file, Shrake Archives, SWWC.
4. Bud Shrake, email to author, 22 May 2002.
5. Martin Weldon, review of *Strange Peaches* by Edwin Shrake, *Houston Chronicle*, 18 June 1972, F3; Bill Warren, review of *Strange Peaches* by Edwin Shrake, *Austin American-Statesman*, 6 August 1972, *Show World*, 33; Olin Chism, review of *Strange Peaches* by Edwin Shrake, *Dallas Times Herald*, 16 June 1972; Jay Milner, review of *Strange Peaches* by Edwin Shrake, *Dallas Morning News*, 4 June 1972, B12.
6. Roxy Gordon, review of *Strange Peaches* by Edwin Shrake, *Texas Observer*, 21 July 1972, 14–15.
7. Pilkington, *State of Mind*, 154; Don Graham, "Don Graham's Texas Classics," *Texas Monthly*, November 2000, online. http://www.texasmonthly.com/mag/issues/2000-11-01/classics.php
8. Shrake, *Strange Peaches*, 286.
9. Ibid., 43–44.
10. Ibid., 204, 205.
11. Ibid., 156.
12. Ibid.
13. Ibid., 189.
14 Ibid., 267.

Chapter 28: *Semi-Tough*

1. MacCambridge, 178-179.
2. Shrake Archives, Austin History Center.
3. Jennings, Diane, "High Profile: Dan Jenkins," *Dallas Morning News*, (23 February 1986), E1.
4. Jenkins, Dan, *Semi-Tough*, (New York: Atheneum, 1972), 4.
5. Ibid., 222.
6. MacCambridge, 180.
7. Cohen, Jason, "Rude Behavior," *Texas Monthly*, (November 1998), 62.
8. Jenkins, *Semi-Tough*, 37-34, 3.
9. Ibid., 3-4.
10. "Dan Jenkins," Gale Group Literary Database, http://www.galenet.galegroup.com/servlet/GLD.
11. Flippo, Chet, "Bestseller, as in Yellow Pages," *Texas Observer*, (3 November

1972), 15; Millhauser, Steven, "A Few Novels," *The New Republic,* (16 September 1972), 31; Flippo, 14; Spencer, Jack, review of *Semi-Tough* by Dan Jenkins, *Saturday Review,* (14 October 1972), 81.

12. Halberstam, David, review of *Semi-Tough* by Dan Jenkins, *New York Times Book Review,* (17 September 1972), 2; Axthelm, Pete, "Scotch on the Jocks," *Newsweek,* (18 September 1972), 106.

13. MacCambridge, 182.

Chapter 29: A New View of Texas

1. Michael Levy, "From the publisher," *Texas Monthly,* February 1973, 1; William Broyles Jr. "Behind the Lines," *Texas Monthly,* February 1973, 2.

2. Gary Cartwright, "The Lonely Blues of Duane Thomas," *Texas Monthly,* February 1973, 47.

3. Ibid., 49.

4. Jan Reid, *Close Calls: Jan Reid's Texas,* 9.

5. Broyles Jr. "Behind the Lines," *Texas Monthly,* April 1978, 5.

6. Bill Brammer, "Sex and Politics," *Texas Monthly,* May 1973, http:///www.texasmonthly.com/mag/issues/1973-05-01/feature3.php.

7. Hank Stuever, "*Texas Monthly* at 25: Make it Mythic," *Austin American-Statesman,* 25 January 1998, A1; Billy Lee Brammer to Bill Broyles, n.d., Brammer Archives, SWWC.

8. Reid, *Close Calls,* 9; Broyles Jr. "Behind the Lines," *Texas Monthly,* April 1978, 5.

9. Stuever, "*Texas Monthly* at 25," A1.

10. Si Dunn, "New York Journalism, Texas Style," *Dallas Morning News,* 9 May 1976, Scene, 24.

Chapter 30: The Cowboy Professor

1. King, *None But a Blockhead,* 157; King interview.

2. King, *None But a Blockhead,* 163; Larry L. King to Billy Lee Brammer, 12 March 1972, King Archives, SWWC; King interview.

3. King, *None But a Blockhead,* 163.

4. Ibid., 163–164; Larry L. King to J. Barlow Herget, 24 January 1973, King Archives, SWWC.

5. Larry L. King to Warren Burnett, 14 February 1973, King Archives, SWWC.

6. Larry L. King to Lanvil and Glenda Gilbert, 13 February 1973, King Archives, SWWC; King, *None But a Blockhead,* 158.

7. King interview; Larry L. King to Richard West, 16 November 1973, King Archives, SWWC.

8. King, *None But a Blockhead,* 158; King to Richard West; King interview.

9. Larry L. King, "Great Willie Nelson Commando Hoo-Ha and Texas Brain Fry," *Playboy,* November 1975, 102; King interview.

10. David Halberstam to Larry L. King, 3 November 1973, King Archives, SWWC.

Chapter 32: Live Music Capital

1. Jan Reid, *The Improbable Rise of Redneck Rock*, 71.
2. Cartwright, "Shrake's Progress"; Cartwright interview.
3. Cartwright, "Shrake's Progress."
4. Reid, *The Improbable Rise of Redneck Rock*, 113.

Chapter 32: North Dallas Forty

1. Peter Gent to Larry L. King, 9 February 1973, King Archives, SWWC.
2. Peter Gent, *North Dallas Forty*, d.j.; Dick Schaap, review of *North Dallas Forty* by Peter Gent, *New York Times Book Review*, 28 October 1973, 44.
3. Gent, *North Dallas Forty*, 230.
4. Ibid., 149; Golenbock, *Cowboys Have Always Been*, 356.
5. Gent, *North Dallas Forty*, 43, 5.
6. Ibid., 283, 268–269.
7. Ibid., 241.
8. Ibid., 267.
9. Ibid., 162.
10. Ibid., 29, 30.
11. Ibid., 69.
12. Lee C. Milazzo, "Money Makes the Ball Move," *Dallas Morning News*, 9 September 1973, C13.
13. George Solomon, "Gent 'Indicts the Whole NFL': Schramm," *Washington Post*, 9 December 1973, C4.
14. Pilkington, *State of Mind*, 147.

Chapter 33: The Regenerator Erection Laboratory

1. Douglas Swanson, "Bud Shrake, Almost Famous," *Pearl*, May 1976, 21.
2. Bud Shrake, *Dime Box* screenplay, 18, Shrake Archives, SWWC.
3. Vincent Canby, review of *Kid Blue* (Twentieth Century Fox movie), *The New York Times*, 1 October 1973, 45.
4. Shrake interview.
5. Edwin Shrake, *Peter Arbiter*, 4.
6. Ibid., 14.
7. Ibid., 117.
8. Ibid., 119.
9. Ibid., 126, 128.
10. Ibid., 146–147.
11. Clipping file, Shrake Archives, SWWC.

Chapter 34: Challenging Texas

1. King, *The Old Man and Lesser Mortals*, x.

2. Christoper Lehmann-Haupt, review of *The Old Man and Lesser Mortals* by Larry L. King, *The New York Times,* (31 January 1974), 31.

3. King, *None But a Blockhead,* 158; Larry L. King to Warren Burnett, 1 February 1974; Larry L. King to Lanvil and Glenda Gilbert, 10 March 1974, King Archives, SWWC.

4. Larry L. King to Geoffrey and Priscilla Wolfe, 1 August 1974, King Archives, SWWC.

5. William Broyles Jr., "Behind the Lines," *Texas Monthly,* (March 1974), 3.

6. William Broyles Jr., "Behind the Lines," *Texas Monthly,* (August 1974), 8.

7. Larry L. King to Bill Broyles, 12 August 1974,King Archives, SWWC.

8. Larry L. King, "Coming of Age in the Locker Room," *Texas Monthly,* (September 1974), 80, 85.

9. Ibid., 93.

Chapter 35: Changes at *Sports Illustrated*

1. Edwin Shrake, "Why is This Man Laughing?" *Sports Illustrated,* 18 September 1972, 119.

2. Edwin Shrake, "Getting Swamped by Gators," *Sports Illustrated,* 20 January 1975, 26.

3. MacCambridge, *The Franchise,* 190.

4. Shrake interview.

5. MacCambridge, *The Franchise,* 202.

6. Ibid., 200.

7. Ibid., 202–203.

8. Larry L. King to Peter and Jody Gent, 17 January 1974, King Archives, SWWC.

9. Dan Jenkins, *Dead Solid Perfect,* 17; Eric Moon, review of *Dead Solid Perfect* by Dan Jenkins, *Library Journal,* 1 October 1974, 2500; Barry Hannah, review of *Dead Solid Perfect, The New York Times Book Review,* 3 November 1974, 69.

10. Moon review; Pete Axthelm, review of *Dead Solid Perfect* by Dan Jenkins, *Newsweek,* 11 November 1974, 112.

Chapter 36: Texas' Gonzo Journalist

1. Larry L. King to Robert Manning, 16 September 1974, King Archives, SWWC.

2. Cartwright, *Heartwiseguy,* 23; Cartwright interview.

3. Cartwright interview.

4. Gary Cartwright, *Thin Ice,* 127.

5. Cartwright, *Confessions of a Washed-Up Sportswriter,* 71.

6. Cartwright interview.

7. Cartwright, "Shrake's Progress."

8. Cartwright, *Confessions of a Washed-Up Sportswriter,* 37.

9. Ibid., 57–58.

10. Ibid., 287, 297.

11 Gary Cartwright, "Candy," *Texas Monthly,* December 1976, 190.

12. Cartwright interview; Shrake interview.

Chapter 37: Texas Brain Fry

1. Correspondence files, King Archives, SWWC.
2. Larry L. King, "Great Willie Nelson Commando Hoo-Ha and Texas Brain Fry," *Playboy*, November 1975, 207.
3. Ibid., 209–210.
4. Ibid., 210.
5. Ibid.
6. King, "The Best Sportswriter in Texas," 92.
7. Larry L. King to Bill Broyles, 8 January 1976, King Archives, SWWC.
8. King, *None But a Blockhead*, 164.
9. Larry L. King, *The Whorehouse Papers*, 21.
10. King interview.
11. King, *The Whorehouse Papers*, 21.
12. King interview.

Chapter 38: LBJ, Speed, and Paranoia

1. Brammer Archives, SWWC.
2. Richard West, "Reporter: Part way with LBJ," *Texas Monthly*, (May 1976), 22; Billy Lee Brammer, untitled typescript, 3; Brammer Archives, SWWC.
3. Brammer, untitled typescript, 1.
4. Ibid., 4.
5. Ibid., 9-10.
6. Ibid., 16.
7. Shrake interview.
8. Billy Lee Brammer, "Austin's Musical History Explored," *Austin Sun*, (17 October 1974), 19.
9. Reinert, "Billy Lee," 169.
10. Ibid., 81.
11. Ibid.; Travis County District Clerk, court records.
12. Reinert, "Billy Lee," 81.
13. Cartwright, *Confessions of a Washed-Up Sportswriter*, 287; Golenbock, 376; Shrake interview.
14. Golenbock, 376; Shrake interview; Frank Gifford, *The Whole Ten Yards*. (New York: Random House, 1993), 22.
15. Cartwright, *Confessions of a Washed-Up Sportswriter*, 287.
16. King interview.

Chapter 39: Hollywood vs. *Sports Illustrated*

1. Bud Shrake, "The Screwing Up of Austin," *Texas Observer*, 27 December 1974, 27.
2. Mark McDonald, "Richards Escort Bud Shrake Leaves Trail of Tales," *Dallas Morning News*, 15 January 1991, A14; Shrake interview.

3. Shrake interview.

4. Axelrod, review of *Limo;* Clippings file, Shrake Archives, SWWC.

5. Shrake Archives, SWWC.

6. Ibid.

7. Jesse Sublett, "A League of Their Own: Austin's Veteran Screenwriters Opened the Doors to Hollywood Without Leaving Home," *Austin Chronicle,* 12–18 March 1999, http://www.austinchronicle.com/issues/vol18/issue28/screens. writers.html.

8. Willie Nelson and Bud Shrake, *Willie: An Autobiography,* 211.

9. Clippings file, Shrake Archives, SWWC.

10. MacCambridge, *The Franchise,* 207.

11. Ibid.

12. Bud Shrake, email to author, 24 July 2002.

Chapter 40: Whorehouse

1. King, *The Whorehouse Papers,* 2-3.

2. Larry L. King, *True Facts, Tall Tales, and Pure Fiction.* (Austin: University of Texas Press, 1997), 184.

3. King interview; King, *None But a Blockhead,* 228.

4. King, *None But a Blockhead,* 229.

5. King, *The Whorehouse Papers,* 35.

6. King, *None But a Blockhead,* 165.

7. Ibid., 227.

8. King, *The Whorehouse Papers,* 10.

9. Ibid., 12-13.

10. Ibid., 17.

11. Ibid., xi; King, N4.

5. Ibid., 9-10.

6. Ibid., 16.

7. Shrake interview.

8. Billy Lee Brammer, "Austin's Musical History Explored," *Austin Sun,* (17 October 1974), 19.

9. Reinert, "Billy Lee," 169.

10. Ibid., 81.

11. Ibid.; Travis Cos, SWWC.

14. King, *The Whorehouse Papers,* 166.

15. Ibid., 273.

Chapter 41: A Fraction of His Talent

1. Cullum, "The Second Act," 13.

2. Reinert, "Billy Lee," 81.

3. Ibid., 83.

4. Travis County District Clerk, court records.

5. King, *None But a Blockhead,* 252; King interview.

6. Will Blythe, review of *The Gay Place* by Billy Lee Brammer, *Esquire*, 1 April 1996, 41; Sidney Brammer, "My Old Man," 20.
7. Reinert, "Billy Lee," 168–169; Brammer Archives, SWWC.
8. Kaye Northcott, "Billy Lee Brammer, 1929–78," *Texas Observer*, 3 March 1978, 21. Marge Hershey, untitled typescript of remarks at Brammer funeral, 2–3, Brammer Archives, SWWC; Reinert, "Billy Lee," 169.
9. Northcott, "Billy Lee Brammer," 21; Cartwright, "Billy Lee Brammer, 1929–78," 21.
10. King interview.
11. Reinert, "Billy Lee," 166; King, *None But a Blockhead*, 252; Shrake interview; Graham, Introduction to *The Gay Place*, ix.
12. King, *None But a Blockhead*, 252.

Chapter 42: Measures of Success

1. Shrake interview.
2. Ibid.
3. Sublett, "A League of Their Own."
4. Willie Nelson and Bud Shrake, 210; Clippings file, Shrake Archives, SWWC.
5; Bud Shrake, email to author, 24 July 2002.
6; Bud Shrake to Larry L. King, 5 August 1980, King Archives, SWWC; Shrake interview.
7. Denise Kessler, "Eccentric Author Finds His Way to Best-Seller List," *Santa Fe New Mexican*, (3 September 1980), B1.
8. Review of *Blood Will Tell: The Murder Trials of T. Cullen Davis* by Gary Cartwright, *Library Journal*, 15 June 1979, 1351; Clippings file, Cartwright Archives, SWWC; Bobby Wiedemer, "Author Terms Cullen Davis Murder Trial Bizarre," *Daily Texan* (University of Texas), 3 April 1980.
9. Robert Sherrill, "A Texas Story," *The New York Times*, (17 June 1979).
10. John Kelso, "Cartwright Writes What It Takes," *Austin American Statesman*, 1 February 1983; Clippings file, Cartwright Archives, SWWC; Gary Cartwright, *Blood Will Tell: The Murder Trials of T. Cullen Davis* (New York: Harcourt, Brace, Jovanovich, 1979), Inscribed copy, Southwestern Writers Collection, Alkek Library, Texas State University-San Marcos.
11. King, *The Whorehouse Papers*, 273.
12. Ibid., 263; Clippings file, King Archives, SWWC.
13. Clippings file, King Archives, SWWC; Larry L. King, *The Kingfish*, 14.
14. King, *The Kingfish*, ix.
15. Sam Attlesley, "Of Outlaws, Con Men, Whores, and Larry King," *Dallas Morning News*, 13 April 1980, G1.

Chapter 43: Hitting the Wall

1. Golenbock, 367, 377.
2. Peter Gent, *The Last Magic Summer: A Season with My Son: a Memoir.* (New York: William Morrow and Company, 1996), 71; Bud Shrake, "My Favorite Place," *Texas Monthly*, (May 1989), 102.

3. Larry L. King to Jay Milner, 11 July 1980, King Archives, SWWC; Larry L. King to Frank Rich, 18 August 1980, King Archives, SWWC.

4. King interview; Pat Oliphant, "Larry of Melwood," drawings, King Archives, SWWC.

5. Bud Shrake to Larry L. King, 17 July 1980, King Archives, SWWC.

6. Ibid.; Bud Shrake to Larry L. King, 12 August 1980, King Archives, SWWC.

7. David Richards, *Once Upon a Time in Texas,* 215-216; Ann Richards with Peter Knobler, *Straight from the Heart.* (New York: Simon & Schuster, 1989), 205-206.

8. Ann Richards, 210.

9. Ibid., 219-220.

10. David Richards, 226.

11. Cartwright, *Heartwiseguy,* 34.

12. Ibid.

13. Gary Cartwright, "Back Home," *Texas Monthly,* (April 1982), 118.

14. Clippings file, Cartwright Archives, SWWC.

15. Cartwright, *Heartwiseguy,* 35-36.

16. Cartwright, *Confessions of a Washed-Up Sportswriter,* d.j.; Kelso.

Chapter 44: A Recovery

1. King interview.

2. Ibid.

3. Ibid.; King, *The Whorehouse Papers,* 269.

4. King, *The Whorehouse Papers,* 271.

5. King interview; Burt Reynolds to Larry L. King, n.d., King Archives, SWWC; Liz Smith to Larry L. King, n.d., King Archives, SWWC.

6. Larry L. King to Norman Mailer, 11 April 1982, King Archives, SWWC.

7. King interview; Larry L. King to Lanvil and Glenda Gilbert, n.d., King Archives, SWWC.

8. CBS Reports, "The Best Little Statehouse in Texas," videocassette, King Archives, SWWC.

9. King interview.

10. Ibid.

Chapter 45: "Ever a Bridegroom"

1. Ronnie Dugger, "To Our Readers," *Texas Observer,* 27 February 1981, 23; Douglas Swanson, "Rebel Without a Pause: Ex-Texas *Observer* Editor Finds Calling as a Crusader Against Corporate Power," *Dallas Morning News,* 24 August 1997, A1.

2. Jan Reid, "Larry McMurtry profile," typescript, 11, Jan Reid Archives, Southwestern Writers Collection, Alkek Library, Texas State University-San Marcos; Larry McMurtry, "The Texas Moon, and Elsewhere," *Atlantic Monthly,* May 1975, 33.

3. Larry McMurtry to Bill Broyles, 25 October 1979, William Broyles Jr. Archives, Southwestern Writers Collection, Alkek Library, Texas State University-San

Marcos. (hereafter cited as Broyles Archives, SWWC).

4. Mark Busby, *Larry McMurtry and the West: An Ambivalent Relationship,* 151; Gene Lyons, review of *Somebody's Darling* by Larry McMurtry, *Texas Monthly,* December 1978, 220.

5. Patrick Bennett, *Talking with Texas Writers,* 29–30; "Table of Contents," *Texas Monthly,* December 1978.

6. Bill Broyles to Larry McMurtry, 24 March 1980, Broyles Archives, SWWC; "Bum Steer Awards," *Texas Monthly,* January 1980, 91.

7. A. C. Greene, "The Fifty Best Texas Books," *Texas Monthly,* August 1981, 158.

8. Ibid.

9. Larry McMurtry, "Ever a Bridegroom: Reflections on the Failure of Texas Literature," *Texas Observer,* 23 October 1981, 11; Bennett, *Talking with Texas Writers,* 17; Reid, "Larry McMurtry profile," 11.

10. McMurtry, "Ever a Bridegroom," 10–11.

11. Ibid., 8.

12. Ibid., 9.

13. Ibid., 14.

14. Ibid., 12, 15.

15. Ibid., 11.

16. Ibid., 15.

17. Ibid.

18. Ibid.

19. Ibid.

20. King interview.

Chapter 46: Third Coast

1. Jane Sumner, "Will *Lonesome Dove* Fly on TV? Austin screenwriter Bill Wittliff Hopes So," *Dallas Morning News,* 22 March 1987; Shrake interview.

2. Sumner, "Will *Lonesome Dove* Fly."

3. Sublett, "A League of Their Own."

4. Shrake interview.

5. Clippings file, Shrake Archives, SWWC.

Chapter 47: Faces in the Fire

1. Gent, *The Last Magic Summer,* 72, 32.

2. Joan Ryan, "Gent Still Exorcising NFL Demons," *San Francisco Examiner,* 5 December 1989, B1; Eric Gerber, "Pros' 'Criminal element' Given a New Meaning," *Houston Post,* 11 December 1983.

3. Peter Gent to Larry L. King, 20 January 1981, King Archives, SWWC; Peter Gent to Larry L. King, 24 December 1981, King Archives, SWWC.

4. Bud Shrake to Larry L. King, 9 April 1983, King Archives, SWWC.

5. Larry L. King to Peter Gethers, 20 July 1983, King Archives, SWWC.

6. Gent, *The Last Magic Summer,* 33, 35.

7. Ibid. 26, 33; Golenbock, *Cowboys Have Always Been,* 377.

8. Gent, *The Last Magic Summer,* 108, 99, 63, 65.
9. Shrake interview; King interview.
10. Gent, *The Last Magic Summer,* 65.

Chapter 48: Jenkins

1. MacCambridge, *The Franchise,* 248, 264.
2. Ibid., 249, 251.
3. Ibid., 249.
4. Ibid., 251.
5. Dan Jenkins, *Baja Oklahoma,* 7, 92.
6. Jeffrey Staggs, *"Play Hurt* Author Blitzes Boneheads, Football Fables," *The Washington Times,* (4 November 1991), D1; Ann Hodges, "Baja Oklahoma: Jenkins' country-western love letter to Fort Worth," *Houston Chronicle,* 14 February 1988, Star 2.
7. MacCambridge, *The Franchise,* 265.
8. Ibid.
9. Ibid., 265-266.
10. Dan Jenkins, *Life its Ownself: The Semi-Tougher Adventures of Billy Clyde Puckett & Them,* 92.
11. Ibid., 298.
12. Shrake interview.
13. Clippings file, Shrake Archives, SWWC; Shrake interview.
14. Sally Jenkins. Foreword to *Fast Copy* by Dan Jenkins (Fort Worth: TCU Press, 2001).
15. Dan Jenkins, *Fast Copy,* 218.
16. Ibid., 333.
17. Dan Jenkins, *You Gotta Play Hurt,* 3.
18. Ibid., 199, 311, 323.
19. Ibid., 88
20. Anne Reifenberg. "Clinton Era Ushers out Bush's 'Ins'," *Dallas Morning News,* reprinted in the *St. Louis Post-Dispatch,* (11 January 1993), D1.
21. Cartwright, *Heartwiseguy,* 47.
22. Cartwright, *Heartwiseguy,* 51; MacCambridge, *The Franchise,* 397.
23. Stephanie Mansfield, "Dan Jenkins, All Tough on Jocks, Women, Writing and Life Its Ownself," *Washington Post,* 10 November 1984, 2.
24. King interview.
25. Review of *Rude Behavior, Publishers Weekly,* 10 August 1998, 368; Dan Jenkins, *Rude Behavior* (New York: Dell Publishing, 1998), 4.
26. Dan Jenkins, *The Money-Whipped Steer-Job Three-Jack Give-Up Artist,* 38.
27. Ibid., 173.

Chapter 49: King

1. Larry L. King to Bud Shrake, 24 March 1984, King Archives, SWWC.

2. Pilkington, *State of Mind,* 105; Larry L. King to Bud Shrake, 19 May 1996, King Archives, SWWC.

3. Morris, Celia, "Requiem for a Texas Lady," in *Range Wars: Heated Debates, Sober Reflections, and Other Assessments of Texas Writing,* Craig Clifford and Tom Pilkington, eds. (Dallas: Southern Methodist University Press, 1989), 87.

4. Morris, Celia, *Finding Celia's Place,* (College Station: Texas A & M University Press, 2000), 146.

5. Morris, Celia, "Requiem for a Texas Lady," 94.

6. Ibid., 95.

7. Larry L. King, "On Critics," typescript, 11, King Archives, SWWC; James Wolcott, "Well, Bust My Bodice," *Texas Monthly,* September 1982, 182.

8. Larry L. King to Jay Milner, 13 September 1985, King Archives, SWWC.

9. Larry L. King to Willie Morris, 27 April 1984, King Archives, SWWC; Clippings file, King Archives, SWWC; Larry L. King to Lanvil and Glenda Gilbert, 8 November 1983, King Archives, SWWC.

10. Christopher Lehmann-Haupt, "Larry King Pens Words of Wisdom on a Writer's Life," *The New York Times* Service, reprinted in the *Austin American-Statesman,* (18 February 1986), Onward 12.

11. King, Larry L., to author, August 15, 2003.

12. Larry L. King, *Because of Lozo Brown,* galley proof, King Archives, SWWC.

13. Larry L. King to Bud Shrake, 4 June 1987, King Archives, SWWC.

14. Larry L. King to Aubra Nooncaster, 30 July 1987, King Archives, SWWC.

15. Clippings file, King Archives, SWWC.

16. Larry L. King to Bud Shrake, 24 March 1984, King Archives, SWWC.

17. Larry L. King to John Bowers, 6 July 1987, King Archives, SWWC.

18. Richard Holland, Afterword to *Larry L. King: A Writer's Life in Letters, Or, Reflections in a Bloodshot Eye,* 394, 398; Kent Biffle, "King Letters Spice up Collection," *Dallas Morning News,* 22 March 1992, A45.

19. Kent Biffle, "Texas Author Rethinks View of LBJ," *Dallas Morning News,* (20 October 1991), A47.

20. Larry L. King to Bill Wittliff, 2 November 1990, King Archives, SWWC.

21. Jerome Weeks, "The Best Little Sequel on Broadway? 16 Years after 'Whorehouse' Made Aggies, Brothels, and Texas Politics a Hit on Stage, a $7 Million Follow-Up Opens Tuesday," *Dallas Morning News,* 8 May 1984, C1; King interview.

22. Skip Hollandsworth, "The Best Little Whorehouse Goes Public (But Just Barely)," *Texas Monthly,* June 1994, 116; Larry L. King to Dick Holland, 20 March 1995, King Archives, SWWC.

23. Larry L. King to Lanvil and Glenda Gilbert, 22 May 1998, King Archives, SWWC.

24. Larry L. King to Bud Shrake, 25 April 1997, King Archives, SWWC.

25. Tom Pilkington, "King Corrals Mostly Scrubs With Some Thoroughbreds," *Dallas Morning News,* 18 May 1997, J8.

26. Larry L. King, *The Dead Presidents' Club,* typescript. 1-1-7. King Archives, SWWC.

27. Larry L. King to Bud Shrake, 22 March 2001, King Archives, SWWC.

28. Larry L. King to Ben Z. Grant, 8 December 1997, King Archives, SWWC.

Chapter 50: Cartwright

1. Shropshire, F1.

2. Reid, *Close Calls,* 10.

3. Hitt, Dick, "Heart Attack Took Many by Surprise," Clipping file, Cartwright Archive, SWWC.

4. Draper, Robert, Foreword to *Turn out the Lights* by Gary Cartwright, xii, xiii.

5. Cartwright, *Heartwiseguy,* 23, 33.

6. Cartwright, Gary, "I Am the Greatest Cook in the World," *Texas Monthly,* (February 1983), 98.

7. Cartwright, *Heartwiseguy,* 36-37; Cartwright, "An Old Five and Dimer," 58, 197.

8. Cartwright, *Heartwiseguy,* 93, 2.

9. Ibid. 3; Anders, John, "A Healthy Dose of Cartwright," *Dallas Morning News,* (9 October 1998), C1, *Heartwisegsuy,* 239.

10 Anders; Cartwright, Gary, "How to Have Great Sex Forever," *Texas Monthly,* (July 1998), 108.

11. Larry King, Foreword to *Confessions of a Maddog* by Jay Milner, xi.

12. Bud Shrake to Larry L. King, 20 August 1997, King Archives, SWWC.

13. Ann Richards, Foreword to *Turn Out the Lights,* ix.

14. Anders. "A Healthy Dose of Cartwright."

Chapter 51: Shrake

1. Clippings file, Shrake Archives, SWWC; Diane Jennings, "High Profile: Bud Shrake."

2. Ray Reece, "A Case of Unearned Grandeur," *Texas Observer,* 24 February 1984, 18-19; Bud Shrake, email to author, 25 June 2003.

3. Clippings file, Shrake Archives, SWWC, Bud Shrake, email to author, 26 December 2002.

4. Clippings file, Shrake Archives, SWWC.

5. Bud Shrake, *The Big Mamoo,* typescript, 104-105, Shrake Archives, SWWC.

6. Clippings file, Shrake Archives, SWWC; Bud Shrake, email to author, 26 December 2002.

7. Bud Shrake, email to author, 26 December 2002.

8. Diane Jennings, "High Profile: Bud Shrake,"; Shrake interview.

9. Cartwright, "Shrake's Progress."

10. Jan Reid, "Novel Approach," *Texas Monthly,* October 1987, 152-153.

11. Clippings file, Shrake Archives, SWWC.

12. Camille Wheeler, "The Book of Bud: Angels Watch Over Austin Author Shrake," *Austin American-Statesman,* 21 October 2001, L1; Mark McDonald, "Richards Escort Bud Shrake Leaves Trail of Tales," *Dallas Morning News,* 15

January 1991, A14; Cartwright, "Shrake's Progress."
13. McDonald, "Richards Escort," A14; Gary Cartwright, "The Old Man and the Tee," *Texas Monthly*, December 1993, 168-170.
14. Cartwright, "The Old Man and the Tee," 170.
15. Shrake interview.
16. Cartwright, "Shrake's Progress."
17. Clippings file, Shrake Archives, SWWC; Cartwright, "Shrake's Progress."
18. Anne Morris, "Shrake's Turn at Texas," *Austin American-Statesman*, 2 April 2000, K6.
19. Steven E. Alford, review of *The Borderland: A Novel of Texas* by Edwin Shrake, amazon.com editorial review,
http://polaris.nova.edu/~alford/reviews/shrake.htm
20. Dick Holland, "Blessed Deliverance," *Austin Chronicle*, 31 March 2000, http://weeklywire.com/ww/04-03-00/austin_books_feature.html; Cartwright, "Shrake's Progress."
21. Bud Shrake, *Billy Boy*, 159.

Chapter 52: "Doing Indefinable Services to Mankind"

1. *Handbook of Texas*, "Dobie, J. Frank,"
http://www.tsha.utexas.edu/handbook/online/articles/view/DD/fdo2.html.
2. Cartwright, *Heartwiseguy*, 33; King, *None But a Blockhead*, 164.
3. Milner, *Confessions of a Maddog*, 115.
4. Swanson, "Almost Famous."
5. Shrake, *Strange Peaches*, 286.
6. Doyal, Tom, "Celebrated for the Least of Reasons," *Austin Chronicle*, (15 October 1999), http://www.austinchronicle.com/issues/dispatch/1999-10-15/books_feature.html; King interview.
7. Larry L. King to Warren Burnett, 3 January 1974, King Archives, SWWC.
8. *Washington Post* review quoted in a letter from Larry L. King to Lanvil and Glenda Gilbert, 17 February 1974, King Archives, SWWC.
9. King, *Warning: Writer at Work*, xix, xx.

BIBLIOGRAPHY

Works Cited

Anders, John. "A Healthy Dose of Cartwright." *Dallas Morning News,* (October 9, 1998), 1C.

Arnold, Ann. *Gamblers and Gangsters: Fort Worth's Jacksboro Highway in the 1940s & 1950s.* Austin: Eakin Press, 1998.

Attlesley, Sam. "Of Outlaws, Con Men, Whores, and Larry King." *Dallas Morning News,* (April 13, 1980),1 G.

Axelrod, George. Review of *Limo* by Dan Jenkins and Edwin Shrake. *Los Angeles Times Book Review,* (October 10, 1976, Clippings file, Bud Shrake Archives, Southwestern Writers Collection).

Axthelm, Pete. "Scotch on the Jocks." *Newsweek,* (September 18, 1972), 106.

——. Review of *Dead Solid Perfect* by Dan Jenkins. *Newsweek,* (November 11, 1974), 112.

Baker, Bobby, with Larry L. King. *Wheeling and Dealing: Confessions of a Capitol Hill Operator.* New York: W. W. Norton & Company, Inc., 1978.

Barthelme, Steve. "Larry King's Confessions." *Texas Observer,* (July 30, 1971), 14.

——. Review of *Moving On* by Larry McMurtry. *Texas Observer,* (October 8, 1971), 13-15.

Bennett, Patrick. *Talking with Texas Writers.* College Station: Texas A&M University Press, 1980.

Biffle, Kent. "Texas Author Rethinks View of LBJ." *Dallas Morning News,* (October 20, 1991), 47A.

——. "King Letters Spice up Collection." *Dallas Morning News,* (March 22, 1992), 45A.

Blythe, Will. Review of *The Gay Place* by Billy Lee Brammer. *Esquire,* (April 1996), 41.

Brammer, Bill. "Tom Reagan's Story." *Texas Observer,* (April 11, 1955), 6.

——. "Hit 'Em Where They Live: The Political Hucksters II." *Texas Observer,* (May 9, 1955), 4.

——. "Unworldly Little Marfa." *Texas Observer,* (June 27, 1955), 1.

——. "Enormous, But Incredible: On Rereading 'Giant'." *Texas Observer,* (July 4, 1955), 7.

——. "A Personal Reminiscence." *Texas Observer,* (August 25, 1961), 6.

——. "A Circus Breaks Down on the Prairie." *Texas Observer,* (July 4, 1955), 4.

——. "A Fragile Subject." *Texas Observer,* (August 17, 1955), 2.

——. "Lyndon Comes Home." *Texas Observer,* (August 30, 1955), 1.

——. "Pow Wow on the Pedernales." *Texas Observer,* (October 5, 1955), 1.

——. "That Old Depleted Feeling." *Texas Observer,* (October 12, 1955), 3.

——. "A Famous Arthur Returns to Dallas." *Texas Observer,* (December 27, 1962), 6.

——. "Mencken and Minnesota Fats." *Texas Observer,* (October 18, 1968), 8.

——. "Apocalypse Now?" *Texas Observer,* (November 1, 1968), 8-10.

——. "Sex and Politics." *Texas Monthly,* (May 1973), http://www.texasmonthly.com/archive/brammer/sexpolitics.php.

——. "Austin's Musical History Explored." *Austin Sun,* (October 17, 1974), 19.

——. *The Gay Place.* New York: Vintage Books, 1983.

Brammer, Sidney. "My Old Man." *Texas Observer,* (April 21, 1995), 20.

Brown, Joe David. "A Big Man Even in Big D." *Sports Illustrated,* (January 21, 1963), 63.

Broyles, William, Jr. "Behind the Lines." *Texas Monthly,* (February 1973), 2.

——. "Behind the Lines." *Texas Monthly,* (March 1974), 3.

—— "Behind the Lines." *Texas Monthly,* (August 1974), 8.

——. "Behind the Lines." *Texas Monthly,* (April 1978), 5.

Buchholz, Brad. "Days of the 'Dillo." *Austin American-Statesman,* (December 10, 2000), K1.

Burst, Ardis. *The Three Families of H.L. Hunt.* New York: Weidenfeld & Nicolson, 1988.

Busby, Mark. *Larry McMurtry and the West: An Ambivalent Relationship.* Denton: University of North Texas Press, 1995.

Canby, Vincent. Review of Kid Blue. *The New York Times,* (October 1, 1973), 45.

Carr, John, ed. *Kite Flying and Other Irrational Acts: Conversations with Southern Writers.* Baton Rouge: Louisiana State University Press, 1972.

Carter, Hodding. Review of *Confessions of a White Racist* by Larry L. King, *Book World,* (July 4), 1971, 3.

Cartwright, Gary. "The Word on Integration." *Dallas Morning News,* (February 12, 1963), Section 2, 1.

——. "Bishop Sheds Its Image." *Dallas Morning News,* (February 21, 1963), Section 2, 1.

——. "Jimmy Ling, The Conglomerate King." *Los Angeles Times West Magazine,* (October 20, 1968), 11, 14.

——. *The Hundred Yard War.* New York: Dell, 1969.

——. "The Lonely Blues of Duane Thomas." *Texas Monthly,* (February 1973), 47-49.

——. *Thin Ice.* Greenwich, Connecticut: Fawcett Publications, Inc., 1975.

——. "Who Was Jack Ruby?" *Texas Monthly,* (November 1975), http://www. texas monthly.com/archive/ruby/ruby.1.php.

——. "Candy." *Texas Monthly,* (December 1976), 190.

——. "Billy Lee Brammer, 1929-78." *Texas Observer,* (March 3, 1978), 21.

——. *Blood Will Tell: The Murder Trials of T. Cullen Davis.* New York: Harcourt, Brace, Jovanovich, 1979.

——. *Confessions of a Washed-Up Sportswriter, Including Various Digressions About Sex, Crime, and Other Hobbies.* Austin: Texas Monthly Press, 1982.

——. "Back Home." *Texas Monthly,* (April 1982), 118.

——. "I Am the Greatest Cook in the World." *Texas Monthly,* (February 1983), 98.

——. "A Old Five and Dimer." *Texas Monthly,* (February 1988), 58, 92-94.

——. "The Old Man and the Tee," *Texas Monthly,* (December 1993), 168-170.

——. *Heartwiseguy: How to Live the Good Life After a Heart Attack*. New York: St. Martin's Press, 1998.

——. "How to Have Great Sex Forever." *Texas Monthly,* (July 1998), 108.

——. *Turn out the Lights: Chronicles of Texas in the 80s and 90s*. Austin: University of Texas Press, 2000.

——. "Shrake's Progress." *Texas Monthly,* (April 2000), http://www.texasmonthly.com/mag/issues/2000-04-01/feature2.php.

Charters, Ann, ed. *The Portable Beat Reader*. New York: Penguin Books, 1992.

Chism, Olin. Review of *Strange Peaches* by Edwin Shrake. *Dallas Times Herald,* June 16, 1972.

Cohen, Jason. "Rude Behavior." *Texas Monthly,* (November 1998), 62.

Cole, Richard Ray. "A Journal of Free Voices: The History of the *Texas Observer*" (master's thesis, University of Texas at Austin, 1966).

Crawford, Ann Fears. *Frankie: Mrs. R.D. Randolph and Texas Liberal Politics*. Austin: Eakin Press, 2000.

Doyal, Tom. "Celebrated for the Least of Reasons." *Austin Chronicle,* (October 15, 1999), http://www.austinchronicle.com/issues/dispatch/1999-10-15/books_feature.html

Draper, Robert. Foreword to *Turn out the Lights* by Gary Cartwright. Austin: University of Texas Press, 2000.

Dugger, Ronnie. "Outgoing, Incoming Editors Talk." *Texas Observer,* (December 16, 1960), 5.

——. "More Thoughts on a Novel." *Texas Observer,* (July 22, 1966), 1.

——. "Observations," *Texas Observer,* (November 11, 1966), 11.

——. "Before the Bar for Pot." *Texas Observer,* (March 20, 1970), 1-2.

——. "Fallow Fields." *Texas Observer,* (November 5, 1971), 21.

——. *The Invaded Universities*. New York: W. W. Norton, 1974.

——. "To a Novelist Dying Young." *Washington Post,* (June 18, 1978), F1-F4.

——. "To Our Readers." *Texas Observer,* (February 27,1981), 23.

Dunn, Si. "New York Journalism, Texas Style." *Dallas Morning News,* (May 9, 1976), Scene 24.

Flemmons, Jerry. *Amon: The Texan Who Played Cowboy for America*. Lubbock: Texas Tech University Press, 1998.

Flippo, Chet. "Bestseller, as in Yellow Pages." *Texas Observer,* (November 3, 1972), 15.

Frady, Marshall. Review of *Confessions of a White Racist* by Larry L. King. *Life,* (June 11, 1971), 16.

Frantz, Joe B. *The Forty Acre Follies*. Austin: *Texas Monthly* Press, 1983.

Friedenberg, Edgar Z. Reviews of *Confessions of a White Racist* by Larry L. King. *New York Review of Books,* (September 2, 1971), 7.

Garrison, Bruce and Mark Sabljak. *Sports Reporting*. Ames: Iowa State University Press, 1993.

Gent, Peter. *North Dallas Forty*. New York: William Morrow & Company, Inc., 1973.

——. *The Last Magic Summer: A Season with My Son: a Memoir*. New York: William Morrow and Company, 1996.

Gerber, Eric. "Pros' 'Criminal element' Given a New Meaning." *Houston Post*, (December 11, 1983), 1J.

Gifford, Frank. *The Whole Ten Yards*. New York: Random House, 1993.

Golenbock, Peter. *Cowboys Have Always Been My Heroes: The Definitive Oral History of America's Team*. New York: Warner Books, 1997.

Gordon, Roxy. Review of *Strange Peaches* by Edwin Shrake. *Texas Observer*, (July 21, 1972), 14-15.

Graham, Don. "Don Graham's Texas Classics." *Texas Monthly*, (November 2000), http://www.texasmonthly.com/mag/issues/2000-11-01/classics.php

——. Introduction to *The Gay Place*. Austin: University of Texas Press, 1995.

Green, George Norris. *The Establishment in Texas Politics: The Primitive Years, 1938-1957*. Norman: University of Oklahoma Press, 1979.

Greene, A. C. "The Fifty Best Texas Books." *Texas Monthly*, (August 1981), 158.

Halberstam, David. Review of *Semi-Tough* by Dan Jenkins. *New York Times Book Review*, (September 17, 1972), 2.

Hannah, Barry. Review of *Dead Solid Perfect* by Dan Jenkins. *The New York Times Book Review*, (November 3, 1974), 69.

Heilbrun, Carolyn G. *The Education of a Woman: A Life of Gloria Steinem*. New York: Dial Press, 1995.

Hershey, Marge. Typescript of remarks at Billy Lee Brammer's funeral. (Billy Lee Brammer Archives, Southwestern Writers Collection, Texas State University-San Marcos, 1978).

Hilburn, Robert. "From the Vaults: A Few Nelson Classics Hidden on His Debut, 'Country Willie." *Los Angeles Times*, (January 28, 2000), F32.

Hitt, Dick. "Would You Believe . . ." *Dallas Times Herald*, (April 13, 1966), Clippings file, Gary Cartwright Archives, Southwestern Writers Collection.

——. "Heart Attack Took Many by Surprise." *Dallas Times Herald*, (October 17, 1988), Clippings file, Gary Cartwright Archives, Southwestern Writers Collection.

——. "Stars of Granite: Four Literary Legends Shine in Austin." *Dallas Times Herald*, (November 8, 1987), Clippings file, Gary Cartwright Archives, Southwestern Writers Collection.

Hodges, Ann. "Baja Oklahoma: Jenkins' country-western love letter to Fort Worth." *Houston Chronicle*, (February 14, 1988), 2 STAR.

Holland, Dick. "Blessed Deliverance." *Austin Chronicle*, (March 31, 2000), http://www.austinchronicle.com/issues/dispatch/2000-03-31/books_feature.html.

Holland, Richard. Afterword to *Larry L. King: A Writer's Life in Letters, Or, Reflections in a Bloodshot Eye* by Larry L. King. Fort Worth: TCU Press, 1999.

Hollandsworth, Skip. "*The Best Little Whorehouse* Goes Public (But Just Barely)." *Texas Monthly*, (June 1994), 116.

Hotchner, A. E. "If You've Been Afraid to Go To Elaine's These Past 20 Years, Here's What You've Missed." New York, (May 2, 1983), 34.

Jenkins, Dan, "Lockwrists and Cage Cases." *Sports Illustrated*, (July 16, 1962), 56.

——. "The Sweet Life of Swinging Joe." *Sports Illustrated*, (October 17, 1966), 42.

——. "A Glory Day for Gay." *Sports Illustrated*, (April 7, 1967), 22.

——. "Life With the Jax Pack." *Sports Illustrated*, (July 10, 1967), 61.

——. "All the Way With O. J." *Sports Illustrated*, (November 27, 1967), 19.

——. "Lee's Fleas Cheer 'Super Mex' to Victory." *Sports Illustrated*, (June 28, 1968), 19.

——. "The Joy of Having a Foe You Know." *Sports Illustrated*, (September 9, 1968), 35.

——. *Saturday's America*. Boston: Little, Brown, 1970.

——. *Semi-Tough*. New York: Atheneum, 1972.

——. *Dead Solid Perfect*. New York: Atheneum, 1974.

——. *Baja Oklahoma*. New York: Atheneum, 1981.

——. *Life its Ownself: The Semi-Tougher Adventures of Billy Clyde Puckett & Them*. New York: Simon and Schuster, 1984.

——. *Fast Copy*. New York: Simon and Schuster, 1988.

——. *You Gotta Play Hurt*. New York: Pocket Books, 1993.

——. *Fairways and Greens: The Best Golf Writing of Dan Jenkins*. New York: Doubleday, 1994.

——. *Rude Behavior*. New York: Island Books, Dell Publishing, 1998.

——. *The Money-Whipped Steer-Job Three-Jack Give-Up Artist*. New York: Doubleday, 2001.

Jenkins, Sally. Foreword to *Fast Copy* by Dan Jenkins. Fort Worth: TCU Press, 2001.

Jennings, Diane. "High Profile: Bud Shrake." *Dallas Morning News*, (January 22, 1989), 1E.

——. "High Profile: Dan Jenkins." *Dallas Morning News*, (February 23, 1986), 1E.

Kelso, John. "Cartwright Writes What it Takes." *Austin American-Statesman*, (February 1, 1983), Clippings file, Gary Cartwright Archives, Southwestern Writers Collection.

Kessler, Denise. "Eccentric Author Finds His Way to Best-Seller List." Santa Fe New Mexican, (September 3, 1980), B1.

King, Larry L. "Happy New Year for Batchelors." *Odessa American*, (January 1, 1954), 1.

——. "Negro Vet Feels Eyes of Race On Him." *Odessa American*, (May 23, 1954), 1.

——. "Border City Scene of Most Politicking." *Odessa American*, (July 4, 1954), 4.

——. "Second Banana Politicians." *Harper's*, (January 1965), 42.

——. *The One-Eyed Man*. New York: New American Library, 1966.

——. "My Hero LBJ." *Harper's*, (October 1966), 54.

——. *. . . and other dirty stories*. New York: New American Library, 1968.

——. "Lyndon Johnson in Literature." *The New Republic*, (August 3, 1968), 30.

——. Review of *Saturday's America* by Dan Jenkins, *Harper's*, (January 1971), 95.

——. *Confessions of a White Racist*. New York: The Viking Press, 1972.

——. "Confessions of a Black-Hearted Loser." *New York*, (May 8, 1972), 37-38.

——. *The Old Man and Lesser Mortals*. New York: The Viking Press, 1974.

——. "The Confessions of an American Father." Typescript, Larry L. King

Archives, Southwestern Writers Collection, Texas State University-San Marcos, (1974).

———. "Coming of Age in the Locker Room." *Texas Monthly,* (September 1974), 80, 85.

———. "Hard Times." *Playboy,* (March 1975), 140, 178.

———. "Great Willie Nelson Commando Hoo-Ha and Texas Brain Fry," *Playboy,* (November 1975), 207-210.

———. "The Best Sportswriter in Texas." *Texas Monthly,* (December 1975), 92, 142.

———. *The Whorehouse Papers.* New York: The Viking Press, 1982.

———. "We've Been Ordered to Make This Thing Work." *Parade,* (February 19, 1984), 4-6.

———. *Warning, Writer at Work: The Best Collectibles of Larry L. King.* Fort Worth: TCU Press, 1985.

———. *None But a Blockhead: On Being a Writer.* New York: The Viking Press, 1986.

———. *The Kingfish.* Dallas: Southern Methodist University Press, 1992.

———. *The Dead Presidents' Club.* Typescript. Larry L. King Archives, Southwestern Writers Collection, Texas State University-San Marcos, 1995.

———. *True Facts, Tall Tales, and Pure Fiction.* Austin: University of Texas Press, 1997.

———. Foreword to *Confessions of a Maddog* by Jay Milner. Denton: University of North Texas Press, 1998.

———. *Larry L. King: A Writer's Life in Letters, Or, Reflections in a Bloodshot Eye.* Fort Worth: TCU Press, 1999.

———. Introduction to *The One-Eyed Man.* Fort Worth: Texas Christian University Press, 2001.

King, Larry L. and Peter Masterson. *The Best Little Whorehouse in Texas.* Final draft script. Larry L. King Archives, Southwestern Writers Collection, Texas State University-San Marcos, (1978).

Kinkaid, Gaines. "A Very Historical Novel." *Texas Observer,* (November 15, 1968), 13-14.

Lala, Jack. "Academic Freedom Under Duress: Political Witch Hunts at the University of Texas, 1939-1952." Master's thesis, Texas State University-San Marcos, (1994).

Lee, James Ward. *Classics of Texas Fiction.* Dallas: E-Heart Press, 1987.

———. Afterword to *But Not For Love.* Fort Worth: Texas Christian University Press, 2000.

Lehmann-Haupt, Christopher. Review of *The Old Man and Lesser Mortals* by Larry L. King. *The New York Times,* (January 31, 1974), 31.

———. "Larry King Pens Words of Wisdom on a Writer's Life." *The New York Times Service,* reprinted in the *Austin American-Statesman,* (February 18, 1986), Onward 12.

Levy, Michael. "From the publisher." *Texas Monthly,* (February 1973), 1.

Lyons, Gene. Review of *Somebody's Darling* by Larry McMurtry. *Texas Monthly,* (December 1978), 220.

MacCambridge, Michael. *The Francgise: A History of Sports Illustrated.* New York: Hyperion, 1997.

Mansfield, Stephanie. "Dan Jenkins, All Tough On Jocks, Women, Writing And Life Its Ownself." *Washington Post,* (November 10, 1984), 2.

McDonald, Mark. "Richards Escort Bud Shrake Leaves Trail of Tales." *Dallas Morning News,* (January 15, 1991), 14A.

McMurtry, Larry. *In a Narrow Grave: Essays on Texas.* Austin: The Encino Press, 1968.

——. "Answer from McMurtry." *Texas Observer,* (February 26, 1971), 22-24.

——. "The Texas Moon, and Elsewhere." *Atlantic Monthly,* (May 1975), 33.

——. "Ever a Bridegroom: Reflections on the Failure of Texas Literature." *Texas Observer,* (October 23, 1981), 8-15.

McNeeley, Dave. "The Courting of Willie Morris." *Austin American-Statesman,* (November 15, 1983), Onward 8.

Milazzo, Lee C. "Money Makes the Ball Move." *Dallas Morning News,* (September 9, 1973), 13C.

Millhauser, Steven. "A Few Novels." *The New Republic,* (September 16, 1972), 31.

Milner, Jay Dunston. *Confessions of a Maddog: A Romp Through the High-flying Texas Music and Literary Era of the Fifties to the Seventies.* Denton: University of North Texas Press, 1998.

Milner, Jay. Review of *Strange Peaches* by Edwin Shrake. *Dallas Morning News,* (June 4, 1972), 12B.

Moon, Eric. Review of *Dead Solid Perfect* by Dan Jenkins. *Library Journal,* (October 1, 1974), 2500.

Morris, Anne. "Shrake's Turn at Texas." *Austin American-Statesman,* (April 2, 2000), K6.

Morris, Celia. "Requiem for a Texas Lady." In *Range Wars: Heated Debates, Sober Reflections, and Other Assessments of Texas Writing* edited by Craig Clifford and Tom Pilkington. Dallas: Southern Methodist University Press, 1989.

——. *Finding Celia's Place.* College Station: Texas A&M University Press, 2000.

Morris, Willie. "Billy Lee Brammer, 1929-78." *Texas Observer,* (March 3, 1978), 20.

——. *New York Days.* Boston: Little, Brown and Company, 1993.

Nelson, Willie with Bud Shrake. *Willie: An Autobiography.* New York: Simon and Schuster, 1988.

Nightbyrd, Jeffrey. Review of *The Austin Music Scene, 1965-1994: Through the Lens of Burton Wilson by Burton Wilson. Texas Observer,* (December 21, 2001), http://www.texasobserver.org.

Northcott, Kaye. "Billy Lee Brammer, 1929-78." *Texas Observer,* (March 3, 1978), 21.

Pardun, Robert. *Prairie Radical: A Journey Through the Sixties.* Los Gatos, California: Shire Press, 2001.

Payne, Darwin. *Big D: Triumphs and Troubles of an American Supercity in the 20th Century.* Dallas: Three Forks Press, 2000.

Pilkington, Tom. "King Corrals Mostly Scrubs With Some Thoroughbreds." *Dallas Morning News,* (May 18, 1997), 8J.

——. *State of Mind: Texas Literature and Culture.* College Station: Texas A&M University Press, 1998.

Powell, Tracie. "Gary Cartwright, Editor/Writer of TM Magazine." *Austin American-Statesman,* (December 31, 1999), J4.

The Rag. Austin, Texas, April 27, 1970, 20.

———. August 3, 1970, 8-9.

Reece, Ray. "A Case of Unearned Grandeur." *Texas Observer,* (February 24, 1984), 18-19.

Reid, Jan. *The Improbable Rise of Redneck Rock.* Austin: Heidelberg Press, 1974.

———. "Novel Approach." *Texas Monthly,* (October 1987), 152-153.

———. *Close Calls: Jan Reid's Texas.* College Station: Texas A&M University Press, 2000.

———. "Return to *The Gay Place.*" *Texas Monthly,* (March 2001), 162-164.

Reifenberg, Anne. "Clinton Era Ushers out Bush's 'Ins.'" *St. Louis Post-Dispatch,* January 11, 1993, 1D.

Reinert, Al. Introduction to *The Gay Place* by Billy Lee Brammer. Austin: *Texas Monthly* Press, 1978.

———. "Billy Lee," *Texas Monthly,* (February 1979), 79-83, 166.

Richards, Ann, with Peter Knobler. *Straight from the Heart: My Life in Politics and Other Places.* New York: Simon and Schuster, 1989.

Richards, David. *Once Upon a Time in Texas: A Liberal in the Lone Star State.* Austin: University of Texas Press, 2002.

Rust, Carol. "Threadgill's Austin Has Lots of Institutions, but Only One Motto: 'Vegetables You Can Drink Beer With.'" *Houston Chronicle,* (August 28, 1994), 2 Star 8.

Ryan, Joan. "Gent Still Exorcising NFL Demons." *San Francisco Examiner,* (December 5, 1989), B1.

Schaap, Dick. Review of *North Dallas Forty* by Peter Gent. *The New York Times,* (October 28, 1973), 44.

Smith, Liz. *Natural Blonde: A Memoir.* New York: Hyperion, 2000.

Shattuck, Roger. "Politics, Its Responsibility and Thrall." *Texas Observer,* (April 8, 1961), 6.

Sherrill, Robert. "A Texas Story." *The New York Times,* (June 17, 1979), Clippings file, Gary Cartwright Archives, Southwestern Writers Collection.

Sherrington, Kevin. "Still a Prose Pro." *Dallas Morning News,* (November 7, 1999), 20B.

Shrake, Bud. "In Barcelona, Glitter Can't Conceal Slums." *Dallas Morning News,* (April 20, 1963), Section 1, 16.

———. "A Story of Thailand." *Texas Observer,* (September 12, 1969), 13.

———. *Dime Box.* Screenplay, Bud Shrake Archives, Southwestern Writers Collection, Texas State University-San Marcos, (1971).

———. "The Screwing Up of Austin." *Texas Observer,* (December 27, 1974), 27.

———. "Cops Eat Kid's Pet." *Texas Observer,* (July 25, 1975), 7-8.

———. *The Big Mamoo* by Bud Shrake. Screenplay, Bud Shrake Archives, Southwestern Writers Collection, Texas State University-San Marcos, (1988).

———. "My Favorite Place." *Texas Monthly,* (May 1989), 103.

———. *Billy Boy.* New York: Simon and Schuster, 2001.

Shrake, Edwin. *But Not For Love.* Garden City, New York: Doubleday & Co., 1964.

———. "Tough Cookie Marches to His Own Drummer." *Sports Illustrated,* (December 14, 1964), 71.

———. "The Once Forbidding Land," *Sports Illustrated,* (May 10, 1965), 83.

———. *Blessed McGill.* New York: Doubleday & Co., 1968.

———. "The Land of the Permanent Wave." *Harper's,* (February 1970), 81.

———. "Why is This Man Laughing?" *Sports Illustrated,* (September 18, 1972), 119.

———. *Peter Arbiter.* Austin: The Encino Press, 1973.

———. "Getting Swamped by Gators." *Sports Illustrated,* (January 20, 1975), 26.

———. *Strange Peaches.* Austin: *Texas Monthly* Press, 1987.

Shropshire, Mike. "The Write Stuff: *Texas Monthly* at 10: A past perfect, a future tense?" *Dallas Morning News,* (February 20, 1983), 1F

Smith, Clay. "Notes on Mad Dogs." *Austin Chronicle,* (January 26, 2001), http://www.austinchronicle.com/issues/dispatch/2001-01-26/books_feature.html.

Solomon, George. "Gent 'Indicts the Whole NFL': Schramm." *Washington Post,* (December 9, 1973), C4.

Staggs, Jeffrey. "*Play Hurt* Author Blitzes Boneheads, Football Fables." *The Washington Times,* (November 4, 1991), D1.

Stevens, Jay. *Storming Heaven: LSD and the American Dream.* New York: Grove Press, 1998.

Stuever, Hank. "*Texas Monthly* at 25: Make it Mythic." *Austin American-Statesman,* (January 25, 1998), A1.

Sublett, Jesse. "A League of Their Own: Austin's Veteran Screenwriters Opened the Doors to Hollywood Without Leaving Home." *Austin Chronicle,* (March 12, 1999), http://www.austinchronicle.com/issues/vol18/issue28/screens.writers.html.

Sumner, Jane. "Will *Lonesome Dove* Fly on TV? Austin screenwriter Bill Wittliff Hopes So." *Dallas Morning News,* (March 22, 1987), 1C.

Swanson, Douglas. "Bud Shrake, Almost Famous." *Pearl,* (May 1976), 20.

———. "Rebel Without a Pause: Ex-*Texas Observer* Editor Finds Calling as a Crusader Against Corporate Power." *Dallas Morning News,* (August 24, 1997), 1A.

Valk, Garry. "Letter from the Publisher." *Sports Illustrated,* (July 24, 1967), 4.

———. "Letter from the Publisher," *Sports Illustrated,* (December 11, 1967), 4.

Warren, Bill. Review of *Strange Peaches* by Edwin Shrake. *Austin American-Statesman,* (August 6, 1972), Show World, 33.

Weeks, Jerome. "The Best Little Sequel on Broadway? 16 Years after 'Whorehouse' Made Aggies, Brothels, and Texas Politics a Hit on Stage, a $7 Million Follow-Up Opens Tuesday." *Dallas Morning News,* (May 8, 1984), 1C.

Weldon, Martin. Review of *Strange Peaches* by Edwin Shrake. *Houston Chronicle,* (June 18, 1972), F3.

West, Richard. "Reporter: Part way with LBJ." *Texas Monthly,* (May 1976), 22.

Wheeler, Camille. "The Book of Bud: Angels Watch Over Austin Author Shrake." *Austin American-Statesman,* (October 21, 2001), L1.

Wiedemer, Bobby. "Author Terms Cullen Davis Murder Trial Bizarre." *Daily Texan* (University of Texas), (April 3, 1980), Clippings file, Gary Cartwright Archives, Southwestern Writers Collection.

Wolcott, James. "Well, Bust My Bodice." *Texas Monthly,* (September 1982), 182.

Wolfe, Jane. *The Murchisons: The Rise and Fall of a Texas Dynasty.* New York: St. Martin's Press, 1989.

Woodward, Stanley. *Sports Page.* New York: Simon and Schuster, 1949.

Wright, Lawrence. *In the New World: Growing Up With America, 1960-1984.* New York: Knopf, 1988.

Archival Collections

Billy Lee Brammer Archives, Southwestern Writers Collection, Alkek Library, Texas State University-San Marcos.

William Broyles Jr. Archives, Southwestern Writers Collection, Alkek Library, Texas State University-San Marcos.

Gary Cartwright Archives, Austin History Center.

Gary Cartwright Archives, Southwestern Writers Collection, Alkek Library, Texas State University-San Marcos.

Larry L. King Archives, Southwestern Writers Collection, Alkek Library, Texas State University-San Marcos.

Jay Milner Archives, Southwestern Writers Collection, Alkek Library, Texas State University-San Marcos.

Jan Reid Archives, Southwestern Writers Collection, Alkek Library, Texas State University-San Marcos.

Bud Shrake Archives, Austin History Center.

Bud Shrake Archives, Southwestern Writers Collection, Alkek Library, Texas State University-San Marcos.

Interviews

Gary Cartwright. Interview by author, Austin, Texas, 16 October 2001.

Larry L. King. Interview by author, Washington, D.C., 19 April 2001.

Bud Shrake. Interview by author, Austin, Texas, 15 March 2001.

INDEX